MANAGING
FINANCIAL *and*
CORPORATE DISTRESS

THE WORLD BANK GROUP

THE INTERNATIONAL MONETARY FUND

THE BROOKINGS INSTITUTION

This book is based on a conference entitled "Emerging Markets in the New Financial System: Managing Financial and Corporate Distress," held on March 30–April 1, 2000, in Florham Park, New Jersey The conference was jointly sponsored by the World Bank Group, the International Monetary Fund, and the Brookings Institution.

The previous volume in this series, Financial Markets and Development: The Crisis in Emerging Markets, *published in 1999, is available from the Brookings Institution Press.*

CHARLES ADAMS
ROBERT E. LITAN
MICHAEL POMERLEANO
Editors

MANAGING FINANCIAL *and* CORPORATE DISTRESS

Lessons from Asia

BROOKINGS INSTITUTION PRESS
Washington, D.C.

NOV 2 8 2000

ABOUT BROOKINGS

The Brookings Institution is a private nonprofit organization devoted to research, education, and publication on important issues of domestic and foreign policy. Its principal purpose is to bring knowledge to bear on current and emerging policy problems. The Institution maintains a position of neutrality on issues of public policy. Interpretations or conclusions in Brookings publications should be understood to be solely those of the authors.

Copyright © 2000
THE BROOKINGS INSTITUTION
1775 Massachusetts Avenue, N.W., Washington, D.C. 20036
www.brookings.edu

Library of Congress Cataloging-in-Publication data
Managing financial and corporate distress : lessons from Asia /
Charles Adams, Robert E. Litan, and Michael Pomerleano, editors.
  p.   cm.
Papers presented at a conference sponsored by the World Bank, International
Monetary Fund, and the Brookings Institution, held in March 2000.
  Includes bibliographical references and index.
  ISBN 0-8157-0103-9 (alk. paper)
  1. Debt relief—Congresses. 2. Corporate debt—Congresses. 3. Debts,
External—Congresses. 4. Debt relief—Asia—Congresses. 5. Corporate
debt—Asia—Congresses. 6. Debt, External—Asia—Congresses.
7. Financial crises—Asia. I. Adams, Charles F., 1945 II. Litan, Robert E., 1950
III. Pomerleano, Michael. IV. Title.
  HG3891.5 .M334 2000   00-010110
  336.3'435—dc21   CIP

9 8 7 6 5 4 3 2 1

The paper used in this publication meets minimum requirements of the
American National Standard for Information Sciences—Permanence of Paper for
Printed Library Materials, ANSI Z39.48-1992.

Typeset in Adobe Garamond

Composition by R. Lynn Rivenbark
Macon, Georgia

Printed by R. R. Donnelley and Sons
Harrisonburg, Virginia

Contents

PART THREE
Facilitating Restructuring

PART FOUR
Risk Management

Foreword

THE FINANCIAL CRISES affecting several emerging market economies have underscored the need for a regular forum in which cutting-edge issues associated with financial sector development in developing countries, as well as deepening financial integration and globalization, are systematically and consistently explored. Toward that end, the World Bank Group, the International Monetary Fund, and the Brookings Institution are collaborating on an series of annual conferences designed to be of interest to investors, analysts, and policymakers throughout the world with the objective of stimulating policy dialogue and sharing global experiences. The program was very effective in distilling the lessons of the massive corporate and bank restructuring efforts currently underway in many East Asian countries for other developing countries.

This book is the product of the second of these conferences, which brought together individuals from a variety of disciplines and sectors—including senior policymakers from developed market countries, practitioners from the financial services industry, officials of multilateral organizations, and selected academicians—to explore the challenges of private capital flows to developing countries, frontiers in financial risk management, and the opportunities for corporate and financial restructuring posed by financial globalization.

Many individuals contributed to the success of the conference and to this volume, including the formal discussants and speakers at the conference shown in the following pages. Many others participated as moderators or as informal discussants: David Atkinson, Manuel Conthe, Donald R. van Deventer, Jonathan L. Fiechter, Hoon Mok Chung, Vijay Kelkar, Richard Newfarmer, Hogen Oh, Vincent J. Palermo, Gary Perlin, Leslie Rahl, Barry W. Ridings, and Peter Tufano. Special thanks are also owed to Donald Mathieson at the International Monetary Fund, who along with the editors, helped organize the conference.

In addition, Kimberly Bliss at Brookings, and Aizaz ul Haque and Sarah Johnson at the World Bank provided valuable assistance throughout the planning and organizing of the conference. We also acknowledge the editorial, proofreading, and indexing assistance of Charles Dibble, Carlotta Ribar, and Mary Mortensen.

Funds for the conference were generously supplied by the World Bank Group, the International Monetary Fund, and the Brookings Institution.

MICHAEL H. ARMACOST
President, Brookings Institution

HORST KÖHLER
Managing Director, International Monetary Fund

JAMES D. WOLFENSOHN
President, World Bank

MANAGING
FINANCIAL *and*
CORPORATE DISTRESS

CHARLES ADAMS
ROBERT E. LITAN
MICHAEL POMERLEANO

1

Introduction

M ORE THAN THREE YEARS have elapsed since the East Asian financial and economic crisis erupted and, for a time, threatened economic and financial stability in the rest of the world. Remarkably, however, most economies in the region—and indeed other emerging market economies around the world—have since staged a significant turnaround. Exchange rates and interest rates in Indonesia, Malaysia, South Korea, and Thailand, the economies at the epicenter of the crisis, have stabilized and economic growth has returned, aided by an improvement in commodity prices and continuing strong exports. Governments in most countries in the region also have done their part, abandoning pegged exchange rate regimes that encouraged excessive and mispriced short-term foreign currency borrowing, increasing their usable foreign currency reserves, and recapitalizing their banks through both government support and foreign direct investment.

Still, the consensus inside and outside the region is that much additional restructuring and reform remain necessary. Several of the microeconomic conditions that underlay the crisis—including the absence of transparency in financial reporting, imperfect regulation and supervision of financial institutions, weak corporate governance, and ineffective bankruptcy systems, among others—still need to be fully addressed. Given the magnitude of the initial economic shock and its political fallout, experts may dispute whether reform has proceeded as rapidly as could be expected, but the V-shaped recovery pattern since the crisis ironically has diminished interest within the region in finishing the job of reform. This is a worrisome development.

In March 2000 the World Bank, the International Monetary Fund (IMF), and the Brookings Institution convened a second annual conference on finance in emerging markets to focus on one especially important aspect of adjustment to the crisis: restructuring the debt of financial institutions and many of their borrowers, many of which were effectively bankrupted when local exchange rates and domestic output sharply dropped.[1] The conference brought together 175 academic scholars, financial experts, regulators, and policymakers from around the world to discuss the papers that address this topic and related issues and that appear in this volume.

The papers and the conference asked some basic questions. Why does debt restructuring—the partial writedown of debt or the conversion of a portion of debt into equity—matter in the first place? How rapidly has it been proceeding? What are the most effective mechanisms for debt restructuring? What further steps should governments and companies in the region take to resolve remaining problems? And what steps should both sets of actors take in the future to prevent recurrence of another crisis? We hope that readers will find some of the answers to these questions—at the very least, different perspectives on the issues these questions raise—in the papers that follow.

Why does debt restructuring matter, especially when the debts are owed to foreign creditors? The first two papers address this deceptively simple question, which turns out to have complicated and very different answers supplied by each of two authors.

To Benjamin Friedman, the major reason why restructuring of debts that cannot be serviced makes a difference is that until this occurs borrowers are not likely to attract new funding. The larger the number of such borrowers and the greater their importance to local economies, the more difficulty these economies will have in mounting a strong recovery or in maintaining healthy rates of growth.

---

1. The initial volume in this series (*Financial Markets and Development*, edited by Alison Harwood, Robert E. Litan, and Michael Pomerleano [Brookings, 1999]) was sponsored by the World Bank and the Brookings Institution.

That said, Friedman cautions that not all nonperforming debts should be restructured. Some defaults, where the debtor is unable to pay and the creditors seize control of assets or the firm itself, are necessary and healthy—necessary because no amount of restructuring can restore the firm to a viable position, and healthy because both creditors and debtors should consider the risk of default when entering into a debt contract in the first place. Without the threat of default, there will be too much credit extended at an insufficiently low price, so that when real conditions render the repayment of the debt impossible, the drag on the economy will be that much greater. In this sense, it is wrong in Friedman's view for analysts to focus on the aggregate volumes of credit flows to countries as measures of the confidence (or lack thereof) in a local economy. What is important is that the right amount of credit be extended at the *right price.*

By the same reasoning, while maximizing economic output is a plausible national objective, avoiding lost output associated with temporary macroeconomic adjustments is not. The real costs of transition are necessary to restrain both borrowers and creditors from future imprudent behavior. When this occurs, output will be maximized *over the long run.*

This line of analysis leads Friedman to conclude that debt restructuring should not be made "too easy." Of course, this is not to say that it should be made unnecessarily difficult either, as has been true in Asian countries that lack effective bankruptcy systems. But the surprising result of Friedman's argument is that the various impediments to debt restructuring in the region that other authors in this volume identify (and some condemn) may not turn out to be as costly in the long run as they have appeared to many observers over the past several years.

Richard Portes takes an entirely different approach to the issue of why debt restructuring matters, focusing primarily on sovereign debt (which did not figure prominently in the Asian crisis but was at the heart of the Mexican and Russian debt crises). Although Portes agrees with Friedman that it should never be too easy to restructure debt, the Asian crisis demonstrated the problems that may ensue when the contractual language of the debt instruments themselves makes debt too difficult to restructure.

In particular, Portes argues that while there has been widespread acceptance inside and outside the official community (governments and international financial institutions) on the need to revise bond contracts to require more "bailing in" by creditors—notably, through collective action clauses and standing creditor committees—effectively no action has been taken to implement these steps. Market participants strongly oppose such measures, claiming they run a major risk of redlining emerging market borrowers from international credit markets.

Portes strongly criticizes this stance, claiming that large rescue packages from the IMF could be avoided in the future if debt contracts were revised to force more orderly debt restructurings. This could be accomplished, in his view, if governments of the G-10 countries simply were to change their sovereign bond contracts, a step that he believes would be taken up by the private bond market in relatively short order. The alternatives to easing workouts are either additional large rescue efforts, with the attendant problems of moral hazard, or default, which Portes finds to have significantly worse effects on borrowers than orderly restructurings.

How rapidly has troubled debt been restructured in the countries caught up in the Asian crisis? Moreover, what lessons can private firms and policymakers draw from the restructuring process for future use? The next four papers in the volume address these questions.

Masahiro Kawai, Ira Lieberman, and William Mako examine the pace of debt restructuring in the Asian corporate sector by outlining what they believe are "best practices" for debt restructuring and then using this list to benchmark actual practice. Among other things, their best practices include the prompt appointment of a receiver; the presence of a court-supervised reorganization framework that protects debtors from asset seizures; substantial institutional capacity to handle the restructuring; a strong regulator that can encourage creditors to resolve differences among themselves; a well-developed market for corporate debt (including distressed debt); and a legal presumption, which can be altered during negotiation, that the equity interests of all shareholders will be wiped out in case of insolvency.

Measured against these criteria, the authors find that the responses of corporate sectors and systems in the region varied widely. Furthermore, because so many companies were rendered insolvent or subject to distress simultaneously during the 1997-98 crisis and its aftermath, the great majority of the debt restructurings proceeded out of court, through less-than-formal bankruptcy procedures. In addition, the authors find that governments displayed different degrees of proactivity and that all eventually used some form of workout agency to facilitate the process.

The authors conclude by assessing various "contextual factors" that, in their view, influenced the pace of debt restructuring in the region. In particular, they point to South Korea's political cohesion, which enabled the government to take the lead in facilitating workouts among the country's principal banks and many borrowers. All of the East Asian economies, however, suffered from a shortage of institutional capacity to deal with the overwhelming number of workout situations and the sheer magnitude of the debt involved. To prevent a recurrence of such crises in the future, the authors urge governments to be more aggressive in discouraging their corporate sectors from imprudent investment and excessive borrowing. They also counsel governments to create and stimulate the development of markets for distressed assets, so that debt resolution may proceed more efficiently and promptly in the future.

In the next paper, Joel Binamira and William Haworth provide their best estimates of the extent of debt restructuring through September 1999—the latest date for which figures were then available. Their findings (see p. 143) are summarized in the following table.

Country	Percent of corporate debt cases resolved	Percent of corporate debt restructured, by value
South Korea	78	50
Malaysia	22	35
Thailand	14	15
Indonesia	1	13

The table essentially confirms the more qualitative assessments of Mako and his colleagues. It indicates that, relative to other countries in the region, the corporate sector in South Korea had made the greatest strides in restructuring debts. Thailand and Malaysia had made lesser progress, while Indonesia trailed significantly behind. The authors warn that as long as large portions of troubled corporate debt remain, the banking systems in the region will continue to display some fragility.

Binamira and Haworth also document the high degree of concentration of ownership in each of the countries, to which they attribute the weakness of corporate governance and oversight before the crisis. Eager lenders also contributed to the crisis by allowing companies to leverage excessively, often with debt denominated in foreign currency. Meanwhile, because of weak minority shareholder rights, enterprises had few incentives to produce positive returns on investment or equity.

The authors note that all of the countries in the region made use of corporate debt restructuring agencies of one form or another. The intensity of the governments' efforts in facilitating restructuring, however, varied considerably; in some cases, financial assistance was provided to borrowers to encourage the process, but often the governments gained only limited commitments from these borrowers to reform their companies. Meanwhile, governments assumed ownership of many banks, but the nationalized banks often lacked the institutional capacity to restructure. Restructuring also has been delayed, in the authors' view, by the unwillingness of many owners to enter the process or to recognize the true extent of their problems, as well as by a shortage of qualified debt negotiators. Binamira and Haworth conclude that the robust macroeconomic growth that has returned to the region has reduced pressure on governments or corporations to undertake significant reforms in the way they conduct business.

Gregory Root and his coauthors consider the pace of restructuring in the region's financial sectors, concentrating on South Korea, Thailand, and Indonesia. In each case, government regulators closed some banks while recapitalizing or nationalizing others. It was not always a smooth operation.

Several countries have made use of asset management corporations (AMCs), which assumed the bad debt of the banks. Root and his coauthors find that Korea's AMC—KAMCO—in which the government has a majority stake, has played a constructive role in easing the burden of banks' nonperforming loans, as well as in disposing of much of the debt afterward. At the same time, they find that KAMCO and the Korean government underestimated the severity of the problem and were forced to add resources to the bank debt restructuring effort several times. The Korea Deposit Insurance Corporation also injected funds into the banking system.

The authors also find that the Korean authorities were among the most aggressive in the region in overhauling the national financial regulatory structure following the crisis. In particular, the government vested much more independence in its central bank than did other governments in the region, while stripping it of its regulatory functions and placing them in the hands of a new, comprehensive watchdog, the Financial Supervisory Commission (FSC). The FSC implemented a system of "prompt corrective action," modeled on that of the United States, in order to expedite regulatory intervention as signs of bank weakness emerged. At the same time, the government became much more receptive to investment in the financial sector by foreign financial institutions, which helped rescue a number of Korean institutions and injected a market-oriented credit culture into the

Korean financial system. The authors are encouraged by evidence that such a culture is beginning to take hold in Korea but are also concerned that the financial sector has placed too much emphasis on a statistical approach to risk management, given the lack of transparency of many Korean corporate borrowers and the inability of bank management to properly interpret the risk control data.

In the case of Thailand, Root and his coauthors note that the government's first step in response to the crisis was to make explicit its formerly implicit guarantee of protection for depositors and all senior creditors of all financial institutions. With this guarantee in place, the authorities were able to force the exit of fifty-six finance companies and the nationalization of seven banks without creating a large panic. (As of March 2000, four of these seven banks had been reprivatized.) The guarantee and the related bank recapitalization efforts, however, came with a high price tag—an estimated 40 percent of Thailand's GDP.

Instead of centralizing their workout operations, the Thai authorities allowed individual banks to establish their own asset recovery vehicles. The authors find that the banks moved slowly to fund and use these vehicles. As a result, restructuring of bad bank debt has proceeded relatively slowly in Thailand. On a positive note, Root and his coauthors applaud the Thai authorities for moving aggressively to restructure the country's financial supervisory system and for improving the central bank's operational efficiency.

Of the three countries surveyed in the paper, Indonesia stands out as the weakest performer with respect to bank restructuring. Indeed, at the time of the conference, about 90 percent of the Indonesian banking system's assets were still in government hands. The authors identify a number of impediments to more rapid progress, including the lack of clear policies and a preexisting environment of pervasive corruption (and thus the absence of an effective legal system). In principle, however, Indonesia took comprehensive action by vesting authority for the restructuring of all the banking sector's bad debts in the Indonesian Bank Restructuring Agency (IBRA). IBRA proceeded to recapitalize many "Category A and B" banks (respectively, those with positive capital or small negative book equity), nationalize others, and close thirty-eight banks. Before implementation of the full scheme, Indonesia suffered a deposit run on several of its banks, which required a massive injection of emergency liquidity support from the central bank.

It is difficult to overstate the difficulties confronting the banking system in Indonesia. Root and his co-authors indicate that, at their peak, nonperforming loans accounted for between 60 and 90 percent of the debt in the lending portfolios of many of the largest banks. The Indonesian government created its own version of an asset management authority to facilitate the removal of the nonperforming loans from the banking system. Smaller troubled loans, however, have continued to be handled by individual banks. Indonesia's asset management unit has moved very slowly, meanwhile, to sell off or otherwise resolve its problem debt.

Before the crisis, financial supervision in Indonesia rested with the central bank, which because it reported directly to the president, was open to direct political interference. The country's banking system was highly fragmented, many banks were owned by commercial conglomerates (and thus were subject to self-dealing), and there was no clear method for closing troubled banks. As a result, the infrastructure of the banking system was not ready for the enormous stresses it soon came under when the crisis erupted.

Since then, Indonesia's central bank law has been amended to give Bank Indonesia a single mission—to maintain the value of the rupiah—and its independence from the presidency has been secured. Until 2003, the central bank also will act as the bank supervisor; thereafter supervision is to be handled by a new independent body. Reporting and supervisory requirements for Indonesian banks also have been strengthened. The authors caution, however, that the jury is still out as to how successful these reforms will prove to be.

Finally, what do the current challenges imply for the future of the East Asian economies? Bernhard Eschweiler takes an optimistic view, arguing that the rapid growth of these economies in the past was neither miraculous nor flawed. The so-called Asian miracle resulted from a combination of abundant capital and labor, together with imported technologies, which enabled the economies to use their ample inputs in a highly efficient manner. Eschweiler believes that these fundamentals will restore growth in the region in the future—with the possible exception of Indonesia—despite the heavy overhang of unrestructured corporate and bank debt. Of particular importance to Eschweiler's forecast is the fact that private saving rates have remained high despite large fiscal deficits, while the economies have been open to trade, foreign investment, and technology transfers.

Nevertheless, the need to complete the job of debt restructuring remains a challenge that Eschweiler does not dismiss. Moreover, in the process of cleaning up the wreckage caused by the crisis, governments in the region have built up their debt burdens substantially, and Eschweiler finds this concern especially troubling for Indonesia.

If debt restructuring is important but has been proceeding at a modest pace at best, what steps can be taken to accelerate the process? This is the focus of the three papers in the third section of this volume.

Stefan Ingves and Dong He make the important point in their paper that the restructuring process requires an effective and well-functioning bankruptcy system, whose judgments can be enforced. Moreover, because the Asian financial crisis affected both banks and their corporate borrowers, the debts of both sectors must be restructured. Ingves and He believe, however, that the banking sector in these countries can and should be restructured first, since banks tend to be more homogeneous than their borrowers and are subject to direct prudential oversight.

The authors survey different countries in the region and find variations among institutional responses to the restructuring that help explain the differing patterns of adjustment discussed earlier. Indonesia and Thailand were relatively slow to establish governmental bank restructuring agencies; Korea was much quicker off the mark. The varying pace of adjustment in these countries seems to be consistent with these facts.

The authors find some common elements among the restructuring efforts, however. In the case of banks in particular, nonviable institutions were separated from those determined to be viable. Those in the latter category have been forced to raise capital—often from foreign institutions—or have been recapitalized with government funds, or both. In the process, bank restructuring has forced governments in the region to relax prior restrictions on foreign ownership of financial institutions, a healthy by-product in the view of the authors (and many others). The governments of Indonesia, South Korea, and Thailand also have nationalized several of their countries' banks, with commitments to return those institutions to the private sector. At the time the paper was written, the authors reported that some progress toward reprivatization had been accomplished in Korea and Thailand (although not in Indonesia). At the end of the day, the authors estimate the gross costs of resolving failed banks in the region to total between 15 and 45 percent of GDP.

The East Asian governments have not been as directly involved in the restructuring of corporate debt as they have been in the case of banks, for understandable reasons: corporations are not subject to direct supervision, and their liabilities are not directly or implicitly backed by the governments. Nonetheless, the absence of effective bankruptcy systems in these countries has contributed to the delay in corporate debt restructuring. Some countries (notably Korea and Thailand) have attempted to expedite the process, however, by providing tax incentives.

The Korean government has encouraged expeditious out-of-court restructurings, encouraging the formation of a consortium of financial institutions to help arbitrate differences among creditors and debtors. During the conference's discussion period, Michael Pomerleano reported on the progress that had been made in Korea through the creation of "corporate restructuring funds," which are managed by foreign investment banks but financed by domestic banks. These funds purchase new issues of equity and bonds of heavily indebted, but potentially viable, small- and medium-size enterprises. The proceeds from these new issues are used to repay existing debts in return for commitments by the enterprises to allow stronger, independent directors to help supervise the operational restructuring of the companies. Pomerleano observed that, by taking large minority positions in companies that can benefit from balance sheet restructuring, the restructuring funds have alleviated the financial distress of Korean companies that were burdened with high levels of debt. The funds have also been instrumental in developing capital markets in Korea.

David Scott agrees in his paper with the view that government-led bank restructuring must take place simultaneously with corporate debt restructuring. In particular, capital-short banks must be given sufficient financial support to absorb losses entailed in writing down or restructuring debt owed by corporate borrowers. Where governments cannot carry out this exercise themselves, Scott urges them to contract with private sector specialists.

Scott explains that economies (and their governments) suffer both direct and indirect costs during financial crises. The direct costs consist of the financial support governments provide to banks to protect depositors. Once depositors are paid off (or their banks recapitalized), governments may also have to carry the costs of nonperforming assets until they can be sold to private purchasers. Indirect costs consist of the reduced national output and tax revenues, higher inflation and unemployment, and political costs associated with financial crises; they can impair the ability of governments to finance direct costs associated with crises, or to take prompt action to minimize those costs. Indeed, Scott points to delay in recognizing the costs of financial crises as a significant reason why those costs can mount.[2]

Scott assesses the use of asset management companies (AMCs), established by governments and banks in the region to take over nonperforming assets. In principle, AMCs can help clean up banks' balance sheets quickly, but they must be managed effectively and used aggressively to restructure or sell troubled loans. In practice, this often has not been the case. Indeed, Scott argues that when AMCs sever the lending relationships between borrowers and their banks—as is inevitably the case—the borrowers have dramatically reduced incentives to repay their debts. Other discussants at the conference shared this assessment.

Scott concludes his paper by comparing what he labels the "bilateral" approach to restructuring, which involves only banks and their borrowers, with the "trilateral" approach, in which the government becomes involved on a case-by-case basis. In particular, Scott advocates that governments provide financial support for banks only as part of a wider process in which the banks' loans to troubled borrowers are resolved concomitantly. Scott details how such a trilateral approach to debt restructuring might best be carried out.

Gerald Meyerman focuses on the London Approach to corporate restructuring and describes how it could be used more widely in Asia. The London Approach was developed when the Bank of England, on its own initiative and without committing its funds, led workouts of corporate debts owed to banks during the recession suffered by the United Kingdom in the mid-1970s.

By the 1990s the Bank of England had abandoned any formal role in debt restructuring but continued to provide informal guidance to banks and other creditors on how to react when corporate borrowers were unable to make their payments. These "London Rules" involve informal arrangements completed outside the bankruptcy process under which the bankers agree to what amounts to an informal standstill during which the creditor(s) and the bank work together, perhaps with a lead bank in charge (where there are multiple lenders) to resolve existing debts. In some cases— in particular, when the enterprise is deemed viable on an ongoing basis— new money is provided pro rata by the existing lenders. Meyerman notes

2. The experiences of the United States with regulatory forbearance granted to insolvent thrift institutions in the 1980s and of Japan with similar forbearances granted to its banks amply demonstrate this point.

that the London Approach was instrumental in avoiding a wave of corporate bankruptcies during the recession that hit the United Kingdom (and other parts of the world) during the early 1990s.

Given its success, Meyerman argues, it is not surprising that something like the London Approach was used in the Asian countries affected by the financial crisis, although the way it was implemented varied across countries. Thailand and Korea, for example, set up informal rules for restructuring in 1998. Especially rapid progress was made in Korea.

Nonetheless, there are key differences between the informal restructurings in Asia and those undertaken in England. In the case of the United Kingdom, the Bank of England played a central role in facilitating restructuring. In Asia, by contrast, many of the borrowers that found themselves in trouble also owned or controlled the banks that had provided their financing. In other cases, notably that of Indonesia, the government owned the banks. Accordingly, the central banks in Asia could not play the neutral, facilitative role that the Bank of England had assumed in the 1970s and again in the 1990s. Instead, Asian governments set up separate organizations, or restructuring committees, to assist the workouts, a strategy that Meyerman finds to be only modestly successful, in large part because participation by debtors has been voluntary rather than mandatory.

Meyerman concludes that the London Approach was more effective in England than in Asia for a combination of reasons, including a greater culture of cooperation in the United Kingdom, coupled with a more effective legal system that was capable of backstopping the voluntary out-of-court settlement process. Various other impediments in the Asian countries— including restrictive labor laws, tax policies, and limitations on foreign participation in workouts (which were gradually lifted during the course of the crisis)—also have slowed the pace of debt restructuring.

Looking ahead, a major challenge for all countries—especially the emerging markets—is to minimize the risk of future financial crises and reduce the severity of crises when they occur. The concluding portion of this volume examines the sources of countries' external vulnerability and considers what national governments and private market participants can do to enhance resilience and better handle liquidity pressures.

Dipak Dasgupta, Dilip Ratha, Dennis Botman, and Ashish Narain focus on the large amounts of short-term external borrowing by the countries at the epicenter of the recent crisis. Consistent with a number of other recent studies, the authors find that a high ratio of short-term debt to reserves has a significant impact on countries' external vulnerability in situations when fundamental economic policies are weak. They also find that short-term capital flows to emerging markets tend to exhibit procyclical behavior—that is, flows rise during favorable domestic times and fall more sharply in bad times. As a result, foreign capital tends not to be available for consumption-smoothing and does not play a stabilizing role when there are unfavorable shocks to the domestic economy. For all these reasons, countries must avoid imprudent short-term borrowing if they wish to avoid future crises.

What factors led to the excessive borrowing that made the Asian countries so susceptible to the crisis when it hit? Dagupta and his colleagues point to premature liberalization of restrictions on short-term cross-border borrowing—before prudential supervision and regulation of domestic financial institutions was strengthened—as a major mistake. This error is now widely recognized. International bank capital rules also favored short-term lending by foreign banks. In 1999 the Basel Committee, which sets these standards, proposed changes to reduce this bias and at this writing, is considering comments on its proposal.

Peter Garber examines methods that the private sector uses, at least in principle, to better manage financial risks, concentrating on various derivative products—swaps, repurchase agreements, options, structured notes—whose volumes have shown explosive growth in recent years, paralleling the growth in cross-border capital movements generally. Garber is not entirely sanguine about this development, and he argues that derivative products so far have been imperfectly supervised at both national and international levels. Using examples from the Mexican crisis of 1994–95 and the recent crises in Korea, Brazil, and Russia, Garber illustrates how off-balance sheet derivative transactions can make individual institutions and financial systems far more vulnerable to disruption than is indicated by their on-balance sheet positions. As a result, the use of derivatives can create uncertainty for regulators about where the risks in international transactions ultimately reside.

Garber also considers how derivatives can skew the information rendered by balance-of-payments accounts. Examples include the way in which on-balance sheet categorizations such as "short-term" and "long-term" flows can lose their information content in the presence of off-balance-sheet maturity transformations and how swap agreements involving equities and bonds can change the interpretation of foreign direct investment data. Garber suggests the need for statistical conventions that go beyond providing health warnings about traditional balance-of-payment classifications to keep better pace with the rapid development of financial innovation, and especially with the growing use of derivatives.

Timothy Wilson develops a number of "good housekeeping" principles for economic agents to follow in seeking to strengthen risk management and considers the role of the private sector and central banks in managing liquidity crises. The principles that Wilson outlines underscore the importance of having economic agents better understand the nature and sources of their risk exposures as a precondition for proper risk management and for the effective use of stress tests and value-at-risk models. He suggests that marking to market (at least internally) should play an important role in helping identify and properly assess risk profiles.

Of particular interest is Wilson's discussion of the responsibilities of the private sector and central banks in managing liquidity crises. Wilson argues that private financial firms are best placed to handle "micro" liquidity pressures affecting small individual institutions. Furthermore, such recent financial innovations as securitization, coupled with different appetites for liquidity across agents, should allow—at least in principle—for the efficient and timely reallocation of liquidity as needed. Having the private sector deal with liquidity demands can also avoid the moral hazard that inevitably accompanies central bank intervention.

Nonetheless, central banks clearly have a crucial role to play in the case of systemic or "macro" liquidity crises. To deal with such events, Wilson suggests that central banks should not provide support free of charge. He proposes that central banks consider selling "liquidity" options, following the lead of the Federal Reserve System in handling potential liquidity problems during the Year 2000 transition. Proper pricing of central bank liquidity support should encourage more efficient liquidity management and reduce moral hazard.

Clearly, liquidity options provided by a central bank may be useful for dealing with particular liquidity events. Their broader use, however, raises many difficult issues of pricing and tradability. Moreover, the question remains whether central banks can credibly pre-commit to provide liquidity solely through options. Accordingly, as Wilson himself notes, more work on the concept is required before making it widely operational.

Kenneth Kletzer and Ashoka Mody focus their analysis of risk management at the country level, considering in particular the costs and benefits of measures that emerging markets can take to deal with readily reversible capital flows. Their analysis is based on two main arguments. First, not all emerging market crises result from the fundamental weaknesses in macro-economic policies emphasized in first-generation balance-of-payments crisis models. Emerging markets can be especially vulnerable to self-fulfilling liquidity crises during the long time needed to achieve complete domestic financial sector development. Second, because of the high economic and political costs of exchange rate variability, freely floating exchange rates are not the panacea for emerging markets that many have suggested. In short, countries cannot practice benign neglect with regard to their currencies.

As a result, the authors argue for specific liquidity-enhancing measures that can help emerging markets better handle international liquidity pressures and avoid their current high costs. Kletzer and Mody suggest that it would be foolish for countries to assume that the international community will provide the levels of support required and that countries therefore must take the initiative themselves.

Kletzer and Mody consider three sets of self-protection measures: accumulating large war chests of borrowed reserves; establishing private and official contingent credit lines; and imposing prudential limits or taxes on short-term external debt (like those that Chile imposed during much of the 1990s). The authors conduct a careful analysis of the various measures and conclude that the choices involve balancing a number of considerations, including fiscal costs and the impact of measures on the terms and conditions of capital market access. They think it unlikely that any single approach would be universally applicable. Kletzer and Mody nonetheless provide a favorable assessment of private contingent credit lines as a means by which countries can protect themselves against sudden reversals of capital flows. They acknowledge that contingent financing provided by private sector institutions may be partially offset by dynamic hedging on the part of the credit providers themselves. Still, the authors believe that contingent credit lines can provide useful and relatively inexpensive insurance for liquidity problems and thereby enhance confidence in a nation's currency and overall economy.

Mansoor Dailami concludes the volume with a broad analysis of how governments can manage the risks of capital mobility. He begins by noting that for roughly the first three decades after the end of World War II, capital was largely restricted to national borders (especially in the case of less developed countries) and exchange rates were fixed. The collapse of the Bretton Woods system of fixed exchange rates, in combination with sharply higher oil prices, intensified currency and interest rate risks during the 1970s and 1980s; increasingly, actors attempted to manage these risks through derivative instruments, such as options, futures, and swaps. The globalization of financial markets in the 1990s—driven by advances in communications and information technologies and the relaxation of barriers to movements of capital across borders—has given rise to an entirely new set of challenges.

Dailami explores, among other topics, the connection between a country's openness to foreign capital and its commitment to redistributionist policies as a way of insuring the population against sudden shifts in international financial sentiment. He finds a positive, statistically significant correlation between the two variables. He also considers capital controls, which represent one means that countries may use to mitigate risks against financial crises. Dailami concurs with those who suggest that, for a time, taxes on short-term capital movements may be a useful risk-minimizing device. But he also argues that the effectiveness of such controls eventually diminishes. What is important from Dailami's study is that, in the long run, openness to foreign capital has both economic and noneconomic (political) benefits that policymakers can all too easily overlook.

At the risk of rushing to policy conclusions, what are some of the key lessons from the recent Asian experience in financial restructuring? In concluding this overview, we offer some tentative views based on our own synthesis of some of the key points in the papers that follow.

We begin, perhaps appropriately, with lessons relating to *crisis prevention*. Well before the Asian crisis of 1997–98, the corporate sector in Indonesia, South Korea, and Thailand was characterized by rapid growth in fixed investment, fueled by debt, and low and declining profitability. Under these conditions, governments are advised to discourage their banks from lending heavily to companies that are already highly leveraged or showing low or negative levels of profitability. Meanwhile, governments should encourage full and prompt disclosure of the financial conditions of their publicly held corporations so that bond and equity investors also can apply market discipline that works in the same direction.

Financial crises will still occur, however, and so governments need to learn from recent experience in fashioning appropriate *responses*. Several lessons emerge from the papers in this volume.

First, even with the best developed legal and institutional mechanisms for restructuring troubled debt—which the Asian countries did not have at the time of the 1997–98 crisis—some financial crises may be so severe that countries will require special structures and procedures, outside of existing formal bankruptcy, to expedite the restructuring of both corporate and bank debt. These informal out-of-court resolution processes will not be fully effective, however, without more backup formal mechanisms so that debtors cannot readily walk away from their commitments.

Second, in order to facilitate this restructuring process, governments must be involved in some fashion, preferably by providing incentives, but if necessary through mandates. Otherwise, the tendencies are too great for troubled companies and banks to ignore the severity of their financial problems and to hope that they will somehow go away if the economy simply recovers. Indeed, a central problem that has plagued efforts to restructure debts throughout the region is that each of the actors—corporate owners, banks, and governments—has been reluctant to allocate the losses from the sharp change in economic circumstances. Praying for recovery, or alternatively willfully ignoring the full magnitude of the problem, are not substitutes for more proactive involvement by governments.

Third, there is no one-size-fits-all solution to the restructuring problem. Countries have different cultures and institutions, and approaches to restructuring must be tailored with those differences in mind.

Fourth, the Asian crisis underscored the close connections between the debt problems of the banking and corporate sectors. This should not be surprising, since corporate debts are assets on bank balance sheets, and if those assets become imperiled, they can threaten the viability of the banks that hold them. Nonetheless, most of the attention of policymakers during the Asian crisis was concentrated on restoring health to the banking sector; comparatively less attention has been paid to facilitating more rapid restructuring of corporate debt. As several of the papers in this volume suggest, either implicitly or explicitly, the imbalance of attention given to corporate debt restructuring was a mistake, and one that should be rectified in the resolution of future crises. The more rapidly corporate debt can be restructured, the more quickly policymakers and the public at large can ascertain the real value of the banks that may hold this debt, and thus troubled banks themselves may be more efficiently assisted and restructured.

As we have indicated, each of the countries in the region used public asset management companies to transfer problem assets out of troubled banks. The AMCs proved to be successful in this endeavor, but far less so in disposing of the assets thereafter. In part, this is because secondary asset markets in the Asian countries were relatively underdeveloped before the crisis. Clearly, therefore, emerging market countries need to develop secondary markets for bonds and real estate. Such markets not only provide better price signals when times are good, but permit the transfer of troubled assets in times of stress.

Finally, as one of the discussants at the conference noted, the countries and their governments at the heart of the crisis are suffering from "reform fatigue," especially with the recovery of their economies. As a result, there is a danger that the momentum behind institutional reforms will falter without ongoing governmental commitment to reform. The papers in this volume help make the case for the value of such a commitment.

PART I

Debt Restructuring: What Does It Matter?

BENJAMIN M. FRIEDMAN

2

How Easy Should Debt Restructuring Be?

B ORROWERS SOMETIMES can't pay what they owe, and most borrowers and lenders know this. As a result, debt contracts are usually more complicated, and the considerations that underlie debt arrangements are more subtle, than would be the case if all that mattered were the time value of money. Two specific distinctions are of particular importance for this purpose: Some borrowers don't pay what they owe because they can't, while others can pay but seek not to. And among those borrowers who can't pay what they owe when they owe it, some can pay later but others can't pay ever. What to do when borrowers don't meet their obligations is therefore not merely a matter of set principles but also of information, inference, and judgment.

Although these basic truths and the practical questions they raise are relevant to all debt markets, the events of the past few years have especially highlighted their importance in the context of borrowers in developing economies and in economies in transition from central planning to reliance on private initiative and incentives—"emerging markets," as they

I am grateful to Richard Cooper, Howell Jackson, Edward Ladd, John Olcay, Dwight Perkins, Michael Pomerleano, Hal Scott, Elizabeth Warren, and numerous other colleagues and friends for helpful discussions, although I alone assume responsibility for the ideas expressed here. I am also grateful for research support from the Harvard Program for Financial Research.

are typically called. From the summer of 1997 until well into 1999, a series of countries, first in Asia and then in Latin America, experienced debt problems severe enough to be widely regarded as crises, typically in conjunction with currency crises. But even in the setting of economic development, such problems were by no means new in 1997. There is a long history of just this kind of event. The Asian crisis in 1997 was not the first such major problem but merely the first since Mexico in 1994–95.

Placing the questions that arise from debtors' actual or potential nonperformance in the specific setting of emerging markets adds several important dimensions to the basic considerations that are already present when the borrower and the lender are both resident in a country like, say, the United States. To begin, when the source of the saving flow that finances the credit is outside the borrower's country—as is often the case for developing economies, which normally rely heavily on foreign capital inflows—then relative currency values become part of the story. Next, many emerging market countries lack the legal or other institutional frameworks that provide standard and well-understood remedies when problems of borrower nonperformance occur in the industrialized countries. Sometimes the requisite legal institutions exist but enforcement is problematic. Many emerging market countries similarly lack the auditing and accounting practices that facilitate monitoring the financial condition of private borrowers in the industrialized world. Finally, in some emerging market countries the borrowers, although nominally private, are often de facto extensions of the government. Sometimes the borrower whose ability to perform is in question is the government itself.

The issue addressed in this paper is what to do when borrowers in emerging markets can't pay what they owe to foreign lenders. The specific question asked is what difference it makes, and for whom, whether the debts of nonperforming borrowers are restructured. Although the presumption here is that the nonperforming debt is owed abroad, the chain from ultimate lender to ultimate borrower may have several steps, and so the nonperforming debts in question are not necessarily owed to foreign lenders directly. But for purposes of this discussion, the fact that it is foreign saving that ultimately stands behind the credit chain is what matters.

In order to pose meaningfully a question like what difference some action or some process makes, it is ordinarily necessary to specify "compared to what?" In the case of debt restructuring, however, specifying a clear-cut alternative is problematic. The logically most obvious alternative to restructuring a nonperforming debt would be an outright declaration that the borrower will not meet the obligation, now or ever, but such a possibility is of little practical relevance in this setting. In the private sector a declaration of this kind conceptually means bankruptcy, but the absence of functioning bankruptcy institutions and procedures is central to the issue in many emerging markets. Among governments, outright debt repudiation is rare apart from revolutionary changes in regime, and even then many postrevolutionary governments carry their predecessors' unpaid debts for decades and eventually reach a settlement with their creditors.[1]

A further reflection of this difficulty in specifying an alternative, which is relevant to much of the argument developed in this paper, is that while the event of default on a debt contract has a fairly precise technical meaning from a legal standpoint, there is no generally accepted *economic* definition of default. One that would make sense for many purposes would be to say that default consists of any action by a borrower that results in a reduction in the present value of what was originally promised to the lenders. (Hence repaying the full amount owed but at a later date would ordinarily constitute default, as would a reduction in the originally stated interest rate or, of course, forgiveness of any part of the stated debt principal.) But default conceived in this way is not very helpful for this paper's analysis either. The question at issue here is what should be done when an emerging market borrower fails to perform as a debt agreement requires, and for practical purposes this situation almost always results in at least some loss of present value to the lenders, whether the debt is restructured or not. The issue here is not whether borrowers should deliver more to lenders, but whether formal debt restructuring is a useful way to proceed once it is clear that a borrower will not perform as the original terms of the obligation specify.

In practice, therefore, the plausible alternative to debt restructuring is hard to pin down precisely. In the reality of actual market practice, there is a large continuum between the poles of formal debt restructuring and formal repudiation. The main conclusion drawn here is that current market practice is at a wrong point on this continuum. Moreover, although

1. For example, although Cuba has long since repudiated all debts of the pre-Castro regime, in 1979 the People's Republic of China settled with the U.S. government on claims against pre-1949 Nationalist China, and Russia recently even settled with holders of pre-1917 Tsarist bonds.

the situation of borrower nonperformance considered here almost always results in at least some loss of present value to the lenders, lenders' sometimes do but often do not recognize that loss for purposes of accounting, regulatory requirements, and the like. Part of what is wrong about the position of current practice on this continuum between restructuring and repudiation is that lenders recognize such losses too infrequently. In terms of a concept that figures importantly in this analysis, the "fiction" of no loss of value is too much a part of current market practice.

To state the argument more fully, the chief conclusions of this paper's inquiry into what difference debt restructuring makes are as follows:

(1) The conventional wisdom that in cases of debt-service difficulties rescheduling and other forms of restructuring help to keep new money flowing to the borrowers is correct.

(2) That said, however, not all nonperforming debts should be restructured. Some frequency of "defaults" (to the extent that default can be considered the alternative to restructuring), arguably greater than that reflected in current practice, is healthy.

(3) With a greater frequency of default, some credit flows to emerging market countries that would take place in a lower-default-rate regime presumably would not happen. This outcome too is not necessarily bad. Judged from the perspective of why debt markets exist in the first place, the highest aim of borrowing and lending arrangements is *not* simply to maximize the volume of credit flows.

(4) Although maximizing economic output and economic development *is* a plausible objective in choosing borrowing and lending arrangements, avoiding lost output and temporarily interrupted development in every case is not. Real costs consequent on borrowers' nonperformance, costs that accrue to debtors as well as creditors, serve an economic function too. The goal of output growth and economic development, construed broadly over time and space, is plausibly enhanced when specific borrowers at specific times suffer real costs, just as it is when specific lenders at specific times sustain losses.

As the discussion throughout the paper makes clear (if it is not apparent already), an important force driving this argument is the problem of "moral hazard" that arises from the differing incentives of borrowers and lenders.[2]

---

2. For a general discussion of moral hazard in this context, see Eaton and Gersovitz (1981). See also Obstfeld and Rogoff (1996, chap. 6), and the many references cited there.

Especially in the context of much of the public debate that has ensued from the emerging markets debt crisis of the past few years, it is worth pointing out explicitly that the moral hazard on which the argument here depends arises from the ordinary conflict of borrowers' and lenders' interests inherent in any debt transaction, rather than any consequence specifically attributable to the role of the International Monetary Fund (IMF) or other official lenders. The actual or potential availability of credit from the IMF or other official sources may exacerbate the moral hazard problem that already exists, and hence may make financial problems of the kind many emerging market countries have recently experienced more likely or, when a problem does occur, more severe. That question is a subject for a different paper. But it is wrong as a matter of history to think that there were no such crises in the past before there was an IMF, and it is therefore wrong as a matter of political economy to believe that simply abolishing the IMF, as some of the institution's recent critics have suggested, would be sufficient to prevent such crises in the future.[3] The more fundamental moral hazard issue that constitutes the heart of the analysis here, and the questions that this paper raises about the "no-loss-of-value fiction," would remain in any case.

The first section briefly sets the stage for the paper's main line of argument by positing a set of patently counterfactual conditions under which it would *not* matter whether a nonperforming loan were rescheduled or otherwise restructured. The second section shows how several ways in which the actual world of international lending to emerging market borrowers departs from these counterfactual conditions give both lenders and borrowers ample reason to care whether nonperforming debts are restructured. The third section shows that one implication of the way in which restructuring matters is that although restructuring is useful to both lenders and borrowers, it nonetheless should not be "too" easy. The fourth section then examines how this line of reasoning leads to the sequence of conclusions stated above: that some nonperforming debts should default, that some credits should not be extended in the first place, and that under some circumstances debt arrangements should impose real economic costs on defaulting borrowers as well as on the holders of defaulted debt. While no ready metric exists (and this paper doesn't develop one) for saying how far current practice should optimally

---

3. See DeLong (1999) for a useful historical review.

move in the direction indicated by these conclusions, as a qualitative matter the warranted direction is clear. The paper concludes with brief comments on two further issues.

A Counterfactual Base for Comparison

Often the logically coherent way to understand why something matters is first to posit circumstances in which it *wouldn't* matter, and then to focus on differences between those circumstances and actual reality. Four plainly counterfactual assumptions are together sufficient to make both lenders and borrowers indifferent to whether a nonperforming debt is rescheduled or otherwise restructured (although certainly not indifferent to whether the loan becomes nonperforming in the first place, nor to the amount, if any, that the lenders ultimately recover):

(1) All lending takes the form of marketable securities, which are regularly traded in highly liquid ("thick") markets. Specific borrowers do not have "relationships" with specific lenders.

(2) All lenders mark their portfolios of such securities to market daily.

(3) Each borrower's obligations are consolidated. There is only one debt security outstanding against each borrower.

(4) Each borrower's debt is a "one-off" transaction—for example, the financing of a freestanding, independent project. There is neither the expectation nor the possibility that the borrower will seek further funds in the debt market.

What happens under these conditions when a borrower has difficulty in meeting its obligations? Once information that this has happened, or even merely information suggesting the possibility that this may happen, reaches the market in which the borrower's debt securities trade, current holders of these securities as well as other potential holders will reduce their assessment of what the securities are worth. In the extreme case that there is no prospect that the borrower will ever pay anything on its debt, the market value of the securities will fall to that of the underlying collateral, if any, less any costs of gaining possession of that collateral and liquidating it. In the further extreme case that the collateral has become either unobtainable or worthless, the market value of the securities will be zero. Because no lenders have privileged information bearing on such matters, current holders of the securities have no systematic reason to disagree with other market participants about their worth. The only question facing each lender is whether to hold or sell the securities (or buy more) at whatever new, presumably lower, market price emerges.

Further, regardless of whether a lender sells its position in the borrower's securities or not, the lender will have to take the reduction in value into account on its balance sheet. If the lender is a bank, or some other financial institution facing regulation similar to that applicable to banks, the reduced asset value passes through to its equity in a way that bears on the lender's ability to meet its capital requirements. If the lender is a mutual fund, the reduced valuation is directly reflected in the fund's quoted net asset value. In either case, no action by the lender can avoid or mitigate these consequences.

The borrower's incentive to meet its obligations is to avoid seizure of its collateral, unless the present value of the debt service owed is greater than the value of the collateral, in which case the borrower would prefer to sacrifice the collateral and stop paying altogether. The lenders' incentive, however, is to receive as much value as possible from the remaining debt obligation under the new circumstances. From the perspective of an *individual* lender—that is, any one holder of the borrower's debt securities—the present value of the borrower's future payments or the proceeds of seizure and liquidation of the collateral is simply priced into the market value of the securities. By contrast, the lenders *collectively* retain an interest in steering the outcome toward whatever course of action will give them greater value, and therefore in whatever process enables them best to achieve this end.

But, importantly, under these circumstances lenders do *not* have an interest in formal restructuring of the debt per se. The borrower's difficulty in meeting the obligation has already resulted in a reduced price of the securities, and each holder of those securities has immediately taken that reduced value on its balance sheet. Although whoever is empowered to act as agent for the lenders will presumably try to persuade the borrower to perform to the greatest extent possible, using the threat of seizing the collateral as its means of compulsion, once the borrower's future performance or failure to pay is taken as given, a formal restructuring would change nothing. At the same time, the borrower's only incentive in this regard is to prevent seizure of the collateral. Moreover, because the lenders have no reason to seek a formal restructuring, the borrower's offering to enter into one would not represent a concession of any value. In short, restructuring simply would not matter.

Why Restructuring Does Matter

None of the four counterfactual conditions listed above corresponds to the actual world in which either sovereign or private emerging market borrowers obtain credit. Focusing on how each of these stated conditions departs from the "real world" makes clear just why restructuring a debt once a borrower has failed to meet its commitments, or even in advance of an actual event of nonperformance, can be important and normally is.

The Role of Banks

Although the bond market now plays a far greater role in funneling credit to emerging market countries than was the case not long ago (though perhaps not any more so than before World War I), it remains true that much of the debt of both public and private borrowers in these countries takes the form of bank loans. Moreover, most borrowers have traditionally attached high priority to staying current on their security obligations. (Among sovereign borrowers, Russia and Ecuador are the only two recent examples of clear nonperformance on the government's bonds, although what would happen to Mexico's dollar-linked tesobonos was a major question during the 1994–95 crisis.) Hence most of the emerging market debt that has been the focus of attention in discussions of restructuring is in fact owed to banks, and much of that is in the form of loans rather than securities.

One reason this matters is that banks, unlike many lenders in the bond market, can and often do maintain ongoing relationships with particular borrowers. The heart of such relationships is that some lenders have information—perhaps privately disclosed data, perhaps specialized knowledge of a country or its banks or its operating businesses, perhaps person-to-person experience with the individuals responsible for the borrower's affairs—that other lenders do not. The enhanced information content of borrower-lender relationships in turn has value to both sides. From the lender's perspective, more information means less risk. To the borrower, the fact of being perceived by some lender as less risky means a lower cost of credit. In extreme cases it may mean the difference between having access to credit and finding none available at any price.

Another reason why the role of banks in lending to emerging market borrowers is important is that banks normally face capital requirements. Loss of sufficient asset value can therefore force a bank into a disadvantaged competitive position—for example, having to stop seeking new business, or being forced to raise new capital on unfavorable terms—and large enough losses can even compromise a bank's viability as an independent institution. (The sharpest counterexample is an open-end mutual fund, where losses on holdings of securities mean a lower quoted net asset value but typically trigger no direct consequences to the fund itself.)

It also matters in this context that much of the credit banks extend to emerging market borrowers takes the form of loans rather than marketable securities. The market for such loans is normally thin. When a borrower experiences difficulties, each lender will have its own assessment of the probability of receiving payment and hence its own notion of what its asset is still worth. The banks that maintain a special relationship with a particular borrower may well have a different sense of the value of that borrower's obligations (either higher or lower) than do other lenders. But there is no readily visible, consensus reference-value for the loan's worth comparable to that given by the price of a bond traded in a highly liquid securities market.

Not Marking to Market

For reasons that derive in part from precisely this absence of thick and liquid markets for loan assets, banks do not mark their loan portfolios to market on anything like a daily basis. Hence the decline in asset value consequent on a borrower's actual or likely nonperformance does not immediately or automatically affect banks' balance sheets in a way that would matter for their capital requirements (although risk-related capital requirements are typically greater for nonperforming loans). If nonperformance has merely become more likely but a loan remains current, normally banks do not reflect this change in their balance sheets at all. Even when a borrower has missed a payment, whether and how soon the lending banks will reduce the stated value of its loan—and by how much—is in the first instance a matter of internal judgment and, beyond that, subject to opinion from the regulators.[4] But neither the banks' internal valuation procedure nor that of bank regulators is likely to track closely the price

---

4. In the United States, for example, the Federal Reserve System, the Comptroller of the Currency, and the Federal Deposit Insurance Corporation render an interagency judgment when they deem that assets are "value impaired."

fluctuation that would take place in liquid security markets in a situation of anticipated or actual borrower nonperformance.[5]

The fact that the lenders are banks and that banks do not immediately mark loans to market (and, moreover, that knowing the market price is problematic anyway) produces one straightforward reason why rescheduling or other formal restructuring can make a difference when a borrower encounters difficulties: Restructuring enhances the lenders' control over the value that they assign to a loan on their balance sheets. This control itself has value. Replacing an old loan with a new one, stretching out payment schedules, adjusting the interest rate and even forgiving missed interest payments (or relegating them to "memo interest") are all ways of maintaining the fiction—for accounting purposes—that a loan is still an asset worth what it was worth before, even though the appropriately risk-adjusted present value of the probable stream of payments to flow from that asset may be diminished.

Such accounting fictions have no direct bearing on the economic value of a lender's business, but they do affect a lender's business if they affect its ability to meet its capital requirements. The ability to maintain the fiction of no loss in value is therefore valuable. Hence *lenders* have a reason to prefer formal restructuring to either default or mere nonperformance. And because restructuring has value to lenders but requires the agreement of both parties, lenders in turn have an incentive to induce borrowers to want (or at least agree) to restructure their problem obligations as well.

Multiple Debts

Few borrowers have only one consolidated debt. Most, including most borrowers in emerging markets, owe different amounts to different lenders or groups of lenders. Often these debts are also of different form: some securities, some loans (of which some are collateralized and some are not), some self-liquidating trade credits, and so on. Often the same lenders participate in providing financing to the same borrower, or group of related borrowers, in several different forms. A bank, for example, might own a country's

---

5. The fact that banks can set aside a reserve against prospective decline in the value of loan assets complicates this story somewhat but represents no fundamental change. The reserve is a counter-asset against the loan, reducing the net (loan minus reserve) value on the asset side of the bank's balance sheet. Reserving against a loan therefore reduces the bank's stated equity just as if the bank had written down the value of the loan itself. For purposes that matter to this discussion, the two are equivalent.

sovereign bonds, extend what amount to uncollateralized loans to the country's government or its banks, and also provide trade credit to operating companies conducting import-export business there.

The multiplicity of debts would not matter if all of a borrower's obligations were strictly independent of one another. In fact they are not. Cross-default and acceleration clauses give lenders in one transaction the ability to demand full and immediate payment if the borrower defaults on an obligation resulting from a separate transaction. To the extent that borrowers prefer not to have their other debts called—after all, there was a reason to borrow the funds in the first place—under these arrangements *borrowers* therefore have a reason to prefer formal restructuring to default. Borrowers may likewise have reason to prefer formal restructuring to merely creating an event, such as a missed payment, that would qualify as default even if they were confident that the lender on that particular transaction would not declare a default. What matters in this case is whether the lenders on the borrowers' *other* transactions would exercise the right to demand payment of *their* claims.[6]

The fact of multiplicity of debts and multiplicity of lenders matters in yet further ways in the emerging markets context because of the connection between a country's foreign borrowing, which is the focus of discussion here, and what happens in its domestic credit markets. In the case of sovereign credits, governments typically borrow both abroad and at home, sometimes via the same securities. Hence nonperformance on obligations to foreign lenders can trigger a collapse of the country's domestic credit market.[7] Moreover, because nonperformance by governments on foreign debt often leads to exchange controls that both block domestic residents' capital mobility and impede debt service payments by private sector borrowers, the most immediate result is often capital flight—which in turn either worsens the crisis or creates a crisis if there was not one already.

6. It is useful to distinguish this reason for *borrowers* to seek debt restructuring from the reason given above for lenders to do so. The lenders' reason for preferring restructuring to default grows out of forces *external* to the direct borrower-lender relationship: specifically, the capital requirements and accounting practices that are a part of the relationship between lenders and their regulators. By contrast, the *borrowers'* reason for preferring restructuring to default or mere nonpayment grows directly out of an aspect of the borrower-lender relationship, albeit a relationship between the borrower and its lenders other than those on whose claim the borrower is not performing.

7. During the 1994–95 Mexican crisis, for example, many tesobono-holders were domiciled in Mexico. Default would almost certainly have made it impossible for the government to borrow from domestic Mexican lenders, and probably would have shut down the country's credit markets more generally.

Ongoing Needs

As is already implicit in the preceding discussion, most borrowers' debts do not arise as one-time needs. Borrowers, including in particular borrowers in emerging markets, have an ongoing need for new credit. At the most basic level, the financing needs of either a single firm or an entire country plausibly increase in pace with the scale of economic activity. Economic growth means increased demand for credit. For countries engaged in international trade where transactions are executed in foreign currencies, some of that credit normally comes from abroad. Moreover, because most trade credits are self-liquidating, even financing a stagnant volume of import-export business requires a constant renewal of credit lines. More generally, as was the case for the United States during much of the nineteenth century, most developing countries rely on repeated inflows of foreign capital, over a period measured in decades, to finance investment at rates in excess of their domestic saving.

The question that then arises—and this is the central focus of the argument in much of the remainder of this paper—is whether, in the event of difficulty in servicing some part of a borrower's debt, restructuring that debt affects the borrower's subsequent ability to attract new financing. The most obvious reason why restructuring versus default matters in this context is that lenders may sensibly fear that a borrower that is not performing on its obligations to other lenders would not perform on an obligation to them either. At the very best, new lenders would see their claims met only on a pro rata basis along with those of previous lenders. Extending new credit would amount to the new lenders' coming to the rescue of the existing lenders.[8] In many circumstances of debtor nonperformance, therefore, resolving the status of outstanding obligations is key to attracting new financing even from a new set of lenders.

As a result, as long as *lenders* have reason to prefer restructuring over default or mere inaction, *borrowers* have reason to do so as well. In effect, contract terms such as cross-default and negative pledge clauses are a way

---

8. A problematic aspect of credit arrangements under such circumstances is the inability of lenders to enforce agreements that would give their uncollateralized claims priority over similarly uncollateralized but subsequently contracted obligations. One possibility would be to rely on negative pledge clauses precluding such subsequent agreements, perhaps enforced by using nonexclusive jurisdiction clauses (when lenders are in different countries) to enable unsatisfied lenders to pursue their claims from other lenders whose claims are honored when theirs are not; but this concept apparently remains a theory untried in actual legal practice.

for lenders to align borrowers' interests with their own. To the extent that the *lenders* want to see a nonperforming loan restructured, these terms give the *borrowers* a reason for seeking a restructuring also. (It is useful to distinguish this line of argument from that made above, based on borrowers' own incentive to maintain knowledge-enhanced relationships with specific lenders. There, borrowers' incentive to restructure derives from the possibility of obtaining further credit from *the same* lenders. Here the incentive to restructure arises from a potential desire to borrow from *other* lenders.)

In settings in which well-established bankruptcy procedures prevail, the need for new credit is a well-recognized motivation for how such matters are normally handled. In the United States, for example, a private borrower that has sought protection under the bankruptcy code can continue in operation by obtaining debtor-in-possession financing, which takes precedence over pre-bankruptcy obligations. But the ability to do so follows only as a consequence of the bankruptcy proceeding, and even then only with authorization from the court, which takes into account (but need not accede to) objections raised by the existing creditors. Such procedures are inoperative or unenforceable in many emerging market countries. Moreover, it is hard to see what the analogue to a formal bankruptcy proceeding (and hence to debtor-in-possession financing) would be for sovereign borrowers.

Finally, it is important to acknowledge explicitly that borrowers' nonperformance often takes on a further, inherently political dimension in the context of debts owed by emerging market borrowers to foreign lenders. Given the importance of trade to most countries' economic existence, maintaining orderly international financial relationships has become recognized almost everywhere as a major element of government responsibility, comparable to (albeit not quite on a par with) maintaining public safety, national security, and so on. Hence any situation that threatens a country's ability to obtain ordinary trade credit, for example, is necessarily not just an economic crisis but a political crisis as well, regardless of whether the initial problem has arisen from the government's debts or those of private borrowers. Governments of emerging market countries facing such a crisis therefore have a political incentive to put it behind them, and normalizing relationships with foreign creditors is a key part of doing so. Hence borrowers facing difficulty in servicing their debts have all the more reason to agree to a restructuring if that is what the lenders seek.

How Easy Should Restructuring Be?

One of the great paradoxes of banking is that repudiating one's debts makes a borrower more creditworthy. The standard explanation is that as long as the borrower has some remaining assets, or even just some prospect of a stream of future income, under the usual me-first rules the bottom tranche of debt is always the least risky. Getting rid of all existing debts gives some new creditor the opportunity to hold what will amount to the first tranche. (The analogy to debtor-in-possession financing, and hence the value of establishing workable bankruptcy standards such that this can be done, should be self-evident.)

Examples of the working of this paradox are not hard to find. In the United States the surest way for an individual to find his or her mailbox overflowing with new credit card offers is to declare personal bankruptcy. In a context closer to the focus of this discussion, global investors in the early 1990s raced to buy bonds issued by sovereign credits that had just written down the principal on their outstanding debt under the Brady Plan. One of the chief motivations underlying the current proposal for organized forgiveness of the debts of the world's fifty or so poorest countries is the hope that once the existing debt is expunged, lenders will promptly extend new credit.

What makes this behavior paradoxical is the commonsense notion that actions follow a pattern, and so reputation matters. If a borrower has defaulted before, why not again? The answer—at least in principle—is that abandoning debts enhances a debtor's creditworthiness only in circumstances that preclude repetition and therefore circumstances that nullify the adverse reputation effect. In the United States personal (as opposed to corporate) bankruptcy is permitted at most once every seven years.[9] Lenders had reason to assume that countries that had restructured their debts under the Brady Plan would not seek another such restructuring any time soon. (The Brady Plan also enabled sovereign credits to put up what amounted to collateral by using U.S. Treasury debt, placed in escrow accounts, to secure the principal and near-term interest payments on what then became bonds.) The current call for debt forgiveness for extremely low-income countries similarly assumes that there will be no repetition of this action within the foreseeable future.

9. An interesting empirical question is whether individuals who have gone bankrupt find their ability to gain credit beginning to erode again after, say, five or six years.

What all of these examples have in common is that by participating in a formal debt restructuring, borrowers in effect reduce the value of what they owe but do so in an orderly way, through procedures that, at least in principle—apart from arm twisting by the regulators—have the consent of their creditors.[10] Hence the borrower acquires a reputation for not servicing debts as promised but also, importantly, a reputation for participating in an orderly resolution of the resulting problem. And, as the discussion above makes clear, lenders have reason to value resolving nonperformance problems in this way.

It is hardly surprising, therefore, that once debt service difficulties arise, a borrower's ability to obtain new financing—including merely the renewal of trade credits—depends in part on debt restructuring. The contrast between the ample flow of new money to developing countries under the Brady Plan (which involved both write-down of principal and below-market interest rates, albeit not necessarily both on the same obligations) and the much different experience under the Baker Plan (which mostly involved rescheduling of principal payments) is one example. Another is the contrast between the rapid economic recovery in Mexico after the recession associated with the 1994–95 debt crisis (which involved debt restructuring supported by IMF and U.S. government credits) and Mexico's much slower recovery from the 1982 crisis (which led to the Baker Plan). Yet another example is the contrast between the rapid recovery now in progress in Korea (which after a crisis in 1997 restructured its large short-term debt, mostly owed by banks at least nominally in the private sector, into government-guaranteed bank credits and then a Eurobond financing) and the sluggish growth in Brazil for some years after that country attempted in 1987 to declare a unilateral debt-payments moratorium. A far more extreme case in point is North Korea, which defaulted on two major loans more than twenty years ago, has since been unable to receive credit from most market sources, and has suffered one of the world's worst economic performances throughout much of this period.

Given that in many situations of nonperformance both borrowers and lenders have a clear interest in rescheduling the problem debt, what seems at first thought much more surprising is that restructuring is not easier to accomplish. The point is especially relevant as securities have come to provide an increasing share of emerging market credits. Bonds issued under

10. Even a pure rescheduling, with interest and other terms left unchanged, would normally be priced by the market as a decline in value.

New York law require unanimous consent of the holders to amend any of the terms of payment, including the interest rate and the schedule for repayment of principal. The sheer mechanics of notifying hundreds or even thousands of bond holders and obtaining consent from each are daunting enough (and all the more so if the bonds are issued in bearer form), but the unanimous consent requirement also creates an obvious incentive for some lenders to game against the others by withholding their consent. Moreover, New York bond contracts typically include no procedure for establishing collective representation of the holders, so that it is difficult to determine how to go about structuring a proposal with at least some claim of procedural legitimacy to present to holders for their consent.[11] Bond contracts also typically do not include the equal sharing clauses conventionally used in bank loan contracts to help maintain a united position among the lenders and especially to discourage dissident members of the lender group from initiating litigation on their own.[12]

Although these specific contract features make bonds significantly harder to restructure than bank loans, loans as well are not always easy to reschedule or otherwise amend. In the case of loans advanced by large syndicates, banks with only a small participation, which poses no threat to their essential business prospects, have less interest in maintaining the no-loss-of-value fiction. When restructuring involves commitment of new money, these banks often prefer simply to write off their loss and drop out. When a borrower owes money to banks in different countries—as was the case, for example, in the 1997–98 Korean crisis—the fact that lenders in different countries face differing regulation and also differing conditions in their respective home economies can be a significant stumbling block. In the Korean example a key part of the story, which was clear at the time, was that the G-10 central banks were pressuring their countries' commercial banks to agree on a restructuring plan that would prevent a situation of broad-scale default.[13] What would have happened if market forces had been left to function on their own remains (and will remain) an unanswered question.

11. By contrast, bonds issued under U.K. law usually include provisions for convening a bond-holder assembly as well as provisions for majority voting.

12. See Buchheit (1998a, 1998b, 1998c) for a detailed discussion of sharing clauses, majority action clauses, and collective representation clauses. See also Eichengreen and Portes (1995) and Eichengreen and Mody (2000).

13. For an account of the Korean restructuring, see "Korea Stares into the Abyss," *Euromoney* (March 1998), pp. 32–37.

The contrast between the readily identifiable interest that both borrowers and lenders often have in achieving a restructuring and the prevalence of these systematic impediments to doing so provides the motivation for much of the interest shown in international debt resolution mechanisms during the past few years. At the grand conceptual level, economists and others have offered various proposals for a "new financial architecture," typically centered around the creation of either an international bankruptcy mechanism or an international lender of last resort, or both.[14] At the level of everyday financial practice, bankers have become more adept at handling London Club negotiations, the bondholder community has begun to make progress in addressing its more complicated representation problem, sovereign borrowers such as Pakistan and Ukraine have shown how to use exchange offers to overcome the impediment posed by the unanimous consent requirement, and other as-yet-untried ideas such as exit consents are receiving widespread attention. Yet all these proposals and actual innovations notwithstanding, debt restructuring in the international arena remains far from easy or straightforward.

Perhaps there is a reason why this is so. As is well known, the conflicting incentives of borrowers and lenders and the asymmetry of information that a borrower and its lenders have about the borrower's financial condition and prospects create a classic moral hazard situation and hence the need for mechanisms to commit borrowers to meet their obligation. The need for such mechanisms is all the greater when the absence of strong auditing and accounting practices and other forms of transparency make a borrower's condition and prospects especially difficult for outsiders to monitor—as is often the case in emerging markets. Transaction by transaction, therefore, lenders always seek ways of committing borrowers to pay what they owe.

But from a perspective that is broader than just one transaction at a time, it is also useful to lenders to have mechanisms that commit *themselves* to press the borrower for payment and even to exercise their rights under whatever mechanisms are in place should the borrower fail to perform. Lenders (and, as developed in the discussion below, borrowers too) have an interest that extends over time to future transactions. That continuing interest may sometimes conflict with a lender's interest in simply gaining the greatest value, net of fully allocated expense, from any one transaction.

14. Prominent examples include Eichengreen (1999); Folkerts-Landau and Lindgren (1998); Goldstein (1998); Rogoff (1999); and Council on Foreign Relations (1999).

None of this is surprising, and in principle lenders should be able to balance these current and future interests in a purely discretionary way. But there are countless examples of situations in which just this kind of balancing of current versus ongoing interests is difficult—in some situations it is impossible—without some form of commitment mechanism to preclude taking actions that would be optimal on a case-by-case basis yet harmful from a more forward-looking perspective.[15]

In the specific setting of what to do when borrowers fail to meet their obligations, the obvious conflict arises from the inferences that future borrowers, including but not limited to those having difficulties at the moment, draw about the likely consequences of their own subsequent nonperformance. As introductory banking textbooks explain, this is why it sometimes makes sense for a lender to pay more to collect a debt, or to seize and liquidate collateral, than the proceeds are worth. The negative net proceeds of such an action are, in effect, an investment in gaining performance by future borrowers. To repeat: that investment is especially valuable in circumstances where verifying the borrower's condition is problematic. Systematic impediments to debt restructuring represent a mechanism that constrains a lender to be more likely to make that investment.

The fact that loans often have multiple lenders compounds the problem. In addition to the inherent conflict that exists between a single lender's interest in the transaction at hand and in the environment in which future transactions will take place, there is also then a potential conflict among the interests of different lenders. Hence lenders, including those that are already creditors to any particular nonperforming borrower as well as those that are not, face a collective action problem. Equal sharing clauses (in bank loan contracts) and unanimous consent requirements (in bond contracts) act as mechanisms for solving that collective action problem among the lenders already participating in a nonperforming credit. Both serve to constrain the lenders *as a group* from acting in any one transaction in ways that may dilute borrowers' incentive to perform on future debts. (As the discussion below makes clear, it is of course possible for such constraints to be too tight.) Cross-default and negative pledge clauses act as a mechanism for solving the analogous collective action problem among lenders more

---

15. The classic formulation of the time inconsistency problem in economics is that of Kydland and Prescott (1977). Now-standard applications in the context of a single country's monetary policy are given by Barro and Gordon (1983) and Rogoff (1985). See Dooley (2000) for an application to debt problems that formalizes parts of the discussion here.

broadly, including those that are part of the specific credit in question and those that are not. More generally, conditioning private credits on a country's receiving IMF loans, or even on its merely entering into an IMF agreement, is also a means of solving lenders' collective action problem. In such circumstances the IMF in effect serves as a cartel coordinator for the lenders.

Hence impediments to debt restructuring have their purpose too. But the straightforward implication of this line of argument is that not all non-performing debts should be restructured, even when it is in the interest of the borrower and also in the (narrowly construed) interest of the lenders to do so. Because the practical alternative to restructuring is hard to specify, whether this means more outright defaults or merely more instances of "muddling on" with debts nonperforming but not in default is ambiguous. But it does mean that failure to restructure a nonperforming debt is not necessarily a failure. And given the role that restructuring normally plays in facilitating the extension of new credit to a nonperforming borrower, it also means that some new loans will probably not be granted. Indeed, the deeper implication is that in a regime in which restructuring is systematically not so "easy," some old credits would not have been extended in the first place.

Real Counterparts of Financial Flows and Accounting Losses

The place to start in assessing whether a regime in which some specific loans are not made is good or bad is to recall that the purpose of credit flows is normally to fund some kind of real economic activity. Hence debt problems, when they occur, are not merely a financial phenomenon. For every financial loss not fully offset by somebody else's gain, there is somewhere a real economic loss. Since the fundamental rationale for having competitive financial markets to begin with is to support the production and use of real goods and services, what it means to do without any given debt transaction is ultimately a matter of real, rather than financial, outcomes.

Thinking about nonperforming debt problems in this way leads to what can sometimes be an awkward question: When things go sour, where did the money go? In cases of ordinary business debt problems, the answer is sometimes straightforward and sometimes not, but rarely interesting in a general way: a firm's product market is unexpectedly weak, its labor or its suppliers become unexpectedly expensive, its production is disappointingly inefficient, its competitors are surprisingly strong, its new technology fails, and so on. Life in a competitive market economy is full of idiosyncratic reverses. But the focus of interest here, spurred by the problems suffered by one emerging market country after another in just the past few years, is not isolated business failure. The issue is instead systemic debt problems that affect a country's borrowers more generally, often to an extent that ultimately threatens the government's own credit as well. Hence asking where the money went is more interesting, but also more difficult.

An example from outside the emerging markets context can perhaps best illustrate the point. The collapse of the savings and loan (S&L) industry in the United States in the late 1980s resulted in a direct cost to U.S. taxpayers of $126 billion.[16] This loss was not just a financial phenomenon. Much of it represented the dissipation of the American economy's resources in constructing office buildings, energy extraction facilities, and other tangible investments that in the end the market did not value. Much of the rest represented the transfer of resources to corrupt and self-dealing S&L operators, some of whom ultimately faced criminal sanctions. In retrospect, it would clearly have been better if many of the credits that led to the U.S. S&Ls' demise had never been extended in the first place.

Turning then to the case at hand, where did the money go in Korea? In Indonesia? In Thailand? In Brazil? The answer is more complex in these cases, not least because of the role of changing currency valuations in what went wrong. Projects that may have looked economically viable at one exchange rate no longer did at another. But even this plain fact is properly part of the story, not an excuse for ducking the issue, and it opens in turn yet further questions: Why were countries' exchange rates supported where they initially were? Given the well-known role of capital flight in initiating most countries' currency crises (not just in this latest round but more generally), were exchange rate policies a thinly disguised mechanism for effecting what amounted to transfer payments? Who ultimately bore the risk arising from the use of unhedged foreign currency obligations to finance investments, the viability of which depended on stable or appreciating currency values? And how did the allocation of that risk-bearing correspond to

---

16. This sum included $42 billion in costs that the government reimbursed to the Federal Savings and Loan Insurance Corporation before putting that entity out of business, $79 billion in costs (net of liquidation proceeds) borne by the Resolution Trust Corporation, and $6 billion in contractual tax benefits awarded to private acquirers of failed S&Ls.

claims on the potential returns from those investments in the event that currency values had remained stable or appreciated?

Nor are currency fluctuations the entire matter. Whether the investments being financed by these loans made sense on other grounds is surely no less of a question in these countries than it should have been in the case of the 1980s office construction spree in the United States. Indeed, the government-business ties and lack of transparency that have received so much discussion ever since the Asian crisis began (with the Thai currency crisis) in 1997 suggest that the economic viability of such investments in many emerging market countries may be even more subject to question than in the industrial world. Either way, however, the questions at issue are about real uses of an economy's resources—importantly, resources that could have been deployed for other purposes—not merely about financial losses. Moreover, leaving aside what led to the financial losses and real resource costs behind the 1997–99 crisis, questions like these are pertinent to future resource uses, and hence future debt transactions, as well.

Thinking about the matter in this way makes clear that simply maximizing the flow of credit to any borrower or group of borrowers, whether in an emerging market country or not, is *not* what competitive financial markets exist to do. The economic function of these markets *is* to transfer resources from ultimate savers to ultimate investors, but not irrespective of the real economic use of the resources that the ultimate investors intend, and certainly not irrespective of the alternative intended use between one would-be ultimate investor and another. The role of competitive financial markets is to discriminate in just this way. Transaction by transaction, lenders do this every day.

But there is also a systemic aspect of this process that arises from the underlying presumptions that both borrowers and lenders carry into their transaction-by-transaction dealings. These include presumptions about whether and under what circumstances borrowers really are supposed to meet their obligations, and what course lenders will take when they don't. To the extent that any competitive situation has elements of a zero-sum game, borrowers and lenders would each naturally prefer that these presumptions be different—more in their own favor, and less to the other side's. Because financial markets make possible real economic activity that could not otherwise take place, however, dealings between borrowers and lenders are not merely zero-sum. Some ways of handling a specific transaction make *both* parties better off. Similarly, some sets of underlying presumptions make both parties better off over time.

The heart of the argument about debt restructuring advanced here is that underlying presumptions that potentially make both borrowers and lenders better off on an ongoing basis are sometimes in conflict with the actions that are potentially to their mutual advantage when any one transaction is viewed in isolation. Creating mechanisms that preserve or even enhance those presumptions, even at the cost of forgoing mutually beneficial actions in some specific transactions, is therefore potentially valuable. Impediments to debt restructuring constitute such a mechanism. That these impediments sometimes impose costs in the context of specific nonperforming debts that are not restructured, and that those costs are sometimes borne by both borrowers and lenders, is certainly true. That as a result some credits are not extended in the first place is not only true, it is precisely the point. It is what makes lenders—and, on reflection, borrowers too—better off.

All this is not to say that restructuring nonperforming debts should be either impossible or maximally difficult. Even the soundest risks, as seen ex ante, sometimes turn out badly ex post. (If not, they wouldn't be true risks.) Borrowers do meet with adverse circumstances that they could not have foreseen, or that genuinely seemed improbable. Events happen that are beyond their control. Some borrowers that can't pay on time will be able to pay later. The point is not that restructuring should be as difficult as possible, but rather that it should not be as easy as possible—arguably, not so easy as is currently the case. The losses sustained by lenders when debts default, and the real costs suffered by borrowers when they cannot obtain new credit, are bad per se. They are worth accepting only as part of a regime governing borrower-lender dealings that justifies itself over time by effectively fostering economic production and economic development. But that regime is not one in which all nonperforming debts are always restructured.

A useful analogy, again from a different context, is the classic prescription for lender-of-last-resort actions in the face of a systemic bank run—namely, to lend on good credit to solvent institutions.[17] This simple maxim rests on the presumption that individual banks are responsible for their solvency (picking good credits is what banks are supposed to do) but not for their liquidity when the banking system as a whole is impaired (maintaining liquid liabilities against illiquid assets is also what banks are sup-

17. See Bagehot (1873).

posed to do). A strict prohibition against lender-of-last-resort actions would prevent a central bank from rescuing banks that are threatened not only for reasons not of their own making but, indeed, for reasons that arise as a consequence of carrying out their economic function as intended. Under such a regime banks would be unable to provide liquidity transformation. But a regime of always rescuing every bank not only destroys banks' incentive to serve their function of allocating resources to good credits. Because of the interaction of limited liability and the competitive market in which banks raise their own capital, such a regime discourages them from serving this function.

The bank-run analogy is not fully apt here for several reasons. Especially in the context of nonperforming borrowers in emerging markets, sorting out insolvency from illiquidity is not straightforward. For sovereign credits, apart from truly extreme cases it is not clear what insolvency would mean. The familiar chain of borrowing, in which a country's banks act as conduits for channeling foreign-source credit to the country's operating companies, while the government often in effect acts as a similar conduit (or provides implicit guarantees) for the banks, further compounds the problem. But the basic idea remains valid nonetheless: What to do when a borrower fails to perform on its obligations is a matter of information, inference, and judgment. A regime in which restructuring is either impossibly difficult or routinely easy prevents that process from working.

Concluding Thoughts: Restructuring without Rules, and the Role of Official Lending

There is no need to restate here the main conclusions of this line of thinking, which are already summarized at the beginning of the paper. Instead, two final considerations particular to the context of emerging markets are worth noting. First, in the legal setting of many emerging market countries, lenders themselves have to assume a broader range of responsibilities. For purposes of comparison, in a standard corporate bankruptcy proceeding in the United States, the lenders propose changes in debt terms, in the borrower's corporate structure, and in other aspects of the borrower's business, and the borrower either agrees or faces liquidation. But these negotiations take place within the framework of rules that specify majority voting within each class of credits, "cramdown" conditions under which one class of creditors can force another to go along, and ultimately the threat of liquidation—all with a judge to determine whether the relevant tests have been met. Any proposed changes in the borrower's corporate structure likewise stand against the background of the U.S. laws applicable to corporate governance. By contrast, when bankruptcy and corporate governance institutions are inadequate, or when lenders either can't or simply don't force their use, lenders potentially negotiate with borrowers over a much broader range of issues and in a more free-form way.

The point is relevant because some of the debtor nonperformance in the Asian crisis appeared to reflect problems of financial and corporate structure as much as or more than underlying business risk. Any firm is necessarily subject to some volatility in its cash flows, and some firms far more so than others. Some firms' cash flows are also exposed to volatility from foreign currency fluctuations, some to volatility from fluctuations in the price of some particular raw commodity, and so on.[18] A balance sheet that is entirely appropriate for one firm may therefore be highly inappropriate for others. The purpose of any firm's borrowing is to facilitate its nonfinancial operations, but the wrong balance sheet structure can instead place the firm's nonfinancial operations, and potentially the firm itself, at undue risk.

This is the point at which debt restructuring comes into contact with more general balance sheet restructuring, and ultimately with corporate restructuring in the broader sense of combining, separating, or even terminating existing business operations. To a far greater extent than in the industrial world, in the emerging markets context all this is in the province of firms' creditors. It is so because denying new financing is often the only potential sanction capable of effecting change.

Second, unlike most private borrowers, *governments* in emerging markets have another source of credit to which they can turn: other governments on a bilateral basis, as well as the IMF and the World Bank. Hence official lending potentially plays a key role in questions of sovereign credit debt restructuring. Because the borrowing governments in these cases are often conduits for their countries' private sector borrowers, however, official lending is also in effect available more broadly.

The role of official lending complicates the argument advanced in this paper in several ways. As much recent discussion has emphasized, the potential availability of official lending can reduce the disincentives for borrowers to fail to meet their obligations. At the same time, official

---

18. Currency depreciation may also trigger a breach of loan covenants even before any effect on cash flow has appeared.

lenders normally exhibit even greater commitment to the no-loss-in-value fiction than do banks, and far more so than among bond investors. (Another way to put this point is in terms of the fiction that lending and direct assistance are conceptually distinct.) The same argument developed above, to the effect that lenders' reluctance to recognize loss of value is a factor empowering borrowers, applies here as well. It is therefore somewhat surprising that the possibility of official lenders' recording losses—including losses on loans by the IMF and the World Bank—has not bulked larger in discussions of the many issues that the latest emerging markets crisis has raised. But it is important to recognize that the availability of credit from the IMF and other official lenders is certainly not the only source of moral hazard in emerging market debt transactions, and the argument advanced in this paper implies that it is not even the most fundamental source.

The central focus of the argument presented here is instead debt restructuring entered into by emerging market borrowers and their private sector lenders. No one should doubt that, in cases of actual or threatened nonperformance, restructuring helps to maintain (or if there has been an interruption, restore) the orderly flow of new credit. Nor should anyone doubt that, on a transaction-by-transaction basis, doing so not only avoids losses to lenders but also prevents a wide range of real economic costs to nonperforming borrowers. What makes the question of debt restructuring more subtle is that the presumptions that underlie debt transactions more generally also depend on restructuring practices. A world in which nonperforming debts are not easily and automatically restructured is therefore a world in which some credits will not be extended. But that may well be to the benefit of not only the lenders but borrowers as well.

References

Bagehot, Walter. 1873. *Lombard Street*. London: William Cloves and Sons.

Barro, Robert J., and David B. Gordon. 1983. "Rules, Discretion, and Reputation in a Model of Monetary Policy." *Journal of Monetary Economics* 12 (July): 101–21.

Buchheit, Lee C. 1998a. "Changing Bond Documentation:The Sharing Clause." *International Financial Law Review* 17 (July): 17–19.

———. 1998b. "Majority Action Clauses May Help Resolve Debt Crises." *International Financial Law Review* 17 (August): 13–14.

———. 1998c. "The Collective Representation Clause." *International Financial Law Review* 17 (September): 9–11.

Council on Foreign Relations. 1999. *Report of the Commission on the Future International Financial Architecture.* New York: Council on Foreign Relations Press.

De Long, J. Bradford. 1999. "Financial Crises in the 1890s and the 1990s: Must History Repeat?" *Brookings Papers on Economic Activity 2:1999,* 253–94.

Dooley, Michael P. 2000. "Can Output Losses Following International Financial Crises Be Avoided?" Working Paper 7531. Cambridge, Mass.: National Bureau of Economic Research (February).

Eaton, Jonathan, and Mark Gersovitz. 1981. "Debt with Potential Repudiation: Theory and Estimation." *Review of Economic Studies* 48 (April): 289–309.

Eichengreen, Barry. 1999. *Toward a New Financial Architecture: A Practical Post-Asia Agenda* Washington: Institute for International Economics.

Eichengreen, Barry, and Ashoka Mody. 2000. "Would Collective Action Clauses Raise Borrowing Costs?" Working Paper 7438. Cambridge, Mass: National Bureau of Economic Research (January).

Eichengreen, Barry, and Richard Portes. 1995. *Crisis, What Crisis? Orderly Workouts for Sovereign Debtors.* London: Centre for Economic Policy Research.

Folkerts-Landau, David, and Carl-Johan Lindgren. 1998. *Toward a Framework for Financial Stability.* Washington: International Monetary Fund.

Goldstein, Morris. 1998. *The Asian Financial Crises: Causes, Cures, and Systemic Implications.* Washington: Institute for International Economics.

Kydland, Finn E., and Edward C. Prescott. 1977. "Rules Rather than Discretion: The Inconsistency of Optimal Plans." *Journal of Political Economy* 85 (June): 473–91.

Obstfeld, Maurice, and Kenneth Rogoff. 1996. *Foundations of International Macroeconomics.* MIT Press.

Rogoff, Kenneth. 1985. "The Optimal Degree of Commitment to a Monetary Target." *Quarterly Journal of Economics* 100 (November): 1169–89.

———. 1999. "International Institutions for Reducing Global Financial Instability." *Journal of Economic Perspectives* 13 (Fall): 21–42.

RICHARD PORTES 3

The Role of Institutions
for Collective Action

Most Directors agreed that there would be considerable benefits from
the introduction of collective action provisions in new bond contracts. . . . Many Directors felt that this could best be achieved if
industrial countries included such terms in their own bond issues. In
addition, provisions authorizing a trustee to negotiate with the
debtor on behalf of bondholders, but without authorizing the trustee
to legally bind them to any agreement, could also contribute to an
orderly and speedy restructuring process.

INTERNATIONAL MONETARY FUND (1999, PARA. 30)

Creditors' committees could have a role to play in effectively resolving financial crises. While the creation of a single standing committee was generally not considered practical, consideration could be
given to ad hoc arrangements in appropriate cases. . . .

INTERNATIONAL MONETARY FUND (1999, PARA. 33)

THESE RECENT STATEMENTS by the Managing Director of the International Monetary Fund suggest that the argument is over. The proposals of a framework for orderly workouts of sovereign debt put forward

This paper builds on work done in a long-standing collaboration with Barry Eichengreen, in particular Eichengreen and Portes (1995, 2000). I have also benefited from correspondence with Jon
Cunliffe.

by Barry Eichengreen and myself, Rory Macmillan, and others have essentially been accepted.[1] All that remains is implementation.

I shall maintain that this is unfortunately not the case. Market participants—the lenders—still vigorously oppose any official action along these lines. Their opposition is even stronger when it comes to official sanction of payments standstills and IMF lending into arrears, other measures that might be used as part of an orderly workout procedure.[2] More broadly, market participants and the U.S. Department of the Treasury appear to reject any rule-based procedures and any effective action by the official community to promote collective action clauses and creditors committees.

The banks and securities houses, as represented by the Institute of International Finance (IIF), continue to argue against measures that they interpret as making it easier for debtors to default, as well as any official intervention into creditor-debtor relationships—except "relatively large but temporary official support,"[3] that is, IMF-led bailouts. In 1996 they supported

the market-based approach [with] the following key characteristics:
   —case-by-case resolution
   —direct contact between debtor and creditors as necessary rather than official intervention through negotiations directed by bodies such as the IMF. . . .
   —normal levels of public support through operations of the IMF and other multilaterals
   —if arrears have accumulated, delay of IMF disbursements until agreements in principle are reached with creditors on a schedule for elimination of arrears.
   It should also be presumed that if contract revision becomes an issue, it will be on the basis of rescheduling rather than forgiveness, and with no interruption in interest payments.[4]

Their view has been unaffected by the subsequent financial crises in Asia, Russia, and Brazil, and debt servicing difficulties elsewhere. The IIF's 1999 report argues that "crisis resolution based on restoring private sector confi-

---

1. Eichengreen and Portes (1995); Macmillan (1997).
2. See further discussion in para. 33 of International Monetary Fund (1999).
3. Institute of International Finance (1999, p. 7).
4. Institute of International Finance (1996, pp. ii–iii).

dence . . . (the 1990s approach) seems both more feasible and more conducive to maintenance of the robust capital market of the 1990s than alternative approaches emphasizing standstills, reschedulings, and concerted
lending (the 1980s approach)."[5]

The principle evoked to justify this stance is that debtors repay only
when the pain caused by default (loss of trade credit and capital market
access, legal harassment, and other consequences) is unacceptable. Thus
anything that might mitigate these consequences would shift the supply
curve of funds to emerging markets downward (to the left) and the
demand curve upward, as borrowers perceive less likely damage if things go
wrong, and lenders understand that reaction. The price (that is, the interest rate) would rise, and the effect on the "volume of capital flows is
ambiguous but would seem more likely to fall . . . than to rise."[6]

Ignoring the totally unsubstantiated assertion about the volume of
flows, the underlying assumption may be wrong. As Kenneth Rogoff
points out, there are alternatives: the debtor may be concerned only with
its reputation for repayment, or more broadly, its standing in the international economic community.[7] Those concerns would be unaffected by
measures that would facilitate debt restructuring where necessary and make
it less damaging to the debtor country's trade and growth as well as its trade
partners. So the borrowers' demand might not rise. Moreover, such measures might in fact make creditors as a class better off by overcoming the
coordination failures involved in crises,[8] just as bankruptcy codes do in
cases of domestic illiquidity or insolvency. In that case, the effect on the
supply of lending would be positive rather than negative. Thus the effect
of collective action clauses on market terms, for example, is an empirical
question. I return below to some empirical evidence.

First, however, I look at broad evidence on how lenders' perceptions of
the likelihood of crisis and default, as well as their assessment of the authorities' determination to achieve "bailins," have been affected by recent events.
Here I find that just as after the Mexican crisis of 1994–95, the international
markets have been resilient and show relatively little sign of concern that a
fresh wave of debt-servicing problems might lie ahead. This suggests either
very short memory or moral hazard effects of the big bailout packages.

5. Institute of International Finance (1999, p. 7).
6. Institute of International Finance (1996, p. 30).
7. Rogoff (1999).
8. Andy Haldane (1999) argues that "*binding* in" creditors is more important than "bailing in."

But there will always be financial crises, both national and international, no matter how much effort is devoted to prevention. Yet the bailout packages cannot and should not be repeated, and the record on bailing-in is so far very unsatisfactory.[9] What is to be done? This is the underlying issue in the debate on the future role of the IMF.[10] The official community is concerned with bailing in the private sector in order to achieve a degree of burden-sharing that would be politically defensible and would discourage irresponsible lending. Yet so far it has not succeeded in establishing mechanisms that work.

It will not be feasible—economically or politically—to cut back Fund bailouts and moral-hazard-creating activities without an adequate substitute. The historical evidence that I shall discuss shows clearly the need for official intervention and appropriate institutions to deal with international debt problems. Indeed, to get the Fund out of the big bailout package business, there has to be an alternative that will not involve as much pain and suffering as debt default does today or did in the pre-IMF period.

That alternative is an orderly workout negotiated between creditors and the debtor. But organizing such workouts efficiently requires standing committees of creditors, which did exist in the earlier period of bond finance, as well as collective action clauses in debt contracts. These should provide for collective representation of creditors and qualified majority voting, so that no rogue creditor can block a settlement; for sharing debt service pro rata among creditors, so no creditor can secure advantage over the others by taking the debtor to court; and for eliminating acceleration provisions that require immediate repayment of all debts if there is default on a single scheduled payment. These clauses were not common in the earlier period, but there is ample subsequent experience with them. Together with an appropriate negotiating framework, they could substantially ease the pain of default for both debtor and creditors, while not unduly encouraging this outcome. Bailing in and burden-sharing are the language of a zero-sum game. We can do better.

We cannot sensibly restrict the role of the Fund without structures that can replace it. The historical evidence—and developments since the Mexican crisis—indicate that the markets will not spontaneously achieve these outcomes. The equivalent of law is required, although not the kind

---

9. Eichengreen and Rühl (2000).

10. Council on Foreign Relations Task Force (1999); Portes (2000); International Financial Institutions Advisory Commission (2000).

of law that would be needed to establish an international bankruptcy court.[11, 12]

I discuss these institutional changes and deal with the objections that have been raised against them. Finally, I argue that the official sector will have to take a much more assertive stance in order to implement these measures.

Market Reactions

Investors should take risks, and risks mean that some proportion of investments will fail. This is why we have domestic bankruptcy laws that provide for orderly workouts when investments and the firms that made them do fail. Similarly, if the international capital markets are functioning well, mistakes will be made. Then one or another country (or its private sector borrowers) will fail: a crisis. History records many. We should not expect or even wish to prevent them all. That would be at the cost of insufficient, excessively risk-averse investment. So such crises will always recur—but capital markets forget.

What did the markets learn from the Mexican crisis of 1994–95? Spreads above comparable U.S. Treasury instruments for Eurobonds of emerging market economies fell considerably during the period mid-1995 to mid-1997—but no more than spreads for high-yield U.S. corporate bonds,[13] so it is hard to argue on that evidence that the markets became more circumspect about emerging market lending (or that the Mexican bailout simply encouraged them). The volume of lending, too, does not show any negative reaction (see figure 3-1).

Did the Asian crisis and other subsequent debt-servicing difficulties have noticeable effects on the willingness to lend to emerging markets? Market participants might have concluded that bailouts on the 1997–98

11. "Law may mimic rules evolving through private ordering, and therefore may reinforce the spirit of trust necessary for cooperative repeat-play relationships . . . an important role of law is to preserve trust. . . . Economists generally agree that markets function properly only within a well-defined legal and institutional framework, although there is debate about whether such institutions must be created by concerted action (which is really simply helping markets to work, and not inappropriate governmental intervention). . . ." Partnoy (2000).

12. Eichengreen and Portes (1995) and Eichengreen (1999) discuss in detail why such a court is not a feasible proposition. The "bankruptcy reorganization approach" that Schwarcz (2000) proposes for implementation by an international convention is also unrealistic.

13. Cline and Barnes (1997).

Figure 3-1. *Gross Capital Flows to Emerging Countries, 1980–98*

Billions of U.S. dollars

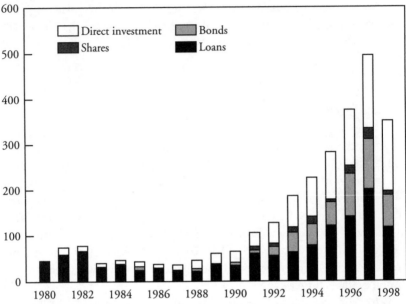

Source: Haldane (1999, p. 186), citing Capital Data and World Bank.

scale would be infeasible in future, because either the resources or the political support would not be forthcoming; or they might have taken fright at the expressed determination of the official community to achieve private sector bailins and burden-sharing.

It is again hard to see in the aggregate data any evidence for this perception. The volume of gross flows to emerging countries in 1998 was not substantially below that of 1996 and was greater than any previous year, as are the bank loan and bond investment components of the total. The Emerging Markets Bond Index spread jumped sharply during third quarter 1998 and by first quarter 1999 was at its 1995 previous peak, but it then fell by 300 basis points, despite the problems of Ecuador, Pakistan, Romania, and Ukraine. This index mainly tracks Brady bonds, which are not representative, according to Steven Kamin and Karsten von Kleist.[14] The index's movement from 1992 to 1999 and those for a wider range of

14. Kamin and von Kleist (1999).

Figure 3-2. *Spreads on Emerging Market Bonds, by Credit Rating,*
1992–99[a]

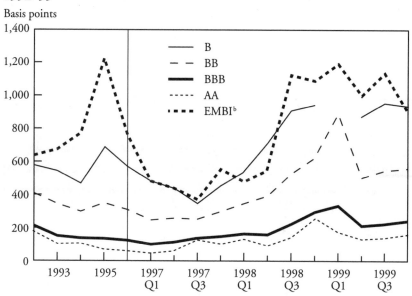

Basis points

Source: Bank for International Settlements (2000, p. 25), citing Bloomberg; Capital Data; J. P.
Morgan; BIS calculations.

a. Estimated credit spread on a 10-year rated bonds issued by emerging market economies over the
benchmark industrial country government bond. No data available for B-rated issues in 1999 Q1.

b. Emerging Markets Bond Index quarterly average

issues are shown in figure 3-2. The spread on AA issues is above its first
quarter 1997 low, but still below the 1992 level, and that for BBB issues is
also not dramatically higher. All spreads are down from their first quarter
1999 peak. Note also that the emerging market spreads have been moving
substantially in parallel to those on U.S. corporate bonds (figure 3-3).
Finally, the performance of emerging market stock indexes in 1999 suggests that investors have gone back in with enthusiasm (table 3-1).

Market participants seem to have been misled by their perception of
the success of the Mexican bailout in restoring market access. They asserted
in September 1996 that there would be no need for "extraordinary assistance" to limit contagion in future potential crises.[15] They were not much
better at forecasting in January 1999, when they argued that "the risk of

15. Institute of International Finance (1996, pp. 12, 35).

Figure 3-3. *Credit Spreads, January 1998–January 2000*

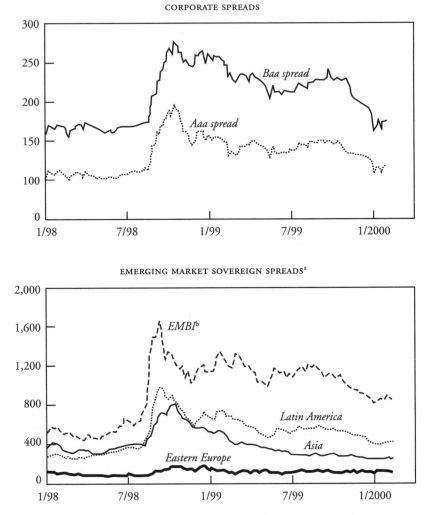

CORPORATE SPREADS

EMERGING MARKET SOVEREIGN SPREADS[a]

Source: Bank for International Settlements (2000, p. 6), citing Datastream; Bloomberg.
a. Average of actively traded international bond spreads (one per country).
b. Emerging Markets Bond Index.

Table 3-1. *1999 Stock Market Performance in Selected Countries: Percentage Gain in U.S. Dollars and Local Currency*

Country	U.S. dollars		Local currency	
	1999	*1999Q4*	*1999*	*1999Q4*
Turkey	126.6	72.6	183.8	86.8
Russia	96.2	55.6	123.2	62.9
South Korea	72.3	26.3	67.9	18.8
Indonesia	66.8	25.8	55.5	17.1
Mexico	58.4	32.1	54.8	32.0
Japan	57.8	16.6	46.0	13.4
Singapore	54.9	18.5	55.9	16.5
Hong Kong	52.0	28.6	52.4	28.7
Brazil	51.2	49.8	95.9	40.9
Sweden	45.3	29.9	50.6	34.0
South Africa	44.5	17.7	49.1	20.3
France	25.9	20.1	41.3	26.1
United States	17.8	13.6	17.8	13.6
MSCI Emerging Markets[a]	50.8	22.1	53.9	20.9
MSCI World[b]	22.7	15.7	24.9	16.5
Dow Jones STOXX	18.3	20.7	33.3	26.7

Source: Bank for International Settlements (2000, p. 4), citing International Finance Corporation, national data.

a. Morgan Stanley Capital International Emerging Markets Index.

b. Morgan Stanley Capital International World Index.

unwarranted retreat from emerging markets finance at least temporarily overshadows any contrary risk of prospective overlending . . .," and they expressed "concern that a major case of . . . disruption of debt servicing could impose a severe shock on emerging capital markets globally."[16] As we saw, the peak of spreads occurred precisely in first quarter 1999, and the problem countries cited above have apparently not created significant spillovers.

Bailouts and Bailins

The debt strategy of the 1980s did not include the large bailout packages that we have seen in the 1990s. The 1990s strategy for dealing with debt

16. Institute of International Finance (1999, pp. 10, 50).

crises has involved commitments to provide $34 billion in support of Thailand, $40 billion for Indonesia, $57 billion for Korea, and $42 billion for Brazil, not to mention the short-lived commitment of $22 billion to Russia. These amounts range from 50 percent to 130 percent (Korea) of annual export revenues, from 6 percent (Brazil) to 30 percent (Indonesia) of gross domestic product (GDP) and up to nineteen times IMF quota (for Korea).

At the very least, this magnitude of IMF-led intervention is politically unsustainable, and we hear rising calls to cut the Fund back or even abolish it. The resources may not be there—whether because G-7 governments will not be able to provide the "second-line" funding behind the IMF allocations, or because the size of the package necessary the next time around may be yet another order of magnitude higher. With full capital account convertibility, and in a world of free capital mobility, bailout lending can never be big enough itself to stem a panic—residents and speculators can short the currency up to the full, IMF-augmented value of reserves, and indeed all of M2 can be exported by residents.

Nor should these large bailouts be continued. There has been much debate about moral hazard, the undesirable effect of insurance on the incentives of those insured. Much of that, in my view, is "hazardous moralizing"—as when market participants solemnly talk about the "sanctity of contracts" or the dangers of contractual changes that would, they say, encourage debtors to default. They are unwilling to concede that lenders may regard official support in crises as an important safety net and that this moral hazard may lead to overlending.[17]

It is difficult to identify moral hazard effects empirically. In my own view, bailouts have indeed reduced the perceived risks in international lending and have thereby encouraged excessive risk-taking. Investor moral hazard has been more important in recent years than borrower moral haz-

17. The only discussion of moral hazard in the text of the 1996 IIF report speaks of the "distorting effects of such an approach [officially elaborated plans for crisis management] on the behavior of emerging economies" (p. 13). Annex A mentions an effect on the behavior of lenders, but it turns out that this would arise from the lenders' perception that borrowers would be subject to moral hazard! The 1999 IIF report estimates total "potential losses" for investors in East Asia and Russia and comes to numbers which, it claims, are "likely to leave foreign investors and creditors chastened . . . distortions of future behavior from recent international support packages are unlikely to be severe." (Institute of International Finance (1999, pp. 9–10, 57–59). The Council on Foreign Relations Task Force (1999, p. 62) shows more historical perspective in remarking, "it is not convincing to argue that because the experience of the Asian crisis has been so wrenching and costly for borrowers, a repetition of overborrowing there or elsewhere in emerging economies is unlikely."

ard. The danger now, however, is that my (long-standing) view is shared by a wide range of opponents of bailouts and by extension, of the IMF itself. All insurance generates moral hazard, yet the existence of insurance does not destabilize markets (and actuarially fair insurance does not involve subsidies). We simply need a better balance between the costs of moral hazard and the benefits of intervention that may create it.

Efforts to limit moral hazard and achieve burden-sharing by bailing in private sector creditors have so far been unsuccessful. Barry Eichengreen and Christof Rühl discuss the cases of Ecuador, Pakistan, Romania, and Ukraine.[18] All involve bonds rather than bank debt, and sovereign rather than private sector debt. They criticize the IMF-World Bank strategy, arguing that conditioning official assistance on "private sector participation" does not change the payoffs to the private sector, nor does it change their set of possible strategies—and hence it cannot affect the equilibrium outcome of the game between the private sector and the international financial institutions (IFIs).

Moreover, since these are not economically big countries with large outstanding debt, their debt problems have no systemic implications. Thus there was never any opportunity for their cases to set credible precedents that could affect lender behavior with systemically important countries and thereby reduce moral hazard significantly. Instead, the IFIs committed themselves to time-inconsistent policies—that they would stand aside, despite the costs of default, if the markets did not "participate" in a resolution—and since these policies were correctly perceived by the markets to be time-inconsistent, they were not credible.

The Historical Evidence[19]

The evidence most relevant to the issue of how to manage debt crises without bailouts may come from the fifty or so years preceding World War I. This was an era of financial globalization, in many respects not unlike the present day. Large portfolio capital flows were intermediated by the bond market, as has been the trend since the early 1990s. Sovereigns and other borrowers experienced crises, halted payments, and restructured their debts. There was no IMF involved in the process.

18. Eichengreen and Rühl (2000).
19. This section relies heavily on Eichengreen and Portes (1989a, 1989b, 1989c).

Initially, bondholders formed ad hoc committees to represent their interests. The committee would negotiate the best deal it could and recommend to the bondholders with whom it was in contact that they accept its terms. If a sufficient majority did so, then the loan was restructured. Generally, committees insisted on full payment of interest arrears but might agree to some write-down of principal and stretch-out of interest. There was no analogue to IMF conditionality: the committee could not insist that the country go back on the gold standard or adopt other reforms, although it might be more inclined to accept the settlement offer of a government that seemed so disposed.[20]

This approach had shortcomings. Ad hoc committees had high administrative costs. Their organizers found it difficult to establish their credentials with investors. A committee that could not claim adequate investor participation had difficulty getting the debtor to take it seriously in negotiations, since it was unlikely to induce adequate participation in the conversion. Insiders sometimes manipulated committees, either by using them to cut a deal that worked to their advantage or by exaggerating administrative costs and skimming the proceeds of membership subscriptions.

In Britain these problems were addressed in the establishment of the Corporation of Foreign Bondholders by a consortium of loan houses and brokers in 1868. The Council, the governing body of the Corporation, constituted committees to deal with particular debtors. Initially the Council was dominated by representatives of banking firms and brokerage houses. The underwriters and brokers recognized that it was bad business to sell bonds that were unprofitable because post-default recovery was impossible; hence the bankers had an interest in creating a framework for orderly restructuring.

In the 1880s and 1890s the Corporation was attacked for serving these "limited interests," that is, for being too willing to settle at the expense of individual bondholders. Its settlements with Cuba, Ecuador, Spain, and Uruguay were criticized for favoring issue houses with an interest in bringing out new loans for the defaulting states and speculators who had purchased bonds in default at depressed prices. As a result, the Council was reorganized in 1897 to include six members who were nominated by the Central Association of Bankers, six nominated by the London Chamber of Commerce, and nine representatives of the investors. In 1898, an Act of

---

20. Specific government revenues (typically, first call on a certain fraction of customs receipts) could, however, be earmarked for loan service, and a bondholders' representative could be installed in the customs house to monitor compliance.

Parliament gave the Corporation a royal charter, removing residual uncertainty about who spoke for the bondholders.

Representing an ongoing body, the committees of the Corporation enjoyed lower administrative costs than the ad hoc committees with which it continued to compete. Through its close connections with the London banking and financial establishment, it could exclude from the market debtors who refused to settle on terms which it regarded as acceptable.[21] The Corporation consequently enjoyed considerable leverage.

A limitation of the Corporation of Foreign Bondholders, a purely British institution, was that it did not have relations with comparable bodies in other countries. This was a problem in the decades leading up to World War I, years of growing lending by Paris, Berlin, and Amsterdam. Nor did the British Corporation have close working relationships with its foreign counterparts (like the Association Nationale des Porteurs Français de Valeurs Etrangères, founded at the instigation of the French Ministry of Finance in 1898). When one national committee offered to settle unilaterally, it undercut the leverage of the others.

These arrangements persisted into the 1920s. What changed was the emergence of the United States as a creditor country. Not having lent abroad on a large scale before World War I, the United States lacked the necessary institutional infrastructure, and so long as lending went well, no one deemed it necessary to organize.[22] Then came the debt defaults in Latin America in 1931, Central Europe in 1932, and Germany in 1933. The response was the formation of the Foreign Bondholders Protective Council (FBPC). The FBPC was not a spontaneous creation of the markets: rather, it arose out of the deliberations of a working party sponsored in 1932–33 by the U.S. State Department, which wanted to deflect the pleas of aggrieved bondholders to another entity.[23] Like its British counterpart, it too was

21. From the 1870s, it was customary for the London Stock Exchange to refuse quotation to new loans by a government that had not yet reached a settlement with the Corporation. Sometimes (as in the cases of Austria, Spain, Russia, and Turkey), the Exchange might go further and strike all the loans of the offending government from the list of admitted securities.

22. The Investment Bankers Association had formed a committee on foreign securities in 1918, but this entity proved short-lived and of little consequence.

23. From the day of the formal incorporation of the FBPC, the State Department responded to letters from disaffected bondholders with a form letter reading, "The Department cannot undertake to advise you with respect to these bonds. . . . The Foreign Bondholders Protective Council operates independently of the Government, and this reference is made wholly without responsibility on the part of the Department." Bondholders were driven to seek State Department help partly by the ineffectiveness of the ad hoc committees. By the end of 1934 some forty of these committees had sprung up.

accused of conflicts of interest and favoring some creditors over others. In 1936 some two-thirds of its financial contributions came from issue houses, fiscal agents, brokers, dealers, and their attorneys. The Securities and Exchange Commission convened a panel under the chairmanship of William O. Douglas to investigate these complaints and consider national-izing the Council. Instead, the Douglas panel recommended ousting the issue houses, fiscal agents, bond speculators, holders of commercial credits, brokers, dealers, and lawyers from the Council.[24]

While enhancing the representation of American bondholders, the for-mation of the FBPC compounded the problems of intra-committee coor-dination that had impeded restructuring negotiations before World War I. A Conference of Bondholders Associations was held in Paris in 1938, but to no avail.[25]

As the role of governments in the establishment of these committees makes clear, negotiations were not simply left to the parties concerned before the IMF came on the scene. Diplomats and consuls provided intro-ductions for the bondholders' representatives, provided them information on political and economic developments, and transmitted their com-plaints. The French and German governments, more than the British, hinted that diplomatic relations would suffer from a country's failure to set-tle with its creditors. Actual gunboat diplomacy was generally limited to cases where military intervention was desired for independent reasons (as in Egypt, Mexico, Turkey, and Venezuela), and debt disputes provided a convenient pretext. But there was always some perceived danger, even if a low one, to concentrate negotiators' minds.

In Eichengreen and Portes (2000), we study the effects of defaults under these institutional arrangements. A coherent picture emerges from the results. Default disrupts market access. Considerable periods of time

24. In 1937 the Council's directors amended its bylaws, setting a higher standard for membership so as to eliminate any hint of conflict of interest.

25. The problems that could result are illustrated by disagreements about the seniority structure of the debt. The British regarded secured debt (debts for which specific revenue sources, like customs receipts, or other security was earmarked) as senior and therefore entitled to prior, or at least concur-rent, settlement on terms at least as favorable as those obtained by unsecured claims. Many British loans were so secured. The loans underwritten by U.S. investment banks during the 1920s and subscribed by American investors, in contrast, were typically unsecured, leading the FBPC to dismiss the differ-ence between "so-called 'secured' and so-called 'unsecured' loans" (cited in Eichengreen and Portes [1989a, p. 224]). This disagreement could lead the two committees to conduct separate negotiations with the same debtor, as was the case in Colombia toward the end of the 1930s.

typically elapse between default and rescheduling,[26] during which the creditors grapple with their collective action problems and the two sides try to arrive at mutually acceptable terms. The process is not pleasant—creditors are not paid, debtors lose access to long-term markets and other sources of external finance. Debt restructuring on acceptable terms and a convincing change in regime can, however, succeed in restoring market access. To be sure, the markets remember defaults and reschedulings, which influence the terms on which they lend. Those effects are not dramatic but do persist. The terms are not so onerous, however, as to price borrowers out of the market. A higher cost of borrowing does not imply an inability to borrow.

Orderly Workouts with Collective Action Clauses and Bondholders Committees

If debt restructuring is to be left to the markets and the role of official intervention and financing is to be reduced, then the collective action and collateral damage problems that characterize financial crises must be solved. It is easy to say that the IMF and G-7 countries should not provide finance to bail out private investors, but this is hard to do as long as default is likely to interrupt market access for an extended period, damage other countries, and threaten systemic stability. Absent solutions to these problems, default will often be too painful and disruptive for the official community to contemplate.[27]

If painful default is the alternative to large-scale official financing, then it is unrealistic to expect that the international community will maintain a distance and let private creditors be bailed in by market-based negotiations. Orderly workouts must be made significantly less painful for the parties and the international economy with institutional innovations that make those negotiations easier, faster, and more efficient. Otherwise, assertions that there will be no official assistance to countries seeking to prop up

26. On average, 14 years for the twenty-five defaults in the period 1821–70, 6.3 years for the fifty-two defaults in 1871–1925, and 10.1 years for the thirty-seven defaults in 1926–75.

27. Thus, what the international community will tolerate in the case of a small country like Ecuador (or even Russia, whose economy is smaller than Belgium's at current rates of exchange) will be unpalatable for a South Korea or Brazil (witness the large-scale financing they were provided at the end of 1997 and 1998, respectively).

shaky currency pegs or pay off nervous investors will clearly be time-inconsistent and will therefore lack credibility. Consequently, they will not reduce moral hazard.

It is impossible to distinguish reliably between illiquidity and insolvency for a sovereign debtor.[28] That is one reason why it is unwise to predicate a big bailout package on the hypothesis that the problem is liquidity.[29] And when there is true, large-scale, potentially contagious panic (a run), IMF bailout lending may only fuel it, permitting creditor exit while creating unacceptable moral hazard. Then a payment standstill may be the right response, to "bind in" the creditors and launch negotiations, while stopping domestic capital flight. Only in that framework can it be resolved whether the debtor can in fact pay; only in orderly workouts can (necessarily) incomplete debt contracts be renegotiated successfully.

We discuss here two key features of this framework: standing bondholders committees and collective action clauses in loan agreements.

Bondholders Committees[30]

Restructuring negotiations are most difficult and protracted when information is least complete.[31] The more asymmetric the information environment, the more likely are debtors and creditors to fight a lengthy war of attrition. Establishing a standing committee of representatives of the various classes of creditors—bondholders, banks, and hedge funds, among others—would open lines of communication and help overcome information problems.

When a crisis erupts and debt service is halted, negotiations cannot proceed until the creditors have been identified, which is time-consuming when the process starts from scratch. A representative committee in continuous contact with its constituents would ease this difficulty. Next the debtor must decide with whom to negotiate—who speaks for the creditors.

28. Eichengreen and Portes (1995).

29. This is the fundamental flaw in the recommendations of the International Financial Institutions Advisory Commission (2000), which seeks through "prequalification" conditions to limit IMF lending to the class of "solvent" borrowers.

30. This section relies substantially on Eichengreen (1999), which draws in turn on Eichengreen and Portes (1995).

31. Where the preferences and capacities of all parties are common information, agreement should be immediate. This is a basic premise of bankruptcy theory: in a world of complete information and no transactions costs, there is no need for a bankruptcy code or bankruptcy court, since debtors and creditors will be able to adjust their contracts instantaneously to any unanticipated contingencies.

The existence of a standing committee would answer this question in advance. Finally there is the need to gain the assent of a majority of creditors to the restructuring plan and to buy out those who refuse. A standing committee would create peer pressure for agreement and facilitate the extension of any required side payments.

The difficulties created by the absence of these committees are apparent in recent experience. In Korea, the problem in the last week of 1997 was to get the banks to roll over their maturing short-term loans, to accept a delay in interest payments, and to agree to the principle of converting those short-term credits into long-term loans. The Korean government and the banks came very close to failure, which would likely have led to default. Only through the personal contacts of William Rhodes and considerable luck were the relevant bankers located and pulled from their Christmas dinners. A committee infrastructure would have eased the process.

Russia's experience in August 1998 following its suspension of payments illustrates the confusion that can arise when there exists no committee of creditors. First the Russian authorities met with a small group of Russian and foreign banks to discuss the formation of a creditors committee. Next it was decided that the committee would be formed only after the authorities had somehow managed to draw up a full list of creditors. Finally there were disagreements over the composition of the creditors' club, with hedge funds complaining that they had been denied a seat at the bargaining table.

Such arrangements will grow more complex with the shift from bank to bond finance. That shift will increase the number of interested parties and vest additional power in the hands of a class of creditors less susceptible to moral suasion by their central banks. Standing committees will become essential.

Experience with corporate debt workouts is cited to suggest that committees of creditors can be constituted when required.[32] In fact, the situation for corporate bonds is different from that for sovereign debts. Most corporate bonds are issued in the United States through an indenture trustee, which is responsible for acting as a communications center to coordinate the bondholders. It must communicate with the bondholders and follow the instructions given by a majority. The trustee represents the bondholders in negotiations with the debtor and the court. But the Trust

---

32. The Institute of International Finance (1996) cites the case of AeroMexico as an example of how swiftly negotiations can be concluded in the absence of a bondholders committee. But here there were no negotiations, no trade-offs, no dealing with various categories of creditors.

Indenture Act of 1939 exempts securities issued by foreign governments, their subdivisions, and municipalities. Sovereign bonds are typically issued through a fiscal agent rather than an indenture trustee. The fiscal agent has a much more limited role. In particular, its responsibilities do not extend to acting as a communications center or attempting to coordinate the bondholders.[33]

The idea of creditors committees was resuscitated in the 1990s by Macmillan and by Eichengreen and myself.[34] Macmillan suggested creating two such committees, a resurrected Foreign Bondholders Protective Council to represent and coordinate the holders of government bonds issued under New York law and submitting to New York courts, and a resurrected Corporation of Foreign Bondholders to represent and coordinate holders of government bonds issued under English law. (The vast majority of bonds are subject to either New York or English law and courts.) If problems arose with the debts of a particular country and negotiations had to be convened, these committees, working separately or jointly, would then be in a position to appoint a subcommittee to undertake the task.

It is important to be clear on what these committees can and cannot achieve. By creating a vehicle for exchanging information and a venue for negotiations, they can ease the process of restructuring defaulted debts, which is essential in creating a viable alternative to ever-bigger bailouts. That process will remain difficult, as it must to prevent borrowers from walking away from their debts, but not as difficult as now. What the creation of committees cannot do, except under unusual circumstances, is to get the creditors to exercise collective forbearance and roll over their short-term credits as a way of averting default. The main role of creditors committees will be to facilitate restructuring after the fact.[35]

To date, however, the investor community has been reluctant to act. It fears that standing committees would make it too easy for debtors to initiate restructuring negotiations, making it too tempting for them to suspend debt payments. It is better, in the self-interested view of the creditors, that there be no one at the other end of the line to pick up the phone.

33. Macmillan (1997, pp. 9–10); Yianni (1999, p. 80).

34. Rory Macmillan, "New Lease on Life for Bondholder Councils," *Financial Times,* August 15, 1995; Eichengreen and Portes (1995).

35. This last point is important: these committees would offer only nonbinding recommendations to the bondholders, who would then have the right to accept or reject them. They would play much the same role as bank advisory committees in the debt crisis of the 1980s.

This view is short-sighted, even for the creditors. For those seeking to create a viable alternative to large-scale bailouts of crisis countries and for whom the difficulties of debtor-creditor negotiations render moratoria and restructuring unacceptably difficult and painful, standing committees are desirable precisely because they make it easier for debtors to initiate negotiations. They would help to provide a viable alternative to ever-more-costly bailouts and disastrous Russian-style defaults, neither of which is acceptable. They would give a venue for building up a common understanding of payment capacity; for resolving issues of equity as between creditors; and for developing procedures that ensure comparability over time, from one case to the next (as the Paris and London Clubs have done for negotiations with government and bank creditors, respectively).[36]

The creation of such committees would require moral suasion by G-7 governments, central banks, and the IMF to overcome the markets' reluctance. There would be nothing unprecedented about their involvement. As noted, the Corporation of Foreign Bondholders received a parliamentary charter and other forms of official support. Its U.S. counterpart, the Foreign Bondholders Protective Council, was formed with the encouragement and support of the U.S. State Department.

Some have suggested that such a committee or committees, possibly with rotating membership, should interface with the IMF and other official bodies. This would create more problems than it would solve. IMF involvement would immediately bring objections from market participants that this could be a source of "politicization" of negotiations—and they might be right.[37] Since membership on the committee would be selective, some in the markets might feel that other participants were getting preferential treatment from the IMF. And insofar as the problem of information asymmetries arises in negotiations between the lenders and the borrowers, it is with the debtor that the creditors' representatives most urgently need to interact.

In instances where the IMF was negotiating the extension of financial assistance while the debtors and creditors were at the same time attempting

36. See Eichengreen and Portes (1995).

37. But another objection from the market participants is a complete red herring: "With respect to bondholder councils, the salience of some large securities houses in the sovereign bond market makes representatives of at least some of them extremely suspect of any such initiative. Some of them fear that their firm's very presence on such a committee would make the firm a 'sitting duck' in the event of a debt crisis: a ripe target upon which officials would exert moral suasion in support of rescheduling schemes . . . if an institutional shift toward prearranged bondholders' councils were to occur, one consequence might be a greater reluctance of the large securities houses to become involved in the bond markets for emerging market economies." (Institute of International Finance [1996, p. 40]).

to restructure outstanding debts, there might be occasion for exceptional discussions among the three parties, but it is not obvious why regular meetings between the creditors' committee and the official sector would be essential. And to the extent that there is a need for the Fund and the financial community to exchange information in a time of crisis, this can be done more simply, by asking the central bank or national treasury in each of the creditor countries to identify a representative of their financial community.[38]

Collective Action Clauses

Another approach to making market-based restructurings less difficult is by amending loan contracts to include sharing clauses, majority voting clauses, and minimum legal threshold clauses. Since many international bonds include provisions requiring the unanimous consent of bondholders to the terms of a restructuring, there is an incentive for "vultures" to buy up the outstanding debt and threaten legal action. Unlike syndicated bank loans, most such bonds lack sharing clauses that require individual creditors to share with other bondholders any amounts recovered from the borrower and thereby discourage recourse to lawsuits.

Those who believe that countries may have to suspend payment and restructure debt argue that these provisions in bond covenants should be modified. Qualified majority voting and sharing clauses would discourage maverick investors from resorting to lawsuits and other ways of obstructing settlements beneficial to both the debtor and the majority of creditors. Collective representation clauses, which specify who represents the bondholders and make provision for a bondholders committee or meeting, would allow orderly solutions to be reached. This was suggested by the G-10 in its post-Mexico report,[39] and echoed in a series of recent G-22 and G-7 reports and declarations. The G-7 then placed the issue on its work program for reforming the international financial system.

The summit communiqué, however, went little further than previous official pronouncements on this issue, and in particular maintained the

---

38. The Managing Director's formulation seems quite correct: "The role of the IMF in debtor-creditor negotiations should focus on specifying the broad parameters of financing needs during the program period and assessing the consistency of financing packages with medium-term sustainability. The negotiation of specific agreement with private creditors would be the responsibility of the member concerned. . . . " (International Monetary Fund [1999, para. 33]).

39. Group of Ten (G-10) (1996).

position that such provisions in bond contracts should be voluntary, with no policies to induce borrowers to include them. U.S. Treasury Secretary Lawrence Summers (1999) has recently stated as U.S. policy that the official sector should not "mandate the terms of debt contracts," with a qualification that may not be credible: that if debtors and creditors "choose contractual arrangements that are costly and inefficient in the event of failures, the official sector will not be prepared to shoulder the consequences."[40] Yet again, we have here an example of a time-inconsistent policy that the markets will ignore, because it will lack credibility.

The objection to collective action clauses is that they would raise borrowing costs by making it too easy for countries to walk away from their debts. Collective action clauses would weaken the bonding role of debt, creating moral hazard. They would disrupt credit-market access.

The counterargument is that provision for orderly restructurings would make emerging-market issues more attractive by minimizing acrimonious disputes, unproductive negotiations, and extended periods when no service is paid and growth is depressed by a suffocating debt overhang.[41]

The analogy with domestic corporate bankruptcy procedures supports the latter interpretation. Few of the critics of collective action clauses would argue that countries should abolish their bankruptcy laws and reinstate debtor's prison to discourage borrowers from walking away from their debts; nor that lending rates would fall if bankruptcy laws were eliminated. Rather, they acknowledge the need to balance the ex ante bonding role against ex post procedures that enhance the efficiency with which sunk resources are utilized. They may still object that recent proposals move too far from the first end of the spectrum to the second: it could be that, given the legal immunity sovereign borrowers enjoy and the special difficulties of seizing the assets of foreign borrowers in general, collective action clauses would seriously weaken the bonding role of debt. But this is an empirical question.[42]

The obvious way of answering it is by comparing the spreads on "British-style" bonds incorporating collective action clauses with spreads

---

40. Summers (1999).

41. Haldane (1999) nicely illustrates the argument that collective action clauses could, by precluding a disorderly grab race, lower the cost of sovereign bond finance.

42. The IIF prejudges it: "There could be some utility to a market-based approach to increasing the 'optionality' of bonds. Issuers, both sovereign and private, could incorporate clauses for qualified majority rescheduling, while expecting to pay some additional spread. . . . " (Institute of International Finance [1999, p. 77]).

on otherwise equivalent "American-style" bonds.[43,44] Eichengreen and Ashoka Mody analyze all international bonds issued in the 1990s for which the relevant information is available.[45] There were approximately two thousand bonds in their sample, of which 58 percent were issued under U.K. law, that is, with collective action clauses.[46] As they note, this suggests that neither lenders nor borrowers can have deep-seated objections to such clauses.

Their initial econometric analysis finds that the choice of governing law has a negligible impact on borrowing costs, as if the advantages of orderly resolution and the disadvantages of moral hazard are roughly offsetting. Once issuers are disaggregated by creditworthiness, however, sharper results emerge. Issuers from countries with high credit ratings pay lower spreads on bonds issued under U.K. law, holding constant other issue and issuer characteristics. In contrast, issuers from countries with low credit ratings pay higher spreads.

These results are intuitive. The most creditworthy borrowers will go to the wall to avoid having to interrupt debt-service payments.[47] For such countries,

43. Yianni (1999) explains in detail the collective action features of English law bond contracts that are not present in the New York contracts. See also Buchheit (1998a, 1998b, 1998c). Eichengreen and Mody (1999) put and answer a key question: "How could debt contracts have evolved so differently . . .? The divergence appears to date only to the US Trust Indenture Act of 1939 . . . adopted in response to the belief that corporate insiders had taken advantage of bondholders in the widespread defaults of the early 1930s. . . . " As they note, "the rationale does not obviously apply to sovereigns."

44. The comparison, however, is not in fact straightforward. Not only does one have to control for observable borrower characteristics and market conditions affecting emerging market spreads, but the choice of governing law is likely to be endogenous and depend on the issuer's characteristics. Borrowers who foresee the need to restructure may be attracted to instruments that allow for this eventuality, as will lenders who value quick resolution. Alternatively, borrowers thought likely to default on their obligations may incur the greatest surcharge if they issue a loan with collective action provisions, encouraging them to opt for bonds that exclude these clauses. Thus, while the possibility of bias due to the endogeneity of the choice of governing law cannot be ignored, not even its direction is clear. Indeed, not just the costs of funding but the very ability of developing-country borrowers to access the market may be affected by collective action clauses. High-risk borrowers, far from just being charged more for contracts including these provisions, may not be able to obtain loans at any price. Alternatively, if collective action clauses increase borrowing costs, they may cause high-quality borrowers to quit the market. Either way, the implication is that even estimates of the effect of choice of governing law on spreads that control for the endogeneity of the choice of governing law will still be contaminated by selectivity bias. Any attempt to infer the impact of collective action clauses on borrowing costs from the existing pool of borrowers would still be biased insofar as the composition of that pool could change with the introduction of those provisions.

45. Eichengreen and Mody (1999).

46. Haldane (1999) states that eurobonds issued under U.K. law constitute just under 50 percent of the stock of emerging market eurobonds (excluding Bradys).

47. Think of Hungary's determination to maintain full debt service in the 1990s, with an exceptionally high ratio of debt to GDP and severe fiscal and current account pressure—all in the face of the

moral hazard is likely to be negligible. Provision for orderly restructuring in the event of truly extraordinary events beyond the control of the country is attractive to investors, who take up the bonds in question at lower spreads. For countries with less sterling credit, in contrast, moral hazard remains a concern, perhaps the dominant one. For them, collective action provisions that weaken the bonding role of debt result in higher spreads.

So while adding collective action clauses to loan contracts might make life more difficult for less creditworthy borrowers, it would make life easier for the more creditworthy. But if one of the goals of architectural reform is to encourage the markets to differentiate better among borrowers and reward efforts to improve creditworthiness more generously, then mandating the inclusion of collective action clauses in loan contracts becomes more attractive. And for those concerned with distribution and with the welfare of the least creditworthy countries, it suggests the need to marry this kind of architectural reform to other initiatives (like debt relief) expressly tailored to their problems.

Market Participants and the Official Sector

As we have seen, although the intellectual argument may have been won with the official community, market participants have reacted negatively to proposals to constitute standing committees of creditors and with skepticism in regard to collective action clauses. This raises the issue whether the official sector should take more forceful action to implement these measures.

The official position has not changed since the Köln economic summit of June 1999:

> We have agreed on the importance of stronger efforts to encourage progress in broadening the use of collective action clauses in sovereign debt contracts. We recommend:
>
> —Making the use of such provisions a component of international best practices in debt management and a consideration in determining access to the IMF's Contingent Credit Line

---

example of Poland, which obtained a 50 percent debt reduction in 1994. This takes us back to the "reputation motive" for debt service discussed at page 49. Hungary was not, however, rewarded with a credit rating higher than that of Poland.

—Focusing attention on the use of these provisions in international surveillance and making such provisions a consideration in IMF conditionality . . .

—Considering incorporating these provisions into sovereign debt that is enhanced by the multilateral development banks

—Further considering the possible inclusion of such provisions in our own debt instruments, and otherwise encouraging the use of such provisions in the debt instruments issued by other sovereigns in our markets.[48]

The private sector market participants, on the other hand, are strongly opposed to even this degree of "coercion," and certainly to anything more compulsory:

Any shift toward involuntary mechanisms for private sector participation . . . would tend to defeat a key purpose of the 1990s approach, namely the emphasis on prompt restoration of market access . . . individual borrowing countries may wish to incorporate qualified rescheduling clauses in bond offerings, but any international attempt to make such clauses mandatory would be counterproductive . . . [it] would convey the impression that the public sector was prepared to facilitate default.[49]

Borrowers, too, may have some reluctance. If they are concerned by the "prenuptial agreement problem"—that asking in advance signals you are likely to want out—they might be reassured if the G-7 governments did proceed to issue bonds with such clauses. Here the United Kingdom has led the way. Some U.K. government foreign currency bonds have had majority voting clauses for years, and recently the United Kingdom issued a euronote with such clauses, with considerable publicity.

But the problem may be deeper. Most Latin American sovereigns issue in New York, where there is market hostility to collective action clauses (although, as pointed out above, there is no particular historical justification for the convention). Even if the U.S. government were to issue dollar bonds (it does not issue foreign currency bonds) with these clauses, that might not affect the advice that New York investment houses give to

48. Group of Seven (G-7) Finance Ministers (1999).
49. Institute of International Finance (1999, pp. 11, 12, 78).

emerging market issuers. That advice will change only if it becomes clear that a bond without collective action clauses does not carry extra protection against bailin pressures, compared to a bond with these clauses, but that in fact it just ensures additional complications. The cases of Pakistan and Ecuador may go some way in that direction. Incentives would change if the investment houses that advise the issuers were to suggest collective action clauses because such clauses would lower the spread paid by the issuer. Here we do in fact have evidence that it does so for the most creditworthy borrowers. But even for those whose credit ratings are lower, the costs of omitting collective action clauses in the new bailin environment may be high.

Nevertheless, it appears likely that encouragement and incentives will not be enough. And there is a simple solution which may or may not be interpreted as "mandating" these clauses: The United States and the United Kingdom (and indeed other G-10 governments, but New York and London should suffice) need only require that sovereign bonds issued, listed, or traded in their markets must include such clauses. One could then expect that general use in sovereign bond contracts would spread to private debt instruments. Currently outstanding bonds could be brought into voluntary exchange programs with enhancement financed by the international financial institutions. The institutional framework we need could in fact be created very quickly.

Conclusion

Debt restructuring, the historical record suggests, has never been easy. This is as it should be, of course. Neither debtors nor creditors should regard restructuring as desirable. And if limited short-term assistance from the IMF can help surmount liquidity problems and avoid that outcome without creating significant moral hazard, that is surely a better way. But regular rescue packages that allow investors to escape without incurring losses push the principle too far by undermining the incentive for responsible lending. They disregard the moral hazard consequences and the political fallout. It is therefore desirable to move back in the direction of market-based resolution.

Unfortunately, restructuring remains so difficult under present institutional arrangements that the international community is unlikely simply to stand aside, except in the case of countries that are so small that the risk to

systemic stability can be safely disregarded, or whose record of reckless policies is so blatant that it cannot be ignored. Without institutional changes
to put in place a framework for market-based restructuring, it will be difficult to avoid continued large-scale IMF financial assistance for countries
with debt-servicing difficulties. In particular, the addition of collective
action clauses to loan agreements and the establishment of standing bondholders committees are needed for a market-based solution to be feasible.

References

Bank for International Settlements. 2000. *Bank for International Settlements Quarterly Review* (February).

Buchheit, Lee C. 1998a, "Changing Bond Documentation: The Sharing Clause." *International Financial Law Review* 17 (July): 17–19.

———. 1998b, "Majority Action Clauses May Help Resolve Debt Crises." *International Financial Law Review* 17 (August): 17–18.

———. 1998c. "The Collective Representation Clause." *International Financial Law Review* 17 (September): 19–21.

Cline, William, and Kevin Barnes. 1997. "Spreads and Risk in Emerging Markets Lending." Institute of International Finance Research Paper 97-1. Washington (November).

Council on Foreign Relations Task Force. 1999. *Safeguarding Prosperity in a Global Financial System: The Future International Financial Architecture.* Washington: Institute for International Economics.

Eichengreen, Barry. 1999. *Toward a New International Financial Architecture.* Washington: Institute for International Economics.

Eichengreen, Barry, and Ashoka Mody. 1999. "Would Collective Action Clauses Raise Borrowing Costs?" CEPR Discussion Paper 2343 (December). London: Centre for Economic Policy Research.

Eichengreen, Barry, and Richard Portes, 1989a. "Settling Defaults in the Era of Bond Finance." *World Bank Economic Review* 3: 211–39.

———. 1989b. "After the Deluge: Default, Negotiation, and Readjustment during the Interwar Years." In *The International Debt Crisis in Historical Perspective,* edited by Barry Eichengreen and Peter Lindert, 12–47. MIT Press.

———. 1989c. "Dealing with Debt: The 1930s and the 1980s." In *Dealing with the Debt Crisis,* edited by Ishrat Hussain and Ishac Diwan, 69–88. Washington: World Bank.

———. 1995. *Crisis? What Crisis? Orderly Workouts for Sovereign Debtors.* London: Centre for Economic Policy Research.

———. 2000. "Debt Restructuring with and without the IMF." Paper for the International Financial Institutions Advisory Committee.

Eichengreen, Barry, and Christof Rühl, 2000, "The Bail-In Problem: Systematic Goals, Ad Hoc Means." CEPR Discussion Paper 2427 (April). London: Centre for Economic Policy Research.

Group of Seven (G-7) Finance Ministers. 1999. "Strengthening the International Financial Architecture." Report to the Köln Economic Summit, 18–20 June.

Group of Ten (G-10). 1996. *Resolving Sovereign Liquidity Crises.* Basel: Bank for International Settlements.

Group of Twenty-Two (G-22). 1998. "Report of the Working Group on International Financial Crises." Washington (October).

Haldane, Andy. 1999. "Private Sector Involvement in Financial Crisis: Analytics and Public Policy Approaches." *Financial Stability Review* (Bank of England) no. 7 (November): 184–202.

Institute of International Finance. 1996. *Resolving Sovereign Financial Crises.* Washington.

———. 1999. "Report of the Working Group on Financial Crises in Emerging Markets." Washington (January).

International Financial Institutions Advisory Commission. 2000. "Report to U.S. Congress." Washington: Government Printing Office.

International Monetary Fund. 1999. "Report of the Managing Director to the Interim Committee on Progress in Strengthening the Architecture of the International Financial System. Washington (September 24).

Kamin, Steven, and Karsten von Kleist. 1999. "The Evolution of Emerging Market Bond Spreads in the 1990s." Chapter 6 of *Bank for International Settlements Quarterly Review* (November).

Macmillan, Rory. 1997. "Towards a Sovereign Debt Workout System." Manuscript.

Partnoy, Frank. 2000. "Why Markets Crash and What Law Can Do about It." Finance and Corporate Governance Law Working Paper Series, vol. 2, no. 2 (January) (http://papers.ssrn.com).

Portes, Richard. 2000. "Where the IMF Should Fit in a New International Financial Architecture." Annual Business Faculty Research Dialogue Lecture, Haas School of Business, University of California at Berkeley (March 3).

Rogoff, Kenneth. 1999. "International Institutions for Reducing Global Financial Instability." *Journal of Economic Perspectives* 13 (Fall): 21–42.

Schwarcz, Steven, 2000. "Sovereign Debt Restructuring: A Bankruptcy Reorganization Approach." *Cornell Law Review* 85 (4): 956–1034.

Summers, Lawrence. 1999. "The Right Kind of IMF for a Stable Global Financial System." Address to London Business School (December14).

Yianni, Andrew. 1999. "Resolution of Sovereign Financial Crises—Evolution of the Private Sector Restructuring Process." *Financial Stability Review* (Bank of England) no. 6 (June): 78–84.

PART II

Debt Restructuring in East Asia: How Much, How Fast, and Lessons Learned

MASAHIRO KAWAI
IRA LIEBERMAN
WILLIAM P. MAKO

4

Financial Stabilization and Initial Restructuring of East Asian Corporations: Approaches, Results, and Lessons

A LMOST THREE YEARS after the East Asian financial crisis began, it is reasonable to offer a survey of the role of corporations in Indonesia, Malaysia, South Korea, and Thailand in causing the crisis and the crisis's impact on the corporate sector; the effectiveness of each country's framework for resolving corporate distress; corporate restructuring results achieved;[1] and major lessons to be drawn from this experience. These lessons include the importance of contextual factors in shaping each country's corporate restructuring approaches and results; detailed recommendations on corporate crisis prevention, crisis response, and crisis resolution; and the ongoing need for government support to facilitate corporate restructuring. Our assessment of each country's corporate restructuring framework proceeds from a notional set of international "best practices." Departures from best practices tend, as shall be seen, to reflect contextual factors.

Development of the Crisis and Its Effects

Well before the onset of acute liquidity problems and full-blown economic crises in the second half of 1997, the financial position and performance of

1. Unless otherwise stated, this paper in principle covers developments through the end of 1999. See also Kawai (2000) and Lieberman and Mako (2000) for earlier assessments of corporate restructuring in East Asia.

77

East Asian corporations were deteriorating as a result of imprudent invest-ment and overleverage. Corporations increasingly diversified away from their core competencies into highly competitive sectors (for example, property, construction, environmental, and financial services) and long-payback emerging markets. These debt-financed excursions were abetted by poor standards throughout the region for financial disclosure, corporate gover-nance, and supervision of financial institutions. Corporate finance practice featured elaborate capital structures and cross-shareholdings within con-glomerates, cross-guarantees among related companies and personal guaran-tees never expected to come due, and improper transactions between related companies—often to the disadvantage of minority shareholders. In terms of interest coverage and leverage, the more problematic corporations began showing signs of distress well before the onset of the acute liquidity crisis. As a result of interest and currency shocks, distress spread beyond the most problematic sectors and corporations. Corporations in some countries—depending on the legal protections available to creditors—engaged in whole-sale self-financing through the suspension of debt service.

South Korea

In Korea, warning signs were evident by late 1996. For instance, prof-itability for the thirty largest chaebols in 1996 was a mere 0.2 percent. Returns on equity for the five largest chaebols (Hyundai, Daewoo, Samsung, LG, and SK) declined from an average of 10.7 percent for the period 1987–88 to 6.2 percent for the period 1989–96. At year-end 1996, the cumulative liabilities-equity ratio for the thirty largest chaebols was 363 percent. Ten of the largest thirty had liabilities-equity ratios in excess of 500 percent—and as high as 3,075 percent in one case.

Korea experienced three waves of corporate distress. Chaebol insolven-cies in 1997 constituted the first wave. Five chaebols with cumulative debts of 8.6 trillion won defaulted during the first half of 1997 and were placed under court supervision. Kia followed in July 1997 with cumulative debts of 6.6 trillion won (see table 4-1). By the end of 1997, thirteen chaebols with debts of 28 trillion won had entered court-supervised insolvency. During 1997, liabilities-equity ratios for Korea's thirty largest chaebols rose from 363 percent to 519 percent. The second wave was acute distress among the second-tier ("6-64") chaebols. By year-end 1997, eighteen addi-tional chaebols from the thirty largest were deemed to be at moderate or

Table 4-1. *South Korea: Chaebols under Court Supervision*

Chaebol	Default date	Leverage (percent)	Net borrowings (billions of won)	Status (as of March 2000)
Hanbo	1/23/97	1,896	4,091	Court receivership; sale under way
Sammi	3/19/97	(3,324)	875	Court receivership
Jinro	4/28/97	4,231	1,917	Composition; sale being finalized
Daenong	5/28/97	(2,806)	1,172	Court receivership
Hanshin Construction	6/2/97	649	502	Court receivership
Kia	7/15/97	411	6,624	Sold to Hyundai; reorganization complete
Sangbangwool	10/15/97	711	595	Court receivership
Taeil Media	10/24/97	334	588	Composition
Haitai	11/1/97	658	3,046	Court receivership; sale under way
Newcore	11/4/97	1,222	1,215	Applied for court receivership
Soosan Heavy	11/26/97	476	639	Court receivership
Halla	12/5/97	2,066	6,453	Court receivership
Chunggu	12/27/97	484	728	Court receivership
Sungwon	4/12/99	n.a.	545	Composition
Samsung Motors	6/30/99	n.a.	4,170	Court receivership
		822 (average)	33,160 (total)	

Source: Goldman Sachs.
n.a. Not available.

high risk of insolvency.[2] Small- and medium-size enterprises (SMEs) began failing in large numbers—8,200 in 1997 and 10,500 in 1998. While not themselves overleveraged, SMEs fell victim to cash-conserving payment delays by their chaebol customers. Between September 1998 and mid-1999, sixteen chaebols and thirty-eight stand-alone corporations underwent organized workouts. The Daewoo crisis in the summer of 1999,

2. SBC Warburg (1998).

which threatened both viable business operations and the stability of local capital markets, constituted a third wave of corporate distress.

Accounting for up to 30 percent of real sector output, 50 percent of exports, and 25 percent of financial sector loans, the top five chaebols stood alone within the Korean corporate sector in size, importance, access to resources, and influence.[3] In mid-1998 it appeared that the top five were not in immediate jeopardy because of their ability to generate cash from core operations, tap local and global capital markets, and provide cross-affiliate support. However, the top five chaebols presented longer-term issues as a result of questionable intragroup transactions, expansion into highly competitive businesses and emerging markets, high leverage (averaging 479 percent at year-end 1997), and their potential to absorb a disproportionate share of new capital that might otherwise go to help restructure second-tier chaebols and support SMEs. Indeed, overall profitability and returns on investment had been declining since the period 1988–89.[4] Core businesses generated healthy cash flows, but substantial resources were being used to expand into competitive businesses and emerging markets.[5] Intragroup sales accounted for 30 percent of 1997 revenues, and cross-support in the form of guarantees, financing, and sharing of resources among affiliates was common. The top five chaebols were slow to sell assets in response to the crisis but adept at accessing local and global capital markets.[6] It appeared that they might be able to float over Korea's corporate carnage without undertaking the real restructuring measures necessary for their long-term competitiveness.

3. Daewoo companies represented 5 percent of GDP, 10 percent of exports, and 10 percent of holdings by investment trust companies.

4. Among the top five chaebols, the average ratio of pre-tax earnings to sales declined from 3.9 percent for the period 1988 to 1989 to 2.6 percent for the period 1990 to 1996. Average return on equity declined from 10.7 percent for the period 1987 to 1998 to 6.2 percent for the period 1989 to 1996.

5. A comparison between publicly listed affiliates and nonlisted affiliates for 1997 indicates that the ratio of cash flows (earnings before interest, taxes, depreciation, and amortization, or EBITDA) to assets was 11.9 percent at the listed affiliates but only 4.3 percent at the nonlisted affiliates. Many of these publicly listed affiliates were tempting cash cows. Indeed, Korea's Fair Trade Commission has brought a number of actions against chaebols for transactions under which more established (often publicly listed) affiliates provided a variety of support (for example, low-interest loans) for nonlisted affiliates within the chaebol.

6. The top five chaebols accounted for 57 percent of the year-end 1997 assets of all chaebols, but only 34 percent of asset or affiliate sales during the first nine months of 1998. In contrast, the second-tier (6-64) chaebols held 43 percent of chaebol assets but accounted for 66 percent of asset sales during the period. During the first nine months of 1998, the top five chaebols absorbed about 80 percent of the proceeds for bond and equity issues.

Thailand

For 350 publicly listed nonfinancial corporations, returns on assets decreased from 4 percent in 1993 to 2 percent in 1996.[7] This reflected a three-year increase of 110 percent in assets versus an increase of only 16 percent in profits. Mismatches were particularly evident in the property sector (assets up 115 percent, profits down 69 percent) and construction and building materials (assets up 107 percent, profits down 16 percent). Other sectors—agribusiness, electronics, household, healthcare, communications, pulp and paper, and textiles—suffered from declining returns on assets as well. Among a smaller set of 280 publicly listed nonfinancial companies, the ratio of operating cash flows (defined as earnings before interest, taxes, depreciation, and amortization, or EBITDA) to interest expense declined from 6.3 for 1994 to 3.4 for 1996. High levels of debt financing, with a quarter of it denominated in foreign currency, left Thai corporations vulnerable to interest spikes and domestic currency devaluation. Of 356 publicly traded nonfinancial corporations, those unable to generate enough operating cash flow to cover interest expense increased from 18 in 1994, to 34 in 1995, and to 49 in 1996. During the third quarter of 1997, 114 of 356 publicly traded nonfinancial corporations could not cover interest expense. Fifty-one property, chemical, and construction corporations accounted for three-quarters of the liabilities of all such distressed public nonfinancial corporations.

Nonperforming loans grew to 2.7 trillion baht by year-end 1998—or 48 percent of systemwide credits. Some six hundred large corporations accounted for half of these nonperforming loans. The other half were owed by 400,000 SMEs and 50,000 individual debtors. Motivations for "strategic default" ranged from self-preservation to malevolent intent—for example, concerns about access to working capital and competitive disadvantage, the debtors' desires to improve their bargaining position with creditors, or hopes of postponing debt repayment indefinitely by driving their creditors out of business. The decision early on to suspend fifty-six finance companies and transfer their assets for eventual sale by the Financial Sector Restructuring Authority (FRA) and disposition by loan purchasers (who might include the original debtors buying back loans at deep discount)— without providing for ongoing loan collections or extraordinary powers by the FRA to enforce its creditor rights—probably encouraged strategic

---

7. Phatra Securities (1998).

defaulting. While individual nonperforming loans did not necessarily indicate corporate distress, they cumulatively wrought severe distress on the financial sector.

Indonesia

The roots of Indonesia's crisis stretch back as far as 1982, when the government allowed free access by domestic corporations to international capital markets. Subsequently, in 1988, the government deregulated the financial sector, which expanded the number of commercial banks without making commensurate improvements in transparency and supervision. By 1993 nonperforming loans were estimated at 14 percent of total loans. Rising borrowing from foreign banks by Indonesian corporations increased the exposure of Indonesia's economy. By year-end 1997 domestic private corporations had borrowed $53.6 billion from foreign banks, which left the corporate sector (as well as Indonesian banks exposed to these corporates) highly vulnerable to sudden depreciation. By late 1998 corporate indebtedness was estimated to total $118 billion. Of this, nearly 60 percent was owed to foreign creditors, and about half of the remaining 40 percent was denominated in foreign currency, rendering the Indonesian corporate sector systematically vulnerable to large-scale depreciation of the rupiah.[8] Risk mismanagement appears to have severely aggravated the situation, as a number of corporations did not hedge exchange risk.

Malaysia

Unsustainable debt-financed asset growth also appears to have been the main culprit in Malaysia. While asset growth between 1992 and 1996 averaged 31 percent for nonfinancial corporations, asset growth exceeded 40 percent on average for corporations in construction, diversified holdings, trade, services, and property. Liabilities-equity ratios averaged 163 percent for nonfinancial corporations as a whole, but averaged between 200 and 300 percent for industrial and construction corporations and more than 500 percent for diversified holding companies.

One analysis of publicly listed companies for the period 1995–98 showed a decrease in net profit margins from 12 percent in 1995 to 6.9 percent in 1997. The proportion of firms whose interest expenses exceeded operating cash flows steadily increased from 3 percent in 1995 to

8. Kawai (2000).

6 percent in 1996, and to 17 percent in 1997.[8] An analysis by Goldman Sachs indicated that nonperforming corporate loans increased from 8 percent in 1996 to 11 percent in 1997 and to 18.5 percent in 1998.

Several measures indicated the extent of corporate distress. The number of corporations wound up under the Companies Act for an inability to satisfy debts coming due increased from 681 in 1996 to 1,898 in 1997 and to 4,800 in 1998. In 1998, 32 corporations sought court protection from their creditors under Section 176 of the Companies Act. Other indicators included increases in corporate defaults disclosed pursuant to Kuala Lumpur Stock Exchange requirements and in corporate downgrades by rating agencies.[10]

Frameworks for Corporate Restructuring

Before examining the corporate restructuring frameworks adopted by the East Asian countries in detail, it is useful to establish some benchmarks for comparison. Box 4-1 suggests a set of best practice standards for corporate restructuring, either under normal conditions or in a systemic crisis.

The responses of the East Asian governments to crisis in their corporate sectors varied in terms of the enforcement and reform of legal protections for creditors, the development of voluntary workout regimes and asset management companies, supporting legal reforms, and linkages between corporate restructuring and overhaul of highly distressed financial institutions. Table 4-2 summarizes various institutions that were put in place to deal with corporate and financial restructuring. The agencies for voluntary corporate workouts and asset management or resolution have all been established since the outbreak of the crisis, together with some new bank recapitalization agencies. Bank recapitalization was considered a necessary component of the overall corporate restructuring process because commercial banks, as major creditors of indebted corporations, needed to have a strong capital base to work out corporate debt.

Legal Frameworks and Reform Efforts

During a systemic crisis in which many hundreds of large corporations and tens of thousands of SMEs experience simultaneous distress, the great majority of restructuring efforts must proceed on an out-of-court basis.

9. Claessens, Djankov, and Klingebiel (1999).
10. See Thillainathan (2000).

Box 4-1. *Suggested Best Practice Standards for Corporate Restructuring*

—A prompt ability by unsecured creditors to appoint a receiver to liquidate a company for a general failure to service debts on time

—A prompt ability by secured creditors to seize and sell collateral

—A court-supervised reorganization framework that protects debtors from asset seizures; provides priority for new lending; gives a debtor and its creditors an opportunity to work out a mutually satisfactory restructuring plan; allows a majority of creditors to "cram down" a reorganization plan on a holdout minority of creditors; and converts the case into a court-supervised liquidation if interim milestones and reasonable deadlines are not met

—Substantial institutional capacity, in terms of experienced judges, receivers, and insolvency professionals

—Agreed standards among financial institutions for out-of-court workouts, including appointment of a lead creditor and steering committee; development and sharing of information; priority for new lending; apportionment of losses among creditor classes; thresholds for creditor approval of proposed workouts; and means for the resolution of intercreditor differences

—A strong regulator who can encourage financial institution creditors to resolve differences among themselves on their own

—A well-developed secondary market for corporate debt, including distressed debt

—No legal barriers to the debt-equity conversions or the swift redeployment of corporate shares, real estate, and productive assets—including through foreign investment, hostile takeover, or merger

—A legal presumption, which can be altered in negotiation, that the equity interests of all shareholders, including minority shareholders, are wiped out in case of corporate insolvency

Otherwise the capacity of local courts, administrators, and other insolvency professionals would be overwhelmed and restructurings delayed. Out-of-court restructuring occurs, however, in the shadow of the law. While some debtors might voluntarily cooperate out of the goodness of their hearts, more often the success of out-of-court efforts ultimately depends on the *ability of creditors to impose losses on debtors*—through the seizure of assets, foreclosure, or liquidation. In East Asia, the shadow cast by legal regimes for secured lending, foreclosure, and bankruptcy was relatively robust in South Korea and Malaysia. In Thailand and Indonesia, however, the shadow remains rather attenuated—even after efforts at

—No immediate taxation of noncash corporate reorganizations (for example, mergers or share swaps)

—A strong financial regulator able and willing to force banks to take immediate losses on corporate restructuring and to take over banks whose risk-weighted capital adequacy ratios fall below an acceptable level

—Adequate public resources to recapitalize banks to make up losses from corporate restructuring combined with systematic monitoring by the financial supervisor of corporate restructuring transactions to ensure the adequacy of proposed operational restructuring, financial restructuring, and provisioning

—If a public asset management company is needed (for example, to provide liquidity through purchases of nonperforming loans or take over failed financial institutions), its operations should be based on best commercial and market principles—including uninterrupted efforts to collect loans and enforce creditor rights and maximum prompt use of bulk sales of small nonperforming loans, outsourcing, and outside professionals (compensated on an incentive basis) to work out large corporate nonperforming loans

—Reliance on market participants to structure and negotiate out-of-court workouts based on available information and the participants' commercial interests

—Opportunities and encouragement for banks to set up professionally managed private asset management companies for distressed corporate debt and converted equity

—Except in extreme cases when the government may need to create a public AMC, government involvement limited to eliminating legal or regulatory impediments to corporate restructuring, providing necessary incentives, and maintaining a sound financial sector

reform. Thailand illustrates the important point that uncooperative debtors will have no incentive to seek protection through a court-supervised reorganization if creditors have no prompt ability to seize assets or force a debtor corporation into liquidation or receivership.

SOUTH KOREA. The existence of a credible threat of foreclosure and court-supervised receivership has distinguished Korea's approach to corporate restructuring. As indicated above in table 4-1, thirteen chaebols were placed under court supervision in 1997. Eleven of these were placed in receivership, entailing a complete loss of ownership and management control. Korea has streamlined its processes for composition, reorganization, and bankruptcy,

Table 4-2. *Institutional Arrangements for Corporate and Financial Restructuring*

Country	Voluntary corporate workout agency	Asset management/ resolution company	Bank recapitalization agency
Indonesia	Jakarta Initiative Task Force (JITF)	Indonesian Bank Restructuring Agency (IBRA)	Indonesian Bank Restructuring Agency (IBRA)
Malaysia	Corporate Debt Restructuring Committee (CDRC)	Danaharta	Danamodal
South Korea	Corporate Restructuring Coordination Committee (CRCC)	Korea Asset Management Corporation (KAMCO)	Korea Deposit Insurance Corporation (KDIC)
Thailand	Corporate Debt Restructuring Advisory Committee (CDRAC)	Financial Sector Restructuring Authority (FRA) and Asset Management Corporation (AMC) for nonbank finance companies	Financial Restructuring Advisory Committee (funded by the Financial Institutions Development Fund)

Source: World Bank (2000, p. 85).

and some large companies, such as Kia, have emerged from reorganization. Court-supervised insolvencies in Korea would benefit, however, from further streamlining (for example, prepackaged reorganizations) and greater flexibility on the part of receivers to respond to the commercial and financial needs of corporations under reorganization. Indeed, the Financial Supervisory Commission (FSC) recently concluded that half the chaebol affiliates under court supervision had made insufficient progress on reorganization. Concerns that receivership would strangle viable business segments of Daewoo Corporation led the authorities to make extraordinary efforts to facilitate a buyout of foreign creditors by Korean lenders. These procedural shortcomings aside, repeated demonstrations of an ability by Korea's courts and creditors to seize ownership and control of a debtor corporation must have encouraged others to cooperate with voluntary workout efforts. While voluntary workouts typically resulted in close ongoing supervision by creditors, conversions of debt into equity, and substantial dilution, controlling shareholders usually retained management control and a significant equity share. Half a loaf apparently seemed better than none.

MALAYSIA. Two traditional remedies available to creditors are "winding up" (that is, liquidating) a corporation or reorganizing the corporation as a going concern.[11]

Under Sections 212–318 of Malaysia's 1965 Companies Act, creditors may petition the High Court to wind up a corporation for failure to pay its debts. The Act provides for appointment of a liquidator or receiver, defines the powers of the receiver, and establishes priorities between and within classes of creditors. From the perspective of an unsecured creditor, commencement of liquidation proceedings is often the best way to pressure a distressed debtor to pay its debts and preserve the debtor's assets from seizure by other creditors. Secured creditors can enforce their security outside liquidation proceedings. In Malaysia, a receiver can even be appointed without court involvement if the underlying legal document is a mortgage or debenture that entitles the mortgage or debenture holder to appoint a receiver.

Under Sections 176–181 of the Companies Act, the High Court can enforce a reorganization or compromise plan that attracts support from 75 percent of a corporation's creditors—debt-weighted. The court can also issue orders temporarily restraining creditors from proceeding against a corporation. While Malaysia lacks guidelines for the rehabilitation of troubled corporations through judicial management and is hampered by a

11. See Thillainathan (2000).

cumbersome reorganization process and the limited experience of the courts, the Companies Act provides incentives for debtors to seek the protection of a court-supervised reorganization or to cooperate with out-of-court restructuring efforts.

THAILAND. The Kingdom of Thailand has undertaken extensive reforms of its insolvency regime and made some progress, but significant gaps remain. Reforms include amendment of Thailand's 1940 Bankruptcy Act to permit court-supervised reorganization as an alternative to liquidation (passed April 1998); further amendments to streamline court-supervised reorganizations (passed March 1999); amendments to the Code of Civil Procedure to expedite foreclosures (passed March 1999); and establishment of a Central Bankruptcy Court (opened June 1999).

Whereas it might formerly have taken more than ten years to seize and sell collateral, local lawyers now suggest that the process could be completed in about two years. The process, however, is still too long and uncertain. Thus, debtors have felt insufficient pressure to cooperate with voluntary restructuring efforts or to seek protection through court-supervised reorganization.

Introduction of an option for court-supervised reorganization has provided a useful means for a supermajority of creditors (representing at least 75 percent of debts) to cram down a reorganization on dissenting creditors. In cases where there is insufficient agreement between creditors and the debtor, however, debtors and creditors remain reluctant to petition for court-supervised reorganization because of three uncertainties. First, an uncooperative debtor who has generally failed to pay debts as they come due may rebut the presumption of insolvency by claiming that assets (possibly inflated) exceed liabilities, as happened in the infamous Nikko Hotels case.[12] Second, because selection of the outside planner—who develops a corporation's reorganization plan—is so important to controlling the corporation and shaping its reorganization, a debtor may be reluctant to seek reorganization without support from one-third of outstanding credits while creditors may be similarly reluctant to seek reorganization without controlling a two-thirds block of credits. Lastly, provisions for exit from

12. In March 2000, Thailand's Bankruptcy Court ruled that the TPI reorganization case could proceed, despite the debtor's claims of solvency. While this indicates that the reorganization chapter in Thailand's Bankruptcy Act can be used to forcibly reorganize a recalcitrant debtor with positive equity, it does not create a strong precedent in a civil law system. A debtor's acceptance of insolvency and a reorganization petition may remain largely discretionary, weakening incentives for debtors to cooperate with voluntary restructuring efforts.

court-supervised reorganization or conversion would benefit from further clarification.

Some cases have emerged from court-supervised reorganization (for example, Alphatec), and the pace of reorganization petitions has increased since additional improvements to the Bankruptcy Act's reorganization chapter in March 1999. Reorganization petitions averaged a value of 7 billion baht per month from April 1998 through April 1999 and then increased to an average of 34 billion baht for the period May–December 1999. Although reforms in insolvency law have expedited consensual cases, recalcitrant debtors still face little or no immediate consequences for failing to service their debts or cooperate with voluntary restructuring efforts.

INDONESIA. A new revised bankruptcy law, together with a special Commercial Court, became effective in August 1998. Important changes include more efficient and transparent procedures; an opportunity to appoint receivers and administrators from the private sector; greater protections against preferential or fraudulent transfers; limits on the ability of secured creditors to foreclose on collateral during proceedings; and recognition of out-of-court settlements approved by as few as 50 percent of unsecured creditors so long as they represent two-thirds of outstanding claims. The consensus among local creditors is that Indonesia's insolvency law is workable but that its credibility has suffered from uneven and uncertain implementation. The threat of imposing loss on recalcitrant debtors remains too low to induce cooperation with voluntary restructuring efforts.

Voluntary Workout Regimes

All four countries introduced procedures and institutions for facilitating out-of-court workouts based on the so-called London Approach or its variants.[13] The details of implementation of these voluntary regimes have differed: Korea has focused on arbitration of intercreditor differences; Thailand's central bank has promulgated and enforced a contractual approach to corporate restructuring; Indonesia has attempted to rely on a

---

13. The London Approach, formulated by the Bank of England in the 1970s and developed further in the 1990s, consists of a set of nonbinding principles to guide debt restructuring processes. It has three objectives: to minimize losses to creditors and other parties; to avoid unnecessary liquidations of fundamentally viable debtors; and to ensure continued financial support to viable debtors. See pp. 300–03

set of principles and active facilitation; and Malaysia has used a loose process overseen by its central bank.

SOUTH KOREA. The FSC assigned specific lead banks to oversee the development of workout agreements for the most troubled smaller chaebols from among the second tier—the so-called 6-64. Recognizing that differences among creditors (for example, between banks and nonbank financial institutions) would quickly come to the fore, in June 1998 the FSC encouraged 210 Korean financial institutions to sign a Corporate Restructuring Agreement (CRA) that provides for the following: (1) creation of a seven-person Corporate Restructuring Coordination Committee (CRCC) empowered to advise on the viability of corporate restructuring candidates, arbitrate intercreditor differences, provide guidelines for workout plans proposed by creditors, and enforce substantial fines for failure to implement CRCC arbitration decisions; (2) an initial standstill of one to three months, which may be extended for an additional one to two months; (3) a 75 percent credit-weighted voting threshold for creditor approval of a proposed workout; and (4) CRCC arbitration if creditors cannot achieve 75 percent agreement after three attempts. The CRCC also provided extensive guidelines on the organization, structuring, and documentation of workout agreements.

The CRCC provided arbitration decisions in twenty-one cases involving second-tier chaebols or other stand-alone companies, and played a major role in the Daewoo case. The CRCC arbitrated among CRA signatories (all of which were Korean financial institutions) on the development of workouts for two Daewoo affiliates. More strikingly, the CRCC mediated a proposal by Korean creditors to buy out $4.8 billion in debt held by foreign creditors in Daewoo Corporation, Daewoo Heavy, Daewoo Motors, and Daewoo Electronics.

THAILAND. Thailand initially took a purely consensual approach to out-of-court restructuring. A Corporate Debt Restructuring Advisory Committee (CDRAC) was formed in June 1998, consisting of representatives from debtor and creditor interest groups—including the Federation of Thai Industries, the Thai Bankers' Association, and the Foreign Bankers' Association—and chaired by the governor of the Bank of Thailand. CDRAC members identified priority cases, promulgated a set of principles for voluntary workouts based on the London Approach (the "Bangkok Rules") in September 1998, and endeavored to facilitate negotiations and identify legal or regulatory impediments.

When it became clear that a purely consensual approach to corporate restructuring was not producing sufficiently timely progress, the Bank of Thailand stepped up its efforts and became the main champion for corporate restructuring. In January 1999, the Bank of Thailand created a CDRAC Office within the central bank to track progress on more than seven hundred large high-priority cases. The CDRAC Office also encouraged the development of two contracts—the Debtor-Creditor Agreement (DCA) and Inter-Creditor Agreement (ICA). DCA signatories agreed to defined procedures for acceptance of a case, a six- to eight-month schedule for developing and agreeing on a workout plan, information sharing, and thresholds for creditor approval. Approval by 75 percent of the creditors (credit-weighted) is necessary to finalize a restructuring—the same threshold as for a court-supervised reorganization. In cases of between 50 to 75 percent creditor approval, an issue or proposed plan must be submitted for ICA arbitration. If fewer than 50 percent of creditors approve the plan, the DCA obliges creditors to petition the court for collection of debts, foreclosure, or insolvency. Violation of DCA obligations exposes financial institution signatories to reprimands or fines by the Bank of Thailand. Differences among creditors are to be arbitrated, according to the ICA, by a three-person panel, which can vary from case to case. Since March 1999, eighty-four Thai and foreign financial institutions have acceded to the ICA and to corporation-specific DCAs.[14] As of year-end 1999, more than four hundred large debtors have acceded to DCAs.

The Bank of Thailand's CDRAC Office has recommended, and creditors have pursued, court sanctions (such as collection of debts or foreclosure) against debtors who have refused to sign a DCA. The CDRAC Office has attempted to smooth corporate restructuring by identifying individuals who could serve as mediators and encouraging parties at interest to avail themselves of mediation, to be paid for by the debtor corporations. The CDRAC Office has also promoted a simplified "lite" version of the DCA for resolution of SME debts.

INDONESIA. As part of its corporate restructuring strategy, the government of Indonesia established the Jakarta Initiative and the Jakarta Initiative Task Force (JITF), in September 1998, to facilitate voluntary

---

14. Notably, an ICA signatory can opt out of ICA application in any case where debts total 1 billion baht or more. This escape clause responds to concerns that some creditor groups—for example, unsecured foreign creditors—might be systematically disadvantaged in arbitration decisions.

negotiations between debtors and creditors for corporate restructuring and
to provide a regulatory "one-stop shop" for administrative procedures per-
taining to debt resolution.[15] The Jakarta Initiative introduced a set of principles based on the London Approach to guide voluntary out-of-court corporate restructuring. The JITF was intended to facilitate negotiations
between debtors and creditors and to obtain necessary regulatory approvals
for deals. While 320 companies with $23 billion in debts have registered
with the JITF, only six cases (representing less than $1 billion in debt) have
been resolved. Uncertain enforcement of laws to protect creditors has given
debtors little incentive to agree to restructuring deals likely to result in
debt-to-equity conversions and substantial dilution of their shareholdings.
In an effort to energize the JITF, the government has recently approved
time-bound procedures for JITF mediation of its cases and agreed that the
JITF may refer cases of uncooperative debtors to the government's
Financial Sector Policy Committee for action by the attorney general's
office in Bankruptcy Court.

MALAYSIA. With the support of Malaysia's central bank, Bank Negara
Malaysia (BNM), a Corporate Debt Restructuring Committee (CDRC)
was established in August 1998 to provide a framework for out-of-court
workouts for complex cases involving debts of 50 million ringgit or more
and three or more creditors. Key principles governing the CDRC
approach include efforts to preserve viable businesses, establishment of
creditors' committees representing at least 75 percent of outstanding
debts, full information disclosure and sharing, appointment of independent consultants, a sixty-day standstill (which can be extended), and continuation of existing credit lines. Workouts can apparently be approved
with 75 percent creditor support. Danaharta—Malaysia's public AMC—
has been used to buy out dissenting creditors. In addition, the BNM has
been willing to persuade hold-out banks who oppose workouts supported
by a majority of creditors. CDRC acts as an adviser and mediator between
debtors and creditors. Once an application is made to CDRC by either
debtor or creditors, an independent consultant is appointed to develop
a restructuring program. Applications for sixty-two cases have been made
to CDRC, and forty-five were accepted. The others were rejected, trans-

15. To assist the voluntary process, in June 1998 the Indonesian Debt Restructuring Agency
(INDRA) was established to provide foreign exchange cover for Indonesian corporations with debt
denominated in foreign currency once they had reached debt restructuring agreements. However,
progress as been slow and only one external debt workout (PT Danareska) had been reached under the
INDRA scheme by June 1999.

ferred to the Danaharta AMC, or rejected for failure to meet Danaharta's viability test.[16]

Role of Asset Management Companies

Public asset management companies (AMCs) can play many roles, including provision of liquidity support through purchases of nonperforming loans and resolution of failed financial institutions. Public AMCs can also bundle and sell loans, work out real estate–backed assets, or restructure corporations in distress.[17] While Korea and Thailand's public AMCs have so far focused on on-selling bad loans, Malaysia's and Indonesia's public AMCs are positioned to play a major role in corporate restructuring. Malaysia's Danaharta has enjoyed some success, but it is too early to assess the performance of the Indonesian Bank Restructuring Agency (IBRA). It is fair to say, however, that IBRA has many obstacles to overcome before it can function effectively.

SOUTH KOREA. As of end-January 2000, the Korea Asset Management Corporation (KAMCO) had purchased loans with a total book value of 74.5 trillion won, including 18.5 trillion won of Daewoo debts. By late 1999, KAMCO had sold only about 5 percent of the assets it had acquired. Although KAMCO is exploring joint venture liquidation and restructuring funds with potential investors, so far it has not actively engaged in corporate restructuring.

THAILAND. The Financial Sector Restructuring Authority (FRA) took over loans with a book value of 600 billion baht from fifty-six failed financial institutions and auctioned these relatively quickly. By November 1999, the FRA had obtained 152 billion baht from the sale of these loans—about 25 percent of book value. In addition, as of September 1999, the FRA had auctioned noncore assets of finance companies (such as automobiles and securities) valued at 65 billion baht for about 53 percent of book value. The FRA has been commended for its speed and thoroughness in on-selling the assets of failed financial institutions, but the FRA was not set up or given extraordinary powers to collect on debts, enforce its rights as a creditor, or restructure debtor corporations. This probably encouraged "strategic defaulting" by other debtors in the belief that they could drive additional creditors out of business.

16. Thillainathan (2000).
17. Klingebiel (1999).

Significant FRA assets were sold to a public AMC, the Asset Management Corporation, which was set up to prevent assets from being sold for too low a price to private investors. Like the FRA, the public AMC has not been active in corporate restructuring. In addition, private AMCs are being set up by many private banks (notably Thai Farmers Bank and Bangkok Bank) and by some of the state-owned banks, including Krung Thai. Thai Farmers has retained Goldman Sachs and GE Capital to work out the 80 billion baht book value of loans transferred to its private AMC at 50 percent of book value. Some observers worry, however, that such a valuation is still too high to encourage a private AMC to take necessary losses on restructuring. In general, it is unclear whether these private AMCs will focus more on loan sales or liquidations or on working out the underlying assets and companies.

MALAYSIA. Danaharta was established in August 1998 to acquire non-performing loans or assets of distressed borrowers from banks in order to provide liquidity, facilitate an orderly resolution of distressed debt and underlying assets, and restructure or liquidate distressed corporations with outstanding debts of 50 million ringgit or less.

As noted in one assessment, at the onset of the crisis Malaysia's Companies Act did not provide for the rapid acquisition and disposal or smooth management of a distressed corporation.[18] The necessary legal framework to engage in these activities was provided in the September 1998 Danaharta Act and in amendments to the National Land Code. This legislation empowered Danaharta to acquire title to assets while preserving existing registered interests in the assets and to foreclose or sell the assets through public auction, public tender, or direct negotiation without consent of the borrower so long as the sale was at market value and 30 days' notice was provided. Danaharta is also empowered to appoint special administrators to manage the affairs of distressed corporations. Under the Companies Act, practically speaking, such an appointment could be made only by a debenture holder. Enabling Danaharta to appoint a special administrator seeks to compensate for the lack of well-defined procedures for judicial management of corporate insolvency cases.

Danaharta's approach to resolution of corporate nonperforming loans is intended to restructure viable corporations, sell its interest in distressed corporations in viable sectors, and sell the underlying assets in cases where neither the corporation nor its industry appears viable. If Danaharta can-

18. Thillainathan (2000).

not reach agreement on a loan workout within three months, the loan is deemed nonviable, presumably setting the stage for a liquidation. Danaharta's loan workouts are supposed to follow certain principles—for example, the debtor's shareholders should bear most of the loss; the debtor's management has only one opportunity to implement an agreed workout, with no opportunities for revision; and the debtor's business operations must be closely monitored. Danaharta has also developed nonbinding guidelines for corporate workouts that include the following: restructured debt should provide a yield commensurate with cash flow, rather than be of a zero-coupon variety; the repayment period for restructured loans should not exceed five years; existing shareholders should be prevented from diluting shareholdings obtained by creditors through debt-equity conversions; and the workout agreement should include monitorable covenants regarding intercompany lending, disposal or transfer of assets, dividend payments, and additional borrowing.

INDONESIA. Progress on corporate restructuring will depend on the Indonesian Bank Restructuring Agency (IBRA), which has acquired extensive corporate sector assets. IBRA includes two asset management units: Assets Management Credit (AMC)—established to work out or sell nonperforming loans; and Assets Management Investment (AMI)—established to manage company shareholdings acquired in satisfaction of related-party lending violations and liquidity support provided by Bank Indonesia to commercial banks that later failed.

IBRA/AMC manages a loan portfolio of more than 207 trillion rupiah. Although these monies are owed by about 170,000 debtors, the credits are concentrated: 1,339 debtors each owing more than 50 billion rupiah account for 82.8 percent of the portfolio, and another 1,572 with loans of between 1 billion and 50 billion rupiah account for 12.4 percent; nearly 168,000 borrowers account for a mere 4.8 percent of the portfolio. Moreover, many of the large debtors are related and can be grouped under single obligors. Thus the fifty largest obligors account for 54 percent of IBRA/AMC's portfolio. IBRA/AMC is itself attempting to restructure nonperforming loans larger than 50 billion rupiah; smaller loans are to be sold, outsourced, or settled (including discounts on accrued interest). While initially adamant in refusing to take haircuts on debt rescheduling, IBRA is now seeking indemnification of its staff and government approval for circumstances in which IBRA might agree to debt write-offs or discounts. Unfortunately, IBRA is vulnerable to charges of KKN (that is, corruption, cronyism, and nepotism), a climate that has not been helped by the Bank Bali affair. It appears that IBRA staff are sensitive to the possibility of unfounded KKN allegations for proposing any transaction that involves a loss to IBRA. This could have a chilling effect on IBRA's ability to resolve its large caseload on reasonable commercial terms in any timely manner.

Of 760 major debtors that IBRA/AMC has categorized, 31 percent are considered cooperative and viable; 53 percent cooperative but questionable; 3 percent uncooperative but viable; and 13 percent uncooperative and questionable. Since mid-1999, IBRA has been gauging cooperation by requiring its largest debtors to sign letters of commitment. While it may use bankruptcy proceedings against uncooperative or nonviable debtors, IBRA faces the same uncertainties as any other creditor in going through the court system. To compensate, effective October 1999 IBRA has been given extraordinary powers (the so-called PP17 powers) to seize the assets of uncooperative debtors. In an attempt to send a message, IBRA used its PP17 powers for the first time in December 1999, seizing two properties— including fourteen hectares of land in Jakarta from a firm owned by a Suharto family member. IBRA had earlier announced that it would sue a number of other uncooperative debtors, and is continuing to fight several lower court decisions that have impeded its debt collection efforts.

Meanwhile, IBRA/AMI has taken equity positions in corporations (mostly convertible rights issues) with a face value of 112 trillion rupiah in settlement by eight commercial banks of violations on affiliated lending and central bank liquidity support. More than half the assets are in agribusiness and real estate. These stakes are organized in as many as eight holding companies. IBRA/AMI plans to rely on private sales and public offerings to exit from these equity positions. IBRA/AMI is seeking to raise 12.8 trillion rupiah in 1999 and plans to sell its 40 percent stake in the automobile manufacturer Astra; three financial investors have expressed an intention to bid on the company. IBRA/AMI's dispositions of its equity holdings could effect significant changes in corporate ownership, but the agency's effectiveness will ultimately depend on its ability to achieve adequate monitoring and governance over its holdings and to exit from these holdings in a timely manner without depressing share prices.

Segmentation and Prioritization

In a climate of systemic distress among many hundreds of large corporations and tens of thousands of SMEs, an efficient response requires some segmentation of the problem and establishment of priorities. As noted above, IBRA/AMC is segmenting its treatment of the 170,000 debtors in its credit portfolio—focusing its efforts on the 0.8 percent that account for 82.8 percent of its portfolio and designating the rest for sale, outsourcing, or standardized settlement. Danaharta's approach to its cases is based on its assessment of corporate and industry viability.

Following initial dalliances with ill-conceived "bankruptcy avoidance" loans,[19] the Korean government eventually settled on an effective crisis-segmentation strategy that included court supervised insolvency for the most difficult companies; an immediate focus on the most-distressed second-tier (6-64) chaebols; multiple efforts to impose financial discipline on the top five chaebols; and a systemic response to SME distress. Thirteen chaebols were placed under court supervision. No additional large bankruptcies occurred during 1998. Between June and September 1998, however, the CRA/CRCC framework was put in place and Korean creditors agreed on workouts for sixteen highly distressed second-tier chaebols and about thirty-eight stand-alone corporations between September 1998 and mid-1999. Although not in immediate danger in mid-1998, the top five chaebols posed longer-term concerns because of problematic business investments and high leverage (479 percent at year-end 1997) and because these chaebols threatened to absorb a disproportionate share of new capital that might otherwise go to help finance second-tier chaebols and SMEs. In response, the FSC attempted to impose financial discipline by requiring chaebols to implement capital structure improvement programs (CSIPs) and bringing a host of legal and regulatory pressures to bear (described below) to forestall avoidance of greater financial discipline by the top five chaebols.

The Korean government also applied several pressures to encourage the top five chaebols to conclude various "big deals"—acquisitions, mergers, or joint ventures designed to rationalize capacity in sectors suffering from overcapacity.[20] For SMEs, the financial supervisor adopted several support schemes: banks were required to roll over SME loans due by December

---

19. Between October 1997 and May 1998, Korean creditors with government encouragement provided 1.9 trillion won in "bankruptcy avoidance" loans to nine chaebols. These were accompanied by little or nothing in the way of commitments by the chaebols to undertake serious restructuring. Eight of the nine chaebols subsequently entered court-supervised insolvency or corporate restructuring agreement (CRA) workouts.

20. "Big deals" have been agreed for semiconductors (for example, Hyundai Electronic's acquisition of LG Semiconductor), oil refining, rolling stock, aircraft, power generation, and ship engine companies. A petrochemical deal is still under consideration. The proposed swap of Samsung Motors for Daewoo Electronics has been scuppered by court receivership for the former and Daewoo's mid-1999 crisis.

1998; commercial banks were required to cancel compensating balances for SMEs between January and November 1998 to all credit flows to SMEs; and the relatively larger and stronger commercial banks were required to provide additional loans to SMEs. In addition, the government made working capital and trade finance available to SMEs through a number of facilities and established four investment funds, mostly to provide debt and equity financing to SMEs.

Supporting Legal and Regulatory Measures

The East Asian governments undertook a wide variety of legal and regulatory initiatives to encourage corporate restructuring. These included both "carrots" (that is, positive incentives and elimination of disincentives or obstacles) and "sticks" (that is, disciplinary procedures and punishments for failure to restructure adequately). Many of these measures appear to have been useful or perhaps necessary, but they are generally not sufficient to induce corporate debtors to sell cherished assets, accept equity dilution, or hand over management control. The measures listed below nonetheless provide a checklist of useful actions for future crises.

TAXES. Some countries provided tax relief for debt restructuring, typically limited to debt restructuring by financial institutions so that the relief might not be abused through debt restructuring transactions between related parties. Typically, the creditor could deduct the debt-restructuring loss from its taxes and the offsetting gain to the debtor would not be taxed. Thailand attempted to strengthen this incentive by limiting its duration from January 1, 1998, until December 31, 1999. This incentive had no noticeable effect on debt restructuring. Recently extended through year-end 2001, this tax incentive may yet prove useful as debtors and creditors become more ready to restructure corporate debt. Some countries have also provided relief on various registration taxes, stamp duties, and transfer taxes. Other measures have included exemptions for SMEs on capital gains from the sale of real estate used to repay debt and for real estate transferred in mergers and acquisitions (M&A). Tax treatment of M&A transactions remains a sticking point in Thailand, where noncash transactions (for example, mergers or share swaps) create an immediate tax liability. One tax "stick" considered in Korea has been to limit or eliminate deductibility of interest on "excessive" debt.

FOREIGN INVESTMENT AND OWNERSHIP. After a series of liberalizations, Korea and Indonesia have essentially eliminated restrictions on foreign ownership of domestic corporations. Thailand has amended its Alien Business Law and somewhat eased restrictions on foreign ownership of land or condominiums. Malaysia had abolished significant restrictions on foreign ownership of corporations before the crisis hit the country.[21]

CORPORATE TAKEOVERS. Korea has made it possible for outside investors to acquire larger blocks of a corporation's shares without approval from the corporation's board.

CORPORATE REORGANIZATIONS. While it has not posed a problem in Thailand, debt-equity conversions are legally considered a two-part transaction between the debtor and the converting creditor, which could give rise to challenges from other creditors as a preferential transfer to converting creditors. The law also requires a waiting period of six months before concluding a merger to enable creditors to object. Lastly, in several countries, it appears that minority shareholders of insolvent companies continue to enjoy substantial rights and are positioned to block restructuring transactions that disadvantage them.

LABOR. Korea amended its Labor Standards Act to allow companies involved in restructuring or an M&A transaction to lay off employees. In addition, Korea somewhat broadened and extended its program of unemployment insurance to mitigate damages to laid-off workers.

CORPORATE GOVERNANCE. Several countries have moved to improve financial disclosure through adoption of international accounting standards and other shareholder protections. Korea, for instance, is requiring chaebols to provide consolidated financial statements for 1999; appointment of independent directors to one-quarter of board seats; and lower thresholds for inspections and lawsuits by minority shareholders. In recognition of the issue of weak corporate governance (for example, inadequate safeguards of minority shareholders, connected party transactions, inadequate financial disclosure, and lack of independent oversight at the board level), the Malaysian government formed the Finance Committee on Corporate Governance in March 1998. Its recommendations have been published and implementation begun.

LOSSES FROM DEBT RESTRUCTURING BY STATE-OWNED BANKS. State-owned banks may be legally constrained from taking losses on debt restructuring. For instance, Article 157 of Thailand's act on state-owned enterprises (SOE)—which holds employees personally liable for losses

21. In all the affected East Asian countries, however, foreign ownership restrictions are still maintained in certain strategic sectors, including utilities.

caused to the SOE—has probably made it more difficult for Krung Thai or other state-owned banks to agree to debt write-offs or restructurings that pose a present-value cost. Similar strictures have applied to IBRA. The Indonesian government, however, has moved forward with a policy specifying conditions under which IBRA may agree to haircuts or discounts with indemnification for IBRA employees.

LIMITS ON BANK SHAREHOLDINGS. Recognizing that Korea's massive corporate debt overhang made debt-equity conversions inevitable, the government amended the banking law to increase the percentage of a corporation's shares that a bank could hold—from 10 to 15 percent, or more with FSC permission. In Thailand, the banking law has been amended to allow private AMCs to hold assets other than debt instruments. This issue apparently remains to be addressed in Indonesia, where banks are required to sell converted equity in profitable companies within two years.

COMPETITION POLICY. The practice of having stronger affiliates in a chaebol cross-guarantee debts of weaker start-up affiliates complicated the liability structure of Korean chaebols. It often worked to the disadvantage of public shareholders, encouraged chaebols to make imprudent, over-leveraged investments, and made it more difficult to jettison nonviable affiliates. In response, in early 1998, the government prohibited new cross-guarantees and required existing cross-guarantees to be eliminated by March 2000. In addition, the Fair Trade Commission has conducted three rounds of investigations into improper transactions between related affiliates within major chaebols. These included purchases of commercial paper, subordinated debt, and real estate at above-market prices.

EXPOSURE LIMITS. More stringent loan exposure limits have served to reduce lending by Korean banks to the top five chaebols.[22] A July 1998 rule limited the ability of a chaebol's financial affiliate to hold the commercial paper of related affiliates. At the end of October 1998, bondholdings in a single group were limited to 15 percent of their total for investment trust companies and 10 percent for banks—still high enough to threaten a bond market meltdown when Daewoo came under stress.

---

22. Banks have been required to include in their calculation of a single borrower and group exposure limits all off-balance exposures, including guarantees; reduce their exposure to a single borrower or group from 45 percent to 25 percent of their equity by year-end 1999; and reduce single-group exposure to large shareholders and affiliates from 45 percent to 25 percent of their equity by January 2000. Net lending, including guarantees, from commercial banks to the top five chaebols dropped from 81 trillion won at year-end 1997 to 58 trillion won at mid-year 1999.

MANDATED EXITS. At the FSC's direction, Korean banks identified fifty-five nonviable chaebol affiliates in June 1998 and forced their sale, merger, or liquidation.

CAPITAL STRUCTURE IMPROVEMENT PROGRAMS. In Korea, since April 1998, the FSC has required each chaebol seeking new credits or a credit rollover to agree on a capital structure improvement program (CSIP) with its lead bank. Each CSIP was to identify measures to enhance management transparency, focus business operations on core competencies, reduce liabilities-equity ratios to 200 percent by year-end 1999, and eliminate cross-guarantees. Following an uneven start-up, quarterly reviews of CSIP implementation have provided a useful means for disciplining at least four of the top five chaebols. Daewoo's migration from the top five to near bankruptcy represented a "too little too late" lapse in the government's ability to impose greater financial discipline on Korea's largest chaebols. If CSIPs provided the anvil for restructuring Korea's largest chaebols, more stringent exposure limits for their lenders, mandated elimination of cross-guarantees, and fines for improper intrachaebol transactions served as the hammer.

Linkages to the Financial Sector

If corporate debtors are likely to suffer losses from corporate restructuring—through forfeiture or sale of cherished assets and businesses, equity dilution, and diminution or loss of management control—their bankers can expect to suffer as well, through credit write-offs, allowance of grace periods, rate reductions, term extensions, or conversions of debt into equity or quasi-equity for which there may be no market. Recognition of the present-value effects of these concessions and provisioning to reflect the future likelihood of repayment can drive a bank's capital below acceptable levels. Capital shortfalls may prompt government seizure of the bank or necessitate recapitalization of the bank from private or public sources, the latter of which would dilute existing shareholder interests and threaten the loss of management control. Thus the controlling shareholders and managements of banks will be reluctant to undertake corporate restructuring initiatives that threaten their equity position and control. Bankers are also reluctant to offer concessions on debt restructuring out of concern for moral hazard. Forcing asset or business sales and acquiring a controlling equity interest in the debtor's business, however, should mitigate such concerns.

To ease the reluctance of bankers to take losses on corporate restructuring, governments may provide various types of forbearance. For example, a government could give banks more time to reduce their capital to reflect losses on corporate restructuring (forbearance on provisioning) or require full provisioning immediately but allow banks to operate for some time with inadequate capital (forbearance on capital adequacy).

If a government ends up taking ownership and control of financial institutions, the dilemmas faced by private bankers convey to the government. For example, what losses on corporate restructuring can state-owned banks absorb, and how much additional recapitalization must be funded by the taxpayers? How can state-owned banks make concessions on debt restructuring without creating moral hazard? The cases of Thailand, Indonesia, and Korea illustrate the dilemmas for private and state-owned banks and the consequent effects for corporate restructuring.

THAILAND. The crisis led to the government taking over a large additional portion of the country's financial sector assets. This included the assets of fifty-six finance companies closed in December 1997, four medium-size banks intervened in January and February 1998, and two additional banks intervened in August 1998. As noted earlier, the decision to close the finance companies and transfer their assets to the FRA for auction—a process that took a year to complete and was unaccompanied by either extraordinary powers or normal loan collection efforts—may have encouraged "strategic defaulting" by debtors who were convinced that they could thereby drive their creditors out of business and escape repayment. Nonperforming loans quickly rose to a peak of 48 percent of outstanding loans in mid-1999 and remained at high levels throughout the year. This represented an ongoing drain on bank capital and a continuing source of frustration for the government (as well as for the World Bank and the International Monetary Fund). The government did not want to force the banks to recognize all capital losses—for example, from any debt restructuring—immediately, for to do so might have resulted in nationalization of most or all of Thailand's financial system. The foremost impediment to corporate restructuring was the inability of Thailand's legal system to impose losses on nonviable or recalcitrant debtors. It would have been unfair and ill advised to force Thailand's banks to assume all of the loss from corporate restructuring. Thai banks may have engaged in imprudent lending, but they were not responsible for the Thai legal system's weak protections for creditors. Nationalizing Thailand's large banks in a rush to resolve nonperforming loans could have politicized the process of resolving distressed corporations.

Instead, the government responded by granting forbearance on the recognition of losses from corporate restructuring and offering public funds—linked to progress in corporate restructuring and new business lending—for bank recapitalization. In early 1998, the Bank of Thailand promulgated regulations requiring banks to upgrade their provisioning to international best practice but gave banks more than two-and-a-half years to decrease their capital to reflect losses from corporate restructuring. Banks could take capital decreases in five semi-annual increments—of 20 percent each—starting year-end 1998 and finishing at year-end 2000. Restructured loans could be reclassified as performing once the debtor resumed consistent debt service (for example, for three consecutive months). Risk-weighted capital adequacy standards remained at 8 percent.

In August 1998, the government followed up with a program for financial sector restructuring that would provide up to 300 billion baht in public funds for bank recapitalization. For Tier 1 recapitalization (preferred stock), the government would recapitalize the institution up to 2.5 percent if, following immediate write-off of nonperforming loans and full provisioning, an institution's Tier 1 capital adequacy ratio fell below 2.5 percent. Beyond 2.5 percent, the government would match Tier 1 capital raised from private investors. The government would not necessarily change the bank's management, but reserved the right to do so. Tier 2 capital (subordinated debt) would be provided at 100 percent of losses from Bank of Thailand-approved corporate restructuring transactions and 20 percent of increases in business lending.

The response of Thailand's private banks revealed their determination to avoid additional state ownership, control, or influence. Thai banks aggressively raised capital from private sources by means of various strategies, including the issuance of preferred shares and subordinated debt, and conversion of deposits.[23] Between January 1998 and October 1999, Thailand's private banks raised 305 billion baht in Tier 1 capital and 53 billion baht in Tier 2 capital. Only 45 billion baht came from public sources—42 billion baht in Tier 1 and 3 billion baht in Tier 2. While avoiding acceptance of public capital except to avoid being intervened, it appears the banks have also carefully staged their losses from corporate restructuring so as to

---

23. Deposits were converted into capital through instruments referred to as SLIPS (stapled limited-interest preferred securities) and CAPS (capital augmented preferred securities). Deposits converted into capital earned interest of between 11 and 22 percent and had first call on bank profits until redeemed. This is a temporary solution, since these instruments will need to be refinanced in five years. See Kawai and Takayasu (2000).

keep their capital write-downs under control. Observers suggest that as banks have become more fully provisioned, they have become more willing to conclude corporate restructuring transactions that include loss-making concessions on debt.[24]

INDONESIA. Moves in the financial sector have included the closure of sixteen banks in July 1997, the transfer of fifty-four distressed banks to IBRA in February 1998, IBRA's closure of seven banks and takeover of another seven in March 1998, and the government's announcement in March 1999 of plans to close thirty-eight additional banks, nationalize seven, and help recapitalize nine. As announced in September 1998, a bank could qualify for joint recapitalization if, after full provisioning of its impaired loans, its capital adequacy ratio was anywhere between 4 percent and *minus* 25 percent. In a joint recapitalization, current owners and the government would share 20:80 in contributions of new capital, related-party nonperforming loans would have to be repaid, the bank's management would have to submit a business plan to achieve viability, and the bank would have to comply with prudential regulations. While requiring immediate full provisioning, the government would give banks until year-end 2001 to achieve 8 percent risk-weighted capital adequacy ratios.

Although Indonesia's remaining private banks may thus have a grace period within which to complete corporate restructuring transactions, many of these deals will necessarily involve IBRA. IBRA's mandate, however, focuses on maximizing collections. Indeed, IBRA is expected to collect and contribute 17 trillion rupiah to the government budget for fiscal year 1999/2000. IBRA has also been adamant in resisting debt write-downs or loss-making reschedulings. Underlying this has been an insistence that flight capital be brought back to Indonesia to satisfy debts. Although there is a good rationale for insisting that capable debtors make good on their debts, IBRA's own analysis raises questions about the business prospects of two-thirds of the major debtors it has analyzed. Especially for such cases, IBRA needs the flexibility to make concessions on debt restructuring, take losses on necessary debt restructuring, and resolve differences on an equitable basis with other creditors.

---

24. This raises some key policy questions: Would corporate restructuring have moved faster in Thailand (or elsewhere) if the government had allowed capital adequacy to drop below 8 percent for some period (for example, two years) but required immediate full provisioning for all loans? Or would such forbearance merely have encouraged banks to take bigger risks and ultimately raised the cost to Thailand's taxpayers?

SOUTH KOREA. By the end of May 1999, four of the lead banks in Korea (Seoul, Korea First, Hanvit, and Chohung) were more than 90 percent state-owned. In theory, this might have enabled the government to be more aggressive in restructuring corporations—for example, seizing assets, changing management at debtor companies, writing off debts, or converting additional debt into equity. Several factors, however, worked against this, including depressed asset values, limited numbers of qualified corporate managers, the concern for leaving existing managers with sufficient equity incentives to turn their companies around, regulatory limits on holdings of corporate equity, and the reluctance of banks to consolidate the financial results of distressed corporates with their own. Perhaps most important, the government did not want to exceed the 64 trillion won ceiling on public sector liquidity and capital support for the financial sector that had been agreed with the National Assembly. Indeed, as resolution of the crisis progressed, officials responsible for financial sector restructuring looked for ways to "recycle" the 64 trillion won. Throughout the crisis, the government displayed two approaches toward its banks—at times directing solutions (for example, mandated exits or "big deals") and at other times taking a relatively hands-off attitude and expecting bank managers to negotiate corporate restructuring transactions based on their best commercial judgment.

In Malaysia, the government created an institutional framework to accelerate bank nonperforming loan resolution, bank recapitalization, and corporate debt restructuring. Danaharta, established as an asset management company in May 1998, has acquired nonperforming loans from financial institutions to clean up their balance sheets and enhance their lending ability. Financial institutions whose nonperforming loan ratios exceeded 10 percent were required to reduce the level of their nonperforming loans either through loan workouts or by selling them to Danaharta. Danaharta was given the power to appoint special administrators to manage the affairs of the distressed corporations to facilitate their restructuring. Another agency, Danamodal, was established as a special vehicle to recapitalize financial institutions whose capital adequacy ratios fell below 9 percent, thereby officially supporting institutions to strengthen their capital base. The authorities thus adopted a deliberate policy of maintaining a functioning financial system and using the official asset management company as part of the overall corporate restructuring strategy.

Corporate Restructuring: Initial Results

The magnitude of corporate restructuring activity in Korea—reorganizations and workouts underway and transactions completed—probably represents the most that can reasonably be expected in terms of a short-term response to East Asia's systemic crisis. Despite the two countries' weak legal incentives for debtors to cooperate with voluntary restructuring efforts, corporate restructuring is progressing in Thailand and Indonesia, and the main agents for corporate restructuring—the Bank of Thailand's CDRAC office and Indonesia's IBRA—have each identified a pipeline of transactions in process and time-bound goals for their completion. Malaysia has made progress through combined use of court-supervised processes, Danaharta, and CDRC under the oversight of Bank Negara Malaysia.

Given that many discussions of East Asian corporate restructuring distinguish between financial restructuring and "real" operational restructuring and allege lack of progress on the latter, it is important to provide some definitions and perspective. The discussion that follows distinguishes between corporate "self-help" and concessionary debt restructuring. Corporate self-help includes sales of businesses or noncore assets, cost reductions, and capital infusions through equity contributions from existing owners or outside investors. Given the time needed to sell businesses or real estate and other assets for above fire-sale prices, to shed marginal business lines and employees, and to focus on core competencies, operational restructuring can easily take between eighteen and thirty-six months to complete. Concessionary debt restructuring—which includes grace periods on interest or principal, rate reductions, term extensions, or conversion of term debt into equity or convertible bonds—can be accomplished almost immediately.

South Korea

Large corporate restructuring efforts amounting to at least 187 trillion won are proceeding along several tracks:

(1) Thirteen chaebols' debts, totaling 33 trillion won, are being resolved through court-supervised insolvencies. Some major reorganizations have been completed (for example, Kia) and other negotiations for significant asset transfers are underway.

(2) Workouts for 44 trillion won in debt at sixteen second-tier chaebols and other large companies have been agreed. These workouts contemplate

a 4-to-1 mix of debt restructuring and self-help, including asset or affiliate sales, new equity investment, and cost reductions. Controlling shareholders have been diluted and some managements replaced.

(3) The top four chaebols (Hyundai, Samsung, LG, and SK) appear to have completed about 20 trillion won in asset or affiliate sales and 27 trillion won in new equity issues by year-end 1999.

(4) The Daewoo case serves as a warning that no chaebol is "too big to fail." Complete changes in ownership and control are underway at the twelve workout affiliates. Domestic creditors have agreed on restructuring 63 billion won in Daewoo debts. Assuming a proposed buyout of debts owed to foreign creditors is completed, strategic sales, spin-offs, operational restructuring, and liquidation of nonviable operations can proceed.

CRA WORKOUTS. By September 30, 1999, CRA workout plans had been agreed for forty-one affiliates of sixteen second-tier chaebols and for thirty-eight large or medium stand-alone corporations (a total of seventy-nine corporations, excluding Daewoo affiliates). These plans represent more than 44 trillion won in planned restructuring (see table 4-3), of which 21 percent is to come from self-help (for example, asset sales and new equity) and 79 percent from debt restructuring. Given pre-workout debt levels and the potential glut of assets and equity issues on offer, this mix of self-help and debt restructuring is not surprising. Of the 34.9 trillion won in proposed debt restructuring, 81 percent is to come in the form of rate reductions or payment deferrals and 12 percent in conversions of debt into equity or convertible bonds. In most (if not all) cases, debt-equity conversions have substantially diluted existing shareholders and given financial institutions a controlling equity interest. So as to ensure needed operational restructuring and maximize share values, these financial institution shareholders will need to exercise effective corporate governance. Payment deferral periods range from two to five years and average four years. Operational restructuring or self-help is to continue during this period. Thus the 34 percent implementation of planned self-help achieved by the end of September 1999 represents reasonable progress. In addition, the sixteen chaebols involved in workouts have committed to disposing of 237 affiliates through sale, liquidation, merger, or court-supervised processes. As of the end of September 1999, 113 affiliates had been disposed of.

TOP FOUR CHAEBOLS. As part of their capital structure improvement programs, the top four chaebols (Hyundai, Samsung, LG, and SK) committed to more than 20 trillion won in asset or affiliate sales and more than

Table 4-3. *South Korea: Summary of Corporate Restructuring
Agreement Workouts*

Category	Agreed amount (billions of won)	Actual implementation at September 30, 1999 (percent)
Self-help		
Real estate sales	3,956	23
Affiliate sales	1,047	7
Other asset sales	995	46
Foreign capital	1,650	58
Rights issues	433	53
Cost reductions or capital contributions	1,262	44
Total self-help	9,343	34 (average)
Debt restructuring		
Rate reduction and deferral	23,302	96
Deferral	4,857	93
Conversion to equity or convertible bonds	4,329	78
Other[a]	2,412	105
Total debt restructuring	34,900	94 (average)
Total	44,243	81 (average)

Source: Financial Supervisory Service.
a. Includes repayments and write-offs.

27 trillion won in new equity issues for 1998 and 1999. These amounts
were intended to produce liabilities-equity ratios of 200 percent by year-
end 1999. These chaebols completed 13.6 trillion won of asset or affiliate
sales and new equity issues in 1998 and sales and issues totaling 26.7 trillion won during the first nine months of 1999 (see table 4-4). As of
September 30, 1999, it appeared that Samsung, LG, and SK were well on
their way to full implementation of their capital structure improvement
programs. Although questions were raised about Hyundai's ability to raise
5.9 trillion won during the fourth quarter of 1999, the company's management announced in December 1999 that it had also achieved a 200 percent liabilities-equity ratio for 1999. Liabilities-equity ratios must be
viewed with caution, and the top four chaebols will warrant continued regulatory attention. While the Financial Supervisory Service (FSS) has eliminated the effects of asset revaluations from the calculation of liabilities-
equity ratios, a significant amount of new equity was sold within these

Table 4-4. *South Korea: Implementation of Capital Structure Improvement Programs at Top Four Chaebols*
Trillions of won

Chaebol	Actual 1998	Actual 1999 Q1–Q3	Required 1999 Q4	Expected 1998–99
Hyundai	2.6	10.3	5.9	18.8
Asset or affiliate sales	0.9	2.7	1.2	4.8
Equity issues	1.7	7.6	4.7	14
Samsung	4.5	5.8	–0.5	9.8
Asset or affiliate sales	2.1	1.9	0.5	4.5
Equity issues	2.4	3.9	–1.0	5.3
LG	5.5	7.3	1.4	14.2
Asset or affiliate sales	3.1	5.2	0.8	9.1
Equity issues	2.4	2.1	0.6	5.1
SK	1.0	3.3	0.1	4.4
Asset or affiliate sales	0.3	1.2	0.2	1.7
Equity issues	0.7	2.1	–0.1	2.7
Total	13.6	26.7	6.9	47.2
Asset or affiliate sales	6.4	11.0	2.7	20.1
Equity issues	7.2	15.7	4.2	27.1

Source: Financial Supervisory Service.

chaebols to related affiliates. Once groupwide financial statements prepared according to international accounting standards become available in mid-2000, a fresh assessment of the financial position of the top four chaebols and longer-term reform requirements should be undertaken.

DAEWOO. While the top four chaebols seemed to make steady progress in deleveraging, the liabilities-equity ratio steadily increased for Daewoo companies from year-end 1997. Despite the availability of analyses indicating that Daewoo experienced a 12.2 trillion won *negative* cash flow from its operations during 1998 and increasingly onerous credit terms during 1999, many local and foreign creditors were surprised at the onset and magnitude of Daewoo's distress. Despite the extraordinary complexity of the Daewoo case—involving more than a hundred individual corporations in sixty-five countries, with almost two hundred foreign lenders and $54 billion in debt—only six to eight weeks were allowed for preliminary due diligence. This reflected the urgency of stabilizing local capital markets and preserving viable but vulnerable business operations among Daewoo companies. Significantly, eight of the twelve workout affiliates were deemed insolvent and three affiliates—Daewoo Corporation, Daewoo Motors, and Daewoo Electronics—were estimated to have negative equity of 23 trillion won. With support from the CRCC, CRA signatories agreed on workout plans for all twelve affiliates by December 2. These plans provided for the restructuring of 63 trillion won in debt. As indicated in table 4-5, 27 trillion won (42 percent of the total) of this restructuring would come from conversion of debt into equity or essentially zero-yield convertible bonds. Especially after ongoing due diligence indicated that Daewoo Corporation had transferred $7.5 billion offshore to support other operations, foreign creditors agitated for additional due diligence and those most exposed to Daewoo Corporation sought substantive consolidation of the four biggest cases in hopes of larger recoveries.

On January 22 the CRCC, the steering committee of foreign creditors, and Daewoo representatives announced agreement on an offer to purchase up to $4.8 billion in loans made by foreign creditors to the four major Daewoo affiliates (Corporation, Heavy, Motors, and Electronics.). Although the prices offered vary according to the debtor and guarantor, proposed purchase prices average about 40 percent of the face value of the debt. This is substantially more than earlier estimates of liquidation value, and it approximated projected returns from CRA workouts. In addition, tendering creditors will be entitled to receive out-of-the-money warrants, the terms of which remain to be finalized. Foreign creditors can either participate in the agreed CRA workouts or sell their claims for the aforementioned discount. For this buyout to go forward, more than 90 percent of foreign claims should be committed to the buyout arrangement or to the CRA workout. The CRCC sought decisions by individual foreign creditors by mid-March 2000 and expected to complete the debt buyout by early April. Assuming this buyout is completed, local creditors can proceed with plans for strategic sales (for example, of Daewoo Motors), spin-offs, transfers of dubious assets and investments into "bad companies" for liquidation, and more complete operational restructuring. At the end of this process, it is expected that Daewoo will have undergone a complete ownership change and substantial restructuring of its operations.

FINANCIAL PERFORMANCE IN 1999. Agreed data on the 1999 financial performance of the top thirty chaebols and their year-end financial position were not expected from the Fair Trade Commission until April 2000, and consolidated financial statements for 1999 may not be available until July 2000. The top four chaebols appear to have floated over Korea's

Table 4-5. *South Korea: Overview of Proposed Daewoo Workouts*

Billions of won

Daewoo unit	Debt deferral		Debt conversion			Total	New money
	Reduced rate	Normal rate	Equity	Convertible bonds	Other[a]		
Daewoo Corporation	6,044	0	2,000	16,700	251	24,995	1,909
Daewoo Heavy	7,556	0	1,349	0	0	8,905	148
Daewoo Motors	6,751	0	1,470	1,878	0	10,099	2,154
Sangyong Motors	1,587	0	130	0	19	1,736	264
Daewoo Telecom	1,054	0	200	1,145	18	2,417	318
Daewoo Motor Sales	0	539	0	0	0	539	0
Daewoo Electronics	3,689	0	395	1,065	1,144	6,293	0
Daewoo Electronic Companies	117	36	0	0	0	153	5
Orion Electronics	1,230	121	0	0	0	1,351	38
Kyungnam Enterprises	92	85	134	0	218	529	10
Daewoo Capital	4,757	0	40	138	0	4,935	0
Diners Club	1,238	0	0	0	0	1,238	0
Total	34,115	781	5,718	20,926	1,650	63,190	4,846

Source: Financial Supervisory Service.

a. Includes monies already on deposit and available to offset claims.

corporate carnage by virtue of their size, cash-generating capacity, opportunities for cross-affiliate support, and access to local and global capital markets. The top four chaebols reduced their debt from 178 trillion won at year-end 1997 to 160 trillion won at June 30, 1999 and—by one means or another—improved their liabilities-equity ratios from between 350 and 575 percent at year-end 1997 to 200 percent at year-end 1999.

The picture is less rosy among the second-tier chaebols and other companies that went through CRA workouts. As a group, the thirty-seven affiliates of the sixteen chaebols that went through CRA workouts achieved 89 percent of their sales targets for the first half of 1999, while the thirty-three stand-alone corporations that went through workouts achieved 99 percent of their revenue goals. While actual "current income" losses (that is, earnings before extraordinary items and taxes) for the thirty-three stand-alone corporations were 6 percent better than plan, actual current income losses for the sixteen chaebols' thirty-seven workout affiliates were two-and-one-half times larger than expected. Given Korea's macroeconomic turnaround, such underperformance suggests unrealistic business plans or failure to implement necessary cost reductions, or both. The viability of CRA workout chaebols (which remain heavily indebted) when grace periods expire in one to four years is uncertain. Eight chaebols have reportedly already entered a second-round CRA workout. It would not be surprising to see ten of the sixteen workout chaebols forced into second-round CRA workouts, court-supervised reorganization, or receivership over the next six to eighteen months.

Thailand

Through December 1999, the Bank of Thailand reported that 1,015 billion baht in corporate restructuring transactions had been completed (see table 4-6). The pace of corporate restructuring has accelerated somewhat. Completed transactions averaged 63 billion baht a month from end-December 1998 through June 1999 and 80 billion baht a month from June through end-December 1999.

CDRAC and the Bank of Thailand's CDRAC Office are separately tracking progress on about seven hundred large and one thousand medium-size restructuring cases, which together account for 2.1 trillion baht in debt. As indicated in table 4-7, 271 of these cases (representing 704 billion baht, or 33 percent of outstanding debt) are complete or essentially complete—either by recovering to normal status, achieving resolution under the old

Table 4-6. *Thailand: Completed Debt Restructuring*
Millions of baht

Sector	December 1998	June 1999	Increase, December 1998–June 1999	December 1999	Increase, June–December 1999
Agricultural	2,573	11,887	9,314	23,841	11,954
Mining	1,911	3,840	1,929	6,309	2,469
Manufacturing	51,088	181,698	130,610	318,422	136,724
Commercial	29,446	108,856	79,410	211,044	102,188
Construction	2,869	14,922	12,053	33,144	18,222
Real estate	33,733	81,480	47,747	166,478	84,998
Public utilities	4,728	12,613	7,885	40,430	27,817
Services	20,086	80,707	60,621	131,796	51,089
Consumption	7,721	38,811	31,090	83,448	44,637
Total	154,155	534,814	380,659	1,014,912	480,098

Source: Bank of Thailand.

Table 4-7. *Thailand: Pipeline of Large and Medium-Size CDRAC Cases*

Disposition	Number of cases	Outstanding debt (millions of baht)	Percentage of debt
Completed	271	704,002	33
Cases under way (for example, under debtor-creditor agreement)	357	436,904	20
Awaiting debtor-creditor agreement accession	872	545,715	25
Voluntary cases under way	1,229	982,619	46
Recommended for legal action by CDRAC	192	366,860	17
Independent legal action by creditors	35	94,973	4
Troublesome cases for legal action	227	461,833	21
Total	1,727	2,148,454	

Source: Corporate Debt Restructuring Advisory Committee.

CDRAC/Bangkok Rules framework, or under the Debtor-Creditor Agreement (DCA) framework. Another 1,229 cases representing 983 billion baht (46 percent of the CDRAC total) are in process. These include 357 cases that are proceeding according to debtor-creditor agreements. *If* debtor-creditor agreement timetables are adhered to and enforced, these cases should be resolved by mid-2000—through agreement on a restructuring plan or court petition for collection of debts, foreclosure, or insolvency. In another 872 cases, the debtor has not yet signed a debtor-creditor agreement. Some 227 cases representing 462 billion baht (21 percent of the total) are destined for legal action. These include 35 cases where debtors have failed to sign debtor-creditor agreements or are otherwise uncooperative and 192 cases where creditors failed to agree on a restructuring plan after a second vote. In the latter cases, CDRAC recommends legal action and creditors are obliged within sixty days to seek court-sanctioned remedies.

Restructurings to date—both CDRAC and purely self-directed—have included a mix of concessionary debt restructuring (for example, forgiveness, term extensions or rate reductions, and conversions of debt into equity) as well as self-help (for example, refinancings through debtor bond issues, capital increases, and asset sales). These efforts are expected to total 221 billion baht (see table 4-8) and involve a 30-70 mix of concessionary debt restructuring and self-help. The favored self-help techniques are debt refinancings (for example, through bond issues) and capital increases (for example, through issues of new equity)—only 6.3 billion baht in asset sales are involved.

Court-supervised reorganizations have not yet played a major role in Thailand's corporate restructuring. By year-end 1999, the Bankruptcy Court had approved reorganization plans for a mere seven corporations.

Table 4-9 presents both interest coverage (EBITDA-interest expense ratios) and leverage (liabilities-equity ratios) by sector from 1996 through September 30, 1999, for 280 nonfinancial companies listed on the Bangkok Stock Exchange. Even though some sectors (agribusiness, electronics, food, pharmaceuticals, and printing) show favorable trends in cash flow and deleveraging, others remain distressed and vulnerable. Communications, energy, packaging, textiles, and transport show reasonable interest coverage but high debt levels. Another cluster of corporations in chemicals, electrical products, health care, household products, property, and miscellaneous suffer both from an inability to cover interest costs with operating cash flows and high debt.

Table 4-8. *Thailand: Allocation of Techniques in Selected Restructuring Cases*[a]
Millions of baht

| Sector | Debt restructuring | | | Debt refinancing | Self-help | | Total |
	Forgiven	Rescheduled	Converted		Capital increase	Sales of assets	
Agribusiness	0	0	100	0	3,200	120	3,420
Automotive	0	0	1,200	0	5,400	0	6,600
Building materials	0	46,410	2,310	50,000	28,037	4,000	130,757
Chemical	0	0	0	0	10,200	0	10,200
Computers	0	0	1,700	0	1,700	0	3,400
Contractors	6,033	1,722	1,060	0	3,082	1,186	13,083
Electronic components	738	0	0	0	1,573	0	2,311
Energy	0	0	0	0	0	0	0
Entertainment	292	0	0	0	3,238	0	3,530
Hotels	0	0	369	0	1,885	0	2,254
Household	0	0	0	0	0	0	0
Manufacturing	0	0	300	0	0	0	300
Property	1,400	0	3,834	5,000	20,714	1,088	32,036
Telecommunications	0	0	0	0	13,530	0	13,530
Transport	0	0	0	0	25	0	25
Total	8,463	48,132	10,873	55,000	92,584	6,394	221,446

Source: SEAMICO Securities.

a. The emphasis on financial self-help reflects the fact that the list includes some viable and proactive companies. For instance, although not a CDRAC case, the table includes Siam Cement's planned 50 billion baht debt refinancing, 400 million baht capital increase, and 12 billion baht debt rescheduling. Notably, TPI is not included.

Indonesia

Corporate restructuring in Indonesia is a work in process. Some significant restructurings have occurred, most of them outside official structures.[25] More than three hundred cases have registered with the Jakarta Initiative Task Force (JITF). IBRA's AMC and AMI have debt and equity positions in, respectively, about 950 and 200 large companies.

JAKARTA INITIATIVE. At year-end 1999, 323 firms with combined external debt of $23 billion and about 15 trillion rupiah in local debt had registered with the JITF (table 4-10). Modest increases in JITF's caseload occurred during the second half of 1999. JITF has restructured the debts of only 6 corporations, with total indebtedness of less than $1 billion. Another 58 cases have reached either a formal standstill agreement, agreement in principle, or final agreement presumably awaiting documentation. Thus, resolution of the remaining 259 cases is presumably in a very preliminary stage. In hopes of giving JITF more teeth, the government recently agreed that JITF would adopt time-bound mediation procedures and that JITF mediators could refer recalcitrant debtors to the Financial Sector Policy Committee for consideration and possible referral by the attorney general to the Bankruptcy Court.

IBRA. Through year-end 1999, IBRA's AMC had collected 4.5 trillion rupiah on its 207 trillion rupiah loan portfolio, from 8,450 debtors—mostly small.[26] Table 4-11 shows IBRA/AMC's pipeline of 959 large cases, which represent $6.9 billion in foreign currency-denominated debt and 60 trillion rupiah in local debt. Only about 5 percent of these cases were complete or close to finalizing a restructuring proposal at year-end 1999. Another 40 percent were in the middle stages of a workout (assignment of advisers, due diligence underway, initiation of restructuring negotiations), while 55 percent were still in the preliminary stages (initial meetings or agreement on a standstill). IBRA's resolution of these cases on more or less satisfactory terms will depend on its ability to use the courts or its own special administrative powers to enforce creditor rights; insulation of IBRA from political pressure—including unfounded KKN allegations; and flexibility to take losses if so warranted by the debtor company's asset base and operating cash flows.

25. Included are the restructuring of $1.1 billion in debt of the automobile manufacturer Astra, $289 million in debt of PT Ariawest International, and $219 million in debt of the pharmaceutical company PT Kalbe Farma. In addition, Bakrie Brothers has reached preliminary agreement to restructure debt totaling $1.2 billion, including with IBRA.

26. Twenty large debtors accounted for a mere 587 billion rupiah in settlements.

Table 4-9. *Thailand: Corporate Interest Coverage and Leverage by Sector, 1996–99*

Sector	EBITDA–interest expense ratio[a]				Liabilities–equity ratio			
	1999: (first 9 months)	*1998*	*1997*	*1996*	*1999: (first 9 months)*	*1998*	*1997*	*1996*
Agribusiness	4.51	2.67	2.24	2.94	1.25	1.51	2.68	1.72
Building	1.37	0.89	0.56	3.01	3.72	3.14	5.14	2.78
Chemicals	0.89	1.37	0.92	3.53	3.89	2.08	5.49	1.74
Commerce	3.54	1.54	1.97	5.78	1.52	1.49	2.58	1.38
Communication	2.04	1.60	1.03	3.52	5.08	4.43	9.22	1.99
Electrical products	0.77	0.11	1.03	2.74	42.89	n.a.	8.38	2.41
Electronic components	12.29	3.71	6.54	7.45	0.68	0.90	1.30	1.27
Energy	4.27	3.33	2.91	3.28	2.05	1.78	2.80	1.52
Entertainment	1.98	(4.87)	9.30	18.20	0.74	0.49	0.54	0.29
Foods	10.58	3.64	2.29	4.49	1.01	1.10	1.71	1.39
Health	0.72	0.33	1.01	3.55	14.76	5.14	4.92	1.42
Hotel	2.42	2.82	1.68	5.37	1.12	1.06	1.14	0.91
Household	(0.97)	0.93	1.09	3.08	77.43	3.76	3.44	1.73
Packaging	2.70	1.11	2.07	4.58	4.75	2.84	3.24	1.52
Pharmaceutical	7.22	2.16	1.73	4.41	0.45	0.48	0.76	0.64
Printing	4.08	1.53	2.18	5.04	0.96	0.29	1.52	0.89
Property	0.50	(0.40)	0.36	3.73	10.43	3.52	3.17	1.88
Pulp and paper	2.57	1.94	1.51	1.11	2.02	1.81	3.13	2.79
Textiles	1.47	1.15	1.72	1.86	2.96	2.04	3.33	1.70
Transportation	2.59	6.08	8.09	3.77	6.32	7.36	14.71	2.77
Vehicles	3.58	1.94	2.89	5.75	1.82	1.98	4.64	1.78
Miscellaneous	0.66	(2.36)	(0.07)	1.79	(8.04)	(24.19)	27.39	1.44
Total average	1.69	1.25	1.66	3.42	3.58	3.16	4.34	1.93

Source: Merrill Lynch.

n.a. Not available.

a. EBITDA = earnings before interest, taxes, depreciation, and amortization.

Table 4-10. *Indonesia: Jakarta Initiative Task Force, Registered Restructuring Cases*

Sector	Number of cases[a]		Debt estimate[b]			
			Billions of U.S. dollars		Billions of rupiah	
	June 1999	December 1999	June 1999	December 1999	June 1999	December 1999
Agribusiness	5 (1)	5 (1)	0.4	0.4	6.9	6.9
Basic industry	27 (3)	34 (6)	5.5	6.8	3,104.0	3,980.8
Chemicals	10 (2)	10 (2)	3.5	3.5	604.0	604.1
Consumer goods	4 (3)	6 (3)	0.4	0.4	65.9	5.9
Textile and garment	21 (1)	22 (2)	2.9	3.0	2,680.0	2,683.1
Finance	12 (1)	16 (2)	1.3	1.3	1,277.0	1,290.1
Infrastructure and utilities	9 (2)	10 (3)	0.5	1.0	386.0	386.3
Mining	5 (0)	5 (0)	0.5	0.5	0.5	0.5
Property and real estate	62 (1)	76 (7)	1.2	1.3	3,668.0	3,797.7
Trading, services, and investment	43 (7)	63 (13)	3.6	3.7	731.0	763.7
Transportation	4 (0)	4 (0)	0.8	0.8	613.0	613.8
Various	49 (3)	72 (19)	0.7	0.7	469.0	533.7
Total	251 (24)	323 (58)	21.4	23.4	13,605.3	14,666.7

Source: Jakarta Initiative Task Force.

a. Cases that have reached a final binding restructuring agreement between parties, a standstill agreement in principle, or an agreement in principle. Numbers in parentheses include the latter two categories.

b. Aggregate indebtedness, as reported by companies and their creditors. Given the existence of undisclosed recent additional or paid debt, these numbers may be over- or understated.

Table 4-11. *Indonesia: Active Debt Restructuring Cases of the IBRA/AMC, December 1999*

Restructuring stage	Number of cases	Debt estimate	
		Billions of U.S. dollars	Billions of rupiah
Initial negotiation	515	1.85	19,553.8
Standstill agreement	16	0.0	1,239.0
Advisory assignment	199	1.82	17,071.3
Due diligence under way	141	1.5	13,196.0
Restructuring negotiation initiated	46	0.4	6,777.5
Restructuring proposal finalized	35	1.2	2,445.7
Restructuring proposal implemented	7	0.1	65.0
Total	959	6.9	60,348.3

Source: Indonesian Bank Restructuring Agency.

IBRA's AMI is in the process of acquiring equity interests in about two hundred corporations (table 4-12). IBRA/AMI is planning to exit these positions through public offerings or private sales. Presently, IBRA is discussing sale of its 40 percent stake in Astra—acquired from Bank Central Asia (BCA)—with three potential financial investors. In theory, IBRA/AMI could be in a position to use these shareholdings to promote corporate restructuring. In practice, its ability to do so will depend on a host of factors—its ability to exercise governance and monitor companies to preserve the value of its assets, its rights as a (typically) minority shareholder, interest from institutional investors and the ability of local equity markets to support public offerings, readiness to open ownership and control to foreign investors, and political pressures on IBRA—including for ongoing contributions to the state budget.

MALAYSIA. More than forty companies have filed for reorganization under Section 176 of the Companies Act. In thirteen cases, reorganization schemes have been proposed, and in another three cases the reorganization proposals have been approved. However, court-based workouts have proceeded relatively slowly in comparison to CDRC- or Danaharta-led restructuring. Amendments to Section 176 and opportunities for creditors to sell their loans to Danaharta have been helpful. The ability of debtor firms to ask for extensions of stay orders against their creditors, however, continues to hamper some restructuring efforts.

Table 4-12. *Indonesia: IBRA/AMI Shareholdings*

Bank	Holding company	Book value (billions of rupiah)	Number of companies	Status
BCA	PT Holdiko Perkasa	52,726	108	Holding company staffed or operational
BDNI	PT Tunas Sepadan I	28,408	12	Holding company staffed or operational
BUN-Hassan Group	PT Kiani Wirudha	5,340	30	Eight transfers complete[a]
BUN-Ongko Group	PT Arya Mustika MA	8,347	20	Final closing due March 21, 2000
Danamon	PT Bentala Kartika A	12,533	26	Completed
Modern	PT Cakrawala Gita P	2,663	10	Completed
Surya	Direct	1,886	5	Four completed
Hokindo	TBT	331	12	Closing in progress
Total		112,234	223	

Source: Indonesian Bank Restructuring Agency.
a. In addition, ten conditional and nine to be replaced with cash.

Table 4-13. *Malaysia: Danaharta's Pipeline of Workout Companies at Year-End 1999*

	Borrowers		Debts	
Stage of process	Number	Percent	Amount (billions of ringgit)	Percent
Not yet started	686	29	5.7	12
Awaiting submission of proposal	182	8	4.1	9
Proposal submitted for evaluation	585	25	15.8	35
Proposal evaluated and awaiting finalization	103	4	2.5	6
Workout proposal finalized	582	25	12.6	28
Fully settled	68	3	1.7	3
Performing	139	6	3.1	7
Total	2,345	100	45.5	100

Source: Thillainathan (2000).

By year-end 1999, Danaharta's portfolio included nonperforming loans from 2,345 borrowers with a book value of 45.5 billion ringgit. As table 4-13 indicates, 17.4 billion ringgit of these loans (that is, 38 percent of Danaharta's portfolio) had undergone loan restructuring, asset restructuring, or disposal as of year-end 1999. By the end of February 2000, Danaharta had appointed special administrators to fifty-three companies.

By December 1999, the CDRC had received applications from sixty-two corporations with debt of more than 36 billion ringgit. Of these, sixteen cases with cumulative debts of 13.1 billion ringgit have been resolved. Another twenty-nine cases with total debt of 16.9 billion ringgit were in process at year-end 1999. Seventeen cases were withdrawn, transferred to Danaharta, or rejected for failure to meet CDRC's viability test.

Of 13.3 billion ringgit in corporate debt restructured by CDRC as of year-end 1999, 87 percent had been effected through conversion of loans into bonds (see table 4-14). Debt-equity conversions accounted for only 5 percent of restructured corporate debt, with other methods accounting for less. As noted in R. Thillainathan's analysis, the prominence of bond refinancing is largely due to the restructuring of two corporations, Renong and UEM, whereby 16 billion ringgit of zero-coupon bonds

Table 4-14. *Malaysia: Summary of Restructuring Approaches for Completed CDRC Cases*

Method	All cases		Excluding Renong and UEM	
	Amount (billions of ringgit)	Percent	Amount (billions of ringgit)	Percent
Rescheduling	277	2.1	277	5.8
Debt-equity conversion	661	5.0	661	13.8
Conversion into term loans	185	1.4	185	3.9
Conversion into bonds	11,632	87.3	3,083	64.5
Equity injection	110	0.8	110	2.3
Debt write-off	71	0.5	71	1.5
Sale of assets	211	1.6	211	4.4
Capital reduction	183	1.4	183	3.8
Total	13,330		4,781	

Source: Thillainathan (2000)

were issued.[27] Excluding Renong and UEM, CDRC restructuring is more balanced. Conversions into bonds decrease to 64.5 percent of total restructured debt, while debt-equity conversions rise to 14 percent.

According to Thillainathan, CDRC has been criticized for approaching each workout on a case-by-case basis and for failing to adopt Danaharta's approach of providing guidelines (for example, on use of zero-coupon bonds) for its workouts. Given BNM's preeminent position in the CDRC process, Thillainathan questions whether participating financial institutions were acting freely. His review of major CDRC restructurings, especially that of Renong and UEM, concludes that there has been a bailout of creditors—especially foreign creditors—and perhaps of existing management (although not of shareholders) and that the fear of systemic risk was used to justify a government-facilitated and financed restructuring rather than a market-based approach. He questions the extent to which the CDRC-sponsored restructuring of Renong and UEM meets Danaharta's viability criteria. Danaharta's approach is driven first by what new capital shareholders can provide and only secondarily by a debtor's cash flow debt-service capacity.

27. Thillainathan (2000).

Lessons Learned

Contextual factors powerfully affect a country's corporate restructuring approach and results. Even so, it is reasonable to make detailed recommendations on the prevention of, response to, and resolution of a systemic corporate crisis. Clearly, there is a need for effective government management of any systemic crisis. Once some financial stabilization of the corporate sector has been achieved, as has occurred in East Asia, ongoing effort—with government support—at operational restructuring of distressed corporations is almost certainly needed.

Contextual Factors

Six factors had an overwhelming influence on the extent and nature of corporate restructuring in the East Asian crisis:

1. the speed of the macroeconomic recovery,
2. political cohesion within each country,
3. institutional capacity,
4. the magnitude of the corporate debt overhang,
5. differences across countries in the ability of each legal regime to impose losses on debtors, and
6. the willingness or ability of creditors—or governments—to recognize losses from corporate debt restructuring.

MACROECONOMIC RECOVERY. The crisis surprised most observers—in terms of both the depth of the crisis and the speed of the recovery. As indicated in figure 4-1, economic growth resumed in 1999. This has been attributed to several factors, including rising exports, fiscal stimulus, restocking of inventories, resumption of consumer demand, global liquidity, and judicious monetary policy actions by the U.S. Federal Reserve. While the prompt macroeconomic turnaround benefited the citizenry in East Asian crisis countries, the recovery may have saved corporations from having to undertake more fundamental operational restructuring needed for short-term survival—for example, massive employee layoffs, closure of loss-making or noncompetitive businesses, sales of noncore assets, greater acceptance of foreign equity ownership. Thus concerted efforts by government regulators (for example, financial supervisors, securities commissions, tax authorities, competition authorities) will be needed in lieu of the discipline that might otherwise have been provided by the marketplace. Unfortunately, surviving East Asian corporate

Figure 4-1. *GDP Growth Rates of Crisis-Affected East Asian Countries,*
1995–2000 (Projected)

Percent

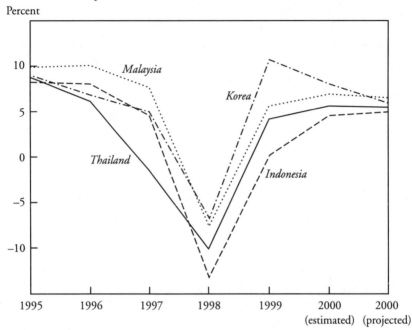

Source: International Monetary Fund, *International Financial Statistics;* estimates and projections for
2000 and 2001 derived from May 2000 Consensus Forecast.

managers may have concluded that—rather than undertaking needed
operational restructuring—they can rely on rapid macroeconomic upsurge
in any future crisis to refloat their corporations.

POLITICAL COHESION. In Korea, a new government committed to reform shepherded a host of legislation through the National Assembly in
February 1998, providing a more conducive legal and regulatory environment for corporate restructuring. As noted earlier, Korea's legal environment going into the crisis already provided strong protections for creditors.
Although Korea's approach to economic management has sometimes been
criticized as overly *dirigiste*, this hands-on approach facilitated relatively
crisp responses when action was needed, for example, taking over the six
largest banks, organizing a workout process to stabilize the most-distressed
second-tier chaebols, orchestrating government efforts to impose financial
discipline on the top four chaebols and facilitating a financial restructuring

by local creditors and their buyout of foreign creditors in the Daewoo case. By contrast, corporate restructuring elsewhere has been hampered by an inability to achieve sufficient strengthening of legal protections for creditors or to enforce available protections through the courts in a timely and dependable manner.

INSTITUTIONAL CAPACITY. To varying degrees, all the Asian crisis economies need to develop their capacity for dealing with court-supervised insolvencies. More experienced judges, receivers, and insolvency professionals are needed to develop sensible solutions in a timely manner. While banks have gained useful experience, a lack of experience with corporate restructuring—for example, among Korean banks—led to superficial, cookie-cutter restructurings. Although Danaharta shows some promising results, the operation of a large-portfolio AMC can be daunting. Public AMCs would be well advised to follow the lead of Thai Farmers' private AMC in outsourcing case management to experienced professionals operating on an incentive compensation basis. Korea's government showed good coordination in using available powers—for example, prudential regulation, fair-trade investigations, tax authority—to impose more financial discipline on its largest conglomerates. It might be difficult for other crisis countries to develop a similarly coordinated government program.

MAGNITUDE OF CORPORATE DEBT. It was unrealistic to expect that East Asia's corporate crisis could be addressed in a timely manner without massive restructuring of corporate debts—for example, through rate or term adjustments, grace periods, and conversions of debt into equity. The corporate debt overhang at the start of the crisis was massive. For example, in 1998 total corporate debts, including those owed to domestic banks and foreign creditors, in Korea ($444 billion), Thailand ($196 billion), Malaysia ($120 billion), and Indonesia ($118 billion) were respectively 144 percent, 162 percent, 171 percent, and 111 percent of GDP. Though Malaysia had the highest corporate debt relative to GDP, this debt was largely owed to domestic financial institutions. Indonesia had the lowest corporate-debt-to-GDP ratio, but a substantial part of the debt was denominated in foreign currency.

In Korea, for instance, the liabilities-equity ratio for the thirty largest chaebols (including their financial affiliates) was 604 percent at year-end 1997. There were not enough asset or equity buyers and not enough of an opportunity for immediate operational restructuring to reduce corporate leverage to a reasonable level (such as the 200 percent mandated by the Korean government) through incremental improvements—for example, from asset or business sales, issuance of new equity, or increases in retained earnings from improvements in operational efficiency—within a reasonable time period (for example, by year-end 1999). Under normal circumstances, it can easily take from eighteen to thirty-six months to restructure a large corporation.

The difficulty in Korea was greatly compounded by the fact that hundreds or thousands of large corporations were simultaneously exploring the possibility of asset or business sales or equity issues to strengthen their financial position—creating the potential for an asset glut and fire-sale prices. Thus, the corporate debt overhang had to be dealt with—either through conversions into equity or through concessionary debt restructuring. An analysis from May 1998 (table 4-15) indicated that even using optimistic assumptions about deleveraging through increases in retained earnings, court-supervised insolvency, asset sales, foreign investment relative to historical norms (for example, as a percentage of GDP), new equity issues relative to historical norms (for example, as a percentage of market capitalization), and debt-equity conversions up to the 15 percent regulatory limit, Korea's thirty largest chaebols would still be 343 percent leveraged at year-end 1999. In fact, Korea has probably exceeded expectations at the start of the crisis for asset or business sales and new equity issues. An immediate focus on the financial stabilization of the most distressed corporates (for example, the second-tier chaebols in late 1998 and Daewoo in late 1999) and a 4:1 ratio of debt restructuring to self-help in a corporate debt crisis of Korea's magnitude is hardly surprising. Financial stabilization of distressed corporations, however, must be promptly followed with more basic operational restructuring.

IMPOSITION OF LOSSES ON DEBTORS. Multiple demonstrations in Korea of an ability to wipe out the equity interests of controlling shareholders through court-supervised reorganization and replace existing management with a receiver played a key role in encouraging other corporate debtors to cooperate with voluntary restructuring efforts. Because they did not face comparable threats of court-imposed loss, debtors in Thailand and Indonesia had little or no incentive to agree to corporate restructuring transactions that would cause them some loss—for example, forfeiture or sale of assets or cherished businesses, equity dilution, or diminution or loss of management control. Mediation and workout contracts, even those enforced by the financial supervisor, are at best a weak substitute for a robust regime for creditor protection.

Table 4-15. *South Korea: Options for Deleveraging the Thirty Largest Chaebols, 1997–99*

Balances	Liabilities (billions of won)	Equity (billions of won)	Liability-equity ratio (percent)	Resolution method
At December 31, 1997	456,308	75,592	604	
	(48,647)	(1,947)		Court-supervised insolvency
	(12,000)			Foreign investment or asset sales
		1,200		Normal increase in retained earnings
		2,500		Increase in retained earnings from restructuring
	(8,250)	8,250		Domestic equity issues
	(5,250)	5,250		Offshore equity issues
Subtotal	382,161	90,845	421	
		0		Asset revaluations
	(16,031)	16,031		Debt-equity conversions (to 15 percent of equity)
Subtotal	366,130	106,876	343	
	(76,190)	38,095		Other (to be determined)
Total at December 31, 1999	289,940	144,971	200	

Source: World Bank staff estimates, based on SBC Warburg Dillon Read (1998).

READINESS OF CREDITORS OR GOVERNMENTS TO TAKE LOSSES.
Even if losses can be imposed on debtors, the managers and controlling
shareholders of private banks must be prepared to take losses—voluntarily
or at the behest of financial supervisors. If major portions of the financial
sector are nationalized, the extent of corporate restructuring (and accounting for it by state-owned banks) will depend on the government's willingness to use public monies to recapitalize banks. If a weak legal framework
makes it difficult to impose losses on debtors, forcing banks to take a disproportionate share of the losses could jeopardize their controlling shareholders or management.

Lessons on Structural Approaches to Systemic Corporate Crisis

Contextual factors aside, the recent crisis indicates that governments can
perform more effectively in terms of corporate crisis prevention, crisis
response, and crisis resolution.

CRISIS PREVENTION. In a world of free access to international capital
markets, a financially disciplined corporate sector is required so as to avoid
excessive risky borrowing. Sustainable leverage and a comfortable excess
cushion of cash flow over interest expense are needed for corporations to
weather exchange rate and interest rate shocks. This requires prudent
financial management and a transparent governance structure for the corporate sector. It also requires effective monitoring of corporations by creditors and financial supervisors. As noted below (items 1 and 8), governments should also be prepared to take countervailing steps when
monitoring indicates the development of unsustainable overinvestment by
corporations. It is also important to create and stimulate markets for distressed assets, especially including debt and real estate. Finally, it is important to stimulate the development of local capital markets and equity
financing. An active market for corporate bonds and other debt can serve
both as a warning and an exit or redeployment mechanism, while equity
financing is obviously needed to cushion against currency and interest rate
shifts.

CRISIS RESPONSE. Upon the development of a systemic corporate crisis, a government needs to ensure that a coherent framework for resolving
corporate distress is put in place. This framework needs to include court-
based measures for reorganization, liquidation, and protection of secured
and unsecured creditors; a well-structured out-of-court process for corporate restructuring; and an enabling tax, legal, and regulatory environment.

Governments also need to segment the crisis and prioritize their responses—for example, to the most-distressed large corporates and to SMEs. If governments choose to create public AMCs, these should be insulated from political pressure and operated according to best commercial and market principles (items 2, 3, 4, 5, 7, and 9 below).

CRISIS RESOLUTION. In addition, governments must actively "work the problem" until the crisis eases. Macroeconomic stabilization is essential, including restoration of confidence in the currency and financial markets. Resolution of external debt is also needed early in the crisis, as in the case of Korea. Throughout, as noted below (item 6), governments will need to ensure that major financial institutions remain reasonably sound and conclude necessary corporate restructuring transactions in a timely manner.

Summary of Lessons

The lessons of the East Asian financial crisis can be summarized in nine points:

1. *It being possible to see systemic corporate crises developing, governments should monitor the financial health of major corporate sectors and respond to early warning signs of overinvestment and distress.* Indications that large corporations and sectors were overinvesting and overborrowing were available in Indonesia by 1993, Thailand by 1995, and Korea by 1996. Assuming that financial disclosure standards for listed companies are adequate, it should be possible to anticipate a crisis by monitoring such measures of financial position and performance as returns on assets, returns on capital employed, profitability, leverage, and operating cash flows relative to interest expense. Governments—especially financial supervisors—should monitor these indicators and make precautionary responses to signs of widescale overinvestment. Possible responses include more stringent exposure limits, additional provisioning for loans to overinvested sectors, tougher tax treatment (for example, nondeductibility of interest on "excessive" debt), and requirements for banks to require capital structure improvement programs from large borrowers.

2. *In a systemic corporate crisis, governments need to segment the crisis and prioritize responses, both by the government and by the banks.* Financial regulators should require banks to identify nonviable companies early on, exit from these companies (for example, by forcing their sale or liquidation), and take the loss. For highly distressed but viable corporations, standardized workouts may be needed. Notwithstanding longer-term opportunities

for asset or business sales and improvements in operating efficiency, a company's short-term debt capacity depends on its operating cash flow. Debts in excess of this debt service capacity will need to be restructured. While financial restructuring is thus likely to figure prominently in responses to a systemic corporate crisis, financial stabilization needs to be followed closely by ongoing operational restructuring to eliminate marginal businesses, assets, and—with appropriate safety nets—redundant employees. For problematic corporations that are not necessarily in immediate peril, concerted government actions (for example, CSIP requirements, tighter exposure limits, fair trade investigations) may be needed to encourage these companies to embrace greater financial discipline. Lastly, in a systemic crisis banks will not have the institutional capacity to resolve distress among tens of thousands of SMEs one by one. Systemic responses to SME distress are needed. These may include, for instance, regulatory forbearance to encourage banks to roll-over SME debts for a certain period, say six months.

3. *Efficient resolution of a systemic corporate crisis depends on out-of-court processes, preferably formal, well organized, and purposeful.* In a systemic crisis involving many hundreds of large corporations, frequent recourse to court-supervised processes would overwhelm the capacity of courts and insolvency professionals. Thus efficient resolution of the crisis must rely on out-of-court processes. An informal unstructured process, however, is not enough. Notably, Thailand initially adopted a soft approach of relying on a set of principles (the Bangkok Rules) modeled after the London Approach, which proved ineffective. Korea dallied with government-sanctioned "bankruptcy avoidance" loans, which did not give creditors sufficient access to perform due diligence and develop restructuring plans and which merely postponed the problem. These initial efforts were abandoned in favor of the more structured CRA/CRCC process in Korea and CDRAC Office/DCA process in Thailand.

Corporate restructuring in Thailand has increased since the Bank of Thailand's promulgation of formal restructuring contracts (that is, debtor-creditor agreements). Experience suggests that such contracts should provide for (1) a time-bound standstill (for example, three months); (2) complete creditor access to all records for due diligence; (3) joint management-creditor teams to monitor performance, develop cash flow projections, and control asset disposals; (4) priority for fresh working capital; (5) interim milestones for completion of due diligence, development of a restructuring plan, and creditor votes; (6) voting thresholds for creditor approval of a reorganization plan; (7) mediation or arbitration of intercreditor differences;

(8) conversion of the case into court-supervised insolvency for failure to meet interim milestones; and (9) penalties for noncompliance by financial institution signatories—including failure to petition the court for debt collection, foreclosure, or insolvency if interim milestones are not met. The financial supervisor could serve to enforce workout contracts, including penalty provisions, as has been done by Thailand's central bank and Korea's FSC.

4. *Some mechanism is needed to resolve intercreditor disputes.* The willingness of creditors to agree to debt restructuring and provide new money will vary—for example, depending on whether they are secured or unsecured and on their provisioning and capital adequacy. Intercreditor differences may be particularly sticky when foreign creditors are involved. On the one hand, the foreign creditor may feel particularly disadvantaged (for example, by language barriers, access to information, or comfort with the local business culture) and hang tough so as to make a point. In other circumstances, well-provisioned foreign creditors with a strong offshore capital base may be more willing to agree to a debt restructuring discount. While a given loss might be painful for a foreign creditor, the same size loss could be life-threatening for a local creditor. While the CRCC arbitration mechanism worked in Korea, it applied only to Korean financial institutions. When foreign creditors became heavily involved—notably in the Daewoo matter—they were unwilling to expose themselves to CRCC arbitration. Similarly, Thailand's Inter-Creditor Agreement allows any financial institution signatory to opt out of the ICA in any case involving total debts of 1 billion baht or more. In the Daewoo matter, issues with foreign creditors will likely be resolved through a buyout by local creditors of foreign creditor claims. In general, centralized buyouts or secondary trading in claims may be the most expeditious way for resolving differences between local and foreign creditors. To make it easier to deal with future crises, countries should facilitate the development of secondary markets in corporate debt.

5. *To be effective, an out-of-court process for corporate restructuring needs to be backed up by credible court-supervised processes for seizure of assets, foreclosure, liquidation, receivership, and reorganization.* Without the threat of court-imposed loss, there is not enough incentive for corporate debtors to cooperate with voluntary efforts and agree to the asset or business sales, equity dilution, and diminution of management control that may be part of a fair deal. Ideally, corporate debtors should face a continuum of threat—beginning with the possibility of prompt seizure of assets. Debtors should feel encouraged to seek protection in court-supervised reorganization as an

alternative to liquidation or foreclosure. Without a strong "shadow" of creditor protections, an emphasis on reform of court-supervised reorganization will produce only limited results. In Thailand, for instance, efforts by recalcitrant debtors to avoid court-supervised reorganization (for example, in Nikko Hotels) indicated that the legal regime for collection of debts was too weak. Court-supervised reorganization needs to be a serious option for restructuring distressed but viable corporations—and not just a forum for a reorganization plan "cram-down" on dissenting creditors in cases where the debtor happens to be cooperative.

As it can be extremely difficult to reform legal regimes for protection and enforcement of creditor rights during a crisis—when the personal "downside" to parliamentarians and other powerful persons may be all too obvious and imminent—necessary reforms should be implemented in good times—that is, before a crisis.

6. *Financial institutions need some breathing room to support real corporate restructuring and take losses, without necessarily threatening current controlling shareholders.* Financial sector restructuring is outside the purview of this paper, but the motivations of the controlling shareholders and bank managers need to be considered in developing a strategic response to systemic crises. Unless it is prepared to nationalize all or most of a country's financial sector, the government will need to give banks an opportunity to take necessary steps in corporate restructuring—that is, loss recognition—without necessarily exposing these banks to a state takeover or government control. The experience of Thailand indicates that banks will sequence corporate restructuring deals so as to avoid threats to their own ownership and control. Real corporate restructuring—including debt restructuring down to sustainable levels—will require banks to take losses. Without some regulatory forbearance, banks will resist these losses. Thailand's experience suggests consideration of forbearance on capital adequacy rather than on loss recognition. Admittedly, governments would have to minimize the risk that forbearance might just lead to a higher eventual cost to the public for financial sector recapitalization.

7. *Supporting legal and regulatory measures—to eliminate obstacles and provide positive incentives—are necessary but will not in themselves induce corporate restructuring.* Real corporate restructuring involves losses for the controlling shareholders and managers of corporations—for example, through sale or forfeiture of cherished businesses and assets, diminished scope of business operations, equity dilution, and diminution of control. Similarly for financial institutions, corporate restructuring will lead to losses from

concessionary debt restructuring, shrinking of capital, and possible dilution and diminution or loss of control. Legal and regulatory incentives—for example, a bank's ability to deduct its debt restructuring losses, or exempting a debtor's gain from taxation—will not be enough to get debtors and creditors to take real losses. The timely resolution of a large volume of distressed companies ultimately depends on the availability of legal coercion.

8. *It can be useful for governments to marshal available powers—both before and during crises—to encourage large corporations to restructure themselves to improve their long-term competitiveness.* Korea provides useful examples, both of ill-advised corporate diversification and a coordinated government campaign to re-impose financial discipline. Debt-financed expansion and diversification—whereby Korean chaebols departed from core competencies for ill-advised diversifications (for example, into luxury automobiles and financial services for a single basic materials producer)—were not sustainable. Although deeply distressed second-tier chaebols had to submit to CRA workouts, in mid-1998 the top five chaebols were not in imminent danger but posed a longer-term problem. As noted earlier, the government orchestrated its various powers—including prudential regulation of financial institutions, tax administration, investigation of unfair trade practices—to impose greater financial discipline on its largest conglomerates. This longer-term approach is worth considering for conglomerates in other countries.

9. *While public asset management companies are useful in reducing nonperforming loans of distressed financial institutions or in taking over assets from closed institutions, they are not a panacea for resolution of corporate distress.* KAMCO and Thailand's Financial Sector Restructuring Authority (FRA) are not good test cases, as the former is more oriented toward providing financial institution liquidity while the latter is focused on bundling and selling assets taken over from failed finance companies. It can be argued that the wholesale closing of fifty-six finance companies in Thailand and transfer of their assets to the FRA for eventual disposition may have hurt the development of a credit culture in Thailand, as debtors came to believe that they could escape repayment by driving their creditors out of business. Experience elsewhere on public AMCs is mixed.[28] They have not proven adept at restructuring operating companies.

While Malaysia's Danaharta has achieved some success, it is too early to draw definitive conclusions. It is also quite uncertain how effective IBRA

28. Klingebiel (1999).

will be as an agent for corporate restructuring. IBRA's effectiveness at corporate restructuring will depend on its ability to enforce creditor rights (either through the courts or through use of its extraordinary PP17 powers); on insulation from political pressure (notably, to protect well-connected debtors); and on its ability to restructure corporate debts on purely commercial considerations. IBRA must be able to give debt discounts or write-offs without worrying about legal liability or allegations of KKN. If the Indonesian government can muster the institutional capacity, IBRA's efforts would benefit from the orchestrated use of existing government powers against recalcitrant corporate debtors.

Political pressures may mount, and IBRA's ability to do deals may well erode over time. Thus for IBRA to function effectively in its role as the principal restructurer of Indonesia's corporate sector, it needs to resolve its caseload quickly and to greatest commercial advantage through bulk sales of loans, cleaning up loans and conveying them to local and foreign financial institutions as quickly as possible through competitive auctions, and perhaps outsourcing debt restructuring negotiations to outside advisers working on an incentive compensation basis.

Concluding Remarks

The crisis countries have been reasonably successful in achieving financial stabilization for their most-distressed corporations. Some operational restructuring is underway. Much more operational restructuring is needed, however, to assure long-tem viability and industry competitiveness.

A key problem is how to move forward from the emphasis so far on financial restructuring to the needed emphasis on operational restructuring. In Korea, for example, local financial institutions are faced with the task of how to manage converted equity, convertible bonds, and rescheduled loans with a face value of about $80 billion for the sixteen chaebols and smaller companies and for the Daewoo affiliates that went through CRA workouts. Strategic buyers will be found for some. In most cases, however, the creditor or shareholders will need new structures to induce ongoing corporate restructuring and maximize the value of their holdings of corporate debt and equity. Since banks in the region do not have experience in the operational aspects of corporate turnarounds, they would do well to enter into joint ventures with foreign partners who can provide this experience. It is encouraging to see that some banks (such as Thai Farmers) have entered into such arrangements with foreign partners.

While more such partnering is needed, Korea's experience suggests that several issues will first need to be addressed. In many cases, banks will need to take a loss when overvalued corporate equity or debt is conveyed—to the private AMCs, joint venture, corporate restructuring company, or other facilities. The equity may be overvalued because of an illiquid market, agreements among creditors not to sell converted equity except by unanimous agreement, and artificial premiums for minority public shareholders. Local banks will need to negotiate fair valuations with foreign partners. Governments can promote this second phase of corporate restructuring by permitting special-purpose corporate restructuring corporations, providing tax neutrality for these, and encouraging banks to transfer corporate debt and equity at real values through tax incentives or some forbearance on loss recognition.

References

Claessens, Stijn, Simeon Djankov, and Daniela Klingebiel. 1999. *Financial Restructuring in East Asia: Halfway There?* Washington: World Bank.

International Monetary Fund. 1999. *Malaysia: Selected Issues*. Washington.

Kawai, Masahiro. 2000. "Financial and Corporate Restructuring: Building Institutions and Resolution of the East Asian Crisis." Washington: World Bank (March).

Kawai, Masahiro, and Ken-ichi Takayasu. 2000. "The Economic Crisis and Financial Restructuring in Thailand." Washington: World Bank (April).

Klingebiel, Daniela. 1999. *The Use of Asset Management Companies in the Resolution of Banking Crises: Cross-Country Experiences*. Washington: World Bank.

Lieberman, Ira W., and William Mako. 2000. "Assessing the Depth of Corporate Restructuring in Asia: Korea's Corporate Restructuring Program." Washington: World Bank (March).

Mako, William. 2000. "Thailand Case." Washington: World Bank (March).

Phatra Securities. 1998. *Special Issue*. Bangkok.

SBC Warburg Dillon Read. 1998. "Top 30 Chaebol Financial Status: Y/E 1996."

Thillainathan, R. 2000. "Malaysian Financial and Corporate Sector under Distress: A Midterm Assessment of Restructuring Efforts." Washington: World Bank (March).

JOEL A. BINAMIRA
WILLIAM C. HAWORTH

5

Debt Restructuring in East Asia: Government and the Corporate Sector

From 1991 to 1996, Indonesia, Malaysia, South Korea, and Thailand posted average gross domestic product (GDP) growth in excess of 7 percent per annum. Per capita income rose dramatically, and the incidence of poverty in even the poorest countries dropped significantly. The East Asian corporate sector clearly benefited from the energetic growth of regional economies. Corporations and in many cases conglomerates grew rapidly, both in sales and profits and in the scope of their activities. The success of many of these corporations, however, was due not to their strategic advantages, products, or global position but rather to a generally favorable operating environment and to their links to the government bureaucracy.

Rifts in the Asian Model

Close relationships between governments and corporations in Indonesia, Malaysia, South Korea, and Thailand led to an interlinking of interests among a small group of interconnected business, government, and military leaders—the "elites." Many of the largest corporations in these countries were owned, in whole or in part, by the state. National security was often advanced as the primary rationale for state ownership of oil, energy, transportation, construction, steel, automobile, and airline companies. As the economies grew, some of the state-owned companies were privatized, either voluntarily or at the urging of local and foreign entities. While nominally private, many of these companies remained close or sympathetic to the governments that had previously owned and managed them. These powerful and profitable corporations became essential components of the booming economy.

The "Asian Model," as distinguished from the system that operates in the West, was one of active cooperation between business and government for perceived mutual gain. In many cases, these private corporations had direct links to the government, often through personal relationships. Families and friends of government officials were granted exclusive licenses, allowing them them to profit in businesses that were often not subject to normal competitive pressures. With little separation of interests, individuals, corporations, and the government (including the military) worked hand in hand to advance their wealth simultaneously. The largest corporations and banks helped direct government policies that, in turn, helped them succeed. Often controlled by a few individuals in each country (in some cases over a period of many years), the system appeared to work while growth flourished.

As a result of their symbiotic relation with the government, the corporations became increasingly influential and their impact on policy more pronounced. Government licenses, permits, restrictions, and tariffs effectively limited the number of competitors in major industries and favored the existing large players; local enterprises were sustained by protectionist and noncompetitive policies. The presence of large monopolies and oligopolies in particular industries, however, resulted in grave distortions to the underlying economies. As these companies grew, so did their ambitions. Expansion into new business areas increased, and this growth was often funded by debt financing. Large-scale projects (in plastics, petroleum, infrastructure, automobile manufacturing, and telecommunications) blossomed during the 1990s. Governments encouraged such projects to bolster growth and "progress"—with little consideration of the true economic viability or rationale of particular endeavors.

Majority control of publicly traded corporations in most of the East Asian economies was concentrated among their top five shareholders (see table 5-1). That, together with the fact that owners were often also the managers of the corporations, rendered corporate governance and oversight toothless in many instances. Management was politically skilled in working within a particular system but generally lacked strong business

Table 5-1. *East Asian Corporate Sector: Percentage of Total Outstanding Shares Owned by Five Largest Shareholders*

Economy (year end)	Percent	Companies reviewed
Indonesia (1997)	67.5	All listed companies
Malaysia (1998)	58.8	All listed companies
South Korea (1998)	38.1	Eighty-one listed companies
Thailand (1997)	56.6	All listed companies

Source: Asian Development Bank (1999).

skills and had little expertise in dealing with a truly competitive environment. Inadequate reporting standards and lax fiduciary oversight by corporate directors left minority shareholders in particularly precarious positions, with little ability to track and influence the actions of company management. Free from the scrutiny of shareholders (often even that of the majority shareholders), management could in effect operate without supervision. The narrow and protected playing field offered few incentives to become globally competitive, and the unnatural competitive environment that characterized the East Asian economies often drove imprudent investment and strategic decisions. Corporate returns and profits increasingly became a function of exclusive licenses, protective tariffs, or monopoly positions rather than of true business productivity and efficiency.

The measures of corporate success most important to enterprise owners were not profit, shareholder return, or cash flow but rather growth, number of people employed, political clout, and licenses. The quality of corporate managment itself suffered, and in the absence of professional, prudent management, companies expanded without restraint and invested in new and unrelated businesses, often with a heavy reliance on debt financing. Corporations overborrowed systematically, with debt-equity ratios commonly exceeding 10 to 1, and in many cases more than 30 to 1. By the time the Asian crisis hit, many East Asian companies were highly leveraged (see table 5-2); attracted by lower interest rates and their governments' assurances (albeit tacit) of stable exchange rate policies, these companies often had their debt denominated in foreign currencies (U.S. dollars or Japanese yen) without the protection of currency hedges. In most cases, companies wrote off large amounts of their debt simply to break even.

Lenders are perhaps equally to blame for the high levels of debt that characterized the East Asian corporate sector. Credit standards were

Table 5-2. *Corporate Domestic Loans as a Percentage of GDP, 1996*

Economy	Loans/GDP
Indonesia[a]	59
Malaysia	107
South Korea[a]	77
Thailand	105
United States	37

Sources: International Monetary Fund statistics; Casserley and Gibb (1999).
a. These countries also relied heavily on foreign corporate loans, which increased leverage significantly.

undoubtedly weak, and banks frequently ignored traditional lending controls. As the economies of the East Asian countries boomed, so did the banks themselves. With close ties to the largest corporations, banks (particularly state-owned financial institutions) willingly provided the debt to finance rapid corporate expansion, often for projects of questionable value. Even today, the portfolios of these banks show dismal performance, and the institutions require ongoing financial assistance simply to remain in operation.

At the corporate level, then, the booming East Asian economy masked an unusual set of economic circumstances.

CONCENTRATION. One consequence of the high levels of debt financing in the East Asian corporate sector was the crowding out of the capital markets. With sufficient debt financing available, companies did not feel the need to tap capital markets and seek equity financing, which would have imposed requirements of transparency and professional management. This, in turn, supported the continued and even further concentration of business ownership and an increasingly strong bond between corporations and banks as they depended heavily on each other for their funding and profits.

The apparent success of the well-connected companies also had the effect of undermining well-run and economically viable local corporations. As honest and rational businesses found the operating environment increasingly hostile, the tendency to close shop and move assets abroad (together with an accompanying brain drain) increased. Inevitably, this has led to a downward cycle in the quality and viability of companies and management that remain.

FINANCIAL CONDITION AND PROFITABILITY. The financial condition of the government-supported companies was very weak compared to companies that are forced to survive in a more open market environment. Typically, these companies were not very profitable and relied on government to ensure even these weak profits. In many cases conglomerates survived solely on their protected rights to develop selected national commodities or operate selected national monopolies. Government policy or protection created a false demand: in an open market, their products could not have competed with cheaper imports. The conglomerates' reliance on political connections and influence ultimately reduced the level of competition and increased the level of concentration of ownership in these markets.

By Western accounting standards, the core profitability of East Asian corporate enterprises was usually weak and often negative. Profitability in any case was a secondary concern: more important was the enterprise's ability to borrow as much cash as it wanted and to get this cash to the elites on a regular basis. Finally, most companies had invested in a variety of noncore businesses that were usually losing money; focusing on the core activities would have required major restructuring or retrenchment.

STRUCTURAL WEAKNESSES. The East Asian conglomerates tended to practice both horizontal and vertical integration and in doing so created a mire of confusing cross-subsidies that made conventional financing analysis difficult or impossible. The financial structure that evolved was generally dollar dependent and highly leveraged with significant inter-company flows and cross-holdings that masked the extent of the leverage. Especially when adjusted for lower labor costs, subsidized imports, and tariff protection, the efficiency of these enterprises was far below Western benchmarks.

The Corporate Sector in Crisis

Beginning in July 1997, the crisis cascaded across Asian corporations, the banks that financed them, and the governments that supported them. The largest corporations were hit hard, and many of the local banks that had provided them with debt financing were brought to the brink of collapse. To stabilize banks and financial institutions and attempt to repair the damage wrought by the crisis, governments and international donors stepped in to provide liquidity and recapitalization assistance. The largest and most

Table 5-3. *Unemployment in the Asian Crisis Economies, 1996 and 1998*

Economy	Unemployment rate, 1996 (percent)	Unemployment rate, 1998 (percent)
Indonesia	4.9	5.5
Malaysia	2.5	4.9
South Korea	2.0	6.8
Thailand	1.1	5.3

Source: Asian Development Bank statistics.

visible corporations received rapid (some would say preferential) assistance, a function certainly of the large-scale unemployment that would have resulted from their bankruptcy and closure but also of their ties to the government bureaucracy.

Small- and medium-size enterprises received significantly less support at the early stages of the crisis. Thousands of businesses went bankrupt and closed. Although perhaps less reliant on debt, smaller companies also had fewer resources to ride out a lengthy downturn in business.

Hardest hit, perhaps, were the average workers, and particularly so in the poorer economies. Unemployment rose dramatically (see table 5-3) and although unmeasured, underemployment almost certainly increased as well. In Indonesia—the poorest of the four economies—individuals slipped quickly below the poverty line. With the loss of employment and little savings to cushion the fall, the segment of the population that had benefited least from the previous two decades of economic expansion suffered most. Strained resources, morevoer, left the East Asian governments hard-pressed to provide significant assistance to the poorest segments of society.

Corporate Restructuring Efforts

While corporate restructuring has made laudable progress in some of the East Asian countries, and particularly so in South Korea, the pace of that progress has been widely criticized. Efforts have concentrated almost exclusively on financial structures rather than on operational, organizational, or managerial structures. There is no question that many of the companies required (and continue to require) significant restructuring, but there also appears to be a level of complacency that ultimately undermines genuine

Table 5-4. *Corporate Debt Restructuring in the Asian Crisis Economies*

	Applications filed		Restructuring "completed"	
Economy (reporting date)	Number of applications	Book value of debt ($ billion)	Number of applications (percent of total applications)	Book value of debt (percent of book value of applications)
Indonesia	4,251	25	57	3
(August 1999)			(1)	(13)
Malaysia	66	9	15	3
(December 1999)			(22)	(35)
South Korea	102	31	80	15
(September 1999)			(78)	(50)
Thailand	721	40	104	6
(December 1999)			(14)	(15)

Sources: INDRA (Indonesia); CDRC (Malaysia); KAMCO (South Korea); CDRAC (Thailand).

restructuring efforts: many managers still cling to the notion of riding out the storm and returning to business as usual when the economies regain their strength.

Of the four Asian economies, South Korea alone appears to have made significant headway, both in the scope and the value of restructurings (see table 5-4). All the countries focused rapidly on the largest corporations, but Korea made significant efforts to restructure small- and medium-size businesses. (Even here, however, the quality of the restructuring efforts has yet to be tested.) Restructuring efforts in Indonesia, Malaysia, and Thailand have been less successful. Negotiations undertaken over the last year by corporations and banks with new, often foreign-based investors have failed for a variety of reasons—unrealistic asking prices for assets, lack of sufficient guarantees to cover various forms of deal risk associated with transactions, and insufficient legal support or infrastructure.

Several mechanisms have been used in East Asia to facilitate corporate restructuring. Most of these have focused on financial restructuring, including the provision of financial assistance (liquidity assistance, trade finance, and debt relief) during the initial stages of the crisis in order to keep the companies operating. In addition to providing direct assistance to borrowers, governments have acted as facilitators and mediators in debt restructuring negotiations and have established asset management vehicles and corporate debt restructuring agencies to encourage voluntary workouts.[1]

In addition to the debt restructuring agencies, governments have also worked to improve or develop bankruptcy and foreclosure laws and have also pushed for much greater transparency, standardized financial statements, and more comprehensive corporate disclosure. However, despite the various strategies and vehicles established by the East Asian governments to assist in the restructuring efforts, progress has been slow. On one level, the progress of restructuring reflects the extent of the government's effort to facilitate corporate restructuring and ultimately, the quality of the effort itself. In many cases, East Asian governments provided financial assistance to the largest borrowers and banks but obtained only limited commitments to restructure aggressively. The ownership of many banks has been transferred to the government, which lacks the resources and the ability to undertake restructuring on behalf of individual financial institutions.

East Asian governments have sought to improve or develop bankruptcy and foreclosure laws and pushed for greater transparency, standardization of financial statements, and more comprehensive corporate disclosures. The statutory and regulatory changes that were urgently sought at the start of the crisis, however, are being reversed or watered down as the process of obtaining approvals and the demands of competing interests narrow the original scope of the proposed changes. Even with new laws and regulations in place, implementation is extremely difficult given the longstanding inefficiencies of the courts, judges, and law enforcement agencies in many of these countries.

Debt restructuring efforts are likewise hampered by a lack of qualified negotiators and facilitators, as well as by other constraints on resources. Asset management companies are deluged with distressed corporations, and restructuring programs need to be tailored to each individual situation. Finally, well-connected corporations have in some instances been able to delay restructuring efforts in order to protect their interests.

---

1. The Indonesian government created a debt restructuring agency (INDRA) to provide foreign-exchange coverage for Indonesian corporations with foreign-denominated debt once they have reached debt-rescheduling agreements. The Jarkarta Initiative Task Force, formed in September 1998, serves as a mediator between debtors and creditors. The Malaysian government created a corporate debt restructuring committee to assist companies with total debts of more than 50 million ringgit to restructure their debts. Thailand established a similar committee to promote market-based corporate debt restructuring. Most of Korea's large corporate restructurings were entrusted to the chaebols, although the Korea Asset Management Corporation (KAMCO) and the Korea Deposit Insurance Corporation (KDIC) are now involved in the process. See pp. 149–215.

Beyond these somewhat mechanistic implementation-linked issues, corporate restructuring has been delayed primarily because of the unwillingness of most corporations to recognize the true extent of their problems (and their need to part with overvalued assets at market prices), a position supported—in some cases deliberately, in others unwittingly—by many governments in the region.

When the crisis struck, donor institutions rushed into the region to help governments cope with the situation. Implicit in this assistance was the intent to restructure local companies as part of the crisis resolution process. All parties, foreign and local alike, expected that effective restructuring of the region's corporations would encounter serious hurdles—difficult and sometimes hostile legal environments, the absence or ineffectiveness of bankruptcy codes, even collateral issues such as poor registration of land titles. Tremendous effort (though the intensity varied from country to country) was expended to develop improvements to key infrastructure issues in the hope that doing so would accelerate the pace of corporate restructuring.

Instead, what increasingly became apparent to both local and foreign observers was the extent and severity of the actual business problems at many of the region's largest companies. Many of these companies had poor underlying fundamentals, often provided minimal value added, and had invested in assets that had lost significant value (for example, grossly overvalued real estate ventures). The donor community, governments, commercial banks, and investment banks had unrealistic expectations about the actual valuations of the corporations and their assets. This overvaluation slowed recognition of the problems and in many cases led to denying their existence altogether. As a result, overvalued assets were often transferred to governments (usually state-owned or sponsored asset management companies) with overly optimistic estimates of the chances of recovery. The pressures to deny the depth of the problems were widespread: by any prudent standard, many of the enterprises should have gone bankrupt and been closed but doing so would have led to major social implications such as massive job losses and potential civil unrest.

Well-run companies hit by the crisis had very little to lose by restructuring. Their shareholders would most likely trust their managers to take the necessary steps to restore health. Poorly managed companies, with unclear strategies and poor value added recognized a loss of face associated with a painful restructuring and were more inclined to downplay, delay, or simply ignore problem resolution. Governments themselves, confronting rapidly increasing inventories of problem corporations and banks, were content to ride out the storm rather than admit the true extent of the problem and accept responsibility for the losses.

In Indonesia, perhaps the hardest hit of the East Asian economies, most of the companies in distress have negative values. They cannot and perhaps never will be sold for more than the amount of their debts. Restructuring loans offered for ten to twenty-five years at concessional rates will only serve to prolong the problem and result in huge losses for the government over time. In Thailand as well many of the distressed companies have found no buyers; the larger ones continue to languish in asset management companies. Malaysia withdrew from the international scene altogether (except for accepting inflows), and it has delayed the restructuring of banks and companies. South Korea has made the most progress, but it also had the least problems to begin with: from a corporate perspective, Korea was producing many products with significant value added, and the country's change in government in late 1997 facilitated more stringent implementation of restructuring efforts.

Ultimately, the critical issue slowing corporate restructuring in the region today is the failure to admit and take responsibility for the huge losses that will come if assets are sold off at their true market value. Governments, lenders, and borrowers will have to take significant losses in order to jump-start the restructuring process. Many of the flawed enterprises, moreover, are still managed by the individuals who presided over their collapse and will continue to be a drain on the taxpayers and citizens of their respective countries. Fundamental changes to management and ownership of the assets are essential if the problem is to be avoided in future. We can go on accounting for their production and overlooking their debts, but the fact remains that we will eventually need to deal with the fundamental problems. The Asian crisis economies have not yet succeeded in changing the structural relationships between government and business and have not insisted that public and private sector leaders be held responsible for their actions.

Restructuring through a Recovery

Meanwhile, robust macroeconomic growth has returned to East Asia. South Korea, which has pursued the most aggressive reforms and corporate restructurings, is also growing the fastest. Indonesia, Malaysia, and

Thailand are likewise in an economic upswing. Many in the international donor community have been quick to point to this recovery as a sign that the crisis is over. This, in turn, is reducing the pressure on the governments and corporations in these countries to undertake real reforms and restructurings. But many of the conditions that were present before the crisis persist and unless addressed fully, will likely cause the recurrence of similar crises in the future.

Poverty levels (particularly in Indonesia and Thailand) have increased dramatically, and nearly every measure of well-being—caloric consumption per capita, education, medical care—has declined. Even with macroeconomic growth, it will be many years before the masses will feel the gains. Meanwhile, we have effectively saved some of the less efficient but well-connected captains of industry at a tremendous social cost.

The Road Ahead

International donors should continue to press for reform of underlying legal, corporate governance, financial oversight, and other related infrastructure issues in the region. They should continue to press for improvements in the quality and timeliness of financial information and reporting, the establishment of workable bankruptcy and foreclosure laws, and the proper implementation of such laws. They should continue to press for reforms to the capital markets, as well as improvements in banking supervision. They should not reduce the pressure applied because of political or implementation difficulties.

All of these efforts, however, simply lay a foundation for restructuring. The medium term requires effective monitoring of how bankruptcy and foreclosure proceedings are implemented and of the efficiency of the courts, as well as continued transparency in corporate and government dealings. What is also critical is the need to facilitate and create sellers. In cases where a company's equity is affected, reducing or eliminating that equity and transferring ownership to new investors is a critical step. Problem assets need to be sold quickly at open and transparent auctions; prices established by these auctions can be used to value other distressed assets. This would force corporations and governments to recognize the true extent of their losses and bring them a step closer to making good on them. Many of the assets currently in government asset management companies are languishing, and every effort should be made to sell these at true market prices. Once better asset values have been determined, these can be used to value the assets on the books for the hundreds of banks that are now effectively under government control. Many banks should be declared bankrupt and shut down. International donors should not fund the ongoing operations of ill-managed banks or of governments that do not take the appropriate action with respect to their failed banks. As bank loans are written off, the equity of borrowers must be wiped out and the company assets sold. The objective is to get assets into productive hands and not maintain assets in existing companies that suppress competition and development.

What can governments do? Governments need to work toward leveling the playing field and creating a transparent process of restructuring. They must carefully weigh the costs of delay against the difficulty of admitting and taking responsibility for losses today. They must take strong action against individuals or corporations that have broken laws and pursue legal cases to set examples. Every effort must be made to break the cozy link between business and government to ensure that a crisis of this magnitude does not recur.

References

Asian Development Bank. 1999. "RETA 5802: A Study of Corporate Governance and Financing in South East Asia." Draft Final Report (November).

Casserley, Dominic, and Gregg Gibb. 1999. *Banking in Asia: The End of Entitlement.* Singapore: Wiley.

GREGORY ROOT
PAUL GRELA
MARK JONES
ANAND ADIGA

6

Financial Sector Restructuring in East Asia

A LITTLE MORE THAN three years have passed since the advent of the East Asian financial crisis (precipitated by the July 1997 devaluation of the Thai baht), and most indicators suggest that the region is now well along in its recovery. Economic growth has resumed, currencies have stabilized, and foreign investment has returned. On the surface, the overall economic situation seems to have improved dramatically. Yet beneath it all lie banking systems that remain in shambles. Although a great deal of effort has been put forth to repair the damage, the region is still far from claiming victory. In several of the countries the level of problem loans continues to hover at alarmingly high levels, and risk-adjusted capital is woefully inadequate.

This paper examines the events that led up to the crisis and the efforts underway to restore financial stability in three countries: South Korea, Thailand, and Indonesia. The primary focus will be on the banking sector, with particular emphasis on what went wrong and why, what has been accomplished thus far to resolve the problems, and the critical issues going forward. This paper reflects developments through March 2000.

South Korea

Few observers could have imagined the phenomenal changes that have taken place in Korea through the tough times visited on the country by its recent financial crisis. In the depths of despair in the winter of 1997–98, with the country on the brink of default, the outlook indeed looked bleak. In less than three years, however, the scenario is remarkably transformed: the country has posted an astounding rebound, with double-digit gross domestic product (GDP) growth in 1999; the financial system has been overhauled (five banks closed, seventeen merchant banks shuttered, and massive public funds mobilized for the recapitalization and rehabilitation of the system); and a regulatory and prudential framework has been put in place for improved transparency and corporate governance.

It is not the intention of this case study to examine the minutiae of the causes of Korea's—and East Asia's—recent crisis; these have been well documented and examined. However, we would argue that in examining the lessons to be learned and applied from Korea's recent travails, the past is ignored at one's peril.

Although it was impossible to predict the exact timing of any market dislocation or collapse, some observers had raised serious concerns before 1997 about a dangerous assortment of vulnerabilities that lay at the heart of the Korean banking system and that could easily conspire to destabilize local banking institutions. These can best be summarized as a fragmented supervisory regime, lax prudential standards, excessive government intervention in banks' credit allocation decisions, and an appalling lack of acceptable credit culture and credit analysis techniques that resulted in large levels of nonperforming loans weighing down the balance sheets of Korean banks. Even in 1997, before Korea's crisis was fully manifested in the results and underlying performance of the country's banks, the financial system was weak and vulnerable—and as history has shown, being brought to its knees was an easy next step (see table 6-1).

Stabilizing the System

Korea's authorities have responded to the crisis with strong commitment to create a foundation for stabilizing the system. Although ongoing issues regarding the Daewoo Group and investment trust companies have thrown up some uncertainties that need to be overcome (and the Korean government and related parties are working to implement plans to resolve these problems), it is fair to say that the Korean economy, and the financial system in particular, have been stabilized (although the local banking sector remains fragile at this stage of the cycle). This case study will examine in

Table 6-1. *Internal Strength of Korea's Domestic Commercial Banks*
Billions of won (except as indicated)

Category	1997	1998	Third quarter 1999
Capital	18,647	16,024	30,235[a]
Loan loss reserves	7,253	14,655	14,777[a]
Nonperforming loans	22,652	22,225	19,032
Bad debt	10,090	10,224	8,667
Nonperforming loans/capital and loan loss reserves (percent)	87	72	42
Bad debt/capital (percent)	54	64	29

Sources: Thomson Financial BankWatch; Korean Financial Supervisory Commission.
a. Estimated.

detail the steps taken by the government in this process as well as discuss their relative strengths and weaknesses. The main steps include

—allocating public funds to resuscitate and recapitalize the banking system,

—recapitalizing distressed banks,

—resolving nonperforming loans through a centralized bad-asset management vehicle,

—creating a new regulatory framework,

—developing an effective and thorough credit culture among local banks,

—evolving corporate governance and transparency, and

—strengthening the repayment culture of borrowers.

However, in seeking to apply the lessons from Korea's restructuring and rehabilitation process, it would be remiss not to emphasize that despite the positive progress to date, much remains to be done and that the steps taken to date fall short of creating the healthy type of banking system that Korea needs going forward.

If the primary aim of Korea's restructuring process is to create a healthy and safe financial system, then it is clear that a number of significant problems persist among Korea's banks; until these are adequately addressed, the Korean banking system (and by extension the Korean economy) will remain vulnerable to future external and internal shocks. The Korean government is caught between two conflicting aims: providing essential stability to the local markets and pressing forward with corporate and financial sector restructuring in order to ensure long-term competitiveness and a sustained economic recovery. The steps taken to date by the Korean authorities to calm market fears, especially those surrounding the Daewoo Group and the investment trust companies, have been positive and are likely to accomplish their short-term goals. It must be recognized, however, that these are only initial efforts at grappling with the more fundamental weaknesses and fault lines that still crisscross Korea's banking landscape.

Some signs have also started to appear that may cast a cloud over the pace and breadth of reform. Buoyed by faith in their new risk-control procedures, Korean banks are already starting to build up their loan books again, even though their balance sheets remain littered with the debris of bad debts thrown up by the recent crisis. Corporate reform remains ongoing, but the fast-paced recovery threatens to dampen enthusiasm for the need to push forward. Finally, the Korean authorities, though much improved in their commitment to transparency and accountability and equipped with strengthened regulatory and supervisory capabilities when compared to the pre-crisis days, still seem not to have completely thrown off the tendencies of the past to modify stated prudential requirements as needed, in the interests of expediency.[1]

Ultimately, it is important to recall that the rapid pace of change in Korea since the 1997 crisis means that the new systems and control mechanisms being developed and put in place remain essentially untested. Their effectiveness will require time to evaluate. In addition, ensuring that the recent reforms take root could well require a generational and strategic shift in management's attitude toward how banks do business. At this stage, given the enormous challenges that re-creating the banking system and overhauling banking practices pose, it remains uncertain whether management philosophies will adapt sufficiently to the new challenges ahead. Although the main areas of concern have shifted to the medium term, the possibility remains that restructuring efforts will be incomplete and that insufficient time will be given to mastering new risk-monitoring techniques and credit analysis skills as the sector returns too quickly to its old habit of building up loan portfolios in order to compete. The injection of foreign competition may well only increase the sense of urgency.

---

1. This is evident in the recent decision to allow Korean banks to spread the increased provisioning burden related to the new asset classification standards over two years—1999–2000—instead of taking the hit up front.

FISCAL ISSUES. Korea's overall level of public debt to gross domestic product (GDP) remains somewhat low, especially in comparison with that of other countries in the Organization for Economic Cooperation and Development (OECD). Korea's economic development recovery has also been surprisingly strong, providing some evidence of the economy's resilience. The Korean government has already signaled its desire to begin the process of fiscal consolidation and has indicated that it will target a primary deficit of between 1 percent and 1.5 percent for fiscal year 2000. Against these positive trends, a note of caution is warranted about the potential impact of absorbing nonperforming loans as a consequence of the Daewoo crisis. As further details of the loss allocation process emerge, the gross costs of rehabilitating banks could rise to between 30 percent and 35 percent of GDP.

RECAPITALIZING DISTRESSED BANKS—TO RESCUE OR NOT? In any banking crisis, authorities will inevitably face difficult decisions on how to deal with distressed banks. There are arguments on both sides of the ledger as to whether a particular bank should be supported or not. In the Korean context, the decision taken was twofold: (1) to close banks deemed beyond redemption; and (2) to support those banks under acute distress but considered "vital to the sector." The first approach resulted in the closure of several smaller players that were easily disposed of; the second led to the effective nationalization of Korea's banking system as several of the nation's largest banks (Hanvit Bank, Cho Hung Bank, Korea First Bank, and Seoulbank) were supported by the massive injection of public funds (see box 6-1).

Korea Asset Management Corporation. The principal vehicle used by the Korean authorities to combat the growing level of nonperforming loans on the books of local banks has been the Korea Asset Management Corporation (KAMCO). Launched by the government in November 1997 to buy and securitize bad loans, KAMCO—a majority government-owned institution whose funding is generated by the issuance of government-guaranteed bonds—was granted additional authority to purchase at a discount nonperforming loans from Korean banks.[2] (The average discount has varied between 55 percent for collateralized loans and 97 percent for unsecured exposures.) The loans assumed include both ordinary loans in

2. As of December 1999 KAMCO's main shareholders were the Korean government (38 percent holding), Korea Development Bank (31 percent), and other financial institutions (31 percent). KAMCO's authorized (and disbursed) funding base stood at 21.5 trillion won at the same time.

Box 6-1. *Korea First Bank: A Case Study*

In January 1998 Korea First Bank (KFB) was nationalized by the Korean government when the state took a 94 percent stake in the bank (raised to 100 percent
before KFB's sale in January 2000). The bank was particularly hard hit by the surge
of delinquent debt flowing from Korea's economic crisis. At the same time, it was
also the eighth largest commercial bank in terms of lending (with a 7 percent share
of the nationwide bank loan market at year-end 1997) and the sixth largest in terms
of deposits (with an 8 percent share of nationwide bank deposits); it boasted a staff
of 7,965 and was backed by a domestic network of more than four hundred offices
and carried large exposures on its books to many of the country's leading companies
(these lending practices were central to the bank's eventual meltdown).

   Although the Korean authorities moved to stabilize the bank through nationalization, it was agreed as part of the International Monetary Fund's support package
that KFB (along with the equally distressed Seoulbank) would be sold off to international investors as soon as feasible. As of January 2000 the Korean government has
reached agreement with Newbridge Capital to sell a 51 percent interest in the bank,
with the government to hold the remainder.

   The Korean authorities have expended around 8.5 trillion won in propping up
the bank and preparing it for sale. The government is likely to spend a further 3 trillion won over the next three years to purchase those assets unwanted by Newbridge,
including new nonperforming loans from the bank, as part of the sale agreement
with Newbridge.

   Was the decision to rescue KFB rather than shutter the bank the right one? From
the perspective of Korea's public purse (and ultimately the Korean taxpayer), the
answer must be a resounding no. The rescue of KFB (including ongoing contingent
liabilities) is set to cost the Korean government a whopping $10 billion (at current
exchange rates), and the final bill will only be tallied at the end of 2002 when the

default for more than three months, as well as restructured corporate loans
and loans to companies in receivership or undergoing workout procedures.

   KAMCO's first purchases of nonperforming loans from local banks
were concluded on a nonrecourse basis, at least with regard to the principal of the loans. The sale-and-purchase agreement allowed for some
final adjustment of the transaction price, usually in the event that the
final amount KAMCO received for the loan upon sale differed from the
original purchase price. (In most cases, the selling bank was required to
cover KAMCO's losses and book additional credit costs as a result.) A siz-

contingent liabilities related to the commitment to purchase further bad debt from the bank can be quantified. In exchange for this outlay, KFB has been stabilized, its balance sheet (relatively) cleansed, and its operational network streamlined, while an international buyer has been secured. However, the bank remains weak—its franchise has undoubtedly suffered badly and its future remains clouded, with much depending upon the future strategy of its new management team.

On the other hand, could the government have afforded *not* to bail out the bank? Ultimately, the answer to this question is a probable no, as well. Beyond the question of whether the bank was "too big to fail," the peculiar circumstances and timing of KFB's demise dictated that state intervention was unavoidable. Stabilizing the banking environment has been a priority for Korea's authorities since the outset of the crisis. Closing KFB at a time when investor confidence was jittery, the economy was buckling, and the state's capacity to work out the bank's problems was drained by reduced resources would only have worsened the situation.

Finally, should bank rescues like KFB's be countenanced in future? This is a difficult question. However, we can make the following observations.

—To some degree, the question should be academic (at least in the Korean context), provided that the wide-ranging prudential and regulatory changes being implemented by Korea are successful. The aim of Korea's restructuring and reform is to reduce (at best, eliminate) the possibility that another KFB will arise.

—Korea now has the ability and mechanisms (such as improved fiscal position and deposit insurance) to work out even a large bank closure.

—The Korean government is committed to reducing government intervention in the market and disinvestment from the banking sector. So much the better. Market practices and principles must rule and moral hazard must be avoided. Shareholders must be made accountable. Letting a big bank like KFB collapse would no doubt be a severe test of Korea's new market principles, but it should be the inevitable corollary of those very principles.

able portion of loans has now been sold to KAMCO on a recourse basis with regard to the principal of the loan. These loans in general refer to credits made to companies undergoing court receivership programs, where the original underlying valuation of the loan had not been settled by the court.

KAMCO's main role is changing. In April 1999 the legislature approved amendments intended to transform the corporation into a full-scale "bad bank" with additional functions. Although KAMCO remains charged with disposing of its warehouse of bad debts, the corporation's functions have

Table 6-2. *Nonperforming Loans Acquired by KAMCO*
Billions of won

Pricing category	1997	1998	1999	Total
Face value	11,044	33,031	11,936	56,011
Purchase price	7,140	12,767	2,869	22,776

Source: KAMCO.

shifted toward creating joint venture asset management companies to assist it in more productively managing its nonperforming loan stockpile. At the same time, banks have grown reluctant to sell off their bad assets to KAMCO for two reasons: the related high one-off credit costs, and improving market conditions, which have encouraged banks in their belief that they themselves are in a better position to realize value from nonperforming loan sales or recoveries than KAMCO.

KAMCO has played a positive and significant role in working with the Korean banking sector to ease a massive nonperforming loan burden. By our estimates, it has helped deal with approximately 30 percent of the total problem assets (including restructured debt) in the Korean financial system. Tables 6-2 and 6-3 highlight KAMCO's impact to date.

KAMCO has been aggressive in reducing its warehouse of bad debt, and the corporation's disposition plans for 2000 indicate a continuation of its innovative approach. The largest component of KAMCO's bad debt sales has been the repurchase and cancellation of nonperforming loans. A number of banks maintain a contingent liability to take back onto their own books nonperforming loans sold to KAMCO (that is, the "with-recourse" sales). Such putback agreements have several interesting—and significant—implications. On the one hand, they provide KAMCO (and the Korean government) with increased flexibility to recover government funds expended in the support and restructuring of the local banking sector. Feeding these recovered funds back into the state's coffers would help speed up the reduction of the government's fiscal burden (although it should be noted that the authorities are looking to channel the funds liberated from KAMCO's asset sales into supporting other sectors of the financial system in 2000, especially the distressed investment trust companies). On the other hand, the putback option returns to the accounts of local banks a sizable portion of problematic credits. Not only will these

Table 6-3. *Breakdown of Nonperforming Loan Sales by KAMCO,
as of December 1999*
Billions of won

Disposition	Face value	Sale price
Securitization	4,512	1,922
Foreclosure auction	2,327	1,856
Public sales	257	183
Voluntary repayment	1,907	1,865
Repurchase and cancellation	12,088	6,298
Total	21,091	12,122

Source: KAMCO.

need to be funded, but realizing and maintaining their fair value will require substantial effort.

At the same time, it is clear that insufficient attention has been given to quantifying the risks for local banks and reconciling the total amount of nonperforming loans in the system. The fact that KAMCO's available resources have been increased several times (although whether sufficient funds have been allocated to cleanse the system remains debatable even now) indicates the difficulties faced in coming to grips with the size and dimensions of the problem. Markets and investors deplore uncertainty: rather than release crucial information and data piecemeal (as was the case), the preferable course would have been to quantify the actual level of nonperforming loans burdening Korea's banks on the basis of reliable and up-to-date analysis and to lay out a clear response to deal with the problem. To accomplish these goals, however, requires that the authorities have access to effective regulatory and prudential mechanisms. Improved transparency must also play its part.

Korea Deposit Insurance Corporation. The Korea Deposit Insurance Corporation (KDIC) has also been involved in the resolution of Korean banks' bad-debt problems. This has taken the primary form of injecting public funds into troubled financial institutions to provide capital adequacy and liquidity support. KDIC received 31.5 trillion won for this task; the amounts dispersed in 1998 and 1999 were substantial (see table 6-4).

As noted above, the Korean government is considering a blueprint for disinvestment from banks that have been effectively nationalized through the recapitalization efforts of KDIC. Of the four commercial banks that

Table 6-4. *KDIC Activities, 1997–99*
Billions of won

Activity	1997	1998	1999
Equity Participation	30	6,286	11,898
Contributions	0	6,932	2,267
Deposit Reimbursements	0	11,230	1,207
Insurance Claim Reimbursements	0	448	2,816
Liquidity Support	332	192	70
Total value	362	25,088	18,258

Source: Korea Deposit Insurance Corporation.

were nationalized (Korea First Bank, Seoulbank, Hanvit Bank, and Cho Hung Bank), the government's stake in Korea First Bank has been reduced following the successful conclusion in January 2000 of the sale of Korea First Bank to U.S.-based Newbridge Capital.

Creating a New Regulatory Framework

Among the crisis-hit countries of Asia, Korea has led the way in aggressively overhauling its mechanisms for regulatory and prudential control. The Korean authorities are much better equipped than they were before the crisis to supervise the country's banks and have been provided with the necessary legal teeth to accomplish their task. Before the onset of the crisis in 1997, the government had moved to tighten up prudential standards and bring banks more in line with international best practices; this was done on a gradual basis, however, and proved insufficient to adequately monitor the growing risk practices of the country's banking system. The main areas of weakness during the years before the crisis can be summarized as follows:

—*Fragmented regulatory authority.* Two main bodies had direct responsibility for divergent elements of the Korean financial system. The Bank of Korea (through its Office of Bank Supervision and governing Monetary Board) supervised the operations and fiscal prudence of commercial banks; at the same time, control of the country's specialized banks and nonbanking financial institutions came under the purview of the Ministry of Finance and Economy. The dichotomy of such a framework naturally lent itself to insufficient regulation and supervision.

—Lax asset classification and provisioning standards. Until June 1998 the definition of nonperforming loans for Korean financial institutions lagged international best practices by some distance. A loan was considered non-performing only when past due by six months or more (this has now been changed to define a nonperforming loan as a credit overdue for three months or more). At the same time, the provisioning required against problem credits was set at inadequate levels (0.5 percent for "normal loans"; 1 percent for "precautionary" loans; 20 percent for "substandard" loans; 75 percent for "doubtful" loans; and 100 percent for "estimated" losses) and relied excessively on the valuation of underlying collateral.

The Korean authorities' track record in enforcing even the lax standards demanded of the country's banks was (and remains) mixed at best, with a marked tendency to modify or even waive regulations from one reporting season to the next in order to avoid damaging banks' reported results.

In response to Korea's financial crisis, the Korean government undertook a full-scale overhaul of the regulatory framework as it relates to the country's financial system. Legislation enacted in December 1998 provided greater autonomy to the Bank of Korea and granted it principal responsibility for maintaining price stability and implementing monetary policy through the central bank's Monetary Board. In tandem with the Bank of Korea Act, Korea's parliament also passed a new financial supervision act effective 1998 to create a new comprehensive supervisory and regulatory watchdog for the financial system—the Financial Supervisory Commission (FSC). The legislation transferred supervisory authority over banks from the Bank of Korea to the FSC.

The commission oversees the establishment and revision of prudential regulations and authorizes the operations of financial institutions, as well as directing and supervising the new Financial Supervisory Service (FSS), an executive body of the FSC. In addition, the FSC is charged with the task of implementing the restructuring of both financial institutions and large conglomerates. Although it falls under the prime minister's jurisdiction, the FSC performs its duties independent of the prime minister and other government agencies.[3]

3. The FSC directorate is composed of a chairman, vice chairman, standing commission, and six members. In consultation with the cabinet council (and based on the recommendation of the Minister of Finance and Economy and the chairman of the FSC), the president of Korea appoints the chairman, the vice chairman and standing commissioner, and three members of the commission. The remaining three commissioners—the vice-minister of the Ministry of Finance and Economy, the deputy governor of the Bank of Korea, and the president of the Korea Deposit Insurance Corporation—are ex-officio.

THE FINANCIAL SUPERVISORY SERVICE. The Financial Supervisory Service (FSS), formerly the Financial Supervisory Board, began operations in January 1999 and is responsible for the examination of financial institutions. The new FSS unifies the functions of the Office of Bank Supervision, the Securities Supervisory Board, the Insurance Supervisory Board, and the Credit Management Fund (formerly carried out under the supervision of the FSC) to create a single financial supervisory authority under the office of the prime minister. The FSS assumes supervisory authority for commercial banks, brokerage houses, insurance companies, and nonbank financial institutions.

IMPLEMENTING PROMPT CORRECTIVE ACTION. The FSC has established criteria for determining the soundness of financial institutions. For commercial banks, in addition to the capital adequacy standards of the Bank for International Settlements (BIS), the FSC uses CAMELS (capital, asset quality, management, earnings, liquidity, and sensitivity) ratings in order to detect problems at an early stage. Any bank that falls below the minimum 8 percent BIS capital adequacy ratio is subject to prompt corrective action (PCA) procedures. Similarly, if the CAMELS ratings (a numerical scale from 1 to 5) of a bank fall below 3, the FSC has the authority to impose appropriate supervisory actions, including PCA procedures. The PCA measures fall into two categories:

(1) Management Improvement Recommendation (MIR). This applies to banks whose BIS capital adequacy ratio falls between 6 percent and 8 percent under the new calculation guidelines. Under the MIR, a bank is required to meet the minimum BIS capital adequacy ratio following the approval of its stabilization plan through the restructuring of its business (sale of unprofitable branches or subsidiaries); improvement of internal management and reduction of nonperforming loan levels; implementation of cost reduction programs by such steps as freezing senior management pay levels; strengthening internal controls; establishing and operating an independent risk management organization; and reporting quarterly on the progress of its normalization plan. The bank is further prohibited from distributing dividends until it meets the minimum BIS standard.

(2) Management Improvement Order (MIO). Modeled essentially on the MIR, the MIO includes a number of comparatively harsher and stricter requirements. It is designed for banks whose adjusted BIS capital adequacy ratio falls below 6 percent. In addition to the directives of the MIR, measures demanded of banks under the MIO include the prohibition, in principle, of new business development and investment; the need to specify

which business areas will be the bank's main focus; significant cost reductions at all staff levels; freezing fixed-asset investment; replacement of the bank's external auditor; production of financial performance projections. Banks subject to the MIO also undergo quarterly examination of asset quality. For cases in which little expectation of normalization remains, restructuring through mergers or third-party takeovers can be considered.

STRENGTHENING ASSET CLASSIFICATION AND PROVISIONING REQUIREMENTS. The asset classification system has been strengthened to bring it more in line with international best practice. The current system has tightened the definition of credits, as follows:

—Normal: loans where the borrowers' credit standing is good and where debt service ability is considered adequate, including loans overdue up to one month;

—Precautionary: loans that require particular attention, including loans overdue between one and three months, loans extended to highly leveraged corporates, or made to leasing companies with negative worth;

—Substandard: nonperforming for more than three months but adequately collateralized or guaranteed;

—Doubtful: inadequately collateralized or guaranteed portion of substandard debt;

—Estimated loss: principal and interest cannot be recovered.

In addition, commercial paper, guaranteed bills, and private placement bonds in trust accounts are now subject to the loan classification system and need to be adequately provided for.

At the same time, the provisioning levels required against each subcategory of asset have been modified. Banks are now required to book a 2 percent reserve against "precautionary" debt, versus 1 percent previously. Nonetheless, Korean banks in general remain inadequately provisioned in that their capability to build up a sufficient reserve against future problem loans remains weak. Although banks are required to generate a nominal general reserve against "normal" performing assets, the current provisioning regime is more focused on providing against specific problem assets already identified by the bank. In this respect, a further revision in loan classification effective 1999 is important, since banks are now required to evaluate the borrower's ability to service debt and set-aside provisions against payment guarantees outstanding.

DEPOSIT INSURANCE. In April 1998 the government strengthened its deposit insurance system by launching the Korea Deposit Insurance Corporation (KDIC). The KDIC combines previous deposit insurance programs covering commercial banks, insurers, and merchant banks. Effective August 1998, the deposit insurance law was revised to restrict the amount of new deposits guaranteed by law, although deposits made before August 1998 continue to receive full guarantees.

Deposit insurance protection for foreign currency deposits, certificates of deposit, bank debentures, and repurchase agreements is scheduled to terminate by the end of December 2000. Time and saving deposits and guaranteed trust account deposits will continue to be protected, but effective January 2001 deposit insurance will guarantee deposits only up to 20 million won (regardless of the principal amount). At present, deposit insurance protection does not extend to nonguaranteed trust account deposits or bank guaranteed corporate bonds.

Creating a Credit Culture

Since the launch of Korea's first five-year economic development plan in 1962, the government has used Korean banks as a vehicle for implementing successive development plans. Local banks were heavily regulated by the government through the Bank of Korea's Office of Bank Supervision, particularly in the area of credit allocation, and as a result they lacked the necessary systems and expertise to properly manage their own loan portfolios. Lending practices among Korean banks have been based on real estate collateral during periods of high economic growth and inflation, while complying with regulations and directives issued from time to time by the central bank.

No in-depth credit analysis was undertaken for commercial borrowers. Instead, banks had been using a one-page Integrated Credit Scoring Sheet for Corporations designed by the central bank more than a decade ago. This assigns a weighted score based on twelve elements, including capital structure, liquidity, profitability, solvency, and growth prospects. The aggregate score was an important consideration for credit approval. In general, once the loan was booked, around 70 percent tended to be continuously rolled over without meaningful review of the borrower's ability to repay the loan as long as the interest payment remained serviced. Loan delinquency was a major triggering point for classifying assets.

Given the absence of a risk-rating program, there was no system in place to assess and monitor the bank's entire risk profile. In an environment in which lending can be an expression of patriotic pride rather than sound commercial assessment, credit control was unable to function as well as it is supposed to, giving rise to a credit culture in which loan officers were viewed as integral to the bank's success, while credit officers were seen as little more than bookkeepers: what mattered was market share and megadeals, with little balance between credit quality and asset growth.

MOVES TOWARD A NEW RISK MANAGEMENT SYSTEM. Since late 1998 Korea's banks have been galvanized by the aftershocks emanating from the country's recent turmoil. Under the strong direction of the FSC, a number of structural and operational changes have been implemented that should increase the tools at banks' disposal to assess the creditworthiness of existing and new borrowers, as well as improve their ability to appraise and monitor credit risk. The introduction of a new layer of supervision and control has strengthened banks' credit appraisal standards and bolstered the checks and balances governing the extension and monitoring of credit lines.

Perhaps most significantly, a new "forward-looking" asset classification method has been introduced, effective year-end 1999. As noted earlier, the previous asset classification relied primarily on the borrower's past delinquency or default record and the presence of collateral. The new system is more statistically oriented and looks "forward" to factor in the borrower's type of business, financial strength, debts, and interest-servicing capability. Any classification of assets using such criteria will require an advanced credit system, including staff with good credit evaluation skills, who are able to conduct credit analysis and credit risk management, and prudent credit monitoring. The authorities believe that this will change the banks' credit approval system and foster a credit culture in Korean banks over the long term. It should also help banks build up a provisioning cushion against future loans that is more fully reflective of the credit risks undertaken.

The minimum standards for the new forward-looking criteria are set by the FSS. Banks will use these as a basic guideline to assess their own loan portfolios but are empowered to design and implement individual assessment and evaluation models, with the minimum standards as a guide. Each bank's individual standards will be reviewed by the FSS before implementation, and the FSS retains the right to have a bank modify its internal rules in order to ensure that compliance with minimum standards. At the same time, banks will be monitored to ensure that assets have been properly classified in line with the agreed standards and that adequate provisioning levels are maintained. The FSS may require that adjustments be made to provisions as needed.

FOREIGN BANKS TO THE RESCUE? Since the onset of the Korean financial crisis, much attention has been paid to the potential benefits to be derived from increased involvement by foreign banks in the local banking industry. Foreign participants are expected to bring with them international standard risk-monitoring techniques and high-tech and up-to-date management systems, as well as to increase competition by introducing sophisticated financial products to meet the diversifying needs of Korean corporate borrowers and consumers. The expectation is that Korean local banks will have no choice but to improve their own services and management expertise. The argument envisages a "win-win" situation for the Korean banking system, with less competitive names forced to exit (or merge), while the sophistication and skill levels of the local banking industry inevitably rise.

Before the crisis, the influence of foreign banks on local market practices was peripheral. Beyond a handful of joint-venture banks established with foreign partners in the late 1970s and early 1980s, foreign players were not directly involved in the management and business decisions of local banks. No large-scale strategic alliances existed.

In recent months, however, several substantial foreign investments and tie-ups with local banks have been announced (see table 6-5). Although such steps may well prove significant, especially for the individual strategies and performance prospects of the banks involved, at this stage the jury is still out on the extent to which meaningful change can be wrought on the entire banking industry by a handful of foreign players. At the least, the evolution of Korean banking to incorporate international best practice and ensure the mature and sophisticated allocation of risk is a medium-term project. The involvement of foreign banks in this process is positive and welcome, but given the cultural impediments that still exist, foreign participation in the local banking sector is unlikely to produce an immediate or sweeping revolution in banking style and techniques.

CAN KOREAN BANKS DEVELOP A PROPER CREDIT CULTURE? The actions taken and systems implemented to date are a positive move toward strengthening Korean banks' management of credit and treasury risks, but these changes are for the most part related to the credit process. The creation of an appropriate and effective credit culture within Korean banks will require considerable attention going forward and is essential to their ability to avoid excessive credit and risk concentrations and reduce the possibility of inappropriate lending, risk control, and management decisions.

Although a bank's operating and credit culture cannot be changed overnight—its development is an ongoing, evolutionary process that requires periodic reevaluation and enforcement—few Korean banks have yet to develop a fresh philosophy and approach to the business of banking. The focus to date has necessarily emphasized the improvement of appraisal and monitoring systems, but banks will also need to register success in altering their business practices in order to make full use of improved risk-control processes.

At this stage it appears that Korean banks are placing too much emphasis upon the statistical approach to risk management. Effective risk control based upon the statistical analysis of quantitative data can only be effective (1) if the raw initial data concerning a borrower that forms the starting point of analysis are thorough and reliable; (2) if sophisticated risk assessment models are in place; and (3) if management is educated in the new risk management techniques and understands the implications of the risk models sufficiently to make professional management decisions related to the extension (or denial) of credit. A number of weaknesses are discernible at this stage of the evolution of new credit management techniques among Korea's financial institutions,.

Of primary concern is the lack of transparency of Korean corporate accounts. The requirement to present consolidated data was introduced for the main Korean conglomerates only as of year-end 1999. It is uncertain whether Korean bank risk managers have access to sufficient levels of information related to borrowers to ensure that reasonable decisions can be made. If the initial raw data that form the basis of the decision are incomplete or unreliable, the results of the risk management model are essentially flawed.

The ability of management to correctly interpret the risk-control data and make prudent and appropriate risk decisions has not yet been addressed as a significant area of concern. Banks have focused (necessarily) on structural and operational issues. Within the limitations of paper-based processing and reporting methods, Korean banks for the most part appear to operate sufficiently well to ensure that the necessary and relevant information flows to the bank's decisionmakers. A number of institutions have also implemented new computerized systems that should allow decisionmakers easier access to the necessary information. However, the broader question of the experience and education levels of senior management remains less easy to quantify.

Table 6-5. *Main Foreign Alliances with Korean Commercial Banks*

Bank	Foreign partner	Stake (percent)	Date of initial investment	Scope of partnership
Korea First Bank	Newbridge Capital	51	January 2000	Full management control rests in Newbridge's hands.
Housing and Commercial Bank (H&CB)	ING Group	10	August 1999	Cooperation extends to mutual investments in ING's Korean life insurance subsidiary, and H&CB's investment trust subsidiary.
Kookmin Bank	Goldman Sachs Capital Partners	11.3	May 1999	Goldman Sachs is essentially a passive investor, although the strategic alliance offers Kookmin access to Goldman Sachs's investment banking expertise.
Korea Exchange Bank	Commerzbank	27.7	July 1998	Two Commerzbank directors on the board, responsible for developing Korea Exchange Bank's corporate lending, credit analysis and capital market business; plans to help develop risk management, among other key areas.
KorAm Bank	Bank of America	16.8	March 1983	Bank of America has direct representation on the bank's credit committee and provides various advanced banking techniques; KorAm Bank adopted Bank of America's credit procedures and systems from its early days.

Source: Thomson Financial BankWatch.

At the same time, the provision that allows banks to create and develop their own forward-looking criteria-assessment and evaluation models (based on the minimum requirements set by the FSS) has the potential to create substantial differences among the risk models employed by individual banks. The mix and distribution of a credit portfolio can vary significantly from bank to bank, and some flexibility is required in creating a new systemwide framework for risk assessment. Nonetheless, each Korean bank's approach to risk management warrants careful attention, while the role of the FSS in monitoring each bank's internal standards and policing discrepancies will also be crucial in creating confidence in the improved risk assessment techniques of Korean banks.

The improvements made to the credit control systems of Korean banks are very new and remain to a large degree untested. Further time and testing will be required to ascertain the success of the new systems in maintaining the quality and integrity of banks' credit portfolios and their level of risk diversification, particularly since Korean banks have started to increase lending with the rebound in Korea's economic fortunes.

Evolving Corporate Governance and Transparency

Korean banking authorities have identified the concentration of decision-making power at the chief executive officer (CEO) level as one area that contributed significantly to the banking sector's poor lending decisions and lax credit policies. One noteworthy change in this respect has taken place in the corporate governance system.

In the case of banks, at least three members of the board of directors should be outside (or nonstanding) directors. Following shareholder meetings in February 1999, the boards of directors of most banks have been reorganized to empower nonstanding directors. Under the new systems, the roles of standing directors and nonstanding directors have been separated. In a move to decentralize authority from CEOs, nonstanding directors have assumed authority for making strategic decisions at most banks and for evaluating the performance of the standing directors, while the standing directors have responsibility for executing management decisions. In addition, several banks have appointed a nonstanding director as chairman of the board of directors.

In addition, the FSC has taken advantage of the government bailout of several major commercial banks to impose a sounder and more prudent corporate governance structure by enlarging the role of nonstanding directors in

Box 6-2. *Korea: Main Steps Taken to Improve Transparency*

Publish data on usable foreign reserves twice a month

Publish data on external debt once a month

Provide monthly data on the consolidated central government's revenue, expenditure, and financing (effective July 1999)

Strengthen accounting standards to ensure full compliance by financial institutions with the minimum requirements of International Accounting Standard 30

Upgrade standards for disclosure, auditing, and accounting to the level of international best practice (effective January 1999)

Require listed companies to publish quarterly financial statements (as of January 2000)

Require large business conglomerates to submit consolidated financial statements (effective year-end 1999)

Require the appointment of outside directors at listed companies (effective February 1998)

Strengthen the rights of minority shareholders by allowing collective action and the right of appeal (effective May 1998)

Publish on an ongoing basis details of all public support for financial sector restructuring.

Source: Korea's Ministry of Finance and Economy.

the decisionmaking processes of some banks. The timely presentation of reliable and up-to-date information has been recognized by the Korean authorities as an important weapon to maintain investor confidence. The Korean government has undertaken several measures to improve the transparency of corporate Korea (including the nation's banks) and enhance the dissemination of data (see box 6-2).

Strengthening the Repayment Culture of Borrowers

More than two years after the onset of the Korean crisis, bad debt write-offs by Korean banks remain modest and the bad debt overhang considerable, a function, perhaps, of the peculiar circumstances that dictate the ability of

Korean banks to realize and write off debt.[4] It is clear that improvements are still required in this area.

BANKRUPTCY AND LIQUIDATION. Korea's bankruptcy laws (including court receivership and court mediation procedures) are essentially designed to work toward the recovery and rehabilitation of a business on the edge of insolvency if its value as a going concern is judged to exceed its realizable value from liquidation, rather than to expedite the winding up of the company. As a result, companies that should have been quickly liquidated, with losses recognized and creditors' calls on underlying assets cleared, continue to find themselves on life support, even years after lurching into bankruptcy. Many companies have been granted generous rehabilitation and repayment schemes (up to five years in some cases), while banks often continue to provide court mediation companies with funds.

Three related bankruptcy laws (the Firm Liquidation Law, Court Mediation Law, and the Bankruptcy Law) were amended in early 1998 to strengthen creditors' rights and encourage companies to apply for court receivership rather than undergo the less demanding process of court mediation. The main intent of the amendments was to establish a management committee to handle the liquidation, mediation, or bankruptcy of the firm; expand the definition of firms that are eligible to apply for court receivership to include small- to medium-size enterprises; and allow creditors to file for a company's court receivership and provide recommendations as to whether the firm should be liquidated or the terms of the court receivership ended early.

Despite the amendments, current bankruptcy procedures continue to throw up a number of obstructions. In particular, complaints persist over the length of time often required for courts to grant banks' applications for court receivership. At the same time, there is still excessive recourse to court mediation or court receivership procedures (as well as workout programs), with few companies wound up expeditiously once rendered insolvent. In addition, the extension of financial lifelines to "workout" companies has thrown up a number of negative consequences. First, it has forced bank management to participate in the direct management of workout companies. This has diverted and distracted bank management, while the ability

---

4. Some banks continue to carry bad debt on their books from companies such as Sammi Steel and Kia Motors, which were caught up in the first waves of the crisis and placed under court protection more than two years ago.

of creditor banks to run nonbank companies under the workout scheme in an efficient and professional manner is questionable at best. Second, companies that should have been forced to exit under more stringent (and more easily enforceable) bankruptcy procedures have been kept alive and in many cases provided with fresh funds. These practices perpetuate Korean banking's darker traditions of heavy-handed government intervention in bank lending decisions, as well as the large-scale misallocation of credit, while starving more deserving and financially viable companies of much-needed funding. Finally the Korean banks involved in the workout schemes continue to carry the associated debt on their balance sheet, thus adding to their stockpile of problem assets.

Korean authorities are reportedly considering further amendments to the country's bankruptcy laws to remedy these deficiencies. In addition, the authorities are considering ways to rationalize the handling of companies currently placed under workout procedures in order to weed out those names that have little or no chance of rehabilitation (by discontinuing debt restructuring programs) and fast-tracking for recovery those companies that have shown improved operating performance.

THE ROLE OF CREDIT-RATING AGENCIES. Three major domestic credit-rating agencies operate in Korea: Korea Investors Service (KIS), Korea Management Consulting and Credit Rating Corporation (KMCC) and National Information and Credit Evaluation (NICE). Although in operation for several years and supported by a legal framework that required local companies wishing to tap the local capital markets to secure a credit rating from at least two agencies, Korea's credit-rating services industry has struggled to assert itself. At the same time, while the crisis unfolded, the credibility of the local industry was heavily undermined as a number of companies that had carried investment-grade ratings one week were reported as having (severe) financial difficulties the next.

The Korean government has recognized the need to develop the country's capital markets. A more sophisticated, robust, and deeper market structure is seen as an essential ingredient in the further reform and development of Korea's economic and financial structure, and the government's latest blueprint for restructuring and development includes broadening the base of Korea's stock and bond markets. Within this context, the authorities remain committed to ensuring the full marking to market of financial institutions' investment portfolios (scheduled to be introduced as of July 2000), while the FSC is insisting that the country's banks regularly tap the market through the issuance of subordinated bonds in order to instill greater market-led discipline within their operations. Against this background, the role of credit-rating agencies is expected to strengthen.

Conclusions

Several systemic weaknesses clearly contributed to the onset of Korea's recent economic and financial meltdown. The Korean government, to its credit, has introduced and implemented a wide-ranging set of new policies to remedy these core problems. Several fundamental crisis-management measures have been adopted by the government in order to avoid or at least alleviate similar problems in the future. These include:

—a unified supervisory and regulatory watchdog, armed with the necessary legal tools to police the financial sector and ensure full regulatory compliance,

—international best practice asset classification and provisioning standards that significantly reduce the system's traditional dependence on collateralized lending and emphasize the borrower's ability to generate sufficient cash flow to service debt as a key determinant in the credit allocation process,

—a framework to enhance credit culture among local banks,

—tougher corporate governance and risk management standards, and

—a limited deposit protection scheme to encourage market confidence and stability.

In addition, the Korean authorities have moved to address several key areas that are essential to their goals of creating a healthy and strong financial system. These include:

—*Corporate sector reform.* The authorities have attempted to deleverage the corporate sector, particularly the overstretched large conglomerates, or chaebols. The 200 percent debt-to-equity ratio imposed on large borrowers is perhaps the most publicized example of these initiatives.

—*Disintermediation of the financial sector.* A core policy imperative for the Korean authorities going forward is to deepen and broaden Korea's capital markets in order to reduce the concentration of lending power traditionally held by local banks; and increase market discipline (and by extension, reduce the necessity for government intervention). To this end, the creation of a healthy bond market has moved to the top of the authorities' action list.

The Korean authorities have recognized that the reform of the country's financial and corporate sectors is a medium-term and multilayered process. Inevitably, the initial policy initiatives were aimed at stabilizing the system by concentrating on the many financial spot-fires that sprang up as a result of Korea's meltdown. The stabilization of Korea's banking system has been accomplished, and with considerable success, although it has entailed massive government intervention and has come at the cost of an enormous recapitalization bill and the nationalization of a large chunk of Korean banking assets. Successfully managing these issues, especially in the context of the prudent management of the country's finances, remains an important challenge for the Korean government going forward.

At the microeconomic level, too, challenges remain. For the most part, the more pressing quantitative issues have been addressed. However, the most significant problem for Korea's banks remains the successful, thorough, and ongoing implementation of the new credit culture and corporate governance frameworks. Inevitably, this will take time. The Korean banking system has only just been stabilized and new risk management techniques and systems of corporate governance have been in place for little more than a year. The return of better economic times (and the consequent reduction in financial distress at many local companies) may well mask the true effectiveness of banks' new risk assessment techniques. It is not difficult for a bank to run low-problem asset levels during favorable economic conditions; only when the cycle turns can banks' risk management and assessment capabilities be accurately ascertained. At the same time, weaknesses in the formal bankruptcy process (and the subsequent preference for informal debt workout programs) need to be addressed in order to help banks manage down their bad debt overhang and establish confidence in efficient debt resolution and corporate liquidation procedures.

Korea has undertaken major structural changes to remedy the deficiencies unmasked by the financial crisis; many of these reforms are fundamental to the creation of a healthy banking system Insufficient attention to the tougher, qualitative problems of the sector, however, may condemn Korea's banks to suffer another major shock in the not-too-distant future. Only in such a context will we be able to judge the true success of Korea's recent banking reforms.

Thailand

The initial responsibility for Thailand's financial and economic crisis must be laid squarely at the door of reckless and excessive investment behavior financed by short-term and largely unhedged foreign capital flows. Such behavior was ultimately and resolutely vetoed by the international foreign exchange markets, which by July 2, 1997, forced the authorities to abandon the policy of pegging the Thai baht to a static basket of currencies (denominated largely in the U.S. dollar). The managed float policy for the currency subsequently adopted by the central bank soon found the currency in a devaluation spiral that triggered a collapse in confidence within business and consumer circles as well as among foreign and domestic agents. The currency crisis precipitated a liquidity crisis, and the domestic financial system and its constituents seized up. The scale and depth of the crisis in confidence initially overwhelmed the best efforts of the authorities to stabilize the financial markets.

Crisis Response

Efforts to arrest the crisis of confidence revolved initially around making implicit guarantees explicit for depositors and senior creditors of all financial institutions. Thus the process of empowering and re-funding the Financial Institutions Development Fund (FIDF) was accelerated. The FIDF, established in 1985 to supplement the role of the Bank of Thailand in funding financial institutions in distress, was re-charged with the principal duties of providing liquidity assistance to distressed financial institutions, providing guarantees to depositors and senior creditors, and acting as agent for the exchange of promissory notes for depositors and creditors.

An amendment to the FIDF Act (signed into law on August 8, 1997), legislated a collective, albeit temporary, guarantee for depositors and senior creditors of all financial institutions. With the guarantee in place, the authorities aggressively pursued an orderly exit strategy for institutions deemed nonviable. Ultimately, fifty-six (out of ninety-one) finance and securities companies were forced out of the system, and seven commercial banks were nationalized. Four of those banks have since been reprivatized, with foreign investors taking up majority equity stakes, one exited, and two are slated to be auctioned off—most likely to foreign interests. Meanwhile, the blanket guarantee that was in due course to have been converted to a self-financing deposit insurance scheme remains in place.

The cost of that guarantee, by the most recent Bank of Thailand estimates, will see the FIDF incur gross debt of 1,007 billion baht ($27 billion). Although proceeds from distressed asset sales, dividend and interest payments, state-owned enterprise privatization receipts, and tax collections may reduce the gross debt to around 800 billion baht, that sum obviously still represents an acute burden. Meanwhile, the best-practices calculation for total public sector debt is estimated to rise to 1,900 billion baht, or roughly 40 percent of GDP. That sum excludes the FIDF debt, as well as other monetary and financial sector debt from the public sector, namely, the total guaranteed and nonguaranteed public enterprise debt (1,300 billion baht) and Bank of Thailand debt (500 billion baht).

The crippling costs of the rescue efforts were aggravated by structural impediments within the financial payments system, the swift evaporation of liquidity for corporates grown accustomed to subsidized credit, and re-infection from the regional financial markets' contagion. The realization that international reserves had been depleted forced the Thai authorities in August 1997 to enlist multilateral assistance led by the International Monetary Fund. On October 22, 1997, the legislature passed the Emergency Decree on Financial Sector Restructuring, which formed the legal basis for the creation of the Financial Sector Restructuring Authority (FRA) and the Asset Management Corporation (AMC).

The primary role of the state AMC was to bid for assets of the closed finance companies. The purpose of the FRA was threefold: (1) to rehabilitate suspended financial institutions; (2) to mediate on behalf of the depositors and creditors of those suspended institutions; and (3) to administer and guide the liquidation process of nonviable institutions. By the end of July 1999, the FRA had auctioned off the bulk of the assets of closed institutions. (The auctions recovered only about 181 billion baht, or 21 percent of the 860 billion baht in reported assets.)

In contrast to other countries in financial crisis that established centralized and theoretically more independent agencies with the authority to transfer and warehouse impaired assets of the commercial banks, the Thai authorities have allowed the individual banks to establish self-determining recovery vehicles. With minor exceptions, however, private sector AMCs have yet to be fully implemented. With contentious tax treatment and regulatory issues related to the functioning of individual AMCs resolved, all nonintervened banks are expected to implement these vehicles in due course. The relative merits and successes of these vehicles will rest upon the pricing and management of asset transfers, but we believe that the risks are sufficiently high that issues of recovery and funding could constrain their success.

Present Crises and Disputes

What is clearly no longer in dispute, on the evidence of recent economic data points and subsequent data series is a confirmed positive trend in economic activity. The balance-of-payments surplus and deeper usable foreign exchange reserves continue to underpin the improving external liquidity profile for the real economy. Export volumes have been revived beyond expectations and have, in conjunction with positive trends in production and select domestic consumption indicators, given rise to estimates of real 1999 GDP expansion of the order of 4 percent year-on-year. (The significance of such growth is evident in the comparison to the dramatic 10 percent contraction from the previous fiscal period.)

What is in dispute, however, is the extent to which claims of a material recovery in the financial economy have taken place over fiscal year 1999. The dramatic ascent in nonperforming loans to approximately one-half of total credits in mid-1999 would appear to have at least stabilized by late 1999. The fact that more than one-half of the borrowed funds in the aggregate lending book had ceased to meet timely repayment schedules is a matter not due entirely to borrowers' inability but also to their unwillingness. Such borrowers are characterized locally as "strategic" nonperformers. The critical questions, then, are what proportion of the total nonaccruing advances are indeed strategic and what would trigger the discharge of the obligations of such borrowers.

Local speculation over the extent of strategic defaults converges on an estimate of at least one-third of the total; public statements by a prominent Thai bank president who claimed that some 400 billion baht ($10 billion) in strategic defaults were owed by local politicians have fueled that speculation. Meanwhile, the costs of a nonpayment culture manifest themselves in

—ineffective and costly financial intermediation,

—prohibited access to global capital markets,

—diminished business and consumer confidence,

—higher risk premiums on all credit transactions,

—deserving economic agents denied credit, and

—retarded economic and social development.

Capturing Potential Troubles in the Balance Sheet Earlier

On March 31, 1998, the Bank of Thailand announced new regulations governing the classification of advances that were designed to recognize troubled advances earlier and oblige the banks to provision more prudently. The guidelines that began to be phased into effect the following July reaffirmed, however, that the manner in which advances are to be classified remains largely at the discretion of bank management when assessing the capacity of a borrower to meet timely repayment schedules. Those guide-lines acknowledged that the uncertainty with respect to collectability of principal and interest from an advance must be tied into an aging schedule.

Although it has introduced a greater focus on the assessment of the credit quality of borrowers, the recognition of troubled advances is still subject to a time line and, more notably, to the discretion of bank management. The process is designed to ensure that troubled debt is subject routinely to credit assessments. For instance, if an advance is fully secured, it should generally be classified at least as substandard when it is more than three months over-due, and at least doubtful when more than six months overdue.

The process, however, does not remove the risk that banks will not fully satisfy the regulations outlined by the central bank. For example, if a bank's substandard loans as a proportion of total classified loans are relatively high, the implication could be that the time-imposed migration to the doubtful classification is being forestalled to avoid more cumbersome spe-cific provisions. Subjective assessments of conservatism or prudence are difficult to make and equally difficult to legislate. Accordingly, a critical appraisal of an individual bank's management culture is crucial to an assess-ment of the asset quality of a balance sheet.

Restructured versus Rescheduled Advances

A thorough understanding of the treatment of restructured or rescheduled loans by banks, especially during an acute crisis, is essential to asset quality assessments. Rescheduled loans are those in which a bank has made con-cessions on a borrower's principal or interest payments (or both)—in other words, advances made on noncommercial terms. Best practices recom-mend that such facilities be classified at least as substandard. Only after such facilities have been serviced on a timely basis over at least a twelve-month period, irrespective of security, should they be upgraded to the nor-mal or "pass" classification.

The process of restructuring bad debt in Thailand, as well as its slow pace, has attracted broad criticism and controversy over what constitutes material workout agreements. The extent to which substantial restructur-ing has taken place over fiscal year 1999 remains in dispute. On the basis of most recently published data for the financial institutions in aggregate (see appendix tables 6A-1, 6A-2), the proportion of reported overdue loans was 2,456 billion baht ($65 billion), or 43.8 percent of total loans. How-ever, the amount of reported restructured loans rose sharply to 826 billion baht—an additional 14.8 percent of total credits (from 2.6 percent at the start of the year), or fully one-third of reported nonperforming loans.

The authorities attribute the swift pace of restructuring to several factors: (1) the new intercreditor and debtor-creditor agreements championed in March 1999 by the Corporate Debt Restructuring Advisory Committee (CDRAC); (2) the enactment of substantive and material amendments, again in March, to foreclosure and bankruptcy legislation; and (3) the installation of a judicial panel dedicated to arbitrating bankruptcy cases (although no case precedents have yet been established). Undoubtedly a significant portion of the CDRAC-approved bad debt restructuring plans have been reasonable renegotiations on delinquent penalty charges and interest rates, debt-equity swaps, and principal maturity extensions. However, the speed and scale of those workout agreements could imply that doubtful and irrecoverable credits were only being rescheduled.

Provisioning

The provisioning need for the unsecured balances of substandard loans is generally 20 percent, 50 percent for doubtful, and 100 percent for loss classifications. Specific provisions should normally be made once an advance is classified as substandard, which is typically 20 percent against the unsecured balance. When the overdue period rises beyond six months, an advance must be reclassified to doubtful. Generally, specific provisions of at least 50 percent against the unsecured balance of such a classified advance are required; however, provisions as high as 100 percent may also be appropriate if realizability of security is unlikely.

Pressed to meet the more demanding loan loss reserve requirements, the banks were eager to reclassify marginal credits and evade taking more crippling provision charges, as well as to continue to accrue interest income. Prospects for such behavior were made easier with the October 1999 revisions to the classification of, and prerequisite provisioning for, all advances. The banks are now allowed to remove credits from nonaccrual status after only one interest payment (that is, one month) versus the twelve-month international best practice (hence our concern that such credits have been misclassified). Further, the provision requirements on normal and special-mention classified advances have been relaxed to 1 percent and 2 percent of the uncollateralized portions of such facilities instead of the nominal outstanding balance. We consider these revisions excessive forbearance in what has been, on balance, a credible program of financial system reform.

Thai generally accepted accounting principles with respect to loan-loss reserve requirements do not address the critical components of the calculation of need, namely, an acceptable valuation of underlying collateral and its realizability. This issue is particularly relevant in Thailand: real estate is the predominant security, and valuations on such security had been maintained at unrealistic levels when that distended asset bubble burst. Owing to a cultural disposition and an as-yet-untested legal mechanism to extract security from creditors in default, the property market remains characterized by severely illiquid conditions and, consequently, bid-offer spreads that are out of all reasonable proportion.

Ideally the banks need to abandon such a practice in favor of provisioning on the basis of international best practices by discounting future interest payments on a flagged credit. Such a change, however, would need to be phased in only after present asset quality and capital levels have improved. Therefore, we would hope to see Thailand adopt, as has South Korea, a more forward-looking provisioning practice.

Recapitalization of Balance Sheets

Vital to the recovery program implemented by the government were the recapitalization schemes to bolster both Tier I and Tier II capital bases of financial institutions. The Tier I capital support facility was designed to induce greater private capital investment. The Tier II scheme aimed to create incentives to accelerate corporate debt restructuring and encourage new lending (which has not taken place in a material way since before the onset of the crisis in mid-1997).

Under the Tier I support scheme, the authorities required that a qualifying bank make full loan-loss reserves on classified loans by fiscal year-end 2000. (At fiscal year-end 1999, approximately 80 percent of all reported nonperforming loans had met regulatory minimums.) If the Tier I BIS-style capital adequacy ratio were to then fall below 2.5 percent, the government would recapitalize the institution by the amount of deficit. Beyond that level, the government would inject Tier I capital up to the amount provided by private investors.

Under the Tier II support facility, capital injections would be made in consideration for the exchange of nontradable government bonds for debentures issued by a qualifying bank, subject to well-defined criteria. As an additional incentive, institutions that satisfied in advance the new full-provisioning rule would be allowed to capitalize portions of bad asset write-

Table 6-6. *Capital Funds Profile of Thai Financial Sector (at November 30, 1999)*

Category	Tier I capital	Tier II capital	Total capital
Thai banks and finance companies			
(millions of baht)	559,145	163,538	722,683
Percent of which:			
Thai banks	89.9	98.7	91.9
Private banks	55.4	85.5	62.2
Government banks	34.6	13.2	29.7
Finance companies	10.1	1.3	8.1
Private banks and finance companies	65.4	86.8	70.3

Source: Bank of Thailand.

downs arising from approved debt restructuring agreements for a five-year period.

Since being offered, these programs have attracted 38.4 billion baht in capital from the Ministry of Finance, with Tier I capital comprising 35.5 billion baht of that total (see table 6-6). Since the end of December 1997, all domestic financial institutions had sourced (directly or indirectly though debt-equity swaps) more than 179 billion baht, which boosted the capital base of the financial system to 723 billion baht ($19 billion) at the end of November 1999. Over the same period, the commercial banks were able to increase Tier I capital by one-third (or 128 billion baht) to 503 billion baht.

Addressing Bank Capital

The recent debt crisis among emerging markets has highlighted the shortcomings of the existing BIS capital adequacy accord, namely, that credit risk has been calibrated by the broad stroke of asset class without a finer appreciation for the inherent risks of dramatic swings in interest rates, liquidity, internal bank operations, or management competence. A new capital adequacy accord, anticipated in 2001, will attempt to synthesize the measures of risk in order to achieve more sensible minimum standards by refining definitions of regulatory capital; measures of risk exposure, and rules specifying the appropriate level of capital relative to such risks; supervisory review; and, for better or worse, market discipline vis-à-vis the

enhanced role of the raters. We agree firmly with the view of the Basel
Committee that the potential benefits to accrue from more refined risk-
calibration techniques cannot substitute for effective bank management.
Meanwhile, we are left with the task of determining an appropriate treatment for the capital reported in the balance sheets of the Thai banks.

At the end of June 1999, Tier I capital within the aggregate banking system was reported by the central bank to be 369.8 billion baht ($9.3 bil-
lion), which produced an averaged BIS-style Tier I capital ratio of 8.14 percent. Coupled with Tier II capital of 206.8 billion baht, the risk-adjusted
ratio climbed to 12.68 percent. Such capital ratio levels suggest observance
of the Basel Accord minimum standard as well as adequate protection for
senior creditors. However, realistic adjustments to reported capital produce
a markedly different reality—one of deep capital deficit. The recalculation
of capital is necessary owing to the huge stock of doubtful advances that
remain largely underprovisioned, misclassification of rescheduled advances
as performing assets, and regulatory forbearance that has overstated Tier I
capital through the relaxed application of capital securities. However, a
good deal of newly raised capital has been in the form of structured capital securities issued through newly created special-purpose vehicles (SPVs).
These legal entities are dedicated to sourcing capital for the banks by raising Tier I qualifying equity in a tax-efficient way. The SPVs issue preferred
shares to investors, with the proceeds then lent back to the banks (or their
branches) through subordinated debentures issued by the bank. The interest payments on these issues are then passed on to the investors as dividends on the preferred shares and are also tax deductible for the banks.

A number of risks and problems are associated with such a recapitalization alternative, not least of which is the excessive future cost. Under a
more strict definition, these instruments would not qualify as Tier I capital, and given that many of the holders of these instruments were former
depositors switching into these securities, limited fresh equity capital is in
fact being brought into the balance sheets. Indeed, the central bank has
moved twice in a matter of months to restrict the use of such instruments
(now limited to one-quarter of a bank's capital measurement) as a qualifying capital constituent.

Strengthening Supervision and Prudential Guidelines

Efforts undertaken by the Thai government to strengthen supervision and
prudential guidelines must be judged as effective in providing a sounder

basis on which to rebuild confidence and credibility in the further development of the country. Since late 1997, the authorities have succeeded in implementing wholesale changes to the regulation and supervision of financial institutions, as well as a raft of changes to standards of financial disclosure.

A new Financial Institutions Act is soon to be enacted with the aim of standardizing the regulatory framework for all financial institutions, and a new Bank of Thailand Act is also to be promulgated with the laudable aim of enhancing the independence and accountability of the central bank. The proposal, expected to be enacted by third quarter 2000, will pave the way for the central bank to pursue explicit inflation targets in conducting monetary policy. Inflation targeting represents an important tool in efforts to anchor price expectations and counter fears that rising public sector debt might need to be monetized soon. The success of this tool, however, will depend upon a high degree of transparency in the conduct of monetary policy. To that end, the legislation also envisages creation of a monetary policy board, composed of five senior central bank executives and four private sector economists, and charged with issuing two-year inflation targets.

The central bank is already undergoing a wholesale restructuring for greater operational efficiency. The structure of the organization has been flattened, with the numbers of deputy and assistant governors rising at the expense of middle management. Training for financial institutions examiners has also been established, with special training schools being set up to certify officers. There also has been a significant drive to improve the quality and timeliness of the publication of data series, with a significant investment in information technology and personnel.

Structural Reform Efforts

Critical to the material, long-term success of any reform effort is the removal of structural impediments from within both the financial and the real economies. The Thai government scores high marks for improving the prospects of, and the foundation for, sustainable economic growth. Fractious coalition governments are often plagued by impotency and short-lived administrations; the achievements of the present government since year-end 1997 are nothing less than miraculous. The net performance of the government has provided the necessary fillip to confidently addressing and removing certain chronic impediments to a responsive legal code (see table 6-7).

Table 6-7. *Amendments to Thai Legal Code, 1999–Present*

Legislation	Main objective
Bankruptcy Court Act (enacted April 8, 1999)	To establish specialized bankruptcy court with specialized procedure
	To deploy specially trained jurists in bankruptcy matters
Amendment to the Bankruptcy Act (en-(acted April 21, 1999)	To allow individuals to file for bankruptcy when debt exceeds 1 million baht (instead of 50,000 baht)
	To allow businesses to file for bankruptcy when debt exceeds 2 million baht (instead of 500,000 baht)
	To allow creditors to claim for repayment if debts are for rehabilitating an insolvent debtor's business
	To allow debtors to retain fixed assets valued at up to 100,000 baht
	To introduce new creditor classifications to expedite rehabilitation plans
	To reduce bankruptcy status from ten to three years
Amendment to Civil Code on Petty Cases (enacted May 3, 1999)	To expedite legal proceedings of petty indebtedness cases
Amendment to Civil Code on Execution of Judgment (enacted May 3, 1999)	To limit court's discretionary power on rescinding auctions to: fraud among bidders and officers' malfeasance
	Restricts appeals of certain court orders
Amendment to Civil Code on Default Judgment (pending in Senate)	To limit defendant rights when defendant is in willful default
Corporatization Bill (pending before Constitutional Court)	To convert state enterprises into corporations; state ownership will be converted into shares
	To establish a corporatization committee to oversee the conversion process
Alien Business Bill (pending before Parliament)	To require foreign investors who ask for permission to conduct business in Thailand to bring in capital (amount of capital depends upon the type of business)
	To allow greater liberalization in the job categories allowed for foreigners
Act on Leasing Property for Commerce and Industry (enacted May 18, 1999)	To extend leasing periods to 50 years, renewable for another 50 years
	To define leasing rights as transferable asset rights
Amendment to Land Code (enacted May 1999)	To allow foreign investors who bring in at least 40 million baht capital to own 1 rai (0.25 acres) of land for residence
Amendment to Condominium Act (enacted April 27, 1999)	To allow foreigners to own more than 49 percent of the space of condominiums in Bangkok, municipal areas, or local if total space is less than 5 rai (1.25 acres)
	To allow foreign ownership up to 49 percent of condominiums outside the above areas
Social Security Law (enacted March 31, 1999)	To extend compensation period from six to twelve months for unemployed who are insured under law

The government has also stressed its commitment to other major planks of reform, namely, the privatization of state-owned enterprises, liberalization of tariff regimes, and the development of long-term capital markets.

Conclusions

If received wisdom maintains that a vigorous financial system is the sine qua non of a robust real economy, then the recent positive signals from the accounts of the real economy, particularly the external accounts position, must appear rather frail against the acute crisis that still characterizes the financial economy of Thailand.

What is no longer in dispute from recent economic data points and subsequent data series is a confirmed positive trend in real economic activity. The balance-of-payments surplus and deeper usable foreign exchange reserves continue to underpin the improving external liquidity profile for the real economy. Export volumes have been revived beyond expectations and, in tandem with positive trends in production and (select) domestic consumption indicators, have given rise to estimates of real GDP expansion on the order of 4 percent year-on-year. The additional significance of such growth is evident by contrast to the dramatic 10 percent contraction during the previous fiscal period.

What is in dispute, however, is the extent to which claims of material recovery in the financial economy have taken place over fiscal year 1999. Although much has been accomplished successfully since the Thai markets were first subjected to convulsive change in mid-1997, policy in respect of the financial system has tended to be motivated more by the desire to postpone the recognition of problems than full rehabilitation. The following points summarize our view of the present state of the banks of Thailand.

First, the bad news about the banks in Thailand at fiscal year-end 1999:

—The financial statements do not reflect a true or accurate financial reality.

—A huge stock of doubtful credits remain on book; these credits are largely underprovisioned.

—Rescheduled loans are being misclassified as performing assets; accordingly, the notional values and ratios of impaired loans are not declining materially.

—Full or partial repayments of interest on troubled advances are being passed generally through the profit-and-loss and are not being applied to reducing principal.

—Provisioning policy on the basis of ill-assessed collateral lends to provisioning shortfall.

—Material debt restructuring has yet to gain momentum.

—Regulatory forbearance has allowed for the overstatement of Tier I capital.

—Crippling provisions resulted in net attributable losses for fiscal year 1999 of 332 billion baht ($9 billion).

—Capital remains in deep deficit at most financial institutions.

Now, the good news:

—Although insufficient, considerable capital, from both domestic public and private sectors as well as from foreigners, has been brought into the principal banks. Prospects are encouraging that much of the additional need can be sourced for the principal banks.

—The state retains further capacity to provide liquidity and capital support and remains committed to reform.

—Substantive changes in bankruptcy and foreclosure legislation in March 1999 have laid the foundation for future bad debt resolution.

—The new, stout wedge of foreign expertise and capital will introduce greater discipline and opportunity in the domestic lending market.

—Capital markets will play a larger role in the provision of finance for the real economy, which in conjunction with foreign participation should lead ultimately to more efficient intermediation.

—The structure of funding (and liquidity) has improved with the higher proportion of baht funding.

Indonesia

Although signs of stability have been emerging in recent months, Indonesia's banking sector remains the most deeply distressed among the countries affected by the Asian financial crisis. The country's response to the crisis has from the beginning been overwhelmed by domestic political events, ranging from the Suharto government's downfall to the independence claims of various provinces. These issues and the uncertainty that they have brought to bear on the country's three recent administrations have hampered the implementation of clear and consistent policy responses. As a result, the rebuilding of Indonesia's banking sector is likely to be the most drawn out and expensive of those experienced by any of the countries in the region.

Indonesia's banking sector, like those of its neighbors, had serious structural problems that have been clearly exposed over the last two years. These included:

—a weak regulatory and supervisory environment,

—an inadequate legal framework for pursuing recalcitrant borrowers,

—ownership nexus between industrial conglomerates and private commercial banks,

—rampant related-party lending by private commercial banks,

—poor and unreliable disclosure by banks,

—politically driven lending by state-owned banks, and

—rapid lending growth in the period before the crisis.

On top of this, a political regime that fostered an environment of pervasive corruption meant that the rule of law was not easy to implement. Such a system also meant that the country's bureaucracy and judiciary had limited capacity or incentive to quickly institute needed policies and reforms. The lack of clear, well-explained, and consistently applied policy responses has been a critical ongoing weakness of Indonesia's reaction to the crisis. The early decision to close a small number of banks was an example. The fact that one of the banks, associated with one of former president Suharto's children, was then able to recommence business under another name raised the specter of political interference. At the same time, a lack of disclosure regarding the health of remaining banks meant that nothing was done to allay depositor concerns about the health of the rest of the sector. This created the conditions that led to bank runs at a number of banks and, in due course, to the introduction of the government guarantee system that has proved exceedingly costly. By issuing a blanket guarantee, the government raised the moral hazard stakes as some bank owners siphoned off central bank support well in excess of realistic levels. The government has yet to reach agreement with several of these bank owners regarding their obligation to repay such money; it is difficult to encourage borrowers to repay if owners of the banks are not obliged to do the same.

The institution central to rebuilding the country's economy is the Indonesian Bank Restructuring Agency (IBRA). Initially set up by the Suharto government and charged with restructuring the banking sector, its reach has grown extraordinary (see box 6-3). IBRA has direct control over most of the Indonesian banking sector (including state banks and major private commercial banks), and it controls roughly three-quarters of all corporate assets. For those reasons, IBRA is under enormous pressure from many competing interests. Progress has been painstakingly slow, although

Box 6-3. *Indonesian Bank Restructuring Agency Objectives*

Bank solvency, restructuring, and sale
IBRA's initial mandate was to help the banking sector back to health. The aim was
to put in place a framework for ensuring the solvency of banks under its control
(through recapitalization), restructuring some names, and then selling its stakes in
the surviving names. The recapitalization program is based on the principle that
proper investment by the government will help to avoid greater losses later. The plan
is to protect well-managed but troubled banks and endeavor to keep them in the private sector. While there is no specified target number of surviving banks, the
Indonesian authorities are working under the broad aim of a core of large national
banking franchises supported by a larger number of smaller niche players.

Loan recovery, restructuring and sale
Bad assets of banks that were closed have been transferred to IBRA, along with problem loans in banks that have been recapitalized and taken over by the government.
IBRA's second objective is to maximize the recoveries from this portfolio. IBRA has
an asset management unit (AMU) responsible for this program. The AMU will seek
to bundle loans into loan pools that can then be sold to investor groups. Some of the
noncore assets controlled by the AMU have already been sold by auction.

Monitoring and sale of corporate assets
As part of the process of achieving commercial settlement with the owners of some
of Indonesia's largest failed banks, IBRA has become custodian of a large swath of
corporate assets. These assets have been pledged to IBRA to offset liquidity credits
and related party lending at the failed banks. An asset management investment
(AMI) unit has been established to handle these. The assets are placed under various
holding companies related to each shareholding group.

the scale of its task should not be underestimated. Initially, IBRA's lack of
progress stemmed from the fact that it was not given the legal teeth to
stand up to the interests fighting it. Steps have been taken to remove some
of the political pressures by placing the agency under the direct control of
the president rather than the Ministry of Finance, and it has been given
substantial extrajudicial powers to deal with recalcitrant debtors. Like
many Indonesian institutions, IBRA has not been particularly successful in
explaining its procedures and implementing them consistently. Given the

extent of what it controls and the role that it is expected to play, such transparency will be essential to its ultimate success.

Indonesia has also instituted a series of reforms that have the potential to substantially alter the structure and workings of the country's financial sector over the medium to long term. These include:
 —the enactment of new bankruptcy laws
 —a narrowed focus for a newly independent central bank
 —the lifting of foreign ownership restrictions, and
 —the promulgation of numerous banking regulations.
However, as has long been the case, the challenge will be effective and consistent implementation of these measures. Policies related to rebuilding the financial sector have suffered numerous reversals and delays, and deeply entrenched interests are fighting hard against reform. Although improving the environment in which the banks operate is a necessary step in strengthening the banking system, there remain a number of areas that need further development.

OWNERSHIP STRUCTURES. The ownership nexus between nonfinancial companies and banks fostered an environment in which many banks lent to related companies far in excess of legal limits. Although rules governing related-party lending have been tightened, former owners of troubled banks participating in the recapitalization scheme are eligible to buy back the government stakes in their banks over the next few years. It remains to be seen whether the penalties will be sufficient to deter the recurrence of such practices.

CREDIT CULTURE. In addition to lending on the basis of group connections, much Indonesian lending has been asset-based, with comparatively little attention given to the underlying viability of the business being lent to. The Indonesian authorities have started to address this by incorporating cash-flow analysis in asset classification criteria, but there is little clear evidence yet of banks incorporating such analysis in credit approval processes.

RISK MANAGEMENT. To date, there is little evidence that Indonesian banks have significantly improved internal risk management systems to recognize potential problems and take action to reduce them.

GOVERNMENT OWNERSHIP OF BANKS. Indonesia's state-owned banks still dominate the domestic banking industry, although it is clear that governments are generally poor allocators of credit. There are plans for the partial privatization of the country's largest state bank, and outside firms are being used to improve the operations of the state banks. However, these changes will take time to filter through under circumstances where new disciplines are needed urgently. With the banking system stabilized, Indonesia now has a long path ahead in its attempt to build a strong industry for the future.

Recapitalizing Remaining Banks

It took until January 1998, under a presidential decree, for the Indonesian government to establish IBRA as the lead agency charged with overseeing the reconstruction of the financial sector. The agency's initial efforts were hampered by a weak legal and regulatory framework (although this was eventually remedied), and it was given special powers to take over, close, and control banks that were in serious financial difficulties. However, this initial weakness meant that IBRA spent longer on the task of trying to stabilize the financial system and closing down nonviable institutions before it was in a position to focus on the future structure of the industry.

IBRA's early actions resulted in the closure of a large number of banks; these had severely negative net worth and no significant value or franchise importance to the system. It was cheaper to close than to rehabilitate these names. However, even among the most deeply troubled banks, there were several that IBRA completely took over. The rationale for "nationalization" of these names was that they either had significant value or franchise importance to the system (for example, Bank Danamon and Bank Central Asia) or had moderate negative net worth, no legal violations and significant franchise value (for example, Bank Tiara and Bank PDFCI). Although in some cases previous shareholders were allowed to retain very minor stakes, the government has sought to rehabilitate the banks through recapitalization and then reprivatize them.

By mid-1998, it was clear that all banks in the sector, even the better names, had been seriously affected by the events of the previous year and a half. The Indonesian authorities decided to review the remaining banks to determine which had the potential to survive. These would form the nucleus of the private banking sector going forward. The early actions of IBRA, and its birth during the last months of the Suharto administration, raised concerns over potential interference in the selection process. As a result, and given the sizable fiscal impact of any bank recapitalization, independent international auditors were contracted to review all remaining banks and classify them into three groups:

—Category A banks, with capital adequacy ratios in excess of the regulatory minimum 4 percent,

—Category B banks, with capital adequacy ratios between 4 percent and –25 percent,

—Category C banks, with capital adequacy ratios below –25 percent. The banks were also required to submit business plans that showed their viability over a three-year period, and their management was required to pass a fit-and-proper test, ensuring that they were both technically competent to run a bank and appropriately law abiding.

On the basis of the review, the Indonesian authorities announced the following findings in March 1999:

—Seventy-three category A banks had already met the 4 percent capital adequacy requirements and were deemed able to compete without public assistance. Some had received capital injections immediately prior to the reviews and these were verified and approved by various evaluation committees to ensure that the funds had been received from appropriate sources.

—Nine category B banks were deemed eligible for recapitalization, and seven category B banks were taken over by IBRA. These banks were in serious financial difficulty, although it was stated that due to their extensive branch networks, they would be taken over (and not closed) to minimize disruption of the payments system. Former owners were blocked from further roles in the management of banks, and IBRA decided on senior management replacements (where needed). The intention was to restructure these banks, improve their financial performance, reduce their burden on the budget, and prepare them for privatization. However, little progress was made, and the condition of these banks has continued to deteriorate. As a result, there is no hope of reviving any of these institutions and they will be merged into Bank Danamon by the end of September 2000. IBRA plans to reprivatize Bank Danamon after the merger of the category B banks.

—Twenty-one category B banks and seventeen category C banks were closed. The banks were all deeply insolvent and considered to have no hope of recovering. Owners were required to enter into agreements to repay related-party lending.

THE RECAPITALIZATION SCHEME. Indonesia is recapitalizing its state-owned banks, provincial development banks, the banks taken over (a necessary step before being able to reprivatize them), and selected private commercial banks.

Clearly the last group is the most controversial. The Indonesian authorities were anxious to avoid domestic criticism that the Indonesian taxpayers were being asked to bail out the country's banks without the banks' owners incurring personal financial loss. The personal liability of bank owners was a particularly pressing issue, since many of the banks eligible for recapitalization were owned by some of the country's major conglomerates. The recapitalization scheme required existing shareholders to provide at least 20 percent (in cash) of the total funds necessary to restore the bank's capital adequacy ratio to 4 percent before IBRA would put in any funds. Once that mark had been reached, IBRA injected the remaining 80 percent in the form of recapitalization bonds. The bonds are held on the balance sheets of the banks (although a portion is to be eligible for trading) and yield an interest rate sufficiently high to allow banks to earn positive interest spreads. As part of the recapitalization process, the banks were also required to transfer the worst of their problem loans (category 5—loss loans) at zero price to IBRA's asset management unit. The banks retain management control and original shareholders have the right to repurchase IBRA's stake within a three-year period at agreed prices.

WHAT WILL IT COST? IBRA's estimate of the government's share of bank recapitalization costs was announced in May 1999 and is shown in table 6-8.

The issuance of bonds for recapitalizing most of the private commercial banks, the major banks taken over (Danamon and Bank of Central Asia), and the provincial development banks has proceeded as planned. However, there have been delays in issuing bonds to the state-owned banks. As a result, the banks have recorded significant further losses throughout the remainder of 1999, thereby further increasing the amount of recapitalization needed. As an example, the recapitalization of Bank Mandiri was originally estimated at around 138 trillion rupiah. However, by the end of December 1999, the bank had received 178 trillion rupiah of recapitalization bonds, and more will likely be needed. Clearly, further delays are adding to the eventual burden of bank recapitalization According to the January 2000 letter of intent that the Indonesian government signed with the International Monetary Fund, the government issued bonds totaling around 500 trillion rupiah by December 1999 for the purpose of bank recapitalization and repayment of liquidity support to the central bank. The letter of intent estimates that another 140 trillion rupiah in bonds will need to be issued by mid-2000, principally to complete the recapitalization of the state banks. This will bring the total to more than 640 trillion rupiah.

Table 6-8. *Indonesian Government's Share of Recapitalization Costs*
Trillions of rupiah

Bank category	Recapitalization needs (estimated)
State banks	233.25
Private commercial banks	24.55
Banks taken over	92.57
Provincial development banks	1.23
Total	351.60

Source: IBRA, May 29, 1999, announcement.

ASSESSING THE RECAPITALIZATION SCHEME. Clearly any scheme that offers public funds in support of private banks will inevitably be subject to careful scrutiny. Indonesia's bank recapitalization scheme has been dogged by criticism, ranging from the time that it took to formulate the scheme to the delays in issuing funds and the types of banks that are being recapitalized.

From the outset of the crisis, the Indonesian authorities shied away from picking winners and, instead, have gone to great lengths to support almost all banks—largely because of early fears about systemic risks arising from bank runs. Even when several banks were closed early in the crisis, a lack of transparency about the processes involved and insufficient disclosure about the health of remaining banks left many doubts hanging over the health of the system itself. It was in this climate, combined with political uncertainties, that runs occurred on several banks, including the two largest private banks in the country, resulting in their eventual nationalization. Before being taken over by the government, enormous amounts of emergency liquidity support were pumped into the banks, even though the weak supervisory powers of the central bank meant that, in a number of instances, this support was well in excess of the banks' asset base (and well in excess of the central bank's internal limits). Reports indicate that after the closure of the first group of banks, President Suharto expressed opposition to any further closures. Given the central bank's lack of independence at that time, this has been cited as one of the major reasons behind the extent of the support given. While it is understandable that the government would choose to nationalize and revive major names through recapitalization, clearly the eventual cost to the taxpayer has been greater than needed.

IBRA appears to have learned some lessons from the earlier experiences, and the criteria for choosing private commercial banks eligible to participate in the recapitalization scheme have been well publicized. However shareholders of the banks being recapitalized were required to come up with only 20 percent of the funds needed to restore capital adequacy ratios to 4 percent. In addition, shareholders are able to repurchase the government stake in the bank after three years at pre-set prices. Given that most of the large, recapitalized banks were controlled by major conglomerates, questions have been raised regarding the appropriateness of such moves. The ownership nexus between banks and conglomerates was one of the major structural weaknesses of the Indonesian banking sector and the recapitalization scheme sets the scene for its continuation.

It also remains to be seen whether the recapitalization scheme results in a healthy banking sector. The scheme restores the capital adequacy ratios of the banks to a paltry 4 percent, and, with many of them continuing to rack up significant losses, clearly much more capital will be needed before these banks can be said to be back on solid ground.

Resolving Nonperforming Loans

The level of nonperforming loans in the Indonesian banking system reached extraordinary peaks, even compared to that of the other banking systems affected by the fallout from the Asian economic crisis. Although peak nonperforming loan levels varied widely between banks, government figures put the levels at between 60 percent and 90 percent of loans outstanding for most names. A lack of reliable statistics and reporting standards in the past has made it difficult to gauge the true level of nonperforming loans in the system; however, with the introduction of internationally accepted standards of classification and quarterly reporting of figures, it is gradually becoming easier to track the level of nonperforming loans.

Clearly, with such extraordinary levels of nonperforming loans, the Indonesian banking system has been severely compromised. Banks incurred huge losses as a result of the need to make substantial provisions against problem loans, while earnings capacity was eroded as recording of interest income on nonperforming loans changed from accrual to cash basis. The huge losses wiped out the capital bases of much of the banking sector, leaving it deeply insolvent. Within the framework of IBRA, the Indonesian authorities established a government asset management unit

(AMU) to facilitate removal of nonperforming loans from the banking system. The AMU is charged with taking over the nonperforming loans and implementing loan recovery plans that involve a variety of methods, including collection, loan workouts, and packaging of the loans for sale to third parties. The rationale for transferring these assets to the AMU is that by removing the burden of problem loans on management and financial resources, the surviving banks will be in a better position to provide new credit to the market and they will be more attractive propositions for new investors.

The AMU has taken over loans from a variety of institutions: closed banks, banks taken over, state-owned banks, and banks participating in the recapitalization scheme. However, not all loans in these banks have been transferred. As mentioned earlier, the introduction of a tighter loan classification system required all banks to categorize their portfolios into five tiers (pass, special mention, substandard, doubtful, and loss). The loans transferred to the AMU are dependent upon the classification of the bank:
—closed banks: all loans transferred to AMU,
—banks taken over: all doubtful and loss loans transferred to AMU,
—state-owned banks: all doubtful and loss loans transferred to AMU,
—recapitalized banks: all loss loans transferred to AMU.
To ensure that the nonperforming loans being transferred are genuine and not simply debt relief for well-connected borrowers, IBRA auditors verify the status of the loans. Additionally, related-party and back-to-back loans have to be repaid before controlling shareholders of the closed banks and banks taken over are released from their liabilities.

Given its limited resources, IBRA has been unable to administer all of these loans on its own. Bad loans of less than 5 billion rupiah are handled by the individual banks; bad loans valued at between 5 billion and 35 billion rupiah are subcontracted back to the individual banks (implementation remains under the supervision of the AMU); bad loans in excess of 25 billion rupiah are handled directly by the AMU. In addition to loans, some noncore assets, including automobiles and office equipment, as well as other fixed assets, have been transferred to the AMU. The Indonesian government indicated that the total amount of problem debt transferred to the AMU as of January 2000 was approximately 250 trillion rupiah. This will continue to grow and is expected to top 300 trillion rupiah.

The IBRA has come under substantial domestic and international criticism for its slow progress in dealing with the assets under its stewardship. The agency is still in the process of consolidating loans transferred from banks in preparation for sale. Has the nonperforming loan burden been substantially reduced? For the closed banks, this is a moot point. For the banks taken over, state-owned banks, and recapitalized banks, transfers of the worst of their nonperforming loan burden has made a significant difference. This does not mean, however, that the portfolios of these banks have been cleansed. Many continue to show a high percentage of problem loans, albeit in less distressed categories. (However, it should be noted that for some of the larger banks, problem loans have been reduced to such an extent that they now represent only a very small portion of total assets.) The ongoing difficult market conditions have meant that many borrowers have migrated downward through the various problem asset categories, a process that will see additional loans being transferred to the AMU. This was highlighted by the January 2000 announcement by IBRA that a further 1 trillion rupiah in category 5 (loss) loans had been transferred from state-owned banks.

Regulatory Framework

Starting with reforms in the late 1980s that spurred rapid growth in the Indonesian financial industry, regulation and supervision of the Indonesian banking sector has undergone substantial change over the last twenty years. New directives have made all banks subject to a uniform set of lending limits and related-party loan exposure levels. Following the collapse of one of the country's largest banks and the near-collapse of several others, authorities quickly put in place additional measures that were codified in the Banking Act of 1992. These measures included minimum capital requirements, adherence to BIS-style capital adequacy measures, ceilings on offshore borrowing by Indonesian banks, and periodic reporting requirements. The regulatory environment continued to be strengthened through the remainder of the 1990s, with the result that, on paper, Indonesia had in place a modern and fairly comprehensive set of banking regulations.

However, without consistent and adequate enforcement by banking supervisors, the regulatory environment quickly eroded. Poor investigation, inadequate enforcement, and backtracking on implementation of rules helped create vulnerabilities in the banking sector. It was widely suspected that several private banking institutions were lending amounts well in excess of legal lending limits, although proving this was impossible given poor transparency and the unreliability of information provided by banks. In the state-owned banking sector, the issue of politically driven lending to well-connected borrowers and projects (without regard to the underlying economic viability of the borrower or project) was frequently raised. However, poor transparency and the inability or unwillingness of state banks' management to resist government interference (understandable, given that it would likely have meant the termination of employment) meant that much was hidden. The regulatory and supervisory environment was compromised in key respects:

—Supervision of the banking system was the responsibility of the central bank, Bank Indonesia, which reported directly to the country's president. This structure left the door open to direct political interference, and it is widely agreed that on numerous occasions, prudential rules were breached by well-connected parties and that no penalties were brought against these individuals. Noncompliance with prudential rules was far from uncommon during the period immediately before the crisis and was only rarely punished by the central bank. Clearly, the absence of penalties raised the moral hazard stakes.

—During the years before the crisis, the Indonesian banking market was highly fragmented, comprising more than 220 commercial banks. The staff and resources of the central bank were insufficient to allow for adequate inspections of the banks under its supervision. During the crisis itself, the lack of resources meant that Bank Indonesia was unable to adequately verify claims for emergency liquidity support before disbursing funds. Subsequent investigations have revealed that during this period, the central bank lent substantial amounts to troubled banks, often in excess of the value of banks' assets. Indonesia's public servants are also comparatively poorly compensated for their work. This fostered an environment in which employees could be tempted by outside incentives.

—The central bank lacked a clear method for closing troubled banks. Before the crisis, the usual mechanism was for Bank Indonesia to engineer a rescue of stricken banks through moral suasion. This ad hoc process, and the lack of a deposit insurance or guarantee system, resulted in lingering threats to public confidence in Indonesia's banking system, demonstrated by the fact that rumors about a bank's solvency often resulted in bank runs. Although during the early stages of the crisis, the Indonesian authorities assumed control of several banks and closed others in attempts to rebuild confidence in the banking system, depositors remained unconvinced. This situation was exacerbated by ongoing political uncertainty, and eventually the central bank issued a blanket guarantee on all bank obligations. The guarantee will run through 2004, after which it will be replaced by a limited deposit insurance fund financed by the banking system.

—Many of Indonesia's largest private commercial banks have long been owned by some of the country's major industrial conglomerates. Though rules governing related-party lending were on the books, significant loopholes allowed conglomerates to lend substantial amounts to related companies or projects related to their groups. Back-to-back lending (under which Bank A would lend to Company B, which would lend the money to Company C, which had the same shareholders as Bank A) was widespread. The central bank did not have the sophistication to monitor these relationships and did not seem to understand the impact that financial problems within the conglomerate could have on banks.

STEPS TAKEN TO IMPROVE SUPERVISION. The most important change to the supervisory environment thus far has been the enactment (in May 1999) of a new law governing the powers and authority of the nation's central bank. The new law stipulates that Bank Indonesia has one central objective: to achieve and maintain the stability of the value of the rupiah. This aim is to be supported by three pillars: a monetary policy backed by prudential regulation, an effective payments system, and a sound banking and financial system.

Significantly, the law seeks to enhance the bank's independence as a state institution outside the administration of the executive branch. It no longer reports directly to the president but to the House of Representatives, and neither of these institutions have the ability to remove the governor or members of the board unless they are found guilty of criminal acts. The law also provides for the establishment of a new, independent supervisory body to replace the central bank as the banking system's regulator from the beginning of 2003. Until that time, banking regulation remains under the control of the central bank.

It will take time to improve the supervisory skills at the central bank. The bank has recently developed a master plan for enhancing supervision, and the IMF has agreed to assist the bank with the implementation of reforms needed to bring supervisory and examination skills up to international standards. Bank Indonesia plans to maintain significant on-site supervision at each of the state banks. In addition, under the letter of intent to the IMF, the Ministry of Finance is scheduled to develop related master plans for the oversight of the nonbank financial sector and the securities market.

Purging corruption at various levels of the Indonesian government and public service is a major aim of the administration of Abdurrahman

Wahid. However, achieving this is certain to be a protracted task. An important first step being undertaken in this regard is to improve the compensation structure of government employees.

STEPS TAKEN TO IMPROVE REGULATION. Indonesia has taken significant steps to improve banking rules and regulations over the last year. The country's banking law has been significantly amended and, as part of Indonesia's commitments to the IMF expressed in various letters of intent, the government has taken steps to review and strengthen banking regulation. Bank Indonesia has issued a number of decrees covering critical areas, including the following:

—*Liquidity monitoring.* Banks are required to submit consolidated liquidity-monitoring reports in domestic and foreign currencies for both domestic and offshore offices. Bank are required to report on a biweekly basis projected cash flow for the coming three months for on- and off-balance sheet exposures and to report balance sheet asset and liability maturity profiles monthly.

—*Legal lending limits.* One of the most significant problems in many of the closed or nationalized banks has been the overconcentration of lending to individual debtors or groups of debtors. As a result, the legal lending limit amounts have been significantly tightened. The legal lending limit for an individual nonconnected debtor or group of debtors is 30 percent of capital until December 31, 2001; 25 percent of capital during the year 2002; and 20 percent of capital as of January 1, 2003. The legal lending limit for connected parties (both individual debtors and groups of debtors) may not exceed 10 percent of capital,[5] and the legal lending limit for the *total* of connected parties may not exceed 10 percent of capital.

Banks are required to submit monthly reports on their legal lending limit positions to Bank Indonesia within fourteen days of month's end.

---

5. "Connected parties" are defined as individual shareholders (or their relatives) owning 10 percent or more of the paid-up capital of the bank; corporate or institutional shareholders owning 10 percent or more of the paid-up capital of the bank debtors; or group of debtors having a relationship with a bank's individual shareholders (or their relatives) owning 10 percent or more of the paid-up capital of the bank; corporate or institutional shareholders owning 10 percent or more of the paid-up capital of the bank; members of the board of commissioners of the bank (or their relatives); members of the board of managing directors of the bank (or their relatives); individuals owning 25 percent or more or taking control of the operation, supervision, or decisionmaking either directly or indirectly; bank officers assigned in the executive function who influence the operational direction of the bank or are directly responsible to the directors (or both); companies in which the parties in the above who hold an interest constituting 10 percent or more of ownership.

Where the legal lending limit is exceeded, banks must submit action plans to the central bank regarding the efforts needed to rectify the excess and specifying the time-frame within which it will be rectified. Subsequent implementation reports are then submitted until rectification occurs.

—*Capital adequacy requirements.* The minimum capital adequacy ratio that banks have to achieve has been reduced to 4 percent. Additionally, the amount of general provisions for earning assets that banks can include as supplementary capital is set at a maximum 1.25 percent of risk-weighted assets. Banks have until December 31, 2000, to achieve an 8 percent minimum.

—*Publication of financial statements.* Banks had previously been erratic about publishing financial data in a timely manner. They are now required to publish unaudited quarterly financial statements within two months of quarter's end and audited financial statements within four months of the end of the reporting year (December 31).

—*Earning asset classifications and allowance for earning asset losses.* Earning assets are now classified in the five following categories. The amounts required to be set aside against these are shown in parentheses: pass (1 percent), special mention (5 percent), substandard (10 percent), doubtful (50 percent), and loss (100 percent). The allowances set aside for substandard, doubtful, and bad assets are net of the value of collateral.

—*Debt restructuring.* The government has issued guidelines regarding the conditions under which debt can be restructured, how it is to be reported, provided against, and accounted for in the financial statements.

—*Net open position.* Banks are required to maintain their net open position in foreign currency at less than 20 percent of their capital. This is to be reported to the central bank on a weekly basis for the consolidated domestic operations and consolidated domestic and foreign operations.

—*Minimum capital requirements.* New commercial banks must have a minimum paid-up capital of 3 trillion rupiah, while new rural banks are required to have between 500 million and 2 billion rupiah, depending on where they are located.

—*Management.* Minimum standards for new members of bank boards of directors and commissioners have been set. In addition, management of all banks are subject to a fit-and-proper test, and the central bank now maintains a list of "bad bankers" who are not allowed to serve in management capacity.

The jury is still out on the Indonesian authorities' efforts to improve the regulatory and supervisory environment. The new central bank law goes some way toward creating a framework for improved supervision, and the tightened regulations plug many of the loopholes that existed before the crisis. However, it remains to be seen how effective these measures will be in improving the supervisory and regulatory environment.

The unwillingness to implement rules and penalties on a fair and consistent basis, free from external interference and pressure, has long been a key weakness in Indonesia. The recent record raises some concerns. There were numerous delays in the announcement of the category A, B, and C banks and their respective fates; this led to widespread speculation that pressure from well-connected banks and owners allowed them to be reclassified and escape closure.

As part of the authorities' review of the Indonesian banking sector in late 1998, senior management and owners of all banks were subject to a fit-and-proper test to ensure that they were both technically competent and law-abiding in their capacity to run a bank. The failure of some owners to meet this test led to their banks being closed during the last round of bank closures. However, the authorities failed to publish a list of the names of these officials, and punishment of their offences has been tardy.

Probably the most damaging evidence of continued weakness in banking supervision has come from the Bank Bali scandal. The case involved the payment of a 546 billion rupiah commission to a company connected with senior members of the Golkar political party in exchange for the company's services in helping the bank to recoup 904 billion rupiah of interbank claims from IBRA. That the issue came to light at all is in itself a positive development, but it is disappointing that the scandal was revealed not by the central bank, IBRA, or the government but rather by an independent banking analyst. Whether the country's regulators will aggressively implement banking laws and regulations on a consistent, transparent, and independent basis remains to be seen.

STRENGTHENING BANK MANAGEMENT AND CREDIT CULTURE. On paper, Indonesia had some of the strongest banking regulations in the region. These included qualitative requirements for eligibility as board members and shareholders.[6] However, the effectiveness of these measures in

---

6. Eligibility requirements provide that potential board members or shareholders have never committed a disreputable act in banking or been convicted of a banking or economic crime; at least 50 percent of the board must have no less than three years' banking experience; and, among other criteria, shareholders or bank management should not have engaged in misconduct or have been convicted of a banking or business crime.

bringing high-quality and reputable management to the sector is questionable. As noted earlier, the supervisory capacity of the Indonesian central bank was seriously compromised before the enactment of legislation that strengthened its powers, and breaches of prudential regulations had gone largely unpunished. But there were significant structural weaknesses in the banking sector as well.

One of these weaknesses was the control of large numbers of private sector banks by industrial conglomerates with diversified interests unrelated to banking. Results of reviews of nationalized banks have revealed that rules to prevent and discourage related-party lending have not been rigorously applied. Tracking this type of lending is extremely difficult, and many banks were skilled at maneuvering around the rules. Moreover, several bank owners abused the emergency liquidity credits disbursed by the central bank to help institutions facing the pressures of deposit runs. Some borrowed far in excess of their asset bases, and there is evidence that they channeled funds offshore. These abuses were behind IBRA's moves to require owners of nationalized and closed banks to surrender their personal assets to guarantee repayment of liquidity credits and related-party borrowings. This has been a difficult task, however, and IBRA is still negotiating with some of the former owners.

The Indonesian authorities have so far taken no steps to examine the ownership nexus between banks and industrial conglomerates. Indeed, IBRA's scheme for recapitalizing private commercial banks allows the previous owners of these banks to repurchase the government's shares over a three-year period, thereby restoring the former ownership structures in some of the sector's largest remaining entities. In the absence of a strong regulator, it may be more effective to consider rules limiting the control or influence that a single shareholder (or group of associated shareholders) has over the policies or operations of a bank.

Part of IBRA's review of the banking sector before its announcement of the banks' recapitalization was an examination of bank owners and management in order to determine whether they were "fit and proper" to run a bank—that is, technically competent and law-abiding. Several hundred Indonesian bankers failed this test; punishments have been slow, and IBRA has come under considerable criticism for not publishing the names. Unfortunately, the lack of decisive action erodes confidence that the country's regulators have at last found their teeth. Bank Indonesia included the fit-and-proper test in the banking regulations that it promulgated in January 2000, and it is to be hoped that the rules will be enforced aggressively.

The quality of management within the country's state-owned banks has also been subject to significant criticism, especially given evidence of extensive lending to politically connected borrowers. To some degree, such attention is misdirected, given the level of corruption that was endemic at the highest levels of the country's administration. Nonetheless, the government has announced that all directors at the country's state-owned banks will be replaced in light of concerns that they may attempt to hide past misdeeds. No clear timetable has been announced for this action, however, and it remains to be seen whether it will indeed be implemented.

Like a number of other countries in the region, Indonesia has concluded that the development of its banking system would benefit from significant investment by the international banking community. On an immediate level, allowing foreigners to own Indonesian banks would bring in an extra source of capital—vital, given the fiscal impact of rebuilding the banking system. However, over a longer period it will also allow the Indonesian banking sector to benefit from a broader range of technological and technical expertise. To date, however, there has been little actual foreign investment in the sector. The high-profile withdrawal of Standard Chartered Bank from its proposed acquisition of a major stake in Bank Bali, continued political instability, and increased nationalist sentiment make the conditions less than ideal for major investment. It may be that, on a more immediate basis, strategic alliances or technical agreements (already effected at some private banks and at the state-owned Bank Mandiri) will introduce much-needed expertise. In addition, some banks have appointed non-Indonesians to senior management positions in order to bolster the international expertise of their teams.

As is true of most of the region, the lack of an in-depth credit culture marks Indonesia's banks. Lending in many cases is name- and relationship based, with collateral values (rather than the fundamental cash flows of the borrower's business or project) often the main determinant of borrowing capacity. The influence of relationships, particularly with parent-owned corporations, goes some way to explaining the extent of related-party lending that has been so damaging to Indonesia's banks.

Although Indonesian banks universally claim to have internal approval and control procedures in place, as well as watchlists for delinquent accounts and procedures for dealing with problems, it has been easy for the institutions to manipulate these requirements. Improved regulation and supervision will go some way toward improving this. Tighter criteria have been set for classifying problem loans, and improved inspections may help to reveal the accuracy of recordkeeping in this regard. However, these are after-the-fact ways of dealing with asset quality, and Indonesia's banks still have some way to travel in the area of changing how credit is allocated.

STRENGTHENING THE BORROWER REPAYMENT CULTURE. Indonesia's economic crisis initially flowed from the inability of the corporate sector to repay its obligations in the wake of the severe currency devaluation. It was compounded by the subsequent economic contraction, systematic banking crisis, and ongoing political uncertainty. In the early stages of the crisis, the extreme currency volatility and high interest rates saw many debtors stop payments on their debt. Although many genuinely could not pay, many simply used stalling tactics to avoid paying their debt, and structural weaknesses in the legal environment meant that debtors faced little pressure from existing bankruptcy laws. This was compounded by the inconclusive steps taken by the Indonesian authorities in the early stages of the crisis to restore confidence in the banking system. Many debtors were unwilling to negotiate debt payments with institutions that faced possible closure.

To build a structure under which debt restructuring could commence, the government established the Indonesian Debt Restructuring Agency (INDRA).

INDONESIAN DEBT RESTRUCTURING AGENCY. To a large degree, INDRA was based on the 1982 Mexican FICORCA model (Fideicomico para la Cobertura de Riesgos Cambiaros). The INDRA scheme was a voluntary plan under which private sector offshore debt would be restructured so that it could be repaid over an eight-year period, the first three of which were a grace period during which only interest was payable. The Indonesian government effectively facilitated the debt repayment by offering debtors a subsidized exchange rate so that they could service their loans. This scheme saw debtors paying INDRA in rupiah and INDRA paying creditors in foreign currencies. Parties were able to join the scheme only if both debtors and creditors agreed. When the scheme was established, parties were given until June 1999 to join the scheme. However, when no deal had been struck, the deadline was extended.

Why has INDRA failed so badly? One of the key reasons has been the inherent lack of incentives for debtors to join the scheme. At the time that INDRA was introduced, large numbers of debtors were already not making any payments on their debt. The INDRA scheme offered no incentive for debtors to begin payments, since the scheme lacked any allowance for debt forgiveness. Given the already stretched resources of the Indonesian government, there was little that it could do in terms of offering debt relief. Under those circumstances, the companies that have actually moved along in terms of debt restructuring have generally done so through direct negotiation with their creditors in order to benefit from mutually agreed discounts.

Moreover, INDRA was established during a period of extraordinary volatility in the Indonesian currency; it offered debtors a way to fix their exposures through this period. However, the currency has since stabilized, and there is little reason for debtors to lock in as they are required to do under the INDRA scheme.

THE JAKARTA INITIATIVE. The enactment of a new bankruptcy law in August 1998 and the prospect of accelerated bankruptcy proceedings were expected to encourage debtors to enter into negotiations with foreign creditors and see them join the INDRA program. However, given the program's intrinsic disincentives, debtors shunned the program. In the case of the bankruptcy proceedings, this was very much the last-case scenario, and many creditors were waiting to see the results of the first cases before testing the waters themselves. Initial decisions by the court discouraged many from pursuing this option. However, the impasse on nonrepayment of domestic corporate debt saw credit virtually evaporate in Indonesia.

As a result, the Indonesian government launched the Jakarta Initiative on corporate debt in September 1998 as an informal arrangement to encourage debtors and creditors into serious negotiations (See appendix figure 6A-1 for an outline of the Jakarta Initiative framework). Unlike the earlier Frankfurt Agreement of June 1998, which dealt solely with private foreign debt, the Jakarta Initiative focused on domestic debt and included other measures for restructuring both foreign and domestic debt and the businesses of corporate debtors. The idea was that mutually agreed, non-judicial agreements would provide better results for both sides. This was based on the rationale that creditors are likely to recover more from restructured corporate debtors than from liquidated enterprises.

Has the Jakarta Initiative been successful? By late 1999, approximately two hundred companies, with a collective debt of around $21.3 billion, had registered with the initiative's task force for assistance in restructuring their debt. As of December 1999, restructuring deals had been struck with only twenty-four companies for amounts totaling little more than $3 billion. While the numbers suggest little progress, they mask the complexity of the procedures involved: single companies may have dozens, and in some cases hundreds, of creditors to deal with.

BANKRUPTCY LAW. Indonesia enacted a new bankruptcy law in August 1998 to replace a statute that had been introduced by the Dutch colonial government at the beginning of the twentieth century. The arcane nature of the proceedings under the old statute meant that any creditor brave enough to pursue debtors through the courts was assured of a long, drawn-out process: relatively few pursued this alternative. The landmark liquidation of Bank Summa in the early 1990s, for example, took seven years to complete.

In the economic crisis that flowed from the fall in the rupiah, large numbers of the country's defaulting corporate debtors halted payments on their debts. Although some borrowers entered into negotiations to restructure their debts, many others simply used stalling tactics in anticipation of improvements in the exchange rate and took advantage of the differing needs of various creditors to avoid payment. Ongoing political instability in Indonesia meant that many debtors were unwilling to enter into serious negotiations. However, given the paralysis in debt resolution, multilateral agencies and foreign creditors pressured the Indonesian government to overhaul the law. It was also thought that if creditors knew that in the worst-case scenario they had the possibility of recovering at least some of their claims under clear and transparent rules and procedures, they would be more amenable to investing in the Indonesian economy.

The statute established for the first time a separate commercial court to deal with the administration of the bankruptcy law. The main principle of the law is to ensure that all creditors have equal rights to the assets recovered as the result of a bankruptcy proceeding. It seeks to give creditors increased power to force debtors to restructure and pay off their debts and also attempts to give creditors greater chance of liquidating the assets of the debtor in the event of a refusal to pay.

Restructuring under the bankruptcy law is achieved through a "suspension of payments" proceeding, which grants debtors temporary relief against claims by unsecured creditors so that the company can continue in business and, at the same time, reorganize so that debts can be repaid. The commercial court decides whether the debtor can repay its obligations and, if there is evidence of business recovery prospects, whether to grant a suspension of payments. After approval by more than half of the creditors (representing two-thirds of total claims) an administrator is appointed, and the debtor has up to 270 days to submit a composition plan to the creditors. If this plan is approved, it becomes binding on all unsecured creditors. If it is rejected or if the court objects to it, the debtor is declared bankrupt and liquidation proceedings begin.

Under bankruptcy proceedings, assets are liquidated to pay creditors' claims according to seniority of claims. If a debtor declares bankruptcy, management retains control of the business under a forty-five-day stay of foreclosure so that it can organize the liquidation. If a creditor files bankruptcy proceedings, management is sacked, the court appoints a receiver, and a ninety-day stay of foreclosure is implemented to organize a fair liquidation.

The early record of the new bankruptcy law has not been encouraging. A relatively small number of cases have been tried, and many of the judgments handed down, especially among the first cases, have been seen as unfavorable to creditors. Much of this was attributed to a lack of expertise in modern commercial transactions among commercial court judges. Additionally, there were claims that some of the judiciary were less than independent in their judgments. The Indonesian authorities have in effect acknowledged these criticisms and, in a July 1999 letter of intent to the IMF, proposed several remedial measures, including increasing the salaries of the commercial court judges and establishing a subcommittee to investigate the financial holdings of members of the court.

Together with an increase in the number of judges, these measures should go some way to improving the operation of the commercial court. The framework of the law should be useful over the longer term as the experience of the judiciary grows.

IBRA. Given the amount of assets now under IBRA control, the agency has a significant role to play in encouraging repayment or restructuring of large amounts of corporate debt. It has worked on constructing an institutional framework and strategy for loan collection and asset recovery, focusing heavily on the largest borrowers. In 1999 IBRA published the names of its largest debtors in order to encourage them to begin negotiations. It then classified all debtors into four categories, based on the viability of their businesses and the extent to which they cooperate in restructuring efforts. However there are still large numbers of recalcitrant debtors, and the agency is now starting to take legal measures against them.

Estimating the Costs of Bank Recapitalization in East Asia

The final costs of recapitalizing banks in Korea, Thailand, and Indonesia remain uncertain. Estimates of the gross costs have risen steadily over the past two years as the extent of the distress in the banking sectors has become more evident. Table 6-9 presents recent figures for the gross costs that have accrued to governments in Korea, Thailand, and Indonesia.

The costs of recapitalization have continued to rise for all three countries. In Korea the FSC has estimated the total figure for recapitalization of the banking sector at 76.7 trillion won ($68.48 billion), but the estimate is likely to rise further. KAMCO has announced that it will continue to purchase nonperforming loans from the country's investment trust companies; these purchases are associated with the sector's large exposure to the Daewoo Group's debt. To the extent that data are available, government estimates of the gross costs of restructuring banking systems in Korea, Thailand, and Indonesia seem overly optimistic (see table 6-10).

Against these high gross costs of restructuring the banking sectors, the three governments expect to raise funds by selling to foreign investors distressed assets acquired by public asset management companies and stakes in distressed banks. Estimating the net costs is rendered difficult by uncertainty about the likely recovery rates on distressed assets. The slower-than-anticipated pace of restructuring, as well as contrasting views held by asset management companies and investors, has hindered price formation in these markets. Calculations of recovery rates are also complicated by the fact that the secondary market for nonperforming loans is relatively illiquid in all three economies.

Some domestic banks have been sold to foreign investors, especially in Thailand. A high degree of foreign investor interest along these lines could help to hold down the net costs to be borne by the fiscal authorities. Foreign investor interest will depend largely on the continuation of strongly pro-reform attitudes. Korea and Thailand both face parliamentary elections in 2000. The outcome of these elections could hasten or slow the pace of bank sales. Indonesia, on the other hand, continues to face an uphill struggle to elicit the interest of foreign investors, despite the ascendance of a democratically elected government. Investor caution regarding Indonesia stems from continued political uncertainty and the scale of the macroeconomic challenges ahead.

The recent experience of Mexico sheds some light on the problem of the costs of bank recapitalization in Asia. Five years after the onset of the "Tequila crisis," problems persist in the Mexican banking sector and the costs of recapitalizing the nation's banks continue to mount. Estimates of the cost of East Asia's bank recapitalization have risen over the past two years and could rise further, particularly if authorities in Korea, Indonesia, and Thailand drag their feet on the remaining tasks.

Table 6-9. *Fiscal Burden: South Korea, Thailand, and Indonesia*
Billions of U.S. dollars

Category	South Korea (mid-1999)	Thailand (year-end 1998)	Indonesia (mid-1999)
Liquidity support	...	20	20
Recapitalization	22	11	40
Purchases of nonperforming loans	17	0	20
Interest cost	7	3	5
Total	46	34	85

Source: International Monetary Fund.

Assessing the Fiscal Sustainability of Bank Recapitalization Efforts

The adverse macroeconomic implications of an unsustainable fiscal burden are well documented. Governments risk a buildup in inflationary pressures if they are forced to monetize budget deficits. Public sector debt can also crowd out private investment and lead to lower trend growth rates.

The low levels of public sector debt that prevailed before the crisis and a track record of conservative fiscal policy management create some flexibility for Korea and Thailand, even though total public debt has risen dramatically in both countries (see tables 6-11 and 6-12). While saving rates have trended downward over the past few years, they remain sufficiently high to provide a strong conduit to fund the rising public burden in both countries (see table 6-13). In addition, the sharp drop in private investment, resulting from the persistence of overcapacity, suggests that domestic saving could be channeled to meet government needs

Table 6-10. *Estimated Gross Costs of Bank Restructuring as a Percent of GDP*

Country	Government estimate	Thomson Financial BankWatch estimate
South Korea	21.2	25–30
Thailand	n.a.	35–45
Indonesia	60	25–30

Sources: South Korea: Financial Supervisory Commission; Indonesia: IBRA.
n.a. Not available.

Table 6-11. *South Korea, Thailand, and Indonesia: Gross Public Sector Debt-to-GDP as a Percentage of GDP, 1992–99*

Year	South Korea[a]	Thailand	Indonesia
1992	6.9	21.6	40.6
1993	5.9	20.8	37.6
1994	6.1	18.9	38
1995	6.3	17.3	33.4
1996	8.8	15.7	27
1997	11.1 (13.3)	29.2	35.5
1998	15.9 (31.9)	38.2	60
1999[b]	19.4 (36.5)	41	102

Sources: OECD, 1992–96, and Ministry of Finance and Economy, 1996–99 (South Korea); World Bank.

a. Contingent liabilities in parentheses.

b. Estimated.

without risking crowding-out effects—at least for some time. The levels of debt relative to GDP currently seen in Indonesia are much more worrisome than in Korea or Thailand. Indonesia has also suffered a sharper drop in its saving rates than the other countries since the advent of the crisis, reinforcing concern about the sustainability of its level of overall public sector debt.

Table 6-12. *South Korea, Thailand, and Indonesia: Budget Deficits as a Percentage of GDP, 1992–99*

Year	South Korea	Thailand	Indonesia
1992	−0.5	2.8	0.2
1993	0.3	2.1	−0.2
1994	0.5	1.8	−0.5
1995	0.4	3.0	0.8
1996	0.3	1.6	0.5
1997	0.0	−0.6	−1.0
1998	−5.0	−4.5	−12.5
1999[a]	−4.6	−5.0	−6.8
2000[b]	−3.5	−5.0	−5.0

Source: Thomson Financial BankWatch.

a. Estimated.

b. Projected.

Table 6-13. *South Korea, Thailand, and Indonesia: Domestic Saving Rates as a Percentage of GDP, 1992–99*

Year	South Korea	Thailand	Indonesia
1992	34.7	31.3	35.7
1993	35.1	32.5	35.2
1994	35.2	33.6	36.1
1995	35.9	34.2	35.8
1996	34.5	38.4	36.0
1997	33.4	34.6	31.0
1998	33.2	41.9	26.2
1999[a]	33.8	36.3	24.5
2000[b]	30.0	32.0	25.0

Source: Thomson Financial BankWatch.
a. Estimated.
b. Projected.

The issuance of domestic bonds has been the primary means of funding bank recapitalization; as a result, the fiscal burden is translated into the ability to meet annual interest payments on these bonds over the short to medium term. The question of sustainability thus involves assessing whether future growth rates can stay ahead of future real interest rates. Banks in all three countries remain weak, and corporates are still burdened by excess investment. Growth prospects over the medium term are thus likely to hinge upon the continued implementation of structural reforms as well as favorable conditions for external demand. Korea and Thailand are ahead of Indonesia in terms of restructuring and have reasonably good prospects for attaining trend growth of between 5 and 6 percent over the medium term. The shift from fixed to floating exchange rate regimes in all three countries means that adjustment to external shocks can now be accommodated through the exchange rate, thus providing some room for interest rates to remain relatively low.

SOUTH KOREA. Korea's gross level of public debt relative to GDP remained relatively manageable at year-end 1999, especially in comparison that of with other OECD countries. The recovery has been surprisingly strong, and medium-term forecasts call for growth rates of between 5 and 6 percent, barring any unexpected shocks from debt weaknesses in the banking or corporate sector. The Korean government has already signaled its desire to begin the process of fiscal consolidation by targeting a primary deficit of 1 to 1.5 percent for fiscal year 2000. The strong recovery also suggests that KAMCO could obtain better-than-anticipated prices for its distressed assets, which would help lower the net costs of recapitalization.

On the negative side, however, the failure of the proposed sale of Seoulbank has delivered a setback to the entry of foreign investors in the banking sector, despite the sale of a majority stake in another bank, Korea First Bank, to a foreign investor. Disagreements between the government and the prospective foreign buyer over valuations were cited as the principal reason for the deal's failure. In addition, caution is warranted about the fallout from the resolution of the Daewoo debt crisis. The government has supported the corporate bond market, Daewoo subcontractors, and some of the investment trust companies in an effort to minimize the risk of financial market destabilization. As further details of the loss allocation process emerge, it is possible that the gross costs of rehabilitating Korean banks could exceed 30 percent of GDP.

THAILAND. In terms of the sustainability of its fiscal burden, Thailand, like Korea, has benefited from its low level of gross public debt to GDP going into the crisis. While Thailand's economic recovery has not been as robust as that of Korea, it is nevertheless significantly stronger than is the case in Indonesia. The government has also limited its fiscal burden by refraining from the purchase of nonperforming loans, unlike the Korean and Indonesian governments. In addition, the Thai government enjoys a high degree of investor confidence, and the country has a record of being relatively open to foreign investment.

The prospects for a pickup in the sales of distressed assets are also improving, in tandem with the country's economic recovery. Of the three countries, Thailand has made the most progress in selling stakes in distressed banks to foreign investors. Four banks have been sold so far, and two more banks may be sold to foreign investors later in the year 2000. Although Thailand's gross costs of bank recapitalization are more significant than those of Korea, these trends could help keep the net costs of bank recapitalization at manageable levels.

Nonetheless, the government faces pressure to begin the process of fiscal consolidation soon. With an election looming in 2000, investor confidence depends upon maintaining a favorable climate for foreign investment and reform. In addition, the persistence of a high level of nonperforming loans raises the possibility that the government may be forced to assume more of the private sector's obligations in 2000, which would lead to a further rise in the overall level of debt to GDP.

INDONESIA. The sustainability of the fiscal burden is most worrisome in Indonesia. Here, debt-to-GDP levels have already climbed dangerously high. Gross public sector debt was almost entirely composed of foreign currency debt until 1997, since Indonesia's balanced budget law precluded the buildup of domestic currency debt. The country's track record of prudent policies is unlikely to comfort investors, given the dramatically altered political and economic environment. The precipitous depreciation of the rupiah has made Indonesia's foreign currency debt much more onerous in local currency terms, and the government has assumed significant liabilities from the distressed banking sector. As a consequence of these trends, public sector debt reached 100 percent of GDP by the end of 1999.

The government is under pressure to start the consolidation process immediately. Indonesia's debt burden appears more onerous than that of Korea or Thailand because the nation's economic recovery is much weaker. The persistence of significant political uncertainty, despite the assumption of power by the new administration of President Wahid, also complicates the fiscal picture in Indonesia. Prospects for asset sales still remain distant. Likely recovery rates could range anywhere from 10 to 30 percent going forward, depending on the extent of future macroeconomic and political stabilization. Foreign investors continue to be wary of investing in Indonesia at the moment. The collapse of the proposed sale of Bank Bali in 1999 and troubles at IBRA have also adversely affected the investment climate in Indonesia.

Evolution of the Loss-Allocation Process

Although the loss-allocation process is subject to uncertainties, trends suggest that taxpayers in all three countries will bear most of the burden of the costs involved in recapitalizing banks. Depositors and most creditors of financial institutions were covered by deposit insurance programs.

In Korea, the government has decided to support, on an as-needed basis, acutely distressed banks considered vital to the sector. This has led to the effective nationalization of the banking system, with several of the largest banks (Hanvit Bank, Cho Hung Bank, Korea First Bank, and Seoulbank) supported by the massive injection of public (that is, taxpayer) funds.

In Thailand, the authorities forced creditors of suspended finance companies to bear sizable losses. The creditors of the sixteen finance companies closed in June 1997 were made to bear a higher share of losses than the creditors of the forty-two companies closed in August of the same year.

Shareholders in Indonesian banks that are in the process of recapitalization (that is, the major private banks that have not been nationalized) have had to inject only 20 percent of the funds needed to bring these institutions' capital adequacy ratios up to 4 percent. Former owners of nationalized and closed banks, by contrast, are expected to repay related-party lending and pledge personal assets to repay credit extended to boost liquidity. IBRA has already entered into deals with some of the largest banks and is negotiating this process with the other names. In addition, many of the major shareholders of Indonesian banks had already recouped their capital investment before the crisis by floating portions of their stock (30 percent of their shares or less) on the Jakarta Stock Exchange. Shareholders did not stand to lose anything in the event of a systemic crisis, since these funds generally exceeded their original investments. This is a structural weakness in the banking sector and has contributed to the burden of Indonesian taxpayers.

Funding Fiscal Shortfalls

Domestic bond issuance is the major source of funding for meeting fiscal shortfalls in Korea, Thailand, and Indonesia. As a consequence of the Asian crisis, the governments of all three countries have been eager to develop the depth and sophistication of local bond markets, viewing these markets as an important means of reducing their reliance on banks. Local banking systems remain distressed and are unlikely to resume significant amounts of new lending in the near future. The motivation to tap alternate sources of financing dovetails with the rising funding needs of the governments, as well as a desire to avoid a buildup in foreign currency debt.

Toward this end, all three countries have moved to reduce regulatory and tax obstacles to bond issuance and to create or enhance the infrastructure for primary and secondary bond markets. Gross issuance of central government bonds in Korea totaled $15.8 billion in 1999, and is projected to reach $22.9 billion in 2000; Thailand issued $10.7 billion in bonds in 1999; year 2000 projections are $4.7 billion (Indonesia's bonds were placed directly with banks). The high saving rates of Korea, Thailand, and Indonesia (as distinct from the low rate of saving in Latin American countries) provide a platform for the development of local bond markets. Much depends on how the authorities boost liquidity and develop secondary bond markets. A greater degree of government issuance would provide much-needed benchmarks and boost liquidity, while an active secondary market would enable banks to manage their liquidity.

BOND ISSUANCE IN KOREA. With more highly developed government and corporate bond markets, Korea has a head start on both Indonesia and Thailand. The country has a pool of domestic institutional investors that constitutes a ready base for purchasing government paper. The government has so far used a combination of bonds and cash to recapitalize the banking system, and the Korean parliament has already approved the issuance of 64 trillion won of bonds to finance KAMCO and KDIC.

In addition to domestic bond issuance, Korea also relied upon external sovereign borrowing and quasi-sovereign borrowing in 1998 and 1999. Quasi-sovereign borrowing has involved borrowing through Korea Development Bank and the Korea Export-Import Bank, institutions that can borrow on terms similar to those of the sovereign. Korea is unlikely to rely to any appreciable extent on external borrowing during the year 2000, even though conditions in the international credit markets have significantly improved. This reluctance probably stems from the desire to limit further foreign currency debt exposure and the need to deepen the domestic government debt market through further domestic issuance.

BOND ISSUANCE IN THAILAND. Thailand issued 337 billion baht in fiscal year 1999 to support the FIDF's efforts to recapitalize domestic banks. Most of the budget deficit in 1999 was financed out of cash reserves and loans from the World Bank. The financing of the deficit in fiscal year 2000, however, is expected to be accomplished through the issuance of domestic bonds. Since the bulk of the recapitalization was accomplished last year, bond issuance is likely to be considerably lower than in 1999.

The Thai government can also tap the international credit markets during the remainder of 2000 and is more likely to do so than either Korea or Indonesia. While the spreads on Thai external sovereign debt have tightened considerably, the Thai government (unlike the Korean government) has not tapped the bond markets since the advent of the crisis.

BOND ISSUANCE IN INDONESIA. The Indonesian government has relied heavily on bond issuance to meet the large costs of its bank recapitalization program. These bonds, however, were not issued into the market but were placed directly with banks, as part of their recapitalization program. In 1999, 260.6 trillion rupiah worth of government bonds were issued. Of this sum, 157.6 trillion rupiah was issued at the end of May, and the remainder was issued later in the year to help recapitalize Bank Mandiri. Since the government's total target for bond issuance is 351.6 trillion rupiah, bond issuance in fiscal year 2000 will be significantly smaller than in 1999. The government is expected to allow banks to start trading these bonds in 2000, to help boost bank liquidity and to aid the process of developing a secondary market. The authorities, however, are concerned about flooding the market and are likely to permit banks to trade only a small portion of these bonds initially.

Unlike Korea, and to a much greater degree than Thailand, Indonesia relies on external borrowing from official aid sources, which come under the umbrella group known as the Consultative Group on Indonesia (CGI). The extent of borrowing is much greater than in Thailand, and it is used to meet the country's large budget deficits. The budget deficit for the period April–December 2000 is projected to come in at 45.4 trillion rupiah, or approximately 5 percent of GDP. This gap is expected to be financed by 23.2 trillion rupiah in foreign funds from CGI. The target for sales of IBRA assets is 16.3 trillion rupiah, while 5.9 trillion rupiah is expected to be collected in privatization receipts. There is some concern about whether the government will be able to meet the targets for domestic financing. The previous administration of Bacharuddin Habibie was unable to meet its targets for IBRA assets or privatization receipts, since both these efforts ran into opposition from vested interests.

Of the three countries, Indonesia has the greatest need for additional sources of financing. Tapping into the international capital markets, however, will prove to be very expensive. Political and economic uncertainties add to the country's already large foreign currency burden and create difficult conditions for foreign bond issuance. Depending on future developments, particularly growth prospects and the level of investor confidence, the possibility that Indonesia might have to resort to monetizing at least part of its budgetary deficits cannot be ruled out.

THE IMPACT OF UNCONDITIONAL DEPOSIT INSURANCE. To restore public confidence in their banking systems, the governments of Korea, Thailand, and Indonesia have all issued formal deposit guarantees over the last two years, covering bank depositors and most creditors but not shareholders. In all three countries, the guarantees are backed by central bank statements of liquidity support. However, to limit the extent of moral hazard, the authorities in all three countries announced that the blanket guarantees were intended only as temporary measures.

The Indonesian government issued the most comprehensive guarantee, covering all deposits and creditors, both in rupiah and foreign currency; the guarantee also covers both on- and off-balance sheet liabilities. The Korean government established a full guarantee for all depositors and most creditors of financial institutions.

It is very likely that the announcement of the guarantees will result in higher gross fiscal costs than would otherwise have been the case. The use of these guarantees suggests that the governments have sharply curtailed the degree to which private creditors can be asked to share the burden of financial restructuring. Given the severity of the collapse facing the banking systems in all three countries, however, these guarantees have proved vital to restoring public confidence in the domestic banking systems. They have also helped to stabilize the situation while creating some breathing room for restructuring to be implemented.

Conclusions

A comparison of the experiences of the three countries in recapitalizing their banking systems reveals that confronting problems upfront and quickly is usually the preferred strategy. Keeping weak institutions afloat means that the task of rapidly reducing systemic risk—which is the primary goal of government intervention—may be needlessly delayed. Each of the crisis countries faces the risk of a systemic crisis as a consequence of an individual bank's failure, a fact that has undoubtedly outweighed the costs of recapitalizing that institution. The case of Korea First Bank suggests that state intervention was probably unavoidable in this instance. Mechanisms to work out even a large bank closure now exist in Korea, indicating a diminished need for state support in the event of another crisis. In Thailand and Indonesia, however, the banking sector is still too weak to absorb the closure of a large bank.

Resolving Nonperforming Loans

Korea's centralized approach to resolving bad loans has brought swifter results over the short term; Thailand's decentralized approach appears to be one factor underpinning the country's slower recovery. KAMCO has played a positive and significant role in working with Korean banks to ease the sector's substantial bad loan burden, and it has been aggressive in managing down its warehouse of bad debt. Centralized asset management companies help standardize the purchase of bad assets and their subsequent sale to investors, thus ensuring greater efficiency. Reliance on such an approach also gives the government greater control over the evolution of the post-crisis banking landscape.

However, it is still too early to conclude that the centralized approach to resolving bad loans is necessarily more effective over the long term. In a country like Korea, this approach carries with it the danger of sustaining the government's heavy role in directing credit in the domestic economy. Excessive government intervention in banks' credit allocation decisions was widely recognized as an important vulnerability in the Korean banking system before the crisis. In Indonesia, which has also relied on a centralized government-sponsored asset management corporation, the perils of this approach are more apparent. IBRA's effectiveness has been undermined as a result of charges of political interference. Despite these problems, a centralized approach was probably inevitable in Indonesia's case, given the greater systemic threat that confronted the country in 1997 and 1998.

No matter what approach is chosen, however, much depends on the manner in which the resolution of nonperforming loans unfolds. The process of asset sales is by no means complete in any of the countries. Both KAMCO and the individual asset management companies in Thailand have substantial assets that still await disposal. IBRA has barely begun the process of asset sales in Indonesia. Both the Korean and Indonesian governments must dispose of their stakes in the banking system as soon as possible. The banking systems of both countries have been effectively nationalized, and investor confidence could be undermined if the two governments are seen to be dragging their feet on divesting their stakes.

Revamping Bank Regulatory Frameworks

Korea has led the way among the crisis-hit countries of East Asia in aggressively overhauling its mechanisms for regulatory and prudential control of the banking sector. However, even in Korea, which has advanced the farthest in improving the regulatory framework, the rapid pace of change means that the new systems and controls being developed and installed remain essentially untested. Their effectiveness will require time to evaluate. In addition, ensuring that the developments to date take root could well require a generational and strategic shift in management's attitude toward how banks do business. At this stage, given the enormous challenges posed by re-creating the banking system, it is uncertain whether management philosophies will adapt sufficiently to the new challenges ahead.

The improvements to the regulatory environment in Thailand and Indonesia have generally lagged developments in Korea. Although the main areas of concern with respect to Korea have shifted to the medium term, even Korea runs the risk that its restructuring efforts will be incomplete and that insufficient time will be given over to mastering new risk-monitoring techniques and credit analysis skills as the sector returns too quickly to its old habit of building up loan portfolios in order to compete. The injection of foreign competition may well only increase the sense of urgency.

Strengthening Credit Culture

A bank's credit culture is, in the broadest sense, the unique combination of policies, practices, experience, and management attitudes that defines the lending environment and determines the lending behavior acceptable to the bank. A strong credit culture should be developed around such criteria as growth balanced with asset quality management; an approval system that delegates authority and holds lenders accountable; the separation of duties; the diversification of risk; carefully selected and developed marketing strategies; the independence of the loan review process and asset grading program; the centralization of credit policies; ongoing lender training; and the incorporation of credit quality into performance evaluations.

A bank's operating and credit culture cannot be changed overnight: its development is an ongoing, evolutionary process that requires periodic review and enforcement. Most banks in Korea, Thailand, and Indonesia have yet to unfold a concrete proposal to inculcate a fresh philosophy and approach to business. The focus to date has necessarily emphasized the improvement of appraisal and monitoring systems, but banks will also need to successfully alter their business practices in order to make full use of improved risk-control processes.

Impact of Entry of Foreign Banks

Foreign bank involvement in emerging markets has generally helped strengthen banking systems by improving transparency and injecting greater market discipline into the system. Foreign banks also introduce international standard risk-monitoring techniques and management systems. Local banks are generally compelled to respond to these changes or risk being left behind.

Thailand has opened up more of its banking system to foreign ownership than Korea or Indonesia. The country has already seen foreign banks take majority stakes in four local banks, and two more are in the process of being sold. In Korea, the setback from the collapse of the proposed sale of Seoulbank has raised questions about the extent of the authorities' commitment to opening up the Korean banking sector to foreign participation. Since, judging from current trends, foreign banks are likely to be smaller players in the Korean banking system than in Thailand's, they are likely to have a greater impact on the latter than on the former. In Indonesia, the persistence of political uncertainty over the past two years has caused negotiating with foreign banks over the purchase of stakes in the local banking system to lag the other two countries.

The Road Ahead

Progress in restructuring the banking sector has advanced the farthest in Korea, followed by Thailand, with Indonesia still lagging in several important respects. Despite the positive progress, especially in Korea, much remains to be done. None of the banking systems can be considered to be in full health yet. The level of problem loans remains inordinately high, especially in Thailand and Indonesia. Ensuring that structural weaknesses are gradually eliminated from all three financial systems will continue to demand the highest level of attention from the governments.

The high growth environment of the years preceding the financial crisis of 1997 was supported by high volumes of bank lending in all three countries. While Korea and Thailand have recovered faster than originally anticipated, sustained growth over the long term is possible only when the banking systems have been placed on a sound footing. Korea and Thailand run the risk of complacency in this regard. Korea's strong cyclical rebound and Thailand's more moderate recovery have already led to declarations that the financial crisis has been overcome. Challenges of great magnitude continue to confront the Indonesian authorities, and although the extent of political changes that have occurred over the past two years is undeniable, the country remains a nascent democracy. The persistence of political uncertainty complicates the task in this country and has seen Indonesia continuing to lag Korea and Thailand in resuscitating its banking sector.

Figure 6A-1. *Outline of Jakarta Initiative*

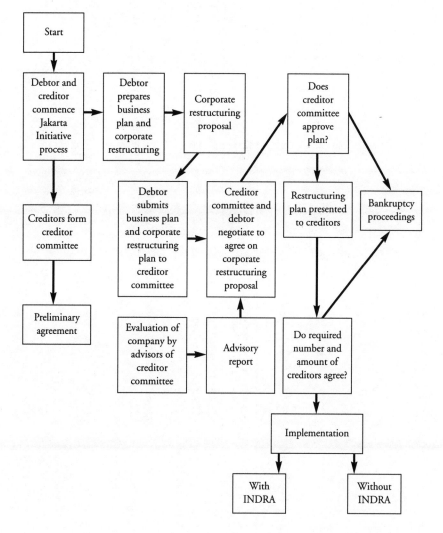

Table 6A-1. *Overdue and Rescheduled Loans Profile of the Thai Credit System, June 1998–October 1999*
Millions of baht

Financial sector	Category[a]	June 1998	September 1998	December 1998	March 1999[b]	June 1999	October 1999	Percent of October totals
Private banks	Loans	3,293,330	3,160,182	3,063,267	3,058,031	2,980,358	2,984,722	53.3
	Overdues	994,230	1,165,549	1,239,944	1,293,788	1,222,689	1,132,842	46.1
	Percent of total	30.2	36.9	40.5	42.3	41.0	38.0	...
State-owned banks	Loans	1,666,308	1,669,450	1,660,068	1,697,091	1,672,741	1,744,496	31.1
	Overdues	786,030	920,467	1,036,654	1,158,199	1,177,467	1,138,662	46.4
	Percent of total	47.2	55.1	62.4	68.2	70.4	65.3	...
Foreign banks[c]	Loans	944,573	838,198	756,505	742,479	696,648	687,035	12.3
	Overdues	52,258	63,142	74,244	85,460	86,300	78,895	3.2
	Percent of loans	5.5	7.5	9.8	11.5	12.4	11.5	...
	Rescheduled	0	0	10,857	18,657	38,938	61,440	7.4
	Percent of loans	...	...	1.4	2.5	5.6	8.9	...

Total commercial banks	Loans	5,904,212	5,667,830	5,479,839	5,497,601	5,349,747	5,416,254	96.6
	Overdues	1,832,518	2,149,158	2,350,842	2,537,447	2,486,456	2,350,289	95.7
	Percent of loans	31.0	37.9	42.9	46.2	46.5	43.4	...
	Rescheduled	0	0	137,158	246,374	499,592	720,115	87.1
	Percent of loans	...	...	2.5	4.5	9.3	13.3	...
Finance companies	Loans	489,786	478,807	461,365	260,482	249,818	188,651	3.4
	Overdues	257,784	288,987	323,691	170,645	168,439	105,835	4.3
	Percent of loans	52.6	60.4	70.2	65.5	67.4	56.1	...
	Rescheduled	0	0	8,561	15,547	27,023	44,640	5.4
	Percent of loans	...	...	1.9	6.0	10.8	23.7	...
Total financial institutions	Loans	6,393,998	6,146,637	5,941,205	5,758,083	5,599,565	5,604,905	100.0
	Overdues	2,090,302	2,438,145	2,674,533	2,708,092	2,654,895	2,456,124	100.0
	Percent of loans	32.7	39.7	45.0	47.0	47.4	43.8	...
	Rescheduled	0	0	156,865	280,936	565,998	826,733	100.0
	Percent of loans	...	...	2.6	4.9	10.1	14.8	...

Source: Bank of Thailand.

a. Loans = total loans; overdues = loans overdue by more than three months.

b. Data of state-owned finance companies transferred to state-owned banks in March 1999.

c. Includes international banking facilities.

Table 6A-2. *Thailand: Rescheduled Loans Profile, April–October 1999*

Loan criteria	April	May	June	July	August	September	October
Rescheduled loans (millions of baht)	383,651	430,013	565,998	628,935	680,187	762,703	826,733
Percent held by:							
Domestic banks	85.2	86.0	88.3	88.7	88.2	87.8	87.1
Foreign banks	9.6	8.8	6.9	6.6	6.6	6.9	7.4
Finance companies	5.1	5.1	4.8	4.6	5.1	5.3	5.4
Crédit fonciers	0.1	0.1	0.1	0.1	0.1	0.1	0.1
Rescheduled loans/total loans (percent)	7.1	8.0	10.1	11.2	12.2	13.5	14.8
Rescheduled loan/loans overdue (percent)	14.2	15.7	21.3	23.7	26.0	29.7	33.7

Source: Corporate Debt Restructuring Advisory Committee.

BERNHARD ESCHWEILER

7

Restructuring in East Asia: Long-Term Growth Implications for the Crisis Economies

THE KEY LESSON of the spectacular recovery of Asia's crisis economies during 1999 is that cyclical drivers matter—that it is a mistake to assess growth prospects purely on the basis of structural factors. Particularly misleading was the view that the plight of East Asia's banks would lead to a prolonged slump. True, bank lending has contributed little or nothing to growth so far, but that is typical of the early stages of any economic recovery. Nevertheless, there is no reason for complacency. Most experts agree that the crisis economies have made substantial progress on the reform agenda but also emphasize that more needs to be done. Sustaining the expansion will eventually require more investment. Corporations and financial institutions must continue the debt workout and complete the restoration of balance-sheet health. To avoid a recurrence of the buildup of excesses and imbalances that contributed to the crisis in 1997, more needs to be done to raise standards and strengthen institutional structures governing the corporate and financial sectors in accordance with global best practice.

I am optimistic that Asia's crisis economies will make further reform progress. Mistakes have been made and reforms are proceeding slowly in some areas, but there are no consistent signs of governments or businesses dropping their reform agendas altogether. South Korea and Thailand are likely to advance the most, although their reform strategies have so far produced very different results. Indonesia faces the highest hurdles, but its track record toward transforming the political system is encouraging. Malaysia has tackled its problems successfully in some areas but has so far resisted addressing the problems of the politically connected conglomerates. The status and prospects of reform in the Asian crisis economies are addressed in depth elsewhere in this volume; in what follows, I focus on implications of the restructuring process for the long-term growth prospects of these economies.

Much can be said about the structural problems hidden behind East Asia's past growth success, but the fact is that the region's economic performance was impressive. During the twenty-six years preceding the crisis, Indonesia, Korea, Malaysia, and Thailand averaged 7.7 percent annualized growth.[1] There were three periods of significant slowdown (1975, 1980, and 1985) but only two recessions (one in Korea in 1980 and the other in Malaysia in 1985). The 1985 slowdown revealed many of the structural problems that are also present today (notably in the financial sector), and yet trend growth subsequently accelerated further, averaging 8.2 percent per annum in the ten years following until the crisis brought the expansion to an abrupt end. East Asia's growth success was not a miracle, but it was real and by no means flawed.

The Asian crisis of 1997 and its aftermath highlight financial soundness and responsible corporate governance as necessary conditions for sustaining strong, long-term growth, but these are not in themselves sufficient. In fact, strong growth was sustained for as much as ten years before the buildup of imbalances and structural flaws became unsustainable and led to crisis and recession. In what follows, I briefly review the key features of the underlying growth process and then discuss the importance of restructuring for maintaining the high saving and investment rates that have been characteristic of the region's past economic expansion. I also focus on the impact of restructuring and other macroeconomic developments on openness, which in the past was often associated with the efficiency of capital use. The findings suggest that with one important exception—Indonesia—

---

1. In contrast, average growth in Latin America over the same time period was a mere 2.9 percent. Moreover, the variance of growth in Latin America was almost twice as large as that of the four Asian crisis economies. Among the economies, Korea was the strongest, growing at 8.1 percent, but the distance to the other three was not large: Malaysia and Thailand both averaged 7.4 percent and Indonesia 6.9 percent.

saving rates have remained high among the Asian crisis economies, thanks in large part to their governments' success in maintaining public confidence and fiscal discipline. Progress in restructuring and recapitalization holds out the promise of revived investment and increased investment efficiency, thanks to a continued high degree of openness.[2] Thus, a return to strong, although less buoyant, long-term growth is in reach.

Catch-up Is Still the Name of the Game

The four Asian crisis economies did not follow the same growth model during their expansion: Thailand's laissez-faire attitude, for example, was very different from the Korean government's promotion of the chaebols. Nevertheless, common to all four countries was their high use of capital and labor resources. Several years prior to the crisis, some observers worried that the growth success of Asia's emerging economies depended primarily, and unduly, on mass mobilization of resources rather than efficiency gains. Indeed, some conventional growth accounting studies ascribed less than a quarter of these economies' growth performance to gains in total factor productivity. Even so, the crisis is not really proof that the past growth model was flawed. Huge excesses during the mid-1990s, especially in investment spending, undoubtedly led to the crisis, but leveraging rich capital and labor resources was not an inefficient strategy. To the contrary, it would have been inefficient for these countries, coming from a low level of economic development, to have emphasized research and development. Asia's emerging economies have done well by combining an abundant labor supply and astonishingly high domestic saving with imported technologies and product designs.

Conventional growth accounting, which is designed to measure the technological progress of a country that is at the frontier of economic development, errs by underestimating the strong efficiency gains made possible by the merger of domestic resources and external know-how. Efficiency gains have been embodied primarily in capital stock. Capital stock increases, especially those effected through technology transfers, have reduced the average economic age of the capital stock by more than its

2. Malaysia runs some risks in this regard if it does not succeed in restoring foreign investor confidence.

average *physical* age, thereby boosting productivity and, in turn, raising output beyond the increase associated with the mere rise in the number of machines. The growth model of Asia's crisis economies was a smart way of playing catch-up, but the crisis was the product of speeding and bad safety standards. With per capita gross domestic product (GDP) and economic standards still well below the frontier of economic development, catch-up (with better safety standards and more effective speed controls) remains the name of the game.[3]

Thus the growth model of the past is likely to remain valid for the future. Furthermore, there are no indications that Asia's crisis economies are looking to shift to a different approach. But the key issue today is whether Asia's crisis countries continue to have abundant resources and are capable of employing them at high and efficient rates to continue the catch-up process. The crisis has led to a sharp decline in investment, which has lagged behind an otherwise exuberant economic recovery. Nonetheless, slow investment should not be seen as a sign of structural flaws or a lack of funds but as the natural fallout of the ongoing restructuring process and the fact that capacity utilization is still low in many sectors, especially real estate. That is likely to change over time as economic recovery and reforms continue. Instead, the limit for investment growth will come to be determined by the availability of funds and the marginal rate of return of every additional unit of investment. A country can borrow to invest more, but the crisis experience has shown that rapidly rising current account deficits are not sustainable—especially if the marginal rate of return of any additional investment falls below the cost of capital. Thus, investments need to be efficient, and the bulk will have to be financed out of domestic saving.

Statistics on Saving Are Poor but Indicative

National income accounting in the four crisis economies has improved visibly over the last two years, but solid saving statistics are still hard to get and often inconsistent. The data situation is by far the worst in Indonesia,

---

3. Only South Korea has come closer to the frontier of economic development, and its ability to raise productivity by leveraging technology transfers is somewhat more limited. However, this applies mostly to the trade sector; the domestic market offers substantial catch-up opportunities.

Table 7-1. *Gross National Saving (GNS) and Gross Domestic Investment (GDI)*[a]

Percent of GDP

Economy	Category	1996	1997	1998	1999 (estimated)
Indonesia[b]	GNS	28.7	28.1	23.0	12.4
	GDI	32.1	31.3	19.1	11.6
Indonesia[c]	GNS	28.0	29.0	16.5	18.2
	GDI	30.8	31.7	31.1	20.5
Korea	GNS	33.7	33.1	32.8	33.0
	GDI	37.9	34.2	21.2	26.8
Malaysia	GNS	38.2	38.5	43.1	41.5
	GDI	41.5	42.9	26.7	22.3
Thailand	GNS	33.2	31.9	31.1	30.1
	GDI	41.7	32.9	20.3	20.7

Sources: Bank Indonesia, Bank of Korea, Bank Negara Malaysia, Bank of Thailand, J. P. Morgan estimates.

a. Saving and investment estimates are based on local national income statistics. Gross national saving equals gross national product minus private and government consumption. Gross domestic investment equals gross fixed capital formation plus inventory changes.

b. Indonesia's national account figures are particularly poor and usually much revised. Huge relative price changes following the crisis have further distorted them, biasing the saving and investment estimates to the low side.

c. Institute of International Finance (IIF) estimates suggest that Indonesian saving and investment rates stabilized at higher levels in 1999. But the IIF figures are also questionable, especially as they imply that Indonesia continued to run an external deficit in both 1998 and 1999.

where the discrepancy between different saving rate estimates can be more than 6 percentage points. But even the Korean data are questionable—Korea's flow-of-funds statistics, for example, suggest that the saving rate rose sharply in 1998, whereas the national account statistics show a small decline. Nevertheless, this paper estimates saving rates from national income accounts to ensure completeness and comparability. The results must be interpreted with caution, but show some important trends (table 7-1): Korea's saving rate has remained roughly unchanged at 33 percent of GDP; the Thai saving rate has inched down a few percentage points to stabilize around 30 percent of GDP; Malaysia's already high saving rate climbed by several percentage points above 40 percent of GDP in 1998 and declined only modestly in 1999; the troubling news comes from Indonesia, where gross national saving has dropped by nearly half—to less than 20 percent of GDP.

Financial Stability and Fiscal Discipline

The stark contrast between Indonesia on the one hand and the other three crisis economies on the other highlights the importance of public confidence in the banking system and stable inflation expectations. Indonesia lost both, which in combination with political uncertainties prompted massive capital flight. Inflation is now under control, and expectations are likely to stabilize over time, but the restoration of financial health and public confidence in the banking system is not only far distant but also no certainty.

In contrast, Korea, Malaysia, and Thailand installed emergency measures soon after the outbreak of the crisis—closing and nationalizing insolvent banks and giving guarantees to depositors—and resisted boosting money in circulation so as to avoid fueling inflationary expectations. That said, what the rise in Malaysia's saving rate manifests is not high public confidence in the banking system and the government but rather the unprecedented collapse of both private consumption and the effectiveness of controls in preventing capital flight.

Fiscal discipline is usually seen as the third factor accounting for East Asia's high saving rates. In the years since the crisis, recession, the use of stimulus measures, and the fiscal cost of bank restructuring have pushed budget balances into deep deficits. Nevertheless, fiscal prudence seems to have prevailed. The governments of Indonesia, Korea, Malaysia, and Thailand have not spent recklessly and with their economies now in recovery mode are shifting their focus to deficit. However, fiscal discipline alone may not be enough. The crisis countries have issued large amounts of bonds to help banks reduce nonperforming loans and raise capital. As a result, government debt has increased sharply. The concern is that despite good intentions rising debt-service expenses could continue to bloat budget deficits and absorb saving needed for recovery of private investment.

In reality, the risk of a debt trap and crowding-out concerns only Indonesia, where government debt as a percentage of GDP is much higher than in the other three crisis economies (table 7-2). Moreover, Indonesia's government debt will continue to rise substantially during fiscal year 2000, coming close to the 100 percent of GDP mark, since the government will probably issue at least another 100 trillion rupiah of bank restructuring

Table 7-2. *Government Debt, 1996 versus 1999* [a]

Economy	$ billion		Percent of GDP	
	1996	1999	1996	1999
Indonesia	73.2	141.0	32.3	86.7
Korea	57.0	202.0	14.0	41.0
Malaysia	35.6	31.7	35.6	41.5
Thailand	28.0	51.0	16.0	38.0

Sources: Bank Indonesia, Bank of Korea, Bank Negara Malaysia, Bank of Thailand, J. P. Morgan estimates.

a. Including bank restructuring debt.

bonds on behalf of the Indonesian Bank Restructuring Agency (IBRA). The implied interest expense burden is already so large that the government will have to tighten policy by close to 4 percent of GDP in fiscal year 2000 and target a primary budget surplus of 1.6 percent of GDP to keep the overall budget deficit no higher than 5 percent of GDP (table 7-3). Needless to say, the tightness of fiscal policy will slow the economy and risks keeping the rate of nominal GDP growth below the level of the effective interest rate that the government has to pay on its liabilities, a shortfall that will compound the debt problem. Generating a robust stream of revenues through asset sales will be critical for Indonesia to avoid a fiscal crisis and its potentially debilitating effects on the economy's long-term saving and growth performance.

Table 7-3. *Government Budget Balances, 1999–2000*

Economy	1999 budget			2000 outlook	
	Plan	Revised	Total	Primary	Thrust [a]
Indonesia	–6.0	–6.8	–4.8	+1.6	+4.0
Korea	–5.0	–2.7	–2.6	–1.1	+0.5
Malaysia	–6.0	–3.4	–4.5	–1.3	–1.1
Thailand	–4.5	–6.3	–6.8	–3.4	–0.5

Sources: Bank Indonesia, Bank of Korea, Bank Negara Malaysia, Bank of Thailand, J. P. Morgan estimates.

a. Policy-driven tax and expenditure changes (positive value denotes tightening).

In contrast, the risks of a fiscal crisis are close to zero in Korea, Malaysia, and Thailand. First, all three countries have substantially lower debt-to-GDP ratios and are unlikely to issue substantially more bank-restructuring bonds in the future.[4] Second, economic recovery is starting to have a positive impact on the countries' tax revenues. This is especially visible in Korea and Malaysia, where budget deficits in 1999 fell well below their initial targets. Finally, policymakers are scaling back fiscal stimulus and in Korea are moving to a slightly restrictive policy stance. Thailand switched to fiscal stimulus measures only in 1999 and policy remains somewhat expansionary in fiscal year 2000. Malaysia leaves some reason for concern, given the greater role of fiscal pump-priming in its recovery and the government's natural reluctance to unwind that stimulus. Moreover, Malaysia's bank-restructuring bonds are zero-coupon and thus will require much larger principal repayments when they mature in three to five years. Even so, the overall level of government debt in Malaysia is not sufficiently high to create a serious threat, especially given the high private sector saving rate.

Investment Has Long Bottomed but Has Not Yet Picked Up

With saving rates staying high in all countries except Indonesia, there is plenty of room for investment to rise. But while inventory investment has risen notably, fixed capital spending remains weak. Replacement investment has picked up, but not strongly enough to push up the total. There is new investment in the high-tech sector, but it is largely confined to Korea and even there has not boosted the overall capital expenditure numbers. Nevertheless, slow investment activity should be seen not as a sign of structural flaws, but as the natural fallout of the ongoing restructuring process and the fact that capacity utilization is still low in many sectors.

Korea's overall manufacturing capacity utilization has returned to normal, but there are large differences between sectors: the automobile industry, for example, continues to carry large excesses, while electronics is running at high operating rates. The largest excesses, however, are outside manufacturing. Real estate in particular, which used to contribute roughly

---

4. Korea announced in April 2000 that it plans to issue more bank restructuring bonds, but although large, the amount is unlikely to distort the overall fiscal balance.

50 percent to overall fixed investment before the crisis, remains plagued by huge vacancy rates across the region.

Moreover, even under less-damaged structural conditions, investment would be unlikely to lead the recovery. Typically, new investment only takes off in the mid-term of an expansion once a period of sustained strong growth has boosted profits and growth expectations. For similar reasons, bank lending is unlikely to bounce upward soon either. That should not trouble the outlook, however: early investments are often funded out of cash flows, and these have recovered nicely.

All said, there is no reason to be alarmed about the slow investment performance. However, there is also no room for complacency. Without the restoration of financial and corporate health, investment is unlikely to recover its full potential. The verdict is still out on whether Korea's and Malaysia's activist policies are better than Thailand's more market-driven approach, but restructuring is not a horse race: different methods may reflect different needs and thus lead to different results. So far, economic indicators favor Korea and to a lesser degree Malaysia, but restructuring in Thailand might ultimately go deeper.

A Glass Half Full and Still Filling

Financial sector reform is far more advanced than corporate restructuring. This is especially true for Korea and Malaysia, whose governments have taken an active approach, pushing nonperforming loans still left in the banking system down close to single-digit percentages of loan books (table 7-4). The Korean government expects to pay another $20 billion or more for additional bad-loan carve-outs and deposit redemptions, in response to the fallout of the Daewoo failure as well as a tightening in accounting standards. The Malaysian government has spent far less and sees no further need for action on its part. However, its optimism rests largely on two assumptions: that Petronas, the national oil company, will continue to support some of the ailing large conglomerates; and that the central bank can keep interest rates sufficiently low to avoid further loan defaults.

In Indonesia, IBRA has spent far more on bad-loan transfers and bank recapitalization than its counterparts in the other crisis economies and may still have to put up as much as another $20 billion (see table 7-5). Even today the banking system is still burdened by a large and potentially rising

Table 7-4. *Nonperforming Loan Estimates*
Percent of total loans

Economy	Peak[a]	Latest estimates[a]	Transferred[b]
Indonesia	70.0	30.0 April 2000	47.0
Korea	25.0	11.3 December 1999	13.2
Malaysia	24.5	11.3 February 2000	13.0
Thailand	46.8	38.2 February 2000	0.0

Sources: Bank Indonesia, Bank of Korea, Bank Negara Malaysia, Bank of Thailand, J. P. Morgan estimates.

a. Nonperforming loans in the banking system.

b. Nonperforming loans transferred to public asset management and bank restructuring agencies (excludes nonperforming loans assumed by Thailand's Financial Sector Restructuring Authority during the closure of fifty-six finance companies in 1997).

amount of nonperforming loans. Moreover, interest payments on the bank-restructuring bonds already (or yet to be) issued threaten to overwhelm the country's fiscal position. The fragile financial and fiscal conditions highlight the need for strong privatization revenues. Here, the recent success in advancing the sale of some key assets—notably IBRA's share in the automaker Astra—is encouraging. Even so, the final outcome will depend largely on political conditions, which have certainly improved but are still not stable.

In contrast, the government of Thailand has provided relatively little financial assistance to its banks. Not surprisingly, Thai banks' nonperforming loans are still high. Even so, there are encouraging signs of

Table 7-5. *Government Assistance for Bank Restructuring*[a]
$ billion

Economy	Nonperforming loan buyouts and deposit repayment	Recapitalization	Total	Percent of GDP
Indonesia	37.3	25.0	62.3	43.3
Korea	41.0	16.8	57.8	14.2
Malaysia	2.9	1.6	4.5	5.7
Thailand	0.0	6.6	6.6	5.4

Sources: Bank Indonesia, Bank of Korea, Bank Negara Malaysia, Bank of Thailand, J. P. Morgan estimates.

a. Funds spent through March 2000.

Table 7-6. *Total Bank Loans Outstanding as Percent of GDP*
End of period

Economy	1996	1997	1998	1999
Indonesia	55.0	60.3	48.6	23.0
Korea[a]	115.7	128.3	120.8	114.6
Net new[b]	15.4	16.7	–3.9	6.0
Malaysia	143.8	162.9	157.1	146.5
Thailand	105.4	128.2	113.0	109.5

Sources: Bank Indonesia, Bank of Korea, Bank Negara Malaysia, Bank of Thailand, J. P. Morgan estimates.

a. To nonfinancial private sector only.

b. Net new loans excluding write-offs and transfers to KAMCO.

progress. Nonperforming loans of private banks have dropped to 30 percent of total loans from a peak of 43 percent, while the bad-loan share at state banks, which account for roughly half of all bank assets, remains above 60 percent. Moreover, 2000 will be the endgame for Thai bank restructuring, since all financial institutions will have to meet the BIS capital adequacy ratios by year-end. Their equity issuance, which has already been stronger than anywhere else in the region, is therefore set to rise further, and the government is likely to spend more money to recapitalize the state banks and match the equity issuance of qualifying private banks.

Given the depth of financial restructuring, it is not surprising that outstanding bank credits appear sluggish. Nevertheless, there are some signs of new lending taking place, especially in Korea (table 7-6). However, the concern is that the pickup in new credits in Korea comes largely in response to government pressure to lend to small- and medium-size enterprises. Thus, while balance sheet health is improving nicely, much remains to be done to improve banking standards and implement new prudential regulations. Policymakers are aware of this challenge, but practices change only slowly.

On the other hand, restructuring needs have led to huge changes in capital markets, which are likely to have lasting effects. In 1999 total equity issuance in Thailand was 12.0 percent of GDP, up from an already strong 8.3 percent of GDP in 1998 (see table 7-7). New equity issuance in Korea also rose sharply over the last two years, but was smaller in relation to GDP (3.2 percent of GDP in 1998 and 6.3 percent of GDP in 1999). In Malaysia, new equity issuance recovered somewhat in 1999, but only to a meager 2.1 percent of GDP, a sign of both lower recapitalization needs (or

Table 7-7. *Private Gross Equity Market Issuance, 1991–99*
Percent of GDP

Economy	1991–97	1998	1999 (estimated)
Indonesia	2.0	0.6	3.0
Korea	1.2	3.2	6.3
Malaysia	4.6	0.6	2.1
Thailand	2.1	8.3	12.0

Sources: Bank Indonesia, Bank of Korea, Bank Negara Malaysia, Bank of Thailand, J. P. Morgan estimates.

efforts) and the absence of foreign investors. Given the heavy issuance burden, it is not surprising that the Thai equity market underperformed most other markets in the rest of the region.

The conversion of equity markets from casinos to potent fundraisers has important implications beyond current recapitalization needs. Banks are likely to remain each economy's financing backbone, given the overall level of economic development and still relatively low per capita incomes. Nevertheless, equity markets are taking on a more prominent role as intermediaries of capital. This is welcome news, as it will make the financial system more stable and facilitate a more efficient allocation of capital. Similar trends are also visible on the bond market side, where issuance has increased sharply over the last two years. So far, this trend is driven by governments' deficit financing needs and issuance of bank recapitalization bonds: in Thailand there has been in addition a notable increase in the issuance of private subordinated debt to support and bridge bank recapitalization. The development of government bond markets, however, is likely to further the expansion of corporate bond markets once investment spending reaccelerates.

On the corporate restructuring side, the glass is probably less than half full, but the trend is positive. Unfortunately, analysis of the degree of corporate restructuring is complicated by the lack of definition and identification. In many cases, analysts just focus exclusively on the progress of registered corporate debt restructuring cases, missing the many cases that occur outside the official process. Besides, corporate restructuring is not limited to debt problems, but includes issues such as ownership, corporate governance, business activities, and costs, especially for employment. Progress along these various dimensions varies from country to country.

Table 7-8. *Corporate Debt Restructuring*

	Number of cases		Debt as percent of GDP	
Economy	Total	Resolved	Total	Resolved
Indonesia	1,434	103	22.3	2.4
Korea	91	n.a.	13.7	6.5
Malaysia	45	16	7.0	3.8
Thailand	1,727	271	46.0	15.0

Sources: Bank Indonesia, Bank of Korea, Bank Negara Malaysia, Bank of Thailand, J. P. Morgan estimates.

n.a. Not available.

On the surface, Korea and Malaysia have made the most progress, while the problems in Indonesia and Thailand appear still overwhelming (see table 7-8). However, Malaysia's apparent progress ignores the fact that many large conglomerate problems are hidden behind the protective shield of the government. The Korean government has been much more willing to confront the large chaebols—with visible success—and it remains committed to its reform agenda despite the recent defeat in the National Assembly election. Some concerns nonetheless linger as to whether the reforms will sufficiently improve business practices.

The Power of Momentum and Low Interest Rates

Putting the pieces together, reform shows substantial progress and its dynamic has not been broken despite some setbacks and slowness. Moreover, one key lesson of last year's recovery is that cyclical drivers matter and that it is a mistake to assess growth prospects purely on the basis of structural factors. Indeed, business cycle forces are strong, and positive for both growth and restructuring progress.

Business cycle conditions point to real GDP growth for the region of 6 percent per year and higher in 2000 and 2001. Only Indonesia will lag, but its growth will accelerate significantly from its zero pace in 1999. These tailwinds improve the outlook for new investment and will facilitate the restructuring process.

Even as growth stays strong, inflation and balance-of-payments conditions should continue to favor a low interest rate environment, which is a plus for investment as well as restructuring. Banks in particular are likely to benefit from an upward-sloping yield curve, a condition that proved a key remedy for the woes of U.S. banks in the early 1990s.

Investment Efficiency and Openness

In all, a return to strong saving and investment performance seems feasible for at least Korea, Malaysia, and Thailand. However, that does not ensure that the capital will be spent efficiently. Overinvestment prior to the crisis led to waste and failures, but the overall use of capital was highly efficient, especially during the years before the final boom and compared to the results in other emerging economies, notably in Latin America. Many factors have contributed to this success, but openness to trade, foreign investment, technology transfer, and training are widely deemed key.

Openness to Trade

Contrary to some fears, the Asian crisis did not lead to trade protectionism in the affected economies. Indeed, the three countries under the International Monetary Fund (IMF) program—Indonesia, Korea, and Thailand—have reduced tariffs and other import restrictions (partly under pressure from the IMF but also voluntarily). Imports fell sharply as a result of the plunge in domestic demand but are now rising again, gradually outpacing the increases in exports. The sharp currency devaluations initially boosted the competitiveness of the crisis economies. More recently, their currencies have regained substantial ground, but the exports of Asia's crisis economies remain competitive, thanks to a lack of domestic cost pressures, as well as the countries' corporate restructuring progress. As a result, export volumes continue to rise and gain market share. This is most evident in the case of Korea, which publishes reasonably reliable and complete trade statistics. Korean export volumes surged more than 20 percent in the course of 1999, even though by year's end the won had regained more than two-thirds of the value it lost during the initial phase of the currency crisis. Korea's share of U.S. non-oil import volumes rose by nearly a third over the same time period.

The balance-of-payments crisis forced sharp cutbacks in investment spending and technology imports. Even so, with the exception of Indonesia, the crisis economies were able to focus investment spending and technology imports on areas that promised to produce the highest rates of output growth and returns. For Korea and Malaysia, this was the electronics sector[5]: the dollar value of Korean information technology exports more than doubled in the course of 1999, and total electronics exports from Malaysia rose roughly 25 percent. In Thailand, agriculture and sunset industries benefited the most from the gains in competitiveness, but the highest growth rates occurred in the electronics sector (production of semiconductors rose more than 40 percent during 1999), although from a much lower base than that of Korea and of Malaysia.

Openness to Foreign Direct Investment

For the right price, Asia's crisis economies have access to almost all advanced technologies and product licenses. However, experience shows that the use of imported technologies and product designs is most efficient when it comes in the form of (or in combination with) foreign direct investment (FDI). The occurrence and importance of FDI have varied: it was lowest in Korea and highest in Indonesia and Malaysia. Persistently high FDI inflows to East Asia have long been seen as a factor in the region's strong growth performance. Many observers believed that the solvency and liquidity problems of Asia's crisis economies would trigger a surge in new foreign investments. However, many foreign investors who came to the region during 1998 and 1999 in search of bargain opportunities returned empty-handed, complaining about high prices and lack of transparency, as well as business, legal, and political uncertainties. Foreign investors' frustrations revealed many structural flaws that even today are not fully resolved, but these same flaws are the product of the rapid improvement in liquidity conditions, which allowed businesses to hold out.

Actual FDI figures, as well as FDI commitments, show some interesting trends (see table 7-9). In Korea and Thailand, actual FDI inflows have increased visibly. In absolute terms, Korea has recorded the highest FDI inflows: roughly $8 billion in 1999 plus new commitments worth $15.5 billion. Relative to GDP, Thailand has attracted more—roughly 4 percent of GDP, three times higher than before the start of the crisis. In

5. It is often claimed that because semiconductors use a large portion of imported intermediate inputs and technologies, they will not generally benefit from a weaker currency. However, this contention is not the whole story. Some 50 to 55 percent of dynamic random access mechanization (DRAM) production costs are local-currency based, in part because of the high share of test procedures in total costs, which gives a net advantage to firms producing in Asian countries with weak currencies.

Table 7-9. *FDI Inflows and New Commitments*

	1996		1999 (estimated)	
Economy	$ billion	Percent of GDP	$ billion	Percent of GDP
Indonesia				
Net inflow	6.2	2.7	–1.0	–0.6
Gross commitments	29.9	13.1	6.8	4.2
Korea				
Gross inflow	2.3	0.5	8.1	1.7
Gross commitments	6.0	1.2	15.5	3.2
Malaysia				
Gross inflow	3.3	3.3	1.7	2.2
Gross commitments	6.8	6.7	3.2	4.2
Thailand				
Gross inflow	2.3	1.3	5.5	4.1

Sources: Bank Indonesia, Bank of Korea, Bank Negara Malaysia, Bank of Thailand, J. P. Morgan estimates.

contrast, actual FDI inflows as well as new commitments to Indonesia and Malaysia fell in the years following the crisis. Indonesia has been worst hit, with net FDI inflows falling into negative territory (–$1 billion in 1999) and commitments tumbling from $30 billion in 1996 to roughly $7 billion in 1999. In Malaysia, both FDI inflows and commitments have declined by roughly half.

The disparity between the improvements in Korea and Thailand and the deteriorations in Indonesia and Malaysia reflects several factors but most importantly suggest that investors have less confidence in Indonesia and Malaysia and see more opportunities in Korea and Thailand. Direct investment in Indonesia fell victim to the country's political turmoil. In contrast, favorable political developments in Korea and Thailand and their new administrations' more positive attitude toward foreign investors and reforms helped promote FDI inflows. Political uncertainties may also have played a role in Malaysia. The main culprit there, however—and not for the first time—was probably the introduction of capital controls, which has undermined the credibility of Malaysia's investment rules and attitude toward foreign investors. The positive trends in Korea and Thailand are likely to persist, and there is even some hope for Indonesia, provided the political situation continues to improve. Whether Malaysia can overcome its credibility problems with foreign investors is less clear.

One area in which future success or failure to use imported technologies and attract FDI will become critical is the information technology sector. The high-tech boom has already had an impact on the economies of Korea and Malaysia (less so that of Thailand), and there seems to be no lack of willingness to explore the new opportunities. To be sure, Asia's crisis countries have little chance to compete across the frontier of information technology developments, and to the extent that they are already trying to do so (as in the case of Malaysia's multimedia supercorridor) this is likely to be a waste of resources. However, there is plenty of room to use information technology developments to create new product markets and raise economic efficiency. The former is already the case on the hardware side, where Korea and Malaysia are among the world's largest producers. Despite its strength as a hardware producer, East Asia, including the four crisis economies, lags far behind on the applications side. This is the area in which the transfer of existing concepts and foreign investments can lead to the largest productivity gains.

Conclusion

It seems reasonable to conclude that high saving rates and a high degree of openness will continue to characterize Asia's crisis economies, although there are notable uncertainties surrounding prospects for Indonesia and to a lesser extent Malaysia. Trend real GDP growth of more than 8 percent per annum is unlikely to return, but a 6 percent pace is feasible. One way to illustrate this is to use the ICOR (incremental capital-output ratio) concept, which defines real GDP growth as the product of the investment rate and investment efficiency (which is the inverse of the incremental capital-output ratio). Compared to the factor growth model, which requires the estimation of an output function, the ICOR concept is more practical, both for analyzing past output outcomes as well as for forecasting future trends.

Applying the ICOR concept to the ten years prior to the crisis shows that the growth of Asia's crisis economies was driven by a combination of high investment rates and high efficiency of capital use. In Korea, Malaysia, and Thailand, average investment was roughly 36 percent of GDP with an ICOR of 4, yielding nearly 9 percent average annual GDP growth. Indonesia's average investment was 27 percent of GDP and its ICOR was around 4 as well, yielding slightly less than 7 percent average growth. By comparison, average investment in the three largest Latin American

Table 7-10. *Incremental Capital-Output Ratio (ICOR), 1998–2000*[a]

Economy	Recovery 1986–87	Expansion 1988–92	Boom 1993–97	Bust 1998	Recovery 1999–2000 fiscal
Indonesia	5.4	3.8	4.3	–1.8	8.5
Korea	2.3	4.0	5.2	–4.3	2.9
Malaysia	7.9	4.2	5.0	–3.0	4.5
Thailand[b]	3.8	3.5	5.2	–4.7	3.8

Source: J. P. Morgan estimates.

a. ICOR is the investment rate (real gross domestic fixed investment/real GDP, in percent) relative to real GDP growth (in percent per year)—the lower the ICOR the higher is investment efficiency (unless growth is negative).

b. For Thailand the boom period ended in 1996.

economies (Argentina, Brazil, and Mexico) over the same period was a mere 18.5 percent of GDP with an ICOR of more than 8, resulting in average growth of only slightly more than 2 percent. However, investment efficiency deteriorated significantly in Korea, Malaysia, and Thailand during the four years preceding the crisis. Average investment increased from 33 percent of GDP to more than 40 percent of GDP, and the ICOR rose from 3.5 to 5.0.

In the current recovery, however, investment efficiency in Korea, Malaysia, and Thailand is high and compares favorably to its levels in the previous recovery during 1986–87 (see table 7-10). However, this combination of high growth and low investment can only last a few years until the average capital stock becomes too old. Investment efficiency in Indonesia, by contrast, is poor, being more reminiscent of the weak performance of Malaysia in the 1986–87 recovery or that of Latin America during the 1980s and 1990s.

Putting the saving, investment, and efficiency factors together suggests two alternative long-term growth scenarios for each country going forward (see table 7-11). For Korea, Malaysia, and Thailand, the average of the two points to a long-term growth potential of around 6 percent per annum—high, but less than in the previous expansion. Indonesia could also reach that pace, but faces distinct downside risks.

The outlook is least uncertain for Korea, but reform slippage and excessive government interference could lead to inefficiencies and lower growth. For Thailand, fiscal discipline and financial reform progress are critical for maintaining high saving. In addition, bottlenecks concerning

Table 7-11. *Two Long-Term Growth Scenarios*[a]

Percent/ratio annualized

| | Investment rate | | | ÷ | ICOR | | | = | Real GDP growth | | |
| | Pre-crisis | Outlook scenarios | | | Pre-crisis | Outlook scenarios | | | Pre-crisis | Outlook scenarios | |
Economy	trend	Positive	Negative		trend	Positive	Negative		trend	Positive	Negative
Indonesia	28.0	27.0	19.5		4.1	4.2	6.5		6.9	6.5	3.0
Korea	34.8	32.5	30.0		4.6	5.0	5.5		7.6	6.5	5.5
Malaysia	41.3	35.0	30.0		4.8	5.0	6.0		8.6	7.0	5.0
Thailand	39.6	30.0	27.0		4.7	5.0	6.0		8.1	6.0	4.5

Source: J. P. Morgan estimates.

a. These projections are built on a simple model that rests on the view that the key factors separating high-growth from low-growth countries are the rate of investment relative to GDP and the efficiency of investment represented by the incremental capital/output (ICOR).

infrastructure and skilled labor supply could become constraints. Malaysia has probably the highest growth potential, given its abundance of saving. But failure to address the hidden problems of the politically connected conglomerates and restore foreign investor confidence could result in a lower growth outcome. For Indonesia, achieving lasting political stability is the first priority. Only then has the government a chance to restore public faith in the banks, accelerate asset sales to avoid a fiscal crisis, and attract fresh FDI to renew the capital stock.

PART III

*Facilitating
Restructuring*

STEFAN INGVES
DONG HE

8

Facilitating Bank and Corporate Restructuring: The Role of Government

I N MANY COUNTRIES that have experienced systemic banking crises, corporate sector restructuring began slowly and lagged behind bank restructuring. In part this stems from the length of the loss-recognition process, the insufficiency of incentives and legal frameworks for addressing corporate restructuring, the unavailability of skills, and the complexity and diversity of the corporate sector. Most important, unlike the banking sector, the private corporate sector is not subject to a unitary regulatory and supervisory agency nor to prudential regulation; policymakers, as a result, are less knowledgeable about the corporate sector. In addition, the corporate sector usually comprises hundreds or even thousands of units; financial institutions are relatively few in number.

From a policy perspective, several preconditions must be in place in order to accelerate corporate restructuring. The most important of these is a strong legal and regulatory framework and effective enforcement, including an efficient judicial process. However, the structure of the corporate sector and its creditors is also an important determinant of the pace of restructuring. Corporate restructuring in Malaysia, for example, has been facilitated by the fact that its legal framework is stronger than that of the

The authors would like to thank Carl-Johan Lindgren and Claudia Dziobek for their comments on an earlier version of the paper.

other crisis countries. South Korea has also made good progress because new laws were adopted fairly rapidly, the corporate sector is concentrated around the chaebols, and the government has clearly specified its restructuring objectives and has provided strong leadership. In Indonesia, the lax enforcement of bankruptcy and foreclosure laws (particularly by state-owned institutions) has slowed the process. Thailand suffered from delays in adopting a new legal framework for bankruptcy and disclosure.

The pace of corporate restructuring must be taken into account in the course of bank restructuring. To be successful, the two processes must proceed broadly in tandem, although bank restructuring may take a lead role. The banking sector tends to be more homogeneous and subject to prudential oversight, which allows for a more focused and more rapid restructuring approach. More important, maintaining a functioning payment system is a public good and must be a policy priority in the process of crisis management.

The Role of Government in Bank Restructuring

Systemic bank restructuring seeks not only to preserve an essential economic infrastructure but also entails major macroeconomic and wealth distribution effects, even if in essence it is a microeconomic process.[1] For those reasons, it requires strong government leadership (see box 8-1). Government policy should provide appropriate incentives to ensure effectiveness and, to the extent possible, avoid problems of moral hazard for all market participants, including bank owners and managers, borrowers, depositors and creditors, asset managers, and government agents involved in bank restructuring and supervision. The restructuring strategy should minimize the cost to the government by managing the process efficiently and ensuring appropriate burden-sharing (by distributing losses among existing shareholders and subordinate-debt holders where possible). To achieve these objectives, governments must ensure effective governance of banks subject to intervention, the presence of appropriate resolution procedures, maximization of the value of nonperforming assets, and optimal involvement of private investors. Experience also indicates that keeping the public well informed is a crucial part of the

1. Lindgren and others (1999).

Box 8-1. *Principal Elements of a Bank Restructuring Strategy*

Institutional and legal frameworks for the restructuring, including the allocation of qualified human resources

Criteria for discriminating among those institutions that are sound and need no public support, those that are viable but require public support, and those which should exit the system

Modalities to assess the financial condition of institutions (deciding who will perform the valuation and the valuation rules to be applied, including loan classification, loan-loss provisioning, and collateral valuation)

Methods for dealing with troubled institutions (liquidation, mergers, nationalization, use of bridge banks, or purchase and assumption operations)

Treatment of existing and new shareholders

Role of government and private (domestic and foreign) sectors in contributing equity and subordinated debt

Financing arrangements, including target level of recapitalization, types of instruments, terms, and conditions for the government's support of restructuring (guided by the principle of minimizing the government's contribution)

Arrangements for loan recovery and workouts, and management of problem assets

Appropriate linkages with corporate restructuring

Operational restructuring of banks

Time frame for the different steps in bank restructuring

Information campaign and transparency on the restructuring strategy to ensure credibility and public confidence

Exit strategy from government ownership of banks

Exit strategy from blanket guarantee

strategy. Conversely, a nontransparent restructuring process may fail to restore public confidence.

The financial involvement of the government in bank restructuring is also conditioned by the government's fiscal stance. The cost of bank restructuring is typically high and largely falls on the public sector—at least initially. The Asian crisis countries were seeking efficient ways to restore banking soundness while limiting fiscal costs. At the onset of the crisis, Indonesia, South Korea, and Thailand had relatively sound fiscal positions; the immense scale of public support, however, increasingly required special attention to preserve medium-term fiscal sustainability.

Institutional Arrangements

Systemic bank restructuring involves a number of government institutions that can lend their expertise to the diverse aspects of bank restructuring. Three steps should be undertaken at the outset: (1) assigning primary responsibility for restructuring to a single authority, including the option of creating a new temporary restructuring authority for that purpose; (2) determining the role of other authorities during the restructuring effort; and (3) ensuring that all available relevant expertise can be utilized in the restructuring process. Vesting a single authority with responsibility for making proposals to the government on bank restructuring principles and measures ensures the internal consistency, credibility, and transparency of the restructuring strategy, as well as clearly defined decisionmaking and prompt corrective action.

Bank restructuring requires skills not necessarily found collectively in existing authorities (including auditing, securitization, auctioning assets, managing nonperforming assets, and evaluating business plans). The skill profile of any existing authority given primary responsibility for restructuring may therefore need to be substantially widened. Furthermore, a significant part of an authority's management resources will—at least for some time—be expended on restructuring issues in addition to the authority's normal responsibilities.

There are thus strong arguments for creating a special (albeit temporary) restructuring authority. This authority should have substantial autonomy for several reasons. Proposals and decisions made by such an authority must be largely based on bank-, enterprise-, and instrument-specific considerations that should not be unduly influenced by other authorities; a need to weigh the differing views of other independent authorities may arise, and some conflicts of interest may otherwise be difficult to avoid.[2]

The allocation of responsibilities for handling the restructuring was a crucial first step in the restructuring process in East Asia. Taking into account technical considerations as well as political circumstances and existing institutional and legal frameworks, the governments put in place a variety of institutional structures. In Indonesia, no institution was in charge of restructuring until the Indonesian Bank Restructuring Agency (IBRA) was established in January 1998 under the auspices of the Ministry

2. Nyberg (1997).

of Finance. Initial problems in providing adequate legal and regulatory powers to IBRA delayed the effective start of bank restructuring and asset management. Bank Indonesia remained the principal supervisory authority, though its powers vis-à-vis state-owned banks and IBRA had not been clearly defined. In South Korea, responsibility for restructuring was given to the newly established Financial Supervisory Commission (FSC), which also coordinated the work of the other agencies involved in addressing the crisis, including the Korea Asset Management Corporation (KAMCO), a bridge bank (Hanaerum Merchant Bank), and the Korea Deposit Insurance Corporation (KDIC). In Thailand, the fact that no agency was given specific responsibilities for bank restructuring has hampered the resolution process. The Financial Institutions Development Fund (FIDF), a semi-autonomous legal entity within the Bank of Thailand (which is also the supervisory authority) was in charge of managing liquidity and providing solvency support to insolvent or troubled banks. However, most decision-making authority remained in the Ministry of Finance, and the FIDF has been hampered by a lack of clear legal powers. The Financial Sector Restructuring Authority (FRA) was set up to assess the viability of the fifty-eight suspended finance companies and to liquidate the assets of the fifty-six companies that had been closed. A public asset management corporation was established to purchase residual assets from the FRA. The Corporate Debt Restructuring Advisory Committee was formed to facilitate corporate debt restructuring.[3]

Asset Valuation and Forecasting

Realistic asset valuation is an important factor in establishing the viability of individual banks but difficult during a crisis, since there is no precise method for valuing nonperforming loans. Differing approaches to valuation were used to improve self-assessments by banks in the Asian crisis countries. Although banks continued to be responsible for valuing their assets and making provisions for losses, they were also subject to intensified on-site examinations by supervisors and in some countries to assessments by external auditors.[4] These on-site examinations and external audits generally revealed situations that were worse than those reported by the banks.

---

3. Lindgren and others (1999).

4. In Indonesia and South Korea, these assessments were further supplemented with audits by internationally recognized accounting firms.

Valuations serve as a basic source of information for the restructuring authority's decisions on the viability of financial institutions. Thus regardless of the valuation methods used, the information collected must allow the restructuring agency to make comparisons among banks on the basis of uniform and transparent criteria. This implies that the restructuring agency or the bank supervisor has to choose the valuation procedures (including the use of external valuation boards) and issue regulations on how banks should assess the value of their assets but be prepared (and have the power) to overrule valuations by others. This power to overrule needs to be used judiciously in order to not discredit the process, particularly in cases where the assessment has been performed by independent outsiders. Moreover, valuations should be subject to revision as economic conditions change. In any event, most prospective private investors will undertake their own due diligence valuations before any investment in or acquisition of assets or financial institutions.

Methods for Dealing with Troubled Institutions

Once nonviable banks were separated from viable ones, governments in all the crisis countries devised strategies to rehabilitate the latter group of institutions. To minimize the fiscal cost for the government and to preserve private ownership of banks, each government's prime goal was to encourage banks to rehabilitate themselves; in instances where market-based solutions were not forthcoming, governments sought to assist in forging such solutions.[5] In cases of insolvency, governments intervened, and the degree of government involvement was in large part determined by the extent of particular banks' insolvency.

The governments' main vehicle for seeking private sector–based resolutions was to request recapitalization and rehabilitation plans from existing shareholders. In all countries, owners of undercapitalized banks were asked to increase their banks' capital to prescribed levels and to provide evidence of their viability within agreed-upon timetables. In South Korea, the government asked banks with capital adequacy ratios below 8 percent to devise plans for reaching that threshold, including contributions of new capital from existing or new shareholders. Approval of these "self-improvement" plans was a prerequisite for banks to keep their licenses and to receive pub-

---

5. See Ingves and Lind (1997) for a description of the hammock approach adopted by Sweden in resolving its banking crisis in the early 1990s. See also Enoch, Garcia, and Sundararajan (1999).

lic sector support in the form of equity through the sale of nonperforming loans to KAMCO. The content of individual plans varied depending on the circumstances and the size and significance of the institution. Memorandums of understanding documented approval of the plans and the associated conditions. The latter typically included operational improvement benchmarks on matters such as cost reduction, labor shedding, and rate of return on assets. The Bank of Thailand asked undercapitalized institutions to provide biannual capitalization plans that detailed their procedures for bringing in equity (domestic and foreign) to meet capital standards. These plans were agreed upon under binding memorandums of understanding with the Bank of Thailand.

The initial lack of private capital in the three crisis countries forced the governments to match (in varying proportions) new private capital contributions. Under Indonesia's joint recapitalization program, owners of banks with a capital adequacy ratio between +4 percent and –25 percent are required to submit a business plan demonstrating medium-term viability, in addition to satisfying a fit-and-proper test. The parties must also agree on schedules to eliminate excess connected lending. Owners providing 20 percent of the capital shortfall are eligible for support, with the government providing the remaining 80 percent. To assist private banks' recapitalization efforts, South Korea followed a case-by-case approach under which the government was prepared to arrange for the purchase of (through KAMCO) nonperforming loans, subordinated debt, or subscription of new capital. In Thailand, the government will match any amount of capital injected by private investors, subject to four conditions: (1) that the bank has brought forward and fully implemented the year-end 2000 loan classification and provisioning rules; (2) that the new capital (public and private) is injected with preferred status; (3) that the government and the new investor have the right to change management; and (4) that an acceptable operational restructuring plan has been presented to the authorities, including procedures for dealing with nonperforming loans and for improving internal control and risk management systems. This scheme has contributed to restoring confidence in the Thai banking system, and, as a result, to inducing private banks to find private investors, with or without public matching funds.

To facilitate foreign participation in the restructuring process, governments have liberalized regulations on foreign ownership of financial institutions. In addition to bringing in foreign capital, these measures have sought to enhance competition by introducing international banking expertise into the domestic financial system. All crisis countries have allowed foreign investment in existing financial institutions. In South Korea, the banking law has been amended to allow foreigners to acquire a controlling interest in domestic banks, including full ownership. Thailand permits foreign entities to hold stock in excess of 49 percent in existing banks.

When self-rehabilitation was beyond reach, governments resorted to a variety of bank resolution methods to deal with troubled institutions. Such methods included interventions, nationalization, mergers, purchase-and-assumption operations, and the use of bridge banks.

A general principle in resolving troubled institutions is that existing shareholders should bear losses until their capital has been fully written off. This principle was generally applied in the crisis countries, although in some countries shareholders were left with nominal stakes in order to take into account legal restrictions on a full write-down or to avoid costly legal challenges by the former shareholders. In Indonesia, for example, existing shares in the largest bank taken over in April 1998 were diluted to 1 percent of total equity. Until its amendment in mid-1998, Korean law prevented shareholder stakes from being written down below the minimum capital required for a bank to operate. In Thailand, the shares of owners in intervened banks have been written down to token values.

New shareholder contributions are essential in strengthening bank finances and governance. All countries have revised their rules and regulations governing new shareholders. Existing shareholders may not continue to hold stock unless they meet fit-and-proper tests; rules regarding shareholder conflicts of interest have been strengthened. Another key issue is the maximum equity share of each individual shareholder: on the one hand, concentration of equity may facilitate governance and capital injections; on the other hand, concentration may lead to excessive connected lending and large exposure risks. New or amended banking laws in Indonesia and South Korea address this trade-off. In South Korea, for example, the law limits the maximum shareholding stake of domestic residents in commercial banks unless that stake is matched by a foreigner's stake.

In Indonesia, South Korea, and Thailand, the insolvency of numerous private banks led to the nationalization of a significant part of the private banking sector. In Indonesia, the IBRA has acquired control of twelve banks, representing 20 percent of the banking sector. However, the authorities continue to distinguish between "banks taken over" and the seven state banks that existed before the crisis: the aim is to resolve the former through privatization, mergers, or closures within a relatively short period. In South Korea, public equity support was extensive because the limits on single ownership of commercial banks meant that no significant strategic shareholders could be called upon to inject funds into the banks. Thus, five of the six major corporate lending banks have ended up with government shareholdings in excess of 90 percent. In Thailand, public equity support has been provided mainly to the six commercial banks and twelve finance companies in which the government has intervened; in the case of one private bank, the government has matched private equity contributions. All the governments have expressed their commitment to privatizing the intervened banks as soon as feasible. South Korea and Thailand have already made some progress in this direction.

Closures, mergers, purchase-and-assumption operations, and bridge banks have proved to be useful techniques to consolidate the financial sectors in most countries, and governments adopted them flexibly under the circumstances. Closures were an important measure in Indonesia, South Korea, and Thailand, as indicated by the proportion of the closed entities in the banking sector. Government-assisted mergers were used in all countries to consolidate the banking system. In South Korea and Malaysia, private sector banks were involved in these mergers. In Indonesia and Thailand, the authorities resorted to such operations mainly on behalf of the state-owned sector. In Indonesia, four of the seven state banks have been merged into a single bank. In Thailand, the authorities are merging some intervened banks and finance companies into three new banks. The liquidation of fifty-six closed finance companies has been largely completed, and the distribution of proceeds to creditors is now under way. Mergers, purchase-and-assumption operations, and bridge banks have been used in South Korea.

In a deep systemic crisis, no standard solution can be prescribed within the broad overall restructuring strategy. The governments of the Asian crisis countries have had to deal with troubled financial institutions on a case-by-case basis. The solution for each institution had to take into account the interest of the parties involved (existing shareholders, potential investors, the government, and creditors), the legal and regulatory framework, the fiscal burden, and often the political situation. As a result, the outcome for the sector as a whole necessarily varied from country to country (table 8-1).

The Public Sector Cost of Restructuring

Covering losses and contributing new capital entails costs both in the private and the public sector (private sector outlays will not be considered

Table 8-1. *Financial Institution Mergers, Closures, and State Interventions, June 1997 to June 1999*[a]

Country	Mergers	Closures	State interventions
Indonesia	Four of the seven state commercial banks to be merged into a single commercial bank (54 percent)	Sixty-four commercial banks (18 percent)	Twelve commercial banks (20 percent)
South Korea	Nine commercial banks and two merchant banks to create four new commercial banks (15 percent)	Five commercial banks, seventeen merchant banks, more than one hundred other nonbank financial institutions (15 percent)	Four commercial banks (14 percent)[b]
Thailand[c]	Three mergers involving five commercial banks and twelve finance companies (16 percent)	Fifty-six finance companies (11 percent) and one commercial bank (2 percent)	Six commercial banks and twelve finance companies (12 percent)

Source: International Monetary Fund.

a. Figures in parentheses refer to the percentage of total banking system assets held by the corresponding group of institutions.

b. Banks with more than 90 percent government ownership. The government owns varying amounts of shares in seven other commercial banks.

c. In Thailand, most of the intervened institutions were later merged.

here). The government's gross costs in bank restructuring arise from paying out guaranteed bank liabilities, providing liquidity support, assisting in meeting capital adequacy ratios, and purchasing nonperforming loans. The net costs will be known only after proceeds from (re)privatization of banks and recoveries of loans accruing to the government have been taken into account. A more complete picture of the cost would also include the indirect effects of the crisis and subsequent reforms. The magnitude of these costs and the need for political support for the process require transparent accounting rules and disclosure of information.

Gross costs of restructuring in Indonesia, South Korea, and Thailand are likely to be on the order of 15 to 45 percent of gross domestic product (GDP). Estimating these costs is an evolving exercise because loss recognition is still taking place as part of the corporate restructuring process. The costs will depend on several factors, including domestic and external macroeconomic conditions, the effectiveness of corporate restructuring, and the efficiency with which bank restructuring is implemented. As a result, there has been a wide range of estimates for the cost of restructuring, with government numbers generally lower than market estimates. Although the staff of the International Monetary Fund (IMF) has regularly made estimates on the basis of different scenarios in order to discuss policy options with the authorities, it has refrained from including any estimates in official documents because of their sensitive and necessarily crude nature.

The need for immediate liquidity support at the onset of the crisis meant that the central banks in the crisis countries were the main providers of funds.[6] In Indonesia and Thailand, formal arrangements to allocate costs between the central bank and the government were weak or nonexistent. In Indonesia, the government has issued 150 trillion rupiah (13 percent of GDP) of indexed bonds to the central bank to compensate it for past liquidity support. In Thailand, the government was authorized to issue bonds for 500 billion baht (10 percent of GDP) to cover losses in the FIDF, and the government has announced its intention to cover additional losses in a similar way.

Bonds issued or guaranteed by the governments of Indonesia, South Korea, and Thailand are the main instruments for financing the public contribution to the costs of restructuring. Market interest rates and regular coupon payments are needed because, unlike zero-coupon bonds, they help banks' cash flows. Tradable bonds help banks manage their liquidity, since the institutions can sell or use the bonds as collateral if liquidity is needed. Given the large amount of bonds to be issued, making them tradable also assists in the development of a government bond market while reducing the government's costs; thus the development of an efficient microstructure for government securities markets becomes critical.

A full and transparent recording of the costs of bank restructuring is important. Although the initial support provided by the central banks was not very transparent, bringing the outlays into the budget would imply more transparency. The budgets of all the crisis countries have factored in interest payments on the governments' recapitalization bonds. However, the cost of earlier liquidity support and the capital cost of government bonds have not yet been accounted for in the budgets. Incorporating the total costs of restructuring into the budget is crucial, not only to allow the

---

6. See He (2000) for a discussion of the resource constraints on the central bank as the lender of last resort.

governments to obtain a clear overview of the total cost but also to enable them to better assess the countries' medium-term fiscal sustainability.

The Role of Government in Corporate Restructuring

The goal of corporate debt restructuring is the timely and orderly transformation and reduction of corporate debt with a view to enhancing profitability, reducing leverage, and restoring credit to viable enterprises. To give creditors and debtors incentives to restructure debt in accordance with this goal, debt restructuring must be tailored to the economic, institutional, and political circumstances at hand.

Comprehensive corporate restructuring typically includes the following components:

—establishing an appropriate macroeconomic, tax and legal environment,

—formulating the debt restructuring framework,

—"triage," or separating the viable corporations for debt restructuring from the nonviable corporations that should be closed, and

—financial engineering involving debt reduction and debt-equity swaps.[7]

Sometimes, the government takes a hands-off approach, and debt workouts are handled between creditors and debtors directly on a case-by-case basis. Government intervention is not needed when the number of troubled corporations is small and their macroeconomic importance is limited. By contrast, a comprehensive debt restructuring framework involving the government is needed when corporate debt problems are widespread or have macroeconomic consequences, when market failures inhibit the debt restructuring process, and when banks are short of the capital and expertise needed to work out debt on a large scale.

Corporate restructuring has been lagging behind bank restructuring in the Asian crisis countries and has been hampered by the lack of leverage of most banks vis-à-vis their borrowers. The countries generally lacked frameworks (such as coordinating credit committees under the guidance of a lead bank) for restructuring failing borrowers. Moreover, in many countries, the courts have tended to be lenient and have provided little support for creditors—at least in the initial stages. Companies have been able to

7. Stone (1998).

continue to operate under court protection, allowing interest to be deferred. This has undermined credit discipline.

Many countries, however, have undertaken measures to address these problems. Where existing law unduly favors borrowers, strengthened bankruptcy and foreclosure procedures have been developed. In some cases, banks and corporations are given incentives to settle out of court. Other initiatives aim at improving court procedures and judicial enforcement and efficiency.

The Legal Framework

A key function of the government in corporate restructuring is to provide an effective insolvency regime. An effective statutory regime can contribute directly to financial stability by allocating risk among debtors and creditors in a predictable, equitable, and transparent manner. An effective insolvency law also protects and maximizes value for the benefit of all interested parties and the economy in general.[8] In the context of a financial crisis in which the entire enterprise sector is in distress, an effective insolvency law can provide a useful means of ensuring that private creditors contribute to the resolution of the crisis. For example, a rehabilitation procedure provides a way to impose a court-approved restructuring agreement over the objections of dissenting creditors. Such a mechanism not only reduces the public cost of the crisis and relieves external financing needs, but it also strengthens the stability of the international financial system by forcing creditors to bear the costs of the risks they incur.

An important aspect of legal reform in crisis countries is to strike the right balance between creditor and debtor interests. A balanced approach allows corporate restructuring proceedings (at the pre-insolvency stage) to be initiated by either debtor or creditor: evidence of inability to pay debts should be required for creditors (but not for debtors) in order to encourage early restructuring designed to avert insolvency. Ideally, a corporate restructuring should allow the debtor to continue to operate the business on a day-to-day basis but under the close supervision of an independent, court-appointed administrator. Where evidence of gross mismanagement or misappropriation of assets exists, courts should have the authority to displace company management. This approach can be viewed as a compromise

---

8. See Dziobek, Hobbs, and Marston (2000) for a discussion of the importance of an effective insolvency regime for systemic liquidity in the financial sector.

between an excessively creditor-oriented approach, which may eliminate the debtor's incentive to seek restructuring at an early point, and an excessively debtor-oriented regime, which may encourage the debtor to take excessive risks in the knowledge that the burden of any losses will fall disproptionately on creditors. A balanced strategy allows creditors to play a full role in a corporate restructuring—for example, through the designation of a lead bank or creditors' committee.[9]

An effective insolvency regime is crucial for court-supervised reorganizations and liquidations; it is indispensable as well for the successful application of out-of-court debt workouts. The effective application of the insolvency law is critical to the success of informal procedures since it provides the necessary incentives for meaningful negotiations.

Reforms other than changes to insolvency law may also be necessary to create a supporting legal environment that facilitates corporate restructuring. Legal limits on foreign ownership of domestic assets (enterprises or properties) can discourage the participation of foreign banks in the workout process by limiting the options available to them for concluding the workout (such as debt-equity swaps). In countries where foreign banks are important creditors (in Indonesia, for example, foreign banks hold about two-thirds of all corporate debt), this can paralyze the workout process. In these cases, lifting the legal limits of foreign ownership must be a precondition for the workout process.[10]

Tax Issues

In addition to corporate restructuring, debt workout often entails reorganization strategies designed to improve the prospects of the company, such as merger, consolidation, and stock acquisition. Under most tax systems, capital gains are not taxable until they are actually realized—that is, when the instruments that generate the capital gains are sold or transferred. In this regard, potential tax liabilities of companies that wish to enter into corporate reorganization can sometimes discourage the reorganization initiatives. To avoid this scenario, some countries have introduced the concept of tax-neutral company reorganization. This exempts companies from capital gain taxes when the reorganization takes place, provided that the stockholders and property are substantially the same before and after restruc-

9. International Monetary Fund (1999).
10. Woo (2000).

turing and that the restructuring is justified on business grounds and is not principally designed to secure tax-neutral treatment.[11]

Some countries introduced specific tax deductions or subsidies to create incentives for debt restructuring. In Thailand, the government provided temporary tax relief on asset sales and on debt restructuring by financial institution creditors. In South Korea, the government provided tax incentives for corporate restructuring, including exemption of small- and medium-size enterprises from capital gains on the sale of real estate used to repay debt to financial institutions. As compared to tax deduction, subsidies have the advantage of being self-terminating (to the extent that they need to be approved annually by the budgetary process), finite (with specific budgetary allocation), and transparent. In general, it is important that any new incentives for restructuring be temporary in order to avoid erosion of the tax base and to preserve sufficient safeguards to prevent abuse.

Government Mediation and Government Schemes

When a corporate crisis is systemic, involving major portions of the corporate sector, the government inevitably has a role to play in mediating between corporations and banks. Excessive negotiating power by either debtors or creditors, or a lack of incentives (often stemming from poor supervision and weak governance) for banks or corporations to work out debt can obstruct the process—either because there is insufficient sharing of information among banks or because the extent of the crisis delays the formation of a common strategy and impedes new credit relations. Such obstruction can prolong or even preclude debt restructuring, resulting in excessive costs and even the unnecessary liquidation of debtors.

To avoid these pitfalls, the government may be forced to mediate either informally or in a more structured framework. Governments can play the role of honest broker by establishing guidelines, providing expertise, facilitating the sharing of information, and contributing to a constructive atmosphere.

The Asian crisis countries have adopted a variant of the so-called London Approach to debt renegotiation. However, in contrast to practice in the United Kingdom, where the government remains in the background, the Asian adaptation has assumed a more formalized structure, with an active role for the government. The countries have given banks a variety of incen-

11. Woo (2000).

tives to address and expedite corporate debt restructuring. The government-led approach, favoring out-of-court corporate restructuring, has so far been applied most aggressively in Korea, where several medium-size corporate groups were restructured through debt rescheduling (with some interest rate reduction), or through issuance of convertible bonds and debt-equity swaps. In South Korea, under the Corporate Restructuring Agreement (CRA), a steering committee composed of representatives from participating financial institutions is responsible for implementing, amending, and terminating the CRA.[12] The steering committee has appointed the Corporate Restructuring Coordination Committee (CRCC), a panel responsible for assessing the viability of corporate candidates for restructuring, arbitrating differences among creditors, enforcing CRCC decisions, and, if necessary, modifying workout plans proposed by participating creditors.

In Thailand, the Corporate Debt Restructuring Advisory Committee (CDRAC), formed by the Bank of Thailand and representatives of debtor and creditor groups, agreed upon a framework for corporate debt restructuring (the Bangkok Approach) based on the London Approach. The CDRAC initially targeted large debt-restructuring cases but has recently expanded its coverage to small- and medium-size cases.

A scheme that would combine government support for recapitalization with corporate debt settlement (Tier 2 options) has also been established to encourage corporate debt restructuring. In Indonesia, the government has adopted a four-way classification of delinquent borrowers, based on their business prospects and their degree of cooperation with the workout process. Under the Jakarta Initiative (which broadly follows the London Approach), state institutions and the IBRA are adopting a coordinated approach in relation to each major delinquent borrower, beginning with the largest.

Financial incentives to facilitate debt restructuring through a pre-set, government-financed scheme can be useful if corporate debt problems are pervasive and implicate the economy at large.[13] Government schemes usually involve insurance or subsidy incentives that are made available to creditors and debtors on a voluntary basis. These incentives include compensation to creditors for lengthening of debt maturities, as well as grace

12. The steering committee is backed by the Financial Supervisory Commission, which is in charge of financial restructuring and supervision.
13. Stone (1998).

periods, interest rate and exchange rate guarantees, and equity injections. The government must trade off the fiscal costs of the scheme against the benefits of more expedient debt restructuring for the players involved and an alleviation of the negative externalities.

The Role of Asset Management Companies

Under certain circumstances, asset management companies can play a crucial role in corporate debt restructuring. Successful debt restructuring requires negotiation between equals. In situations where most of the debtors are large corporations and the creditor banks are small, asset management companies that centralize the claims on the debtors can perhaps negotiate more meaningful and balanced restructuring settlements than a group of small and possibly divided banks.[14]

Workouts often entail debt-equity swaps, and banks therefore sometimes become majority shareholders in the firms with which they enter into a workout. This new role requires banks to become actively involved in the management of the firms, a task that in many cases banks have neither the expertise nor the resources to undertake. These considerations may be sufficiently important to discourage banks from entering into workouts. In such circumstances, asset management companies may have a comparative advantage in orchestrating financial engineering transactions.

Asset management companies can also be given special legal power to facilitate corporate debt restructuring—for example, when the existing legal system is not equipped to deal with the magnitude of the nonperforming assets or when endeavors to reform the system are excessively time-consuming, or when the authorities want to limit certain legal powers of creditors to the asset management companies. In Malaysia, a 1998 law grants an asset management company—Danaharta—the power to appoint special administrators to manage the affairs of distressed companies. When a corporate borrower is unable to service its debt, Danaharta has the right to appoint such an administrator (with the approval of an oversight committee), who will take over the control and management of the assets and affairs of the borrower. The administrator's role is to prepare a workout proposal that, once approved by the oversight committee (and

14. Woo (2000).

the majority of creditors), will then be implemented. This legal power allows Danaharta to take the initiative in order to catalyze the corporate debt restructuring process. Given the lack of expertise in the private sector regarding debt restructuring, the process would have been very time-consuming had it been left entirely to negotiations between creditors and debtors.

Financial Restructuring in IMF-Supported Programs

Structural reforms have been at the core of IMF-supported programs for the Asian crisis countries. Country-specific reform strategies included measures to handle the acute crisis phase,[15] to ensure the exit of nonviable financial institutions, the strengthening of those that remained in operation, the restructuring of the corporate sector, and the adoption of institutional reforms to help prevent future crises (see box 8-2). From the outset, these programs included both immediate actions and medium-term strategies for restructuring. The programs left implementation sufficiently flexible to accommodate the difficulty of determining at the outset the precise nature and timing of future actions. The programs were refined as new information became available and as required by the evolving circumstances in each country.[16]

Several issues arose in adapting complex medium-term restructuring strategies to the format and conditionality of IMF-supported programs.[17] IMF conditionality has usually been quantitative and strictly time-bound, involving actions under the control of the authorities. In the case of bank restructuring, however, conditionality has to be set cautiously, since the process involves steps that are seldom amenable to measurement, often take longer than planned, are not directly under the control of the authorities, require adherence to legal processes, and involve negotiations between different parties in the public and private sector. Moreover, since restructuring actions have a significant impact on private property and wealth,

---

15. See Garcia (2000) for a discussion of the costs and benefits of a blanket government guarantee for bank liabilities as a tool for crisis management.

16. The market sensitivity of certain actions required in the initial stages of the programs ruled out incorporating these actions in letters of intent between the IMF and the governments of the crisis countries.

17. Lindgren and others (1999).

Box 8-2. *Financial Restructuring Measures in IMF-Supported Programs*

Measures to stabilize the system

Provide liquidity support at penal rates and subject to conditionality (Indonesia, Korea, and Thailand)

Introduce a blanket guarantee (Indonesia and Thailand)

Cap deposit rates in order to reduce the ability of weak banks to capture deposits and further weaken the system (Indonesia and Thailand)

Identify and close fundamentally unsound financial institutions. These included commercial banks (Indonesia), commercial and merchant banks (Korea), and finance companies (Thailand)

Require owners of closed institutions to lose their stakes in these institutions (Indonesia, Korea, and Thailand)

Share losses of closed finance companies with creditors; restructure some depositor claims to longer maturities (Thailand)

Measures to restructure the financial sector

Establish a restructuring agency (IBRA in Indonesia)

Complete diagnostic reviews of financial institutions (Indonesia and Korea)

Tighten loan classification and loan-loss provisioning rules (Indonesia, Korea, Thailand, and the Philippines)

Allow for full tax deductibility on income for loan-loss provisioning (Indonesia, Korea, and Thailand)

Establish a transparent timetable for banks to meet capital-asset ratios (Indonesia and Korea) or provisioning requirements (Thailand)

Intervene in insolvent banks (all countries)

Agree on memorandums of understanding between undercapitalized banks and the authorities to specify a timetable for raising capital to meet capital-asset ratios and attain performance benchmarks (Indonesia, Korea, the Philippines, and Thailand)

Issue guidelines on the modalities for the use of public funds to recapitalize banks (Thailand) and to purchase nonperforming loans from private institutions (Indonesia and Korea)

Issue guidelines for stricter bank licensing (Thailand)

Take steps to privatize nationalized banks (Indonesia, Korea, and Thailand)

Measures to reform the institutional framework

Enact legislation to enhance the operational independence of the supervisory authority (Korea) and central bank (Indonesia)

Take steps to strengthen bank supervision (Indonesia and the Philippines)

Improve accounting, disclosure, and auditing standards (Korea, the Philippines, and Thailand)

Issue-strengthened regulations regarding connected lending, liquidity management, foreign currency exposure, and large exposures (Indonesia and Korea); cross-guarantees were also to be eliminated for the top thirty chaebols in Korea

Introduce a new bankruptcy law (Indonesia and Thailand)

they must be undertaken in a manner consistent with each country's legal and judicial framework.

The timing and pace of reforms requires a delicate balance between short-term IMF conditionality and the medium-term nature of the financial restructuring process. On the one hand, reforms need to proceed rapidly in order to maintain momentum and credibility; on the other, the complexity of the process and country-specific constraints must be taken into account. Rapid recapitalization of financial institutions, for example, was a desirable goal in principle in dealing with the Asian crisis, but too rapid a pace would have meant that necessary concomitant measures (such as operational restructuring and banks' search for private capital) would not have been feasible and that credits would have had to be even more drastically reduced, thereby aggravating the crisis. Thus the recapitalization was phased in and strictly monitored under the IMF-supported programs. Similarly, in South Korea, addressing the excessive maturity mismatches between foreign exchange assets and liabilities had to be phased in, taking into account the difficulty at the time in converting foreign financing from short term to longer term. Introducing meaningful benchmarks for measures such as privatization, which involves complex negotiations with private parties, is even more challenging.

Although the Asian crisis showed that the IMF would need to play a central role in assisting the authorities in the management of the initial crisis and in the design of the overall restructuring strategy, it also demonstrated the need for close cooperation with other multilateral agencies, particularly the World Bank. The IMF assumed the lead role in Indonesia, South Korea, and Thailand, and the World Bank made important contributions in specific aspects of program formulation and implementation. The IMF relied on its capacity to develop programs quickly and build linkages between macroeconomic stability and financial sector soundness. The Bank provided expertise and financing to assist the authorities in program implementation and institution-building, increasing its role in the crisis countries over time. In all the crisis countries, IMF and Bank staff have cooperated closely from the early stages, taking into account each other's views in the program discussions with the authorities; these meetings often included staff of both institutions. Bank staff took the lead in the area of corporate restructuring and nonbank financial institutions; work on strengthening legal and regulatory frameworks has been performed jointly.

Concluding Remarks

Countries that experience systemic banking crises most often also suffer profound weaknesses in the corporate sectors. Addressing systemic banking crises, therefore, must go hand in hand with appropriate corporate sector restructuring. A return of banks to solvency requires solvent corporations—and vice versa. Experience suggests that addressing widespread corporate insolvencies is significantly more time-consuming than bank restructuring given the difficulties in reforming bankruptcy law and judicial systems. Corporate restructuring as a result often lags behind bank restructuring, and lags in corporate reform, in turn, slow the progress of bank restructuring.

Bank restructuring provides a lever for corporate restructuring. Tighter and better-enforced prudential regulations can induce the financial restructuring of corporations, especially of those that are highly leveraged. Moreover, banks can play a lead role in inducing corporate restructuring, particularly if they have strong government support to do so.

The rationale for government intervention in corporate restructuring hinges on the systemic consequences of the debt overhang. Restructuring led by the public sector may entail high fiscal costs and raises potential problems of moral hazard, but it should eliminate the debt overhang more quickly, which is of greater concern when corporate debt problems are delaying economic recovery.

References

Dziobek, Claudia, J. Kim Hobbs, and David Marston. 2000. "Toward a Framework for Systemic Liquidity Policy." Working Paper 00/34. Washington: International Monetary Fund (March).

Enoch, Charles, Gillian Garcia, and V. Sundararajan. 1999. "Recapitalizing Banks with Public Funds: Selected Issues." Working Paper 99/139. Washington: International Monetary Fund (October).

Garcia, Gillian. 2000. "Deposit Insurance and Crisis Management." Working Paper 00/57. Washington: International Monetary Fund (March).

He, Dong. 2000. "Emergency Liquidity Support Facilities." Working Paper 00/79. Washington: International Monetary Fund (April).

Ingves, Stefan, and Goran Lind. 1997. "Loan Loss Recoveries and Debt Resolution Agencies: The Swedish Experiences." In *Banking Soundness and Monetary Policy,* edited by Charles Enoch and John Green. Washington: International Monetary Fund.

International Monetary Fund. 1999. *Orderly and Effective Insolvency Procedures: Key Issues.* Washington.

Lindgren, Carl-Johan, Tomás J. T. Baliño, Charles Enoch, Anne-Marie Gulde, Marc Quintyn, and Leslie Teo. 2000. "Financial Sector Crisis and Restructuring: Lessons from Asia." Occasional Paper 188. Washington: International Monetary Fund (January).

Nyberg, Peter. 1997. "Authorities' Roles and Organizational Issues in Systemic Bank Restructuring." Working Paper 97/92. Washington: International Monetary Fund (July).

Stone, Mark. 1998. "Corporate Debt Restructuring in East Asia: Some Lessons from International Experience." IMF Papers on Policy Analysis and Assessment 98/13. Washington: International Monetary Fund (October).

Woo, David. 2000. "Two Approaches to Resolving Nonperforming Assets during Financial Crises." Working Paper 00/33. Washington: International Monetary Fund (March).

DAVID SCOTT

9

Governments as Managers of Systemic Financial Crises: Controlling Costs by Integrating Bank and Corporate Restructuring

S YSTEMIC FINANCIAL CRISES put governments to the test as do few other calamities. Governments facing crises seek to preserve the core value of the financial system, especially basic payment and credit functions. They attach high priority to protecting bank depositors and typically commit to backing most deposits, becoming the guarantors of the bulk of banks' liabilities. When most banks face insolvency, governments make good on this guarantee by providing them with financial support, although often without explicit arrangements for corporate debt restructuring. The failure to integrate corporate restructuring into resolving financial crises, however, can slow crisis resolution and raise governments' costs.

This paper suggests a strategic, policy, and managerial framework for reducing the cost of systemic financial crises by integrating financial and corporate restructuring when providing financial support to banks. The proposed framework is designed to leverage government financial support to change the incentives of banks and debtors in systemic crises. Managers of economically insolvent banks have incentives to avoid making transparent the losses inherent in restructuring assets. Debtors, in turn, have

This paper benefited from advice and comments provided by Stefan Alber, James Darroch, Richard Duncan, Jose de Luna, William Mako, Brian Perry, and Michael Pomerleano. I am grateful to Cintya Vega for extensive production assistance.

incentives to cease servicing their bank debts. Government financial support enables banks to absorb the losses inherent in restructuring debts to levels that can reasonably be serviced by debtors. A critical challenge for governments in providing this support is to ensure that adequate debt restructuring takes place while incurring no greater cost than is necessary to honor their commitment to protect bank deposits and salvage core elements of the financial system.

This paper is based on practitioners' experiences in many countries facing such crises. The framework described here contrasts with a common approach, used recently in several of the so-called Asian crisis countries, under which governments adopt discrete strategies for providing support to banks and for promoting corporate debt restructuring. This paper argues for executing integrated bank and corporate restructuring strategies so as to control the costs of crises.

The focus of the paper is on governments, banks, and corporations in times of systemic financial crisis, during which most banks face economic insolvency and many corporations experience debt service problems. Nonetheless, the suggested framework can be applied to other types of financial intermediaries, to other types of debtors (such as households), and to less severe forms of financial crisis.

This paper takes several things for granted. It assumes that governments will commit to salvage the core elements of the financial system and to protect bank deposits. It assumes that governments will make good on this commitment principally by providing support to open banks, while some lesser amount of support will be used to repay depositors in liquidated banks. It assumes that desirable legal changes are not forthcoming and thus does not rely on them in its suggestions.

Several related topics are not treated here that are nonetheless relevant for governments seeking to tackle financial crises in a comprehensive manner. For example, this paper does not discuss the immediate actions required to stabilize bank liquidity or put in place a macroeconomic program. It does not describe or evaluate different options to resolve failing banks, nor the various means to dispose of the interests in banks that governments might acquire in the course of resolving bank failures (such as bank privatization). The paper does not discuss complementary regulatory and supervisory actions such as granting temporary regulatory forbearance. It does not address the tasks involved in managing corporate equity interests acquired during the course of debt restructuring so as to promote operational corporate restructuring (such as post-workout monitoring and governance). Finally, it does not address means to correct institutional weaknesses (such as dysfunctional bankruptcy regimes) or to achieve the institutional improvements (such as bank regulation and supervision) that should be a part of crisis resolution.

Costs and the Role of Government

Governments incur both direct and indirect costs in the course of restructuring. *Direct costs* are those associated with financing the support that the government provides to banks in order to honor its commitment to protect deposits and to achieve other key objectives. Typically governments either provide financial support to banks that remain open or repay the deposits in liquidated banks. Direct costs are the debt service (principal and interest) on government debt issued to finance those actions.[1] *Indirect costs* can be measured in terms of reduced national output and tax revenues, higher inflation, increased unemployment and social tensions (and related expenditures), political fallout, and the like. Indirect costs can impair governments' ability to finance direct costs.[2]

Controllable Costs

There are at least four controllable sources of direct costs: carrying costs, bailouts, looting, and waste. *Carrying costs* for assets on which debt service has been suspended are potentially explosive. The carrying costs at different interest rate levels (that is, banks' marginal cost of funds) for a loan on which interest payments have been suspended are outlined in figure 9-1. Several observations can be made. The cumulative negative carry is effectively the rate of the bank's decapitalization. The higher the rate of interest, the faster the rate of decapitalization. For example, at an interest rate of 30 percent within three months (the shortest period for which loans on

1. This is a narrow definition of direct costs. More broadly, direct costs are the cost of servicing all obligations incurred by governments, government-owned entities (for example, public banks), and central banks in resolving a crisis.

2. Long-run debt service requirements will be lower than peak requirements since the amount of government obligations will be reduced by the repayment of support (for example, central bank liquidity lines) and the sale of assets (for example, loans or shares in banks acquired in the course of resolving the crisis). Long-run debt service requirements pertain to the net loss incurred by governments, government-owned entities, and central banks in resolving a crisis.

Figure 9-1. *Rate of Decapitalization*
Assumption: $1,000 loan, at 8 percent = $80
Dollars

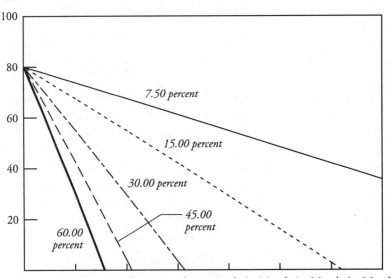

which debt service has been suspended can be classified as nonperforming for regulatory purposes), the cumulative negative carry fully offsets the notional capital supporting the loan.

During the early stages of a crisis, banks incur losses from debtors' suspending interest payments. Aggregate cash-based net interest earnings rapidly become negative, leading to the banks' decapitalization.[3] Over time, the debts are restructured and again begin to generate cash interest payments, though not at the level necessary to fully service the increased real value of the original contractual debt. The government then recapitalizes the bank so as to restore a market-based level of net interest earnings.

Absent other considerations, the shorter the period over which debts are restructured the lower the aggregate level of carrying costs and the lower the government's cost to adequately recapitalize the bank. In the long run,

3. Other factors will further contribute to bank decapitalization in these circumstances. Interest costs for liabilities will rise not only as a result of the interest rate spike but also because of aggressive bidding for funds to cover negative cash flow. See pp. 279–83. Excessive overhead costs may also contribute to decapitalization.

net carrying costs will be determined by the extent to which the original contractual value of debts can be recouped under their restructured terms.

Debtor bailout is a second controllable cost. Crises present opportunities for private parties to escape their obligations at taxpayer expense. Allowing debtors who can reasonably service their obligations to avoid doing so incurs unnecessary costs. The nature of the debt restructuring process will determine the extent to which debtor bailouts are granted. It also may be that the longer the period of time that the government lacks a comprehensive program to resolve the crisis the greater the potential that debtors will be able to secure bailouts.[4]

Looting occurs when bank or corporate shareholders, managers, or employees transfer value from the enterprise for their personal enrichment. Looting tends to increase during periods of prolonged uncertainty, but it can also occur when government support is provided without appropriate conditions and controls. (A common example is using central bank liquidity support to finance offshore transfers to shareholders, managers, or employees.)

Waste is the failure to put government support to effective use, such as failing to undertake necessary restructuring. Waste occurs when support is provided without requiring sufficient action by bank shareholders or managers, or when adherence to agreed actions is not monitored and enforced.

Impact of Government Action on Costs

All four sources of cost are significantly influenced by the nature of the bank support and debt restructuring processes and by the actions of governments and of bank and corporation managers. Key factors governing costs are the speed with which debtors resume debt service, the extent of debt defaults, the level to which debt service is restored (or conversely, the extent to which debt write-downs are granted), and the requirements and controls placed on granting debt relief to debtors and public financial support to banks.

---

4. A related notion is the bailout of nondeposit bank creditors and shareholders. The potential for creditor bailouts is inherent in decisions regarding which bank claimholders government feels compelled to protect. For simplicity, this paper assumes that governments protect all depositors and do not protect (that is, bail out) other bank creditors, although this assumption is not essential to the arguments set out in the paper. The potential for shareholder bailouts is addressed below.

Governments are often slow to respond to crises and may fail to recognize evident signs of distress (such as bank runs) as a reflection of deeper problems in the financial system. Lack of information and poor incentives are probably the principal causes of delayed response (see box 9-1). Delay can raise direct costs by increasing carrying costs as well as the potential for looting. Delay also can raise indirect costs since it allows market uncertainty to persist, which drives up interest rates and depresses the exchange rate, thus further damaging the positions of banks and many corporations. Finally, government delay can forestall needed action in the private sector.

Underestimating the scope of crises often leads governments to respond inappropriately. Early actions may be designed to mask the symptoms of crises rather than solve the underlying problems. A common error is taking steps that improve accounting data and regulatory measures of capital but that do not improve cash-based earnings. Governments often fail to put in place adequate managerial arrangements that enable them to identify and respond to the full range of problems arising in a crisis. Actions limited at the early stage to providing financial support can lead to unnecessary debtor bailouts and increase the likelihood that support will be wasted.

Governments' initial remedial efforts often prove insufficient, and eventually it becomes clear that more comprehensive and profound responses are required. During this period the financial system founders, the availability of credit is reduced, and output suffers. Years may elapse between these initial efforts and the adoption of more viable solutions. Meanwhile, costs can soar to the point that governments are no longer able to achieve even their basic objective of protecting depositors from substantial loss.[5] (Recent experience in Ecuador is one such example.)

More Aggressive Action Might Reduce Costs

Viable solutions for severe systemic crises must address the underlying financial problems. Systemic crises by definition implicate all sectors of the national economy: banks, nonbank financial institutions, corporations and proprietorships, households, and the public sector. Many corporations and

---

5. There may be potential advantages to a "go slow" approach to dealing with crises. Japan's approach over the last decade has led to a decline in prices (real estate, industrial assets) over time and has avoided the potential disruptions and negative wealth effects of marking assets to market at crisis-level prices. It may be that this approach will prove costly in the long run.

Box 9-1. *Why Governments May Be Slow to Respond*

Experience suggests that officials often underestimate the dimensions of a financial crisis in its early stages. This is not surprising given the information constraints and the incentives they face.

Senior government officials rarely have readily available sources of information that would indicate the dimensions of the crisis. Banks' financial statements may inadequately depict their condition, especially in times of rapid deterioration. Regulatory indicators tend to be lagging or inappropriate measures in the context of a systemic crisis. For example, debts on which debt service has been suspended typically are reflected for regulatory purposes as nonperforming only after three months. Bank regulatory capital is oriented to a liquidation scenario and therefore includes many debt obligations that do not contribute significantly to increasing banks' earnings capacity, the key objective in restoring the sector's health. Moreover, accounting reports and regulatory indicators are easily manipulated by bankers, who have incentives to obscure the extent of deterioration. Examples include capitalizing unpaid interest into a loan's principal balance while accounting for the interest as though it was paid (so-called evergreening), deferring losses, accelerating income, and creating artificial gains on asset sales. Bankers are able to obscure both negative cash flow and economic insolvency by increasing liabilities (new deposits and other borrowings).

Since crises reveal pre-existing problems, bank supervisors usually have incentives to underestimate the scope of distress and to not report fully to their governments. Supervisors also may lack the technical capacity to identify the scope of deterioration in banks' condition. Similar incentives may apply to central bank and deposit insurance officials. Central bank loan exposures and deposit insurance fund inadequacy may inhibit recognition of the full scope of the distress.

Finally, senior government officials have incentives to limit the scope of the actions they must take in response to a crisis. These officials will especially wish to minimize the amount of government expenditures that are required. This creates incentives to underestimate the dimensions of distress.

households will have accumulated unserviceable debts that render banks and other financial institutions unable to meet their own liabilities, in turn threatening corporate and household savings. The credit function collapses and the payments system is put at risk. Central banks risk insolvency in lending to insolvent banks or to insolvent nonbank financial institutions. National finances may be threatened by governments' contingent liability to protect depositors and salvage core elements of the financial system. The challenge that governments face under such circumstances is to solve these financial problems simultaneously.

The Interrelated Objectives of Government Action

Governments have three interrelated objectives in addressing systemic crises: to attain a sound banking system, to restore corporate creditworthiness, and to resume economic growth.

Attaining a sound banking system means restoring the cash-based profitability, liquidity, and solvency of those banks (and perhaps other financial institutions) that represent the core elements of the financial system.[6] Ensuring bank soundness protects deposits and moderates the potential for runs, reduces banks' funding costs, and restores their capacity to resume lending to viable corporations. Ensuring bank soundness also offers incentives for corporations to service their existing bank debts, since it preserves the value of the relationship.

Restoring corporate creditworthiness means ensuring that debts of viable entities are restructured to levels that can be serviced on the basis of reasonable projections of future operating results and asset values, which should reflect prudent operational restructuring (for example, downsizing, selling off noncore businesses). Restoring the capacity of corporations to service their (perhaps restructured) debts is a prerequisite to obtaining new financing from banks or other external sources, and ultimately to restoring the health of banks.[7]

Resuming economic growth requires keeping assets in production where that production does not create additional losses. Keeping assets in production means avoiding excessive transfers of corporate ownership and assets in the course of debt restructuring; it also means ensuring that banks are able to provide adequate working capital for needy, viable firms.[8]

---

6. Cash-based profitability is the most useful measure of bank health when defining solutions to crises. Regulatory measures of solvency and accounting measures of earnings are second-best measures, for they may or may not indicate sustainable profitability.

7. Some corporations—perhaps even a significant number—should not be made creditworthy; rather, their assets should be transferred to other owners and managers.

8. A less desirable alternative is for the government to become involved in directing or subsidizing the availability of working capital finance. Lacking a credible program to rapidly restore the creditworthiness of firms and the capital and liquidity of banks, governments may become directly responsible for making working capital available where it may be urgently needed, such as the export sector.

Resuming growth minimizes job losses and social pressures, increases the capacity of corporations to service debts, and increases the capacity of governments to finance the direct costs of crisis resolution.

The fact that these objectives are closely interrelated suggests that governments need to formulate and execute integrated strategies for simultaneous corporate and bank restructuring that are sensitive to the impact of such action on economic growth. These integrated strategies will define how governments provide financial support to banks. The challenge here is to invest public resources in a way that achieves these objectives at the least long-run cost.

Public sector investment in banks can be viewed from two perspectives. From a balance sheet perspective, the investment provides banks with the loss absorption capacity necessary to take the debt write-downs inherent in reestablishing the creditworthiness of debtors, as well as to absorb other losses that will be incurred in their own operational restructuring (for example, severance packages).[9] From an earnings perspective, the investment provides banks with the earnings capacity to bridge the difference between cash-based net interest earnings after debt restructuring and the net interest earnings associated with a market rate of return on equity. It tops-up banks' earnings capacity to ensure sustainable profitability.

The financial support that governments provide to banks is an important tool for creating incentives among banks and corporations to take actions consistent with government objectives. The prospect of financial support can be used to create incentives for banks to take the actions necessary to achieve sustainable cash-based profitability more quickly. It can be used to increase the speed with which banks renegotiate debts so as to reestablish asset cash flows and thus minimize carrying costs. It can be used to create incentives for banks to restructure their operations to increase profit potential and reduce waste. The debt restructuring, write-downs, and resumed lending that are made possible by providing banks with financial support can create incentives for corporate shareholders and managers to undertake the operational restructuring necessary to meet restructured debt service requirements. By restoring banks to health, government financial support preserves the relationship value to corporations of servicing their existing bank debts.

9. Debt write-downs mean that the restructured debt has a lower present value (in local currency terms) than the principal and fully accumulated interest of the original contractual indebtedness.

A key strategic challenge for governments is to obtain maximum benefit from the support they provide. The principal risks are that the beneficiaries (banks directly and corporations indirectly through debt write-downs and restructuring) will seek more support than is necessary and that they will squander the funds provided. Both outcomes will unnecessarily raise the costs to governments of resolving the crisis.

To control these risks, governments can condition their support through explicit contractual arrangements designed to promote the achievement of their objectives, to minimize the risks that support will be wasted, and to facilitate the recovery of as much of the support as possible over the long term. By establishing the terms and conditions for the provision of public sector financial support, such contractual arrangements can be used to ensure that potential beneficiaries know that they have only one opportunity to benefit from support and their performance will be closely monitored.

To apply this policy, governments must be ready to provide banks with an adequate level of support. Failure to do so will undermine the credibility of the policy and the intended incentive effects. (Indeed, it seems to be a leading cause of the multiple rounds of support and high costs seen in many crises.) Providing excessive support, on the other hand, implies either bailouts or the presence of waste or looting, which will result in the need to provide more support than would otherwise be required and raise costs unnecessarily.

Several challenges are inherent in applying this policy. One is to act promptly. The costs of crises tend to increase with time, and governments must act quickly to shape the behavior of bankers and corporate shareholders and managers by improving the private sector's incentives. Prompt action can also reduce uncertainty, which helps reduce costs. Since banks and corporations anticipate the potential availability of government support, delay in putting in place a credible program may inhibit restructuring.

A second key challenge is making the necessary assessments and decisions in an environment of uncertainty. This implies that the contractual arrangements with each beneficiary must provide for flexibility. As will be seen, the contract may provide for adjustments to incorporate changing circumstances or new information. It should also provide for multiple disbursements of the agreed support. Finally, the contract's terms and conditions should be designed to motivate action by beneficiaries consistent with the government's objectives and ensure the provision of no more support than is necessary.

Integrating Bank and Corporate Debt Restructuring Strategies

Restructuring troubled debts is a normal business function for banks. When financial sector distress falls short of being systemic (that is, when distress has reduced bank and corporate solvency but has not led to widespread insolvency), banks and corporations have incentives to work together to achieve mutually beneficial restructuring outcomes. Banks may employ several options to improve their ability to collect on debt over the long term and to ensure the profitability of their relationships with debtors (see table 9-1).

The Nature of Corporate Debt Restructuring

It is normal and appropriate for governments to facilitate restructuring of troubled debts by establishing rules or guidelines for the debts' accounting treatment (for example, income and loss recognition), regulatory treatment (for example, loan classification and provisioning requirements) or tax treatment (for example, deductibility of bank write-offs, taxability of corporate write-offs). Debt restructuring decisions are left to negotiations between banks and corporations, with government involvement limited to oversight of bank performance in restructuring debts as part of the routine supervisory function.

In certain debt restructuring situations, such as those involving large, complex corporations indebted to a large number of banks, governments (usually central banks or bank supervisors) may take a more active role in facilitating the conclusion of a debt restructuring agreement. Techniques such as the so-called London Rules may be used to motivate and coordinate restructuring actions by banks and corporations.

Debt Restructuring in Systemic Crises

In systemic crises, the incentives of banks and corporations to engage in debt restructuring change. Facing a threat that their institution's insolvency

Table 9-1. *Basic Options for Restructuring Troubled Debts*

Option	Applicability	Anticipated benefit to corporation	Anticipated effect on corporate capital	Anticipated benefit (risk) to bank
Extend principal and interest maturity (due date)	For corporations with temporary problems that can service all accumulated debt	Reduces debt service (cash flow requirements) over the near-term	No effect	No economic loss is incurred
Reduce interest rates	For viable corporations unable to service all accumulated debt	Reduces debt service	Increases capital	An economic loss is recognized over time in accounting terms
Forgive a portion of the debt (debt write-downs)	For corporations unable to service all accumulated debt	Reduces debt service	Increases capital	An economic and accounting loss is recognized immediately without the potential to be recovered
Accept assets in lieu of debt repayment	For downsizing or non-viable corporations	Reduces debt service	May increase capital	Bypasses weak foreclosure framework
Accept equity in lieu of debt repayment (debt-equity swaps)	For viable corporations with prospects for recovery	Reduces debt service	Increases capital Changes ownership structure	(Requires management of real estate, plant and equipment, and other assets) A likely economic loss is recognized immediately in accounting terms when equity is recorded at minimal value Increases potential to exert governance over corporations Upside potential to participate in corporation's recovery

will be revealed as a result of necessary debt restructuring, bank managers will either delay restructuring or engage in cosmetic restructuring that defers recognition of the inherent economic losses and postpones necessary operational bank and corporate restructuring.[10] Debtors, suspecting that banks are economically insolvent, may see no long-term relationship value (especially the possibility of new loans) in continuing to service their bank debts, and will conserve cash for internal working capital needs. Both banks and corporations may anticipate that delaying restructuring will increase their opportunities to obtain and benefit from government support. They may defer debt restructuring altogether until the government acts (see box 9-2).

The breakdown of the normal debt restructuring process in a systemic crisis can be costly. Suspension of debt service by even a small number of bank debtors can result in negative cash flow and contribute to bank illiquidity. Banks experiencing this cash-flow problem will respond by bidding more aggressively for funding, raising deposit rates. This increases the carrying costs associated with debts on which debt service has been suspended, accelerating the decapitalization of banks and raising the government's contingent liability as the guarantor of bank deposits (see box 9-3).

Growing illiquidity will make banks increasingly unwilling to lend, which will deepen the credit crunch and may lead to a larger than necessary decline in output. Declining output reduces tax revenues, aggravates social problems (such as unemployment), and increases social expenditures; the condition of banks and corporations deteriorates, further raising the government's potential costs. A downward spiral may ensue. Under these circumstances the stakes for the government become much greater. It becomes appropriate—perhaps essential—for the government to intervene in order to change the incentives of banks and corporations and ensure that debt restructuring proceeds promptly.

Supporting Banks in Systemic Crises

Necessary debt restructuring in systemic crises may well imply losses for banks of a magnitude that will result in their economic insolvency.

---

10. Cosmetic restructuring can take many forms. One is the deferral of required debt service in situations where it is unlikely that the debtor will be able to service the debt in the long run. Another is transferring debts to bank-owned or bank-funded affiliates (for example, so-called bad banks). A third is transferring debt to government asset management companies with recourse to the bank.

Box 9-2. *Impact of Systemic Crises—Financial Gridlock and Reduced Output?*

Systemic crises include interest rate spikes and exchange rate devaluation and over-shooting. On the domestic level, these phenomena increase claims on debtors as accrued but unpaid interest is capitalized as increased principal. Viewed in isolation, this creates windfall gains for domestic lenders (financial institutions) and holders of domestic debt (financial institutions, households, and others). Foreign exchange devaluation (including temporary overshooting) has a similar effect, increasing the local currency value and debt service requirement on foreign currency–denominated debts. Again, viewed in isolation, this creates a windfall gain for domestic foreign currency lenders and holders of foreign currency–denominated debt.

For debtors the result is that the real value of debt and the cost of servicing debt rises. With some exceptions this reduces the value of corporations, reduces their creditworthiness, and reduces or eliminates their access to new credit for working capital and investment. Corporations' debt burden not only becomes greater, but they may be cut off from external funds as well.

Corporations may respond in several ways. They may cease servicing their debts (even if they have the necessary cash flow), delay payments to trade creditors, reduce wages, or lay off workers. The likely effect is reduced firm and national output. Assets that would be otherwise productive are idled.

Because banks themselves are heavily indebted (perhaps unlike other holders of domestic debt), the potential windfall gain associated with their claims on debtors is partially or fully offset by increases in the value of their liabilities (the claims of depositors and holders of other types of interest-bearing claims, whether denomi-nated in local or foreign currency). Banks, in order to meet these claims, have strong incentives to attempt to extract as much as possible from their now more onerous claims on corporations (and households).

In this situation, debt restructuring gridlock may develop. Corporations will be unwilling or unable to service debts to banks, and banks will be unwilling to relin-quish claims on corporate debt. Output is likely to suffer.

Assuming that existing or new private sector bank shareholders will prove unwilling to bear those losses beyond the amount of their existing invest-ment, the government must decide whether to salvage banks or liquidate them. Since the government's interest is to protect the core elements of the financial system, it is likely that a substantial portion of the banking industry will be salvaged. Salvaging banks means restoring their cash-based profitability. For economically insolvent banks, this will require new

Box 9-3. *When Bank Cash Flow Turns Negative*

Depicted in table A is the financial structure of a sample bank. Given this financial structure and the annual level of interest earnings and noninterest expense, table B depicts—under different interest rate scenarios—the point at which debt service suspension can cause the bank's cash flow to become negative, expressed as a percentage of total loans. For example, in a market where the average asset yield is 20 percent and the average cost of funds is 15 percent, cash flow can be negative when debtors cease meeting interest payments on 22 percent of total loans.

Table A

	Balance sheet		
Assets		*Liabilities*	
Cash	50	Interbank deposits	750
Government securities	50	Short-term debt	100
Corporate debt	50	Other liabilities	50
Loans	800	Total liabilities	900
Other assets	50	Equity	100
Total	1,000	Total	1,000
Noninterest income	22.50		
Noninterest expense	40.00		

Table B

Category	*Percent*						
Asset yield	10	10	20	20	20	30	30
Liability rate	5	7	13	15	17	23	25
Spread	5	3	7	5	3	7	5
Nonperforming loan threshold	38	16	33	22	11	24	17

The principal assumptions in this hypothetical example are that all interest expense, noninterest expense, and noninterest income is paid and received in cash. The bank can avoid negative cash flow only by retaining some portion of the interest earned by depositors. In other words, to avoid negative cash flow and eventual illiquidity the bank must continuously increase deposits, either by retaining interest earned on existing deposits or raising new deposits or other funds. As the portion of loans on which interest payments have been suspended rises above the threshold, the pressure on the bank to increase deposits will intensify. Bankers will raise deposit interest rates, which in turn will increase carrying costs on the assets on which debt service has been suspended.

equity capital from the government, perhaps with support in the form of debt. In providing this support, the government may be able to simultaneously attract additional equity or debt financing (or both) from the private sector.

CONTRACTUAL ARRANGEMENTS FOR SUPPORTING BANKS. The basis for providing public financial support to banks might be legislation, either preexisting legislation or legislation passed in the course of the crisis. (There may be instances in which pertinent laws are neither on the books nor forthcoming.) Regardless of the statutory environment, the provision of financial support to banks should involve formal contractual arrangements between the government and beneficiary banks and related parties such as senior bank managers.

A decision that governments often face when providing new capital to banks is whether to nationalize them and assume direct responsibility for governance (as was done in Korea) or to leave existing shareholders in control (as was done in Mexico and Thailand).[11] Standard doctrine for resolving failed banks is that the interests of shareholders should be written off, thereby extinguishing their control. In severe systemic crises, where most banks may be economically insolvent, this prescription may no longer hold. The government may be unwilling or unable to assume even temporary responsibility for governance of all insolvent banks that will be salvaged. Moreover, it might achieve better outcomes (for example, quicker action or lower long-run costs) by allowing shareholders of certain banks to retain governance responsibilities and an ownership stake. Simply leaving banks economically insolvent and their shareholders in control, however, is not an option. Rather, the government should undertake to provide equity capital to insolvent banks in a manner sufficient to achieve its crisis resolution objectives while the shareholders retain certain governance responsibilities and ownership positions. The government may have to choose among the existing bank and shareholder groups.[12]

In cases where the government provides equity capital to nationalized banks, the arrangements might involve two types of contracts. One contract would be entered into between the government and the bank and

11. In nationalizing banks it is possible in principle to simultaneously attract equity capital from new investors in an amount sufficient to warrant granting primary responsibility for governance to those investors. In practice, this is rarely achieved.

12. As a first step in mitigating the potential inherent risks, eligibility criteria might provide that only relatively well-managed banks in which a controlling shareholder (or group of shareholders) is able to exert positive governance over managers and contribute to bank recapitalization would qualify.

would define the terms and conditions for financial support.[13] Another contract would be entered into between the bank or the government (or both) and the bank's senior management. This contract would more specifically address management performance. The interests of existing shareholders would be substantially diluted (if not written off entirely) through local regulatory regimes for identifying losses, writing down existing shareholder interests, and eliminating the role of shareholders in governance.[14]

Where the government decides to retain existing shareholder interests, the contractual arrangements also would involve two types of contracts. As in the case of nationalization, a contract defining terms and conditions for financial support would be entered into between the government and the bank. Another contract would be agreed between the government and the bank's principal shareholders. The contract with shareholders would provide incentives and penalties to promote required actions by bank management and mechanisms for the government to gain ownership control of the bank under defined circumstances. It might also provide for mandatory equity contributions by existing shareholders.

Linking Support to Banks to Debt Restructuring

A government's grant of financial support to banks will be based in large part on the losses that the institutions incur in debt restructuring. These losses need to be made transparent as part of the process of providing the support. Losses inherent in restructuring corporate debt can be made transparent either by selling the debts (most likely to a government-owned or sponsored asset management company, but perhaps to third parties) or by restructuring debts retained by banks.

SELLING DEBTS TO GOVERNMENT ASSET MANAGEMENT COMPANIES. In a systemic crisis, government asset management companies can serve a number of purposes, offer certain benefits, and entail certain drawbacks (see box 9-4). Selling debts to government asset management

13. It might seem that this contract would be unnecessary since the government is providing the new equity capital and is also the bank's sole or major shareholder, but this is not the case: A formal contract will ensure that terms and conditions are clear and provide the basis for monitoring and enforcement.

14. The effectiveness of mechanisms for writing down existing shareholders and reducing or eliminating the rights associated with ownership varies among countries. In some circumstances, shareholders may be able to block government action. A discussion of the various tactics that governments can use to enforce their intended action is beyond the scope of this paper.

Box 9-4. *Purposes, Benefits, and Drawbacks of Asset Management Companies in the Context of Systemic Crises*

Purposes

Recapitalize banks by purchasing assets at greater than market value

Finance support to banks while avoiding explicit fiscal consequences (asset management company buys assets with its own debt, which, though guaranteed by government, is not accounted as a fiscal liability)

Reduce bank capital needs and bolster reported regulatory capital

Reduce uncertainty associated with bank assets when attracting new investment or selling banks

Serve as a repository for credits to nonviable corporations (credit risk and management responsibility transferred to the asset management company)

Raise additional, nongovernment finance (asset management company issues debt to third parties)

Potential benefits in restructuring debts

Benefit from specialized restructuring and collection expertise

Aggregate debts from many banks into a single creditor unit

Achieve economies of scale

Sever personal or economic ties between bankers and debtors that give rise to conflicts of interest

Potential drawbacks

Loss of asset value

Loss of bank relationship value to corporation and associated incentives to achieve debt restructuring

Loss of relevant information regarding the corporation and its prospects

Lost opportunity to develop troubled debt restructuring skills in banks

Possibly less expert management

Potential for self-preservation and pressure to become a permanent (loss-making) institution

companies relieves bankers of further responsibility for debt restructuring and eliminates any future risk for banks associated with the debts.[15] Losses inherent in the debts are made transparent.

Although government asset management companies can be used to improve information (by making losses transparent) and reduce risks (by

---

15. Not all government asset management companies have been designed to achieve these objectives. Under Mexico's Fondo Bancario de Proteccíon al Ahorros (FOBAPROA), for example, banks retained substantial credit risk.

removing the potential for future credit losses) as a way of facilitating the process of providing equity capital support to banks, in practice a primary reason that governments use asset management companies in systemic crises is to strengthen banks' balance sheets through off-budget financing. Debts are purchased from banks (perhaps at inflated values) in exchange for bonds issued by the asset management company. These bonds, although probably guaranteed by the government, usually are not treated as a fiscal liability.

Using government asset management companies in this manner—essentially as an expedient for financing piecemeal support to banks without ensuring that the support is sufficient to restore sustainable profitability—can be counterproductive in terms of achieving government objectives at least cost. Selling debts to asset management companies severs the lending relationship (and perhaps all business relationships) between banks and corporations. Selling the debts of potentially viable corporations may reduce the corporations' incentives to service their debts, lower the chances that the debts will be restructured promptly, and impair the corporations' ability to attract new external financing. This may unnecessarily take assets out of production and may create incentives for looting. The transfer of an excessive number of debts to asset management companies will in the long run increase the government's costs.[16]

Given these risks, governments should adopt policies limiting the use of asset management companies to certain defined circumstances. One appropriate use would be for clearly nonviable corporations with no bank or corporate relationship value. Another would be for debts likely to involve collateral liquidation that can take advantage of asset management companies' specialized liquidation capacity (for example, commercial real estate projects). To the extent that governments nationalize banks in the process of resolving systemic financial crises, asset management companies might be used as an organizational means to handle a broader range of debt restructuring cases.[17] Finally, as discussed below, there may be specific circumstances in which asset management companies can be used to contain uncertainty arising from certain large debts so as to facilitate new investment by the private sector in distressed banks.

---

16. Providing piecemeal support in this manner will also increase waste costs since banks will be unlikely to use the support to maximum effect.

17. Managers of private banks might use asset management subsidiaries in a similar manner.

Table 9-2. *Features of a Bilateral Approach to Debt Restructuring*

Government role	Benefits	Risks
Create enabling environment (accounting, regulatory, and tax treatment)	Minimizes government involvement	Losses may be deferred via cosmetic restructuring, banks may remain weak, and costs may soar
Encourage formation of voluntary creditors' committees		
Upgrade creditor-debtor legal framework		
Oversight via bank supervision process		

RESTRUCTURING CORPORATE DEBTS IN BANKS: A TRILATERAL APPROACH. Two alternative approaches for promoting debt restructuring can be applied to debts that are not sold to government asset management companies, one bilateral, the other trilateral.

A *bilateral* approach leaves restructuring mainly to banks and corporations (see table 9-2). Under this approach, the government limits its role to establishing an enabling environment, promoting the formation by bankers of creditors' committees, upgrading bankruptcy and foreclosure regimes, and perhaps monitoring bankers' decisions and actions. Bankers, either managers of private banks or managers with whom the government has contracted to run nationalized banks, are the key decisionmakers in the process.

A bilateral approach may be inconsistent with a government's need to provide financial support to banks and corporations and achieve its crisis resolution objectives quickly and at least cost. The approach suffers from at least three potential weaknesses in this context. Two relate to the debt restructuring process itself; the third relates to the process of providing support to banks.

A bilateral approach may fail to leverage the financial support that the government provides to banks and corporations as a means to change their incentives to restructure debts. It also implies that the government in effect cedes to bank managers the analytic, decisionmaking, and follow-up authority that will significantly affect the costs of achieving its objectives and its ability to finance those costs.

A bilateral approach also may undermine the process under which banks are granted support and sustainable profitability is restored. Because of its

Table 9-3. *Features of a Trilateral Approach to Debt Restructuring*

Government role	Benefits	Risks
Provide financial support to banks under contractual terms and conditions that promote debt restructuring	Leverages financial support to promote prompt debt restructuring effectively	Requires substantial institutional capacity to implement
Ratify analyses and decisions relating to restructuring of large credits	Reduces the potential for cosmetic debt restructuring	
Evaluate bankers' debt restructuring performance with contractual remedies for poor performance	Makes transparent the outcomes of genuine (noncosmetic) debt restructuring	
Create an enabling environment Upgrade creditor-debtor legal framework	Ties managers' future employment to debt restructuring outcomes	

inherent slowness in revealing the outcomes of debt restructuring, a bilateral approach does not yield adequate information on portfolio losses on which to base bank recapitalization decisions. At best, it may lead to costly delays in restoring banks to health; at worst, it means that the provision of government support will be based on insufficient information regarding inherent losses, which in the end will necessitate additional rounds of financial support. This raises costs and undermines bank incentives and the credibility of the support program.

A *trilateral* approach to promoting the restructuring of debts held by banks casts the government as a principal in the debt restructuring process. The distinguishing feature of a trilateral approach is that government support is explicitly linked by contract (and perhaps law) to debt restructuring outcomes and to bank performance in debt restructuring (see table 9-3).

A trilateral approach may offer the government several important benefits. It can make transparent the losses inherent in debt restructuring and mitigate the potential for cosmetic restructuring. The government would then be more able to ascertain banks' recapitalization needs and provide funds with greater certainty that the support will restore their sustainable profitability. A trilateral approach can be used to accelerate the debt restructuring process, leading to faster restoration of corporate creditworthiness. Restoring bank soundness and making corporations creditworthy lays the groundwork for a resumption of lending under market-based terms and conditions. It can boost output, reduce costs, and improve the government's ability to finance those costs.

DETERMINING DEBT RESTRUCTURING OUTCOMES AND PERFOR-MANCE UNDER A TRILATERAL APPROACH. In general, debt restructuring outcomes under a trilateral approach can be made transparent in one of two ways: a case-by-case method or a pool method.

Under the case-by-case method, the government would track the re-structuring of debts of specific debtors and related groups of debtors. This method is most appropriate for large complex debts where, as is often the case, these debts significantly affect banks' overall financial condition. A case-by-case approach may include a range of options. Two options lie at the extremes: a centralized approach, under which the government takes responsibility for most of the work and makes most of the decisions, and a decentralized approach, under which the government contractually dele-gates to banks most of the work and decisionmaking and monitors the process, while retaining the power to intervene (see table 9-4). Under a centralized approach, the government contracts for extensive support from private sector experts to conduct the work; under the decentralized ap-proach, the government contracts with the banks themselves.

Under either of the options, the government would play an active role commensurate with its intention to provide substantial financial support to banks. At a minimum, it would execute this role under contractual ar-rangements. However, if legislation is attainable, it might grant the gov-ernment explicit legal powers with respect to debtors in arrears to banks benefiting from government support; such powers would enable the gov-ernment to execute a centralized approach while providing the authority to delegate certain responsibilities to others (for example, to bankers) under some form of decentralized approach.

Under a *pool* method, debt restructuring outcomes would be deter-mined for *portfolios* of debts. The method would be most appropriate in situations involving smaller debts, where substantial responsibility for the debt restructuring process must be delegated to banks. The relatively large number of such debts makes a case-by-case approach unfeasible, and the relatively small *value* of such debts does not warrant substantial commit-ment of the government's limited institutional resources. Moreover, for debts of small and medium-size enterprises in particular, decisions would have to be based on close knowledge of the operations of the enterprises; these decisions might best be delegated to bankers at the local branch level.

Table 9-4. *Indicative Options under a Case-by-Case Method for Determining Restructuring Outcomes*

	Primary responsibility	
Steps in debt restructuring process	*Centralized*[a]	*Decentralized*[b]
Obtaining information regarding corporation's financial and operating position	Bankers	Bankers
Verifying completeness and accuracy of information	Government	Bankers
Analysis of corporation's position (debts, contract terms, value of plant or equipment, business-line profitability), restructuring plans, and debt service prospects	Government	Bankers
Formulating debt restructuring alternatives	Government	Bankers
Evaluating alternatives and deciding on a debt restructuring plan	Government	Government
Negotiating agreement with corporations	Government	Bankers
Monitoring corporation's adherence to agreed terms and conditions	Bankers	Bankers
Enforcing corporation's adherence to terms of agreement	Government	Bankers

a. Governments organize substantial capacity, principally by contracting with the private sector, to undertake debt restructuring with corporations.

b. Governments contractually delegate responsibility to bankers.

Under a pool method, banks could be asked to designate their troubled small business and consumer portfolios, and private sector experts contracted by the government would then value these portfolios on a statistical basis. Debt restructuring targets would be set, and the government would provide financial support on the basis of periodic assessments of progress against these targets.

BASIC CONTRACTUAL TERMS AND CONDITIONS. The goal of the contracts involved in implementing a trilateral approach is to maximize the impact of future government outlays (for example, equity investments in banks) so as to promote rapid achievement of the government's crisis-resolution objectives. The contracts are intended to create incentives for managers of banks and corporations to take actions that contribute to achieving those objectives. Incentives for bank managers would derive principally from prospects for (and terms of) future employment and from the potential to obtain the financial support necessary to salvage their institutions. Incentives for corporate managers would derive from the potential to obtain debt restructuring (that is, reduced debt service cash-flow requirements), debt write-downs, and new external finance, all of which may be vital to ensuring the viability of the corporation. A key feature of the approach proposed here for shaping incentives for bank managers (and shareholders where applicable) is that the government would commit to providing once-and-for-all support: failure to meet terms and conditions would exclude existing managers and shareholders from any further opportunity to benefit from public support. This feature would create incentives to avoid cosmetic restructuring (such as postponing losses).

The contract between the government and the bank would define the instruments in which the government might invest, the basis for determining the amount and timing of the investment, the terms and conditions for obtaining government support, and the means of payment. It would establish the basis for monitoring implementation of agreements and provide remedies in the event of nonperformance. They would provide means for the government to recoup its investment to the maximum extent possible.

The instruments in which the government might invest would include (at the least) equity instruments such as common or preferred shares, since these instruments are essential to restoring the sustainable profitability of banks. Additional support might also be available in the form of debt instruments such as medium-term bonds or short-term loans and other forms of support such as asset purchases or the issuance of guarantees.

The forms of support for which the bank might qualify (as well as the process for determining the level of support) would be defined by contract. Losses incurred by the bank in restructuring corporate debt would be a principal determinant of the level of equity capital support, but other sources of loss (such as the bank's operational restructuring costs) might also might be contemplated. In the case of a nationalized bank, the government would likely invest sufficient equity to fully compensate the bank for after-tax losses incurred. For a bank in which shareholders retain meaningful ownership stakes, the government might well agree to compensate the bank for only a portion of losses; new shareholders would provide the additional needed equity.

The contract between the government and the bank would define the timing of the provision of different forms of support. An important feature is that support would be provided in tranches so as to provide an underlying mechanism for monitoring the performance of the bank's managers. For equity capital investments, these tranches would represent ex post compensation for losses realized in restructuring large debts subject to a case-by-case method. Support for losses incurred using a pool method could be provided ex ante or ex post.

The contract between the government and the bank would also define the government's means of payment. These might include government bonds (typically) or cash. Government bonds given in payment would be straight interest-bearing debt at market terms for rates and maturities. Zero-coupon bonds, for example, would not be used, since they undermine bank liquidity and can increase carrying costs.

The contract would provide for means by which the government can recoup its investment in the bank and thereby reduce its long-run costs. There are at least three principal means for doing so. First, the government could invest in bank instruments that are marketable at a future date once restructuring is in process or complete. Second, the government could acquire the equity stakes in large corporations that the bank receives under debt-equity swaps conducted as part of corporate debt restructuring; financial support to the bank could be conditioned on the transfer of those interests to the government.[18] Third, the bank could be required to repay the support provided, which would certainly be the case where the government invested in bank debt instruments, but repayment requirements might also apply to other forms of support. For example, the bank might be required to repurchase certain bank assets that the government had acquired, or shareholders might be required to purchase equity positions acquired by the government in their banks.

Under a trilateral approach, bank incentives are not driven solely by contracts: the government can begin to shape incentives in advance by publicly announcing eligibility criteria and terms and conditions for public support. For example, making it clear that eligibility will be based on analyses of bank actions with respect to all large-debtor relationships and that it may be contingent on specific personnel changes would likely create immediate incentives for banks to cease engaging in cosmetic debt restructuring. Similarly, the terms and conditions of support might provide for new working capital financing to corporations that take defined steps to

18. Viewed another way, part of the government's financial support to the bank could be used to purchase the equity stakes. The purpose in transferring the equity would be to relieve bank managers of the responsibility for the assets and to ensure that it is the government and not the now-recapitalized bank (which may be only partially owned by the government) that benefits from the potential increased value of the equity positions. The government could contract with the private sector to manage those positions and to exert governance on the corporations to promote their operational restructuring.

facilitate their debt restructuring (for example, providing complete and accurate information, or hiring external advisers).

This is not intended as an exhaustive list of all terms and conditions appropriate for contracts between governments and banks. Terms and conditions should also address organizational and operational changes (for example, establishing workout units with specific staffing characteristics, or adopting policies and standards for debt restructuring performance) and specific remedies in situations where performance does not meet agreed standards. Finally, contracts with the managers of nationalized banks should contain many of these same conditions.

DEALING WITH UNCERTAINTY IN LINKING BANK SUPPORT TO DEBT RESTRUCTURING.   A basic feature of the trilateral approach is that government financial support is based on corporate restructuring outcomes. But there may well be situations with respect to certain large debtors or groups of debtors where uncertainties regarding debt restructuring outcomes will have a material impact on the government's ability to ascertain the bank's inherent losses and thus the amount of new equity required to restore the bank's sustainable profitability. Governments can use at least two types of mechanisms to mitigate these uncertainties.

One mechanism is to sell the debts that give rise to excessive uncertainty to a government asset management company, eliminating future risk to the bank arising from these debts and thereby eliminating the source of uncertainty. In this case, the bank's managers would have no future responsibility for restructuring the debts. (Against a decision to sell the debts to an asset management company must be weighed the considerations mentioned earlier, such as the impact of severing the bank relationship on the value of the debts.)

A second mechanism is to use government guarantees to in effect reduce uncertainty regarding the range of possible outcomes in debt restructuring when banks retain the debts. For example, the government might guarantee against losses in excess of a predetermined amount, or the bank might establish a subsidiary to which the debts are sold (a so-called bad bank), while the subsidiary's asset portfolio would receive some form of government guarantee. There are many possible variations on the use of this type of mechanism.

In effect, these mechanisms for reducing or eliminating uncertainty overcome an information constraint that may otherwise undermine implementation of a trilateral approach. They allow for the adequate recapitalization of banks with government support while permitting additional time to determine the outcomes of the restructuring of certain debts. They can be particularly useful for governments in creating inducements in the private sector for new strategic investment in banks as part of the provision of government financial support.

DETERMINING APPROPRIATE DEBT WRITE-DOWNS. Governments face difficult trade-offs in attempting to simultaneously achieve their crisis resolution objectives (sound banks, creditworthy corporations, renewed economic growth) while minimizing their long-run costs (carrying costs, bailouts, looting, and waste), maximizing the recovery of their upfront outlays, and improving their ability to finance those costs. One key trade-off relates to the likely need to grant debt write-downs to certain corporations. Governments have several reasons to seek to minimize debt write-downs. Write-downs beyond some level become debtor bailouts, which raise bank losses and government costs. Write-downs also decrease the extent to which carrying costs can be recouped, again raising bank losses and government costs.[19] But governments also have several reasons for seeking to *promote* debt write-downs. Debt write-downs, in conjunction with corporate operational restructuring, may well be required in order to restore corporate creditworthiness and increase both internal working capital and the corporation's ability to tap external sources of working capital. Debt write-downs may help keep assets in production, which may contribute to renewed economic growth and the government's ability to finance the costs of supporting banks (by increasing tax revenues or by lowering unemployment expenditures). Balancing these trade-offs is a matter of judgment that may well involve complex macroeconomic and microeconomic considerations.

An elaboration on how to approach these trade-offs is beyond the scope of this paper, but several key principles can be defined. In making these judgments, governments will likely wish to prevent substantial transfers to banks of corporate shares or assets. They will wish to prevent the widespread liquidation of corporations and the eventual transfer of their assets to new owners. Debt relief should be available at a level sufficient to keep competent owners and managers in control of corporations. At the same time, incompetent or reckless owners or managers need to be weeded out.

---

19. If banks are able to negotiate with corporations for full repayment of all accumulated interest and principal, carry costs accumulated prior to debt restructuring would be recouped immediately on an economic basis and over time on an accounting basis.

Desired structural change also may imply the transfer of corporate owner-ship, for example, where economic or personal linkages between banks and corporations are an underlying cause of the crisis. Corporate shareholders should not gain as a result of write-downs. It is to be expected that the value of their stakes should decline regardless of whether the corporation benefits from write-downs. Under the principle of burden-sharing, corpo-rate shareholders should become poorer.

Institutional Requirements for Implementing a Trilateral Approach

Implementing a trilateral approach might be seen as a largely technical challenge, much like the challenge faced by private investors in making a major investment in a complex, troubled corporation. But systemic finan-cial crises are also major political challenges. With the country's financial system, economy, and perhaps even social fabric on the line, political lead-ership must play a key role.

THE POLITICAL CHALLENGE. Political challenges associated with restructuring arise in part from the likelihood for significant wealth shifts in the economy. Crisis resolution might appropriately involve poverty for some of the rich, but all manner of vested interests are likely to be affected to some degree. Politicians themselves may be personally affected and may be lobbied heavily on behalf of others. There will be a social and political backlash against the use of scarce public funds to protect banks in a climate of increasing unemployment and poverty. The public and the press will blame the politicians.

Given their personal interests and the interests of those they represent, politicians will likely seek to become involved in the government's response to a financial crisis, especially regarding the use of public funds. This may undermine the potential for promptly resolving crises at least cost. On a political level, direct participation by politicians in the individual analyses, decisions, and actions involved in granting or denying public support to banks (directly) and debtors (indirectly) will open the process to charges of political favoritism or retribution. Given the competing interests, achieving a political consensus on such decisions may prove difficult or impossible. Similarly, gaining public confidence will be more difficult. On a technical level, the *volume* of decisions that need to be made during a financial crisis (especially in the context of executing integrated bank and corporate restructuring strategies) will be too great to accommodate political involve-ment in all key decisions.

While it may be presumptuous to generalize about the nature of politics across a range of countries, one means of accommodating the need of politicians to provide leadership in crises and to be comfortable in their ability to oversee their government's response would be for political leaders to seek consensus on the specific objectives of government actions and the basic principles that should guide those actions. To execute those actions, political leaders should seek agreement on delegating the work to a technically competent government team.

This approach may offer several advantages. Reaching political consensus on objectives and principles is likely to be more feasible than trying to reach consensus on specific actions affecting specific vested interests, such as banks or corporate debtors. The actions required to resolve crises will involve substantial work over an extended period of time (measured in years). The intensity and complexity of the work requires the full-time attention of those responsible. Senior government officials are rarely in a position to drop all other tasks to devote full-time attention to this work, and in practice they will have little choice other than to delegate most of the actual work. Government institutions normally face incentives to underestimate the scope of the problems, which would preclude effective performance. Their effectiveness may be impaired as well by institutional and personal rivalries with other government institutions. Finally, the nature of the work (see table 9-4) requires specialized private-sector skills that do not correspond to those normally possessed by most senior government officials or their staffs.

GOVERNANCE, CHARACTERISTICS, AND POWERS OF THE CRISIS MANAGEMENT TEAM. A purpose-built crisis management team would report to some form of governing body in which political interests, the permanent institutions of government, and probably the private sector would be represented. At the same time, the governance arrangements would be designed such that the team would be seen publicly as operating largely independent of political interference. It should operate transparently, reporting on its analyses, decisions, and actions. Transparency would allow interested politicians, affected parties, the public, and the domestic and international press to judge those actions in terms of politically agreed objectives and principles.

Having publicly agreed on objectives and principles and having put in place these institutional arrangements, politicians may be able to deflect much of the potential criticism and lobbying that otherwise will be directed at them. To a large extent, the heat shifts to the crisis management team.

The work of the team involves a wide range of tasks associated with making a major investment of public resources in a potentially large number of banks. It includes gathering, verifying, and analyzing current and historic information, preparing financial projections, formulating and evaluating investment options, making investment decisions (that is, granting or denying public support), defining investment-specific terms and conditions, negotiating contracts, designing reporting requirements, monitoring performance, and enforcing contracts.

It is important that senior government officials delegate the responsibility and authority for this work in explicit terms. Failure to delegate effectively and explicitly may be one of the most severe errors made by officials dealing with crises. As in any business, effective delegation of the responsibility and authority for financial crisis management depends on several basic elements:

Objectives and responsibilities need to be unambiguously defined. Ideally they should be articulated in terms of explicit outcomes, elaborating on those agreed at the political level. The basic objectives set out above (pp. 289–91) are a starting point.

Basic principles to guide the work must be established. At the political level, these should be of general application in guiding the work of the team. They should be designed to promote transparency, ensure fairness and burden-sharing, minimize bailouts, looting, and waste, and guarantee that the government's financial support has been used to maximum effect. These principles should establish the basic parameters for determining who is eligible to benefit from government support.

The authority and powers available to the team need to be defined. In general terms, the team must be able to obtain information and verify its completeness and accuracy, to make decisions based on that information (including decisions on the investment of public resources), to negotiate contracts with banks, bank shareholders, and bank managers, to monitor performance under the contracts, and to take action where performance standards have not been met. Building public confidence requires that the government speak with one voice, and the team needs the power to act as the chief spokesperson with respect to the actions being taken. It needs a mechanism to be able to coordinate supporting actions that may have to be taken by the government institutions and the authority to arbitrate differences of opinion among government institutions and to refer unresolved differences to the top levels of government, likely through the governing body to which the team reports. The team needs the authority to recruit and to contract for outside expertise. It needs legal protections for team members acting in good faith.[20]

The team needs resources necessary to do the job. The key resource is the government financing necessary for investments in banks and the payment of deposits in liquidated banks. Failure to grant sufficient financing undermines chances for success. The team needs adequate financing for its own operations, including funds to hire experts with necessary skills. Given the nature of the work, this would entail profiles such as specialists in commercial and administrative law, investment bankers, corporate finance and restructuring experts, financial and corporate analysts, strategic experts, forensic and general auditors, and the like.

Conclusion

Executing integrated bank and corporate restructuring strategies so as to control the costs of crises involves aggressive action on the part of governments. The work involved in providing public support to banks while ensuring that no more support than necessary is provided, and that the support is used to maximum effect, is much like the work faced by any private investor contemplating a major investment in a complex, troubled enterprise. Although the payoff for governments in terms of reduced costs of crises may be high, governments can hope to be successful only if they have undertaken to put into place the specialized institutional arrangements capable of effectively executing work of this nature.

20. The team's authority and powers might be granted by special legislation. Special legislation can also be used to overcome weaknesses in the existing legal framework. In many cases, however, effects similar to those created by special legal powers can be achieved by executive decision (in the case of governments), and under contractual arrangements with banks, bank shareholders, and bank managers and debt contracts with corporations. The suggestions made in this paper do not depend on emergency legislation.

GERALD E. MEYERMAN

10

The London Approach
and Corporate Debt
Restructuring in
East Asia

W HEN THE FINANCIAL CRISIS hit East Asia in the fall of 1997, corporate debt in Indonesia, Malaysia, South Korea, and Thailand had
reached high levels. The mechanism that precipitated the crisis was simple:
capital outflows meant that investors and creditors suddenly called in the
loans that they had been aggressively pushing on the East Asian corporate
sector for years. Companies in the region found themselves unable to repay
their debt for a variety of reasons, including mismanagement, unsound
financial practices, lack of accountability, and excessively high leverage.
Local currency devaluations made it harder for local companies with debts
denominated in foreign currencies to repay loans. This led to a stampede,
and as more creditors and investors called in their loans, the "cascade
effect" threatened to bankrupt the entire economy. Had this situation not
been resolved, it would have had vast and unpredictable consequences for
the social welfare, economic development, and political stability of the
region.

The author wishes to acknowledge the contribution of Olivier Butzbach and H. Scott Stevenson.
The findings, interpretations, and conclusions in this paper are entirely those of the author and should
not be attributed in any manner to the World Bank, to its affiliated organizations, or to members of its
Board of Executive Directors or the countries they represent. The World Bank does not guarantee the
accuracy of data included in this article.

The attempt to establish sound insolvency and bankruptcy regimes, however, was not an adequate response to the crisis. The laws enacted and programs put into effect will undoubtedly assist in limiting the impact of future crises, but they were not established in sufficient time to stem the crisis of 1997–98. Company failure sometimes occurs because a company is unable to resolve temporary or other financial difficulties, even though the company's longer-term viability and solvency may be sound. Forcing troubled companies into liquidation, especially if the crisis is caused by macroeconomic circumstances beyond their control, represents a major cost to the economy. It is also a market failure, which can cause or amplify financial instability. Finally, unnecessary liquidation represents a welfare cost in the form of unemployment and misallocation of capital.

Liquidation and court-supervised restructuring were not viable alternatives for the Asian crisis countries; what was needed was an out-of-court, voluntary debt-restructuring process that would have made it possible to distinguish good assets from bad and thereby preserve a particular country's industrial capacity. The countries of the region, however, had no experience with such processes. The crisis called for rapid answers, and the East Asian countries looked to existing models for corporate debt restructuring. Frameworks for corporate debt restructuring have been developed only recently, in the wake of the debt crises of the 1980s in developing countries and the recession of the early 1990s in the United Kingdom and in the United States. Great Britain, in particular, developed a set of guidelines and nonbinding rules—the London Approach—that had positive results during the 1990s.

This paper compares the London Approach with the corporate debt restructuring frameworks developed in East Asia (which, to a certain extent, drew and built on the former), evaluates the approaches taken in different countries, and draws lessons for countries facing similar challenges in the future.

The London Approach

During the mid-1970s, when the United Kingdom entered a period of industrial recession with high inflation, commercial banks had to quickly establish workout units and internal policies in order to deal with a rapidly increasing number of bad loans. The banks, however, had little experience with workouts. Insolvency legislation was outdated and did not provide tools for voluntary restructuring, including protection of new money and processes limiting the ability of a small group of creditors to block a workout settlement between the majority of creditors and the company.

Under these circumstances, the Bank of England chose to become actively involved in individual company workouts. The Bank's main objectives were

—to minimize losses to banks and other parties incurred from unavoidable company failures, through coordinated and well-prepared workouts,

—to avoid unnecessary liquidations of viable companies, through their reorganization and the preservation of employment and productive capacity, and

—to prevent immediate failure by ensuring the provision of interim financial support to companies.[1]

The involvement of the Bank in company workouts was possible because its governing statutes did not limit its activity to a narrowly defined role. In fact, the Bank's policy was entirely unconnected with banking regulation. Companies trusted the Bank to be impartial, independent, and confidential. In many cases, the Bank would call the participating banks together and, in the absence of a lead banker acting on its own, arrange for one of the major lenders to assume that role. The Bank could and did insist on immediate actions such as payment of wages, thus preventing the premature liquidation of companies resulting from a "renegade bank" calling in its loans. Other steps, such as agreements on new money, special arrangements for prioritization of debts, or changes in company management, were undertaken with the Bank's guidance.

During the 1970s U.K. supervisory authorities were prepared to intervene in corporate workout situations without the Bank of England committing any of its own funds. Following the election of more market-oriented governments in the United States and the United Kingdom, long and sustained economic growth during the mid-1980s, and fundamental changes in the financial industry,[2] the Bank reviewed its policy on corporate workouts. It decided to reduce its direct contact with companies in

---

1. Kent (1997).

2. The demand for new corporate finance instruments (for example, hedging, leveraged mergers and acquisitions, and complex syndications), which were financed with short- and medium-term facilities, resulted in high debt ratios. At the brink of the 1989 economic downturn, many U.K. corporations experienced severe liquidity problems as a result. Further, the multiplicity of banking relationships created management problems for borrowers that tried to develop workout solutions.

difficulty, leaving the task of developing restructuring strategies to the private sector. The Bank saw its new, reduced role as that of diplomat and catalyst—to motivate the parties involved in a restructuring to work toward a mutually agreeable workout solution.[3]

After consultations with the banking community in the United Kingdom, the Bank decided in the early 1990s not to formalize its restructuring framework (now popularly termed the London Rules) out of concern that foreign banks might challenge strictly formalized rules in court.[4] In addition, the framework had to remain flexible and adaptable. The Bank therefore chose to define and communicate the framework concerning the conduct of corporate workouts informally—through speeches—rather than through formal policy documents.

The London Approach provides general guidance to banks and other creditors on how to react to a company that faces serious financial difficulties. This guidance, however, is not statutory, and the Bank does not have enforcement powers. The London Approach recognizes that banks and other parties act in their own self-interest. However, by encouraging the parties to observe certain rules for restructuring, it seeks to avoid unnecessary damage and to foster solutions that benefit all parties involved. The key features of the London Approach are as follows:

—Principal creditors must be willing at the outset to consider a nonjudicial resolution to a company's financial difficulties rather than resorting to formal insolvency procedures such as liquidation, administration, or a company voluntary agreement, and without recourse to other enforcement procedures such as receivership or administrative receivership.

—As part of this consideration, creditors must commission an independent review of the company's long-term viability, drawing on information made available by, and shared between, all the likely parties to any workout.

—During the period of the review, the company's bankers holding debt should agree to maintain the company's facilities in place, effectively an

---

3. The principles of the London Approach do not apply to troubled or insolvent banks, since insolvencies intrinsically present unique problems—both for banks themselves and for the central bank in its capacity as supervisor of the banking sector.

4. The term "London Approach" was used until the early 1990s, when David Lascelles published an article in the *Financial Times*, terming the Bank of England's new policy approach the "London Rules." See "Fortunes Vary as Recession Bites," *Financial Times*, November 29, 1990.

informal standstill sufficient to preserve the confidence of suppliers and customers by allowing the company to continue to trade normally.

—Drawing on the independent review, the company's main creditors should work together to reach a joint view on whether, and on what terms, a company is worth supporting in the longer term.

—To facilitate these discussions, a coordinating or lead bank may be designated, and a steering committee of creditors formed.

—In addition to maintaining existing credit facilities, it may be necessary to allow the company to supplement its existing borrowing with new money in the event of an immediate liquidity shortfall. New money may be provided on a pro rata basis by all existing lenders, by specific lenders with priority arrangements, or by releasing the proceeds of asset disposal subject to priority considerations. Other principles during this critical period of financial support include the recognition of existing seniority of claims and the sharing of losses on an equal basis between creditors in a single category.

—If creditors agree that the company is viable, the creditors should move on to consider longer-term financial support, including an interest holiday, extension of loan maturities, further lending for working capital, and conversion of debt into equity.

—Changes in the company's longer-term financing need to be conditioned on the implementation of an agreed business plan, which may well involve management changes, sales of assets or divisions, or even the takeover of the company.

The London Approach does not guarantee the survival of a company in difficulty. Regulatory authorities do not intervene and, because of its voluntary nature, the London Approach can only be effective as long as it is supported within the banking community.

The London Approach was instrumental during the recession of the early 1990s. Many companies survived only because their banks, bondholders, and other creditors sought and achieved a collective solution for the financial restructuring of viable businesses. The Bank has been actively involved in more than 160 restructurings since 1989. However (and more important), many more workouts have been effected by using the principles of the London Approach without the Bank's direct intervention. When successfully applied, the London Approach preserves value for creditors and shareholders, saves jobs, and safeguards productive capacity.

Is the London Approach Replicable? The East Asian Crisis and Corporate Restructuring

The East Asian countries naturally turned toward the London Approach when it became obvious that a general scheme for corporate debt restructuring was needed to pull their economies out of financial crisis. However, a detailed assessment of the frameworks developed in this region show several divergences from the London Approach that are relevant for similar endeavors in the future. In each country, the structure was adapted to meet local conditions and needs. The relationship between business and government, the nature of corporate debt, the extent to which debt was denominated in foreign currency, how much debt was held domestically—all influenced the particular framework adopted.

Corporate Restructuring Frameworks in East Asia

The crisis that hit East Asia in 1997 unfolded against a complex background. The region's economies were (and largely remain) characterized by high concentration, an intricate corporate structure with multiple links between governments, banks, state-owned companies, and the private sector, which frequently created "crony economies" riddled by special interests and corruption. The crisis triggered a wave of large-scale financial and corporate restructuring. None of the countries in the region had either the experience or the resources to conduct such restructuring on their own and all of the economies ran a very real risk of collapse.

In the absence of efficiently functioning systems to resolve financial claims, governments in all the crisis countries have instituted out-of-court mechanisms to encourage financial settlements. As a first step, the governments instituted rules and guidelines for voluntary restructuring, building directly on the London Approach. In Thailand, a framework of principles and timelines for voluntary workouts (the "Bangkok Rules") was promulgated in September 1998. In South Korea the government reached a series of agreements with the chaebols—the country's leading conglomerates—under which the chaebol owners and senior managers committed to take significant steps toward better corporate governance and to reduce their debt through divestitures, concentration on core businesses, and mergers of subsidiaries. In early 1998 the chaebols agreed to a restructuring program based on five elements:

—improving transparency and corporate governance by adopting international accounting and reporting standards, appointing external directors to corporate boards, and strengthening shareholder rights,

—eliminating cross-debt payment guarantees among subsidiaries,

—improving the financial structure of the conglomerates by lowering of debt-equity ratios (the Korean government set the upper limit at 200 percent), and liquidating unprofitable businesses and assets,

—concentrating on core businesses, and

—strengthening the accountability of controlling shareholders and managers.[5]

The Korean government and Korea's president committed to implementing these agreements and intervened several times to speed up restructuring of the chaebols. On December 7, 1998, President Kim Dae Jung met again with the heads of the top five chaebols and reached agreement on a twenty-point action program that followed the principles and the objectives agreed upon in the preceding accords.

These sets of rules and principles, however, were not sufficient to ensure the effective and efficient implementation of corporate debt restructuring. Here lies the first point of difference between debt restructuring in East Asia and the London Approach. In the United Kingdom, the central bank, whose authority and impartiality were widely accepted, was able to play the role of hands-off facilitator while debtors and creditors reached their own agreements in a business environment based on mutual trust and understanding and with clearly defined and functioning market exit and entry mechanisms. In East Asia, the business environment was altogether different. First, a significant part of industrial capacity in these countries took the form of family-owned conglomerates controlling their own banks— that is, their source of financing. A typical instance in the case was (and remains) the Korean chaebols, which had pursued a diversification policy during the 1980s and 1990s that involved them in virtually all sectors of the economy. Second, the East Asian states had a decidedly hands-on attitude toward the private sector, an attitude manifested in the large number of state-owned banks and companies, as well as by the personal holdings of reigning families. In Indonesia, for example, the Suharto family was thought to own 18 percent of the economy. Finally, regulatory authorities

5. Particularly important in this respect were agreements by controlling shareholders to place their personal wealth into recapitalization and loan guarantees. See Yoo Seong Min (1999).

had little enforcement power, and their ineffectiveness was reinforced by the absence of an independent and effective judicial system.

It was obvious, therefore, that the East Asian central banks, lacking authority, power, and experience, could not play the same role as did the Bank of England within the London Approach framework. Instead, East Asian governments put in place a vast array of ad hoc institutions to deal with financial and corporate restructuring (see p. 86, table 4-2).

These institutions, unlike the Bank of England, were given extensive prerogatives, and their power was often amplified and supported by their government's actions. In Indonesia, for example, the Indonesian Bank Restructuring Agency (IBRA) has the power to make creditors and debtors comply with its orders. In Korea, the Corporate Restructuring Coordination Committee (CRCC) set the terms for the restructuring of Daewoo Group,[6] while the Financial Supervisory Commission (FSC) used its enforcement powers to force creditor banks to extend funds and institute debt-equity swaps to twelve units of Daewoo Group under a rehabilitation plan.

Beyond their significant prerogatives, however, the new institutions have assumed an increasing financial and economic importance in their respective countries. In Korea, for example, the FSC—the agency in charge of financial restructuring—was accused in early 2000 of trying to interfere with the central bank's prerogatives when it issued remarks on the future course of interest rates in Korea.[7]

OUT-OF-COURT MECHANISMS. Generally, the special agencies in charge of corporate debt restructuring have included most stakeholders in the debt restructuring process. In Thailand, for example, the Corporate Debt Restructuring Advisory Committee (CDRAC) is chaired by the governor of the Bank of Thailand, and includes representatives from the Federation of Thai Industries, the Thai Bankers' Association, the Board of Trade, the Foreign Bankers' Association, and the Association of Finance Companies. These agencies act as facilitators of the restructuring process, providing expertise and coordinating the work of a vast array of actors. The rationale behind the Jakarta Initiative in Indonesia is fourfold:

—to introduce world-class experts to guide individual debt workouts,

—to provide the restructuring program with sufficient leverage to force parties to participate in good faith,

—to coordinate efforts with the financial restructuring agencies, and

6. See *Korea Herald,* January 31, 2000.
7. See *Korea Times,* February 7, 2000.

—to underpin the framework with an operational bankruptcy system to give all parties incentives to negotiate.

Despite some progress achieved in each of the four countries, the out-of-court mechanisms have produced mixed results, in part because they depend essentially on moral suasion. In fact, in all these countries purely voluntary mechanisms have been superseded by another set of initiatives aiming at channeling and tightening the debt restructuring process. In most countries, the government has used other tools, especially the direct control of lending to the corporate sector and the privatization of state-owned financial corporations, to accelerate corporate restructuring following the cleanup of bad assets.

Thailand's CDRAC (created in January 1999) monitors progress on six- to seven-hundred high-priority cases. In March 1999 the Bank of Thailand promulgated a model Debtor-Creditor Agreement (DCA) and an Inter-Creditor Agreement (ICA) on Restructuring Plan Votes, both of which are enforceable contracts and have been signed by eighty-four financial institutions as of January 2000. The DCA has also been signed by more than four-hundred debtors. In both cases, signatories agree to adhere to defined procedures for case entry, a six- to eight-month process for developing and agreeing on workout plans, information-sharing, development of reorganization plans, negotiation, and 75 percent thresholds for plan approval. These provide for CDRAC-arranged mediation as well as intercreditor arbitration. These agreements empower the Bank of Thailand to enforce creditor compliance through warnings and fines. Creditors are obliged to file a court petition for bankruptcy if fewer than 50 percent of the creditors agree to a proposed workout, or if a debtor refuses to grant the DCA access to all corporate data.

Such compulsory elements clearly signal an evolution from the voluntary London Approach, undoubtedly provoked by the absence of a functioning and reliable insolvency regime. Table 10-1 presents the results of the different approaches followed by the crisis countries.

In Korea, besides the voluntary framework agreed upon by the major chaebols, the government has used its dominant position in the financial sector to overcome the resistance shown by the chaebols' senior management to impose debt rescheduling, rollovers, and repayments. President Kim Dae Jung warned the conglomerates in May 1999 that "if [these] companies fail to show any significant effort to restructure as they had promised to do in December last year, new bank loans will be halted." The cleanup of the financial sector has been followed by a large-scale privatization program.

Table 10-1. *Voluntary Workouts in East Asia, as of September 1999*

Workout strategy	Indonesia[a]	South Korea	Malaysia	Thailand[b]
Out-of-court procedures				
All or the majority of financial				
institutions signed on to accord	No	Yes	Yes	Yes
Formal process of arbitration,				
with deadlines	No	No	Yes	Yes
Provision of penalties for				
noncompliance	No	Yes	No	Yes
Out-of-court restructurings				
Number of registered cases	323	104	53	721
Number of cases filed	157	93	27	406
Number of restructured cases	26	46	10	157
Percentage of restructured debt				
on total debt	n. a.	40	32	22
Court-supervised restructurings				
Number of registered cases	88	48	52	30
Number of cases filed	78	27	34	22
Number of restructured cases	8	19	12	8
Percentage of restructured debt				
on total debt	4	8	n.a.	7

Sources: Claessens, Djankov, and Klingebiel (1999); International Monetary Fund (1999).
n.a. Not available.
a. Within Jakarta Initiative framework.
b. Within CDRAC targets.

Governments throughout the region have systematically encouraged banks to establish asset management companies (AMCs) to work out non-performing loans and maximize debt recovery. In Korea these AMCs are called corporate restructuring vehicles and have a broader purpose, since they provide resources to the banks, giving them time and capital to manage the debt restructuring processes with debtors.

CREATING INCENTIVES, ELIMINATING IMPEDIMENTS. A key aspect of government-led corporate restructuring in East Asia has been a series of statutory and regulatory enactments aimed at facilitating the restructuring of corporate debt, promoting corporate reorganization, strengthening prudential regulation of financial institutions, and creating an environment of open competition. These changes were forced through by powerful government administrations.[8] In the United Kingdom, by contrast, such structures and mechanisms had existed for decades and facilitated the implementation of the London Approach.

Korea's Securities Investment Company Law established the Corporate Restructuring Fund, initially funded with 1.6 billion won in October 1998 to improve the financial status of small- and medium-size enterprises through equity investment and debt rescheduling. Other legislative measures undertaken include the following:

—The government published revised guidelines on credit management by financial institutions to prohibit financial institutions from demanding guarantees from related companies, so-called cross-guarantees.

—The Corporate Tax Law was revised to disallow tax credits for interest payments on any corporate debt in excess of five times equity capital.

—To enable courts to evaluate restructuring applications, the Corporate Reorganization Law adopted economic criteria comparing the liquidation value of a company with its going-concern value. The amended law also simplifies reorganization procedures by facilitating the consolidation of related cases in a single process, shortening the deadlines for approval and submission of reorganization plans to between twelve and eighteen months, and reducing the grace period of debt repayment from twenty to ten years. The law establishes reorganization management committees to advise the court and major creditors.

—The Corporate Composition Law was revised to restrict the conditions for mutual settlement between a corporation and its creditors by specifying cases in which such a settlement might be undesirable. The law also disallows applications for the restructuring of nonviable corporations and strengthens the government's powers to monitor the implementation of mutual settlements. In addition, the law simplified procedures for legal composition and introduced procedural exemptions for small- and medium-size firms.

—Finally, the Foreign Capital Inducement Act was revised to liberalize foreign ownership of Korean corporations. The law also abolished the requirement for prior approval by the Ministry of Finance and Economy for large-scale mergers and acquisitions in all sectors of the economy except

8. Edward M. Graham rightly points to the key role played during the process by the Korean Fair Trade Commission, which, he argues, "emerged as one of the most powerful Korean agencies during the current administration." Graham (1999).

the defense industry. The ceiling on total foreign shareholdings in individual companies was abolished.

Indonesia, South Korea, Malaysia, and Thailand have all undertaken extensive processes of structural adjustment. Evidence of the progress of these undertakings can be found in World Bank and International Monetary Fund documents and policy instruments developed during the crisis and during the recovery phase.

THREAT OF LOSS AND MARKET EXIT MECHANISMS. A fundamental element of corporate debt restructuring is the presence of market exit and entry mechanisms, which act as incentives for companies to engage in out-of-court workouts. In East Asia, the establishment of effectively implemented bankruptcy and insolvency legislation has been critical to the restructuring process; in its absence, there would be no incentives for corporations to pursue restructuring.

In Malaysia, court-supervised restructuring continues to play an important role in complementing the government's efforts. More than forty companies so far have filed for reorganization under Section 176 of the Companies Act. Of these, thirteen have proposed reorganization plans, three of which have been approved. More than a thousand winding-up petitions have been filed.

In Thailand, efforts by the government to reform the country's legal framework for insolvency, foreclosure, and secured lending have resulted in amendment of the 1940 Bankruptcy Act to facilitate court-supervised reorganization (enacted in April 1998 and March 1999), amendment of the Code of Civil Procedure on Legal Execution (enacted in March 1999), and a law establishing a Central Bankruptcy Court (opened June 1999). It is too early to measure the impact of these measures on the resolution of the current crisis.

Introduction of an option for court-supervised reorganization has provided a useful means for a supermajority of creditors (representing at least 75 percent of debts) to impose a reorganization plan on dissenting creditors. Through December 1999, thirty petitions for bankruptcy reorganization have been filed. Of these, twenty-five have been accepted and eight restructuring plans have been approved by creditors.

Indonesia, at the urging of the IMF, enacted a revision of its long outdated, colonial-era bankruptcy legislation. The law accords with international standards and practice, and judges have received significant training on its correct application, but results have been disappointing. Most bankruptcy cases seem to be decided in favor of debtors on seemingly weak legal reasoning, and allegations of corruption are commonplace. The new process has not as yet reached its stated objectives, and this has become a major obstacle to the success of the Jakarta Initiative.

The London Approach in East Asia— Limitations and Considerations

For all of its virtues, the London Approach has several intrinsic limitations. The requirement often contained in the original loan documentation for unanimous agreement among creditors for major changes slows down negotiations and gives an unjustified veto power to minority creditors. The company's main lender must agree to voluntarily support the company during the restructuring while other creditors, such as suppliers, continue to enforce their claims. Large companies frequently have operations in several countries and therefore raise their capital from very different sources. With the globalization of financial markets and the growth of alternative lenders (bondholders, insurance companies, leasing companies, among others), banks are no longer the leading provider of finance.

Because of their different market practices, cultures, and regulatory environment, it becomes increasingly difficult to reconcile the different creditors. Debt trading, which has appeared in the last decade, can be helpful for restructuring, since it allows creditors to opt out of a relationship rather than to continue to hinder the process. However, new parties entering corporate reorganization proceedings as a result of debt trading often require time to gain the necessary level of information and sometimes seek to reopen negotiation on issues that already have been agreed to. Credit derivatives, another relatively new instrument, also weaken the relationship between the original lender and a borrower in financial difficulty. With the transfer of credit risk from the original lender to another institution, the "hedged" lender has little motivation to find a restructuring solution based on the London Approach, since his potential loss may be limited.

The usefulness of the London Approach is linked to the particularities of its origins and context. The London Approach is indeed very much embedded in a set of cultural, economic, and social institutions and organizations that are peculiar to Great Britain. It relies primarily on a set of incentives to cooperate and reach a solution that themselves are linked to several specific elements, including a culture of cooperation, a commitment to justice and a system of equitable dispute resolution, the existence of a legal framework for bankruptcies and insolvency (guaranteeing the ability to exit the market), and the existence of an efficient and effective judicial system that can implement this legal framework.

Many of these elements were not present in the East Asian crisis countries. Indeed, it was the absence of such infrastructure that required the establishment of the agencies and mechanisms described above. However, the lack of an infrastructure has also severely limited the effectiveness of the voluntary approaches. The particular trust placed by all actors in the Bank of England was critical to the success of corporate restructuring in the United Kingdom: such a level of trust does not exist in most countries, and even where it does, it often reflects a country in which government intervention has traditionally been heavy-handed and in which government has been deeply involved in the corporate sector—through direct intervention, state ownership, state-owned banks, directed lending, or other means. In the East Asian countries, the close relationship between governments and corporations undermined the independence that was essential in the Bank of England's ability to implement restructuring in the United Kingdom. The differences among the program designs in the various countries largely reflect two main factors: first, the mix of domestic versus foreign debt and, second, the traditional interaction between government and business. In Korea, for example, senior government officials played a leading role in picking corporate winners, directed lending through domestic banks, and maintained a cozy relationship with chaebol owners; as a result, most of the debt is owed to domestic institutions under the control of the government. The Korean model—"Korea, Inc."—is highly centralized and government-driven, with President Kim Dae Jung playing a direct role in corporate-level and sectoral restructuring and working out debts with largely domestic, government-controlled financial institutions. At the other extreme is Indonesia, where most of the debt (about 75 percent), was owed to foreign banks, and where the relationship between the Suharto government and the business sector became the main political slogan for change. Foreign banks, which held most of the corporate debt, were not easily influenced or intimidated by the Indonesian government or its agencies, and any government involvement in corporate restructuring raised the fear of corruption and the suspicion that some crony would be bailed out at public expense. Under these conditions, early programs sponsored by the IMF expressly prohibited the government from becoming involved in corporate debt restructuring. Even after the fall of Suharto, the Jakarta Initiative was designed to minimize direct government access to corporate information and its ability to influence the outcome of negotiations. This clearly weakened the program, but the experience in INDRA, as evidenced by some highly publicized cases of corruption,[9] demonstrates that the concern was well placed.

Finally, it should be noted that voluntary, negotiated agreements work best when there are alternative, judicially supervised procedures for corporate debt restructuring (for example, statutory rehabilitation procedures, such as under Chapter 11 of the U.S. Bankruptcy Code) that can provide protection against creditors' demands. However, such court-driven procedures can be lengthy and expensive, and they are open to abuse. The difficulties are increased by the presence of foreign lenders and made insurmountable by inefficient or corrupt courts.

An alternative model to the London Approach is the Hausbank model, under which a company's main lender takes responsibility for organizing (and often, funding) a workout. This model is not easily enforceable, however, because of the growing size and complexity of workouts and the unwillingness of banks to assume such a heavy burden.

In most of the East Asian crisis countries, no such credible alternative mechanisms were operational, thus weakening the usefulness of the voluntary approach. Design features of corporate restructuring efforts in each country reflect this weakness and try to overcome it by means of different mechanisms, for example, heavy government pressure in Korea, intercreditor and creditor-debtor agreements in Thailand, and the use of special powers of seizure in Indonesia.

In Thailand, two government organizations explicitly link restructuring of corporate and financial sectors. The Corporate Debt Restructuring Advisory Committee, which is part of the Bank of Thailand, identifies which loans need to be restructured, in principle leaving the negotiation of terms to creditors and debtors. One problem is that some of these loans are being carried on the books of nationalized financial institutions; other loans are being carried by institutions that are being recapitalized by government

---

9. The most widely publicized of these cases—the Bank Bali scandal—broke in late July 1999, when allegations surfaced that a financial firm with close ties to then-president B.J. Habibie's Golkar party had pressured cabinet ministers and IBRA officials to repay a $120 million claim to the recently nationalized Bank Bali, taking a 60 percent commission when the claim was paid. See Jay Solomon, "The Jakarta Jumble: When Investing in Indonesia, Don't Forget Perhaps the Most Important Factor: Politics," *Wall Street Journal*, May 8, 2000. Most recently, Indonesia's attorney general detained the governor of Indonesia's central bank for alleged involvement in the scandal. "Bank Indonesia Chief Is Held in Fund Scandal," *Wall Street Journal*, June 22, 2000.

funds. How the London Approach works when one of the two parties is a government-owned entity is unclear.

A second Thai organization that links corporate and financial sector restructuring is the Financial Sector Restructuring Agency, charged with packaging and auctioning the assets of bankrupt finance companies, including both real estate and business loans. Very few of the tranches of loans have been successfully auctioned because most bids were considered too low. Concern that fire-sale prices would foment national outrage has been augmented by ongoing financial entities that were reluctant (or refused) to further write down their own assets. In the absence of a market price for old financial assets, it is difficult to price new assets, which contributes to the lack of lending and deep economic recession.

In the case of Indonesia, the Indonesian Bank Restructuring Agency (IBRA) was originally created by the Ministry of Finance as an emergency measure to preserve and resuscitate Indonesia's financial sector. By assuming the loan portfolios of bankrupt banks and the nonperforming loan portfolios of recapitalized banks, IBRA has become the single largest creditor of Indonesia's real-estate sector. A major threat to the voluntary workout process has been created by the government's need to quickly liquidate IBRA's assets in order to finance its own fiscal budget deficits. The marching orders for IBRA, then, are to recover assets as quickly as possible, with little regard to the future operations of the corporations to which IBRA is the major creditor. Indeed, IBRA's officers are paid a "success" fee dependent upon the amount and speed of total asset recoveries they can effect in the fiscal year. This time-pressure naturally has caused IBRA to be somewhat suspicious of the London Approach (implemented in Indonesia as the Jakarta Initiative), which is perceived as a barrier to achieving the agency's revenue-collection mandate, and to show little support for voluntary, out-of-court processes.

This situation is further exacerbated by the fact that so much of corporate debt is owed to foreign banks. Many of these banks are suspicious that IBRA will jeopardize their ability to recover assets from a corporation on a long-term basis and that IBRA will use its special powers to prejudice their interests.

Corporate Restructuring Frameworks: The Realities of the Social and Legal Environment

In most of the East Asian countries, commercial society is dominated by a cultural attitude that restricts dispute resolution and problem-solving to nonconfrontational negotiation and mediation. There also appears to be a distinct aversion to the use of strict legal processes (which require a somewhat rigid adherence to legal system organization, function, and methodology) to resolve commercial disputes and problems. This is not intrinsically a bad thing: if commercial disputes can be successfully resolved through negotiation and mediation, then so much the better. Trying to resolve corporate insolvencies, however, frequently implicates a multitude of interests, making it difficult to apply a collective remedial process. Failing a privately negotiated settlement, a more formal, supervised, and facilitated process should be available. An appropriate insolvency regime, which requires a well-functioning legal system with a methodology for effective operation, free of corruption and political interference, should be the last resort, but it should be available.

The purported stigma of insolvency is part of the culture of every country everywhere. Simply stated, it means financial failure, to which few persons would care to admit. Transposed to a corporation, for owners or managers the failure of the corporation represents their personal failure, and it is sometimes accompanied by peer judgment that results in business and social disgrace. One suspects that the cultural elements in many Asian countries may heighten a greater sense of stigma in relation to business or financial failure. The expression "loss of face," for example, commands considerable respect as a compelling and potentially destructive cultural influence. This problem is often a breeding ground for desperate and ill-conceived actions, which may take the form of denial, avoidance, escape, cover-up, secretiveness, or manipulation. Often it results in plain theft, sometimes collusion with cronies in the administration or the government. The effect of the stigma should not be ignored and may prove a powerful incentive to use a voluntary restructuring model.

These are all problems of a human nature and surrounding environment, and they are difficult to deal with. When all of these influences are brought together—as must be done to obtain a sense of the practical difficulties—a significant barrier to the application and operation of both a formal corporate insolvency regime and informal insolvency practice becomes apparent. The "attitude" problem is difficult to overcome. Attitudes may well change over the long term as the process of globalization continues and corporate owners and directors come to understand, through an enlightened self-interest, that hiding from the realities of insolvency regimes will ultimately mean that they will lose their troubled companies. Where there is a clear problem with the court and judicial system, that problem can be overcome only by intensive reform of those institutions, which requires considerable resources and expenditure. Such cultural changes take time.

The status of London Approach–based voluntary restructuring programs in Indonesia, South Korea, Malaysia, and Thailand raises several concerns; these may be summarized as follows:

—experienced workout personnel and advisers are in short supply,

—debtor corporations and banks may be unwilling to engage advisers,

—in a few jurisdictions the insolvency law, in practice, provides an insufficient sanction to encourage the informal approach,

—informal workout initiatives have been launched at a time when, because of the effects of the economic crises, the conditions for their successful promotion are difficult,

—some type of government or quasi-governmental facilitating agency is required, and

—ongoing funding, or new money, is uncertain.

There are three main barriers to the informal approach. The first concerns, among other things, know-how, experience, and commercial knowledge. The second concerns the practical problem of providing for the immediate cash-flow needs of insolvent corporations (the problem of "new money"). The third concerns the level of sanctions that might both promote and encourage informal workouts.

There is a fourth barrier as well, not directly linked to the London Approach but rather to the overall restructuring framework. The links between corporate restructuring and financial sector restructuring are obvious in every crisis country, but the linkages between the corporate and the financial sector crises are only now being fully understood.[10] There is great need for work in the areas of integrated corporate sector vulnerability, restructuring, and risk management. The financial structure of the corporate and business sector, in combination with the policy environment (including exchange rates, interest rates, the financial sector, and capital markets) in many countries can lead to widespread illiquidity and insolvency. This destroys value, reduces growth, and increases poverty. A destabilization of the corporate and business sector can feed back and create an even more severe and widespread economic crisis. This type of crisis is becoming more widespread with larger and more volatile capital flows and

10. Gray (1999).

with liberalization programs, particularly in countries with currencies prone to sharp and sudden devaluations.

Serious problems can occur in the absence of a comprehensive, integrated corporate-financial sector focus. Linkages with financial sector and stabilization opportunities are missed. There are serious consequences for the financial sector from large unhedged foreign currency–denominated debt positions in the corporate sector and high overall debt-equity ratios. Without a corporate sector focus, on the other hand, policy recommendations may be geared to meet financial sector objectives at the expense of corporate sector growth and value generation.

Unfortunately, adequate corporate sector work linked to financial sector reform was missing in the World Bank and IMF programs in East Asia. The piecemeal approach used has been unproductive, in part the result of the inequality of power between a failing financial sector, on the one hand, and a failing corporate sector on the other. The financial sector is always at the heart of the interests of central banks and finance ministries. As a consequence, the corporate sector, when treated through voluntary, London Approach agencies, may be regarded as a problem—the source of the bad loan portfolio and a potential locus to recover money used to bail out the financial sector. Such was especially the case in Thailand and Indonesia. Difficulties in proceeding with the one impede progress on the other. This is an area where close attention needs to be paid to defining the future international financial architecture in order to prevent important policy linkages from falling between the institutional cracks.

For the London Approach to work in any individual country there must be a functioning statutory insolvency regime, and the success of any insolvency system is largely dependent upon those who administer it. If they lack the respect not only of the courts and of debtors and creditors but also of the general public, then complaints will multiply; if remedial action is not taken, then the system will fall into disrepair and abuse. This was the situation in East Asia and, according to most reports, remains so.[11]

11. Thailand's largest corporate debtor—Thai Petrochemical Industry, which defaulted on its $3.4 billion debt in 1997—was declared insolvent by Thailand's Bankruptcy Court only in March 2000, more than two years after the default, and the ousting of its chief executive was bitterly contested. See Robert Frank, "Perception vs. Reality: Yes, the Stock Markets Are Booming, but While Southeast Asia's Economies Are Better, They're Far From Fixed," *Wall Street Journal*, May 8, 2000. In Indonesia, IBRA has reportedly lost eighty out of eighty-four court cases brought against debtors in 2000, prompting the recent appointment of nine outside lawyers to act as judges for a new ad-hoc commercial court. See "Jakarta Plans Special Business Court," *Financial Times*, July 3, 2000.

In addition to ineffective bankruptcy procedures, other obstacles to restructuring that need to be eliminated include tax policies that impede corporate reorganizations, mergers, debt-equity swaps, or debt forgiveness, as well as restrictions on foreigners' participation in domestic banks as investors and as holders of domestic equity. Labor laws, competition policy, and other laws and regulations need to be reformed to create a healthy and competitive business environment. A comprehensive approach requires an active government to eliminate obstacles to restructuring, to facilitate both formal and informal debt workouts, and to establish an effective new legal, regulatory, accounting, and institutional framework.[12] The challenge for policymakers is to undertake comprehensive reform that maintains pressure on all parties in a way that promotes equitable burden-sharing among borrowers, equity holders, workers, taxpayers, the government, short-term creditors, and bondholders; that restores credit to viable enterprises and confidence in the financial system; and that leads to a competitive corporate and financial system that minimizes the chances that a crisis will recur.

The concept of the informal workout using a London Rules approach might be said to be based on a combination of the following elements:

—the fact that there is a significant size of debt owed to a number of different creditors and the present inability to service that debt,

—the attitude that it may be preferable to negotiate an arrangement for the financial difficulties of the debtor both between the debtor and the financiers and also among the financiers themselves,

—the availability of relatively sophisticated refinancing, security and commercial techniques that might be employed to alter, rearrange, or restructure debts of the corporate debtor or the corporate debtor itself,

—the sanction that if the negotiation process cannot be started or breaks down there can be relatively swift and effective resort to the application of an insolvency law, and

—the prospect that there may be a greater benefit for all through the negotiation process than by direct and immediate resort to the insolvency law.

Present experience shows that in most East Asian economies, the elements that are appropriate and relevant with regards to informal workouts are fact, availability, and prospects. Since the sanctions have not been

---

12. Iskander and others (1999).

demonstrated to be clearly effective, there is an adverse effect on attitude. Cultural factors, such as loss of face, may in some instances act as a motivator for a corporate owner or director to pursue a voluntary, London Rules approach to restructuring, but it is clear that in the absence of the credible threat of formal bankruptcy proceedings a great deal of intransigence is being displayed, on the parts of both debtors and domestic creditors. The public is paying a tremendous price for this intransigence, and the vicious cycle must be broken immediately though strict enforcement of existing laws, including criminal penalties where appropriate.

To ensure robustness of the private sector over the longer term, legislation must set the stage for improved performance in the marketplace. A climate of deregulation, trade and investment liberalization, and competition policy that facilitates entry and exit, in which bankruptcy law plays a key role, encourages a more robust private sector that is able to absorb shocks. In addition, appropriate government programs enhance labor-market flexibility and relieve corporations and the financial sector from being the main purveyors of the social safety net. All these factors existed in the United Kingdom, but most are in urgent need of strengthening in East Asia.

Ultimately, both creditor- and debtor-oriented systems of corporate restructuring and insolvency contain elements of optimal regimes; the issue is one of balance. Much depends on the cause of the company's problems. If these problems reflect an external shock or the short-term economic cycle, a debt-oriented approach may be more likely to ensure that viable companies are not wound up. But if they reflect mismanagement by the board of directors or an isolated decline in a company's business, a debtor-oriented approach, which effectively supports rather than penalizes bad management, carries a moral hazard and may also result in the unjustified postponement of the liquidation of nonviable companies, reducing debt recovery. No system should be designed to permit debtors to hide behind the appearance of voluntary restructuring. Clear and time-bound mechanisms must be designed that will lead to immediate liquidation and legal action against directors and other parties responsible in the event that debtors are not viable or are not negotiating in good faith.

Conclusion

Assessing the success or failure of the application of the London Rules in any given country is not meaningful without examining as well that country's total policy and legal environment. Common traits and beliefs of the society must also be examined and compared against those societies in which a voluntary insolvency process has proven successful. It is also worthwhile to study the psychological effect that systemic collapse has on the individual business owner or director. During the early 1980s, when Mexico experienced a similar economic disaster, the business community for many years refused to accept blame for their individual circumstances; it was only when the reality of the situation finally set in that corporate restructuring began in any meaningful way. This was the "lost decade," which led to greater poverty for all—shareholders and workers alike.

In this era of globalization, reforms in East Asia and elsewhere will ultimately be driven by the markets. Capital knows no boundaries, and a country's desire for investment means that it must compete in a global contest. Those countries that represent the best risk-to-return ratio on a given portfolio will be the winners, and investors will increasingly look at a country's total investment environment before committing their funds. The existence, application, and enforcement of a formal and functioning restructuring and insolvency regime will be one of the key determinants in the competition for foreign direct investment. The London Approach cannot and does not provide solutions to rescue nonviable businesses. The high cost of workouts is nearly always at the expense of the restructured company. The solution advanced by the Bank of England is to pool, rather than to grant each creditor individually tailored advisory services.

We live in a world in which restructuring is a constant and ongoing process. Steps should be taken to overcome old taboos and inefficiencies and create a smoothly functioning system that will maximize equitable burden-sharing and the allocation of risk among participants in market economies. The system should be predictable, equitable, and transparent and should protect and maximize value for the benefit of all interested parties and the economy in general. The resulting system should preserve capital and productive capacity and limit the loss of employment. Such timely action will promote social welfare, sustainable development, and political stability in the crisis country and the region.

The London Approach as applied in the United Kingdom and the many recent models in East Asia create a valuable area for further study and can be used, with great caution, in future crisis countries. Each such program will need to be carefully designed and modified, recognizing differences in the cultural, legal, and business environments of each country. Making improvements in the business environment and establishing operational restructuring and insolvency systems should not await crisis.

References

Claessens, Stijn, Simeon Djankov, and Daniela Klingebiel. 1999. *Financial Restructuring in East Asia: Halfway There?* Washington: World Bank.

Graham, Edward M. 1999. "Restructuring the *Chaebol* in Korea." In *The Korean Economy in an Era of Global Competition*, edited by the Korean Economic Institute, 83–104. Washington.

Gray, Dale. 1999. "Assessment of Corporate Sector Value and Vulnerability: Links to Exchange Rate and Financial Crises." Technical Paper 455. Washington: World Bank (December).

Iskander, Magdi, Gerald Meyerman, Dale F. Gray, and Sean Hagan. 1999. "Corporate Restructuring and Governance in East Asia." *Finance and Development* (World Bank) 36 (1) (March).

Kent, Pen. 1997. "Corporate Workouts—A U.K. Perspective." (www.bankofengland.co.uk/londapp.htm [July 2000]).

Yoo Seong Min. 1999. "Corporate Restructuring in Korea." In *Korea and the Asian Economic Crisis: One Year Later,* edited by the Korean Economic Institute (Joint U.S.-Korea Academic Series 9). Washington.

PART IV

Risk Management

DIPAK DASGUPTA
DILIP RATHA
DENNIS P. J. BOTMAN
ASHISH NARAIN

11

Short-Term Debt and Financial Crises

B ETWEEN 1990 AND 1997, the outstanding short-term claims by BIS banks on developing countries nearly tripled, rising from $176 billion to $454 billion. This buildup in short-term foreign debt is widely believed to have played an important role in precipitating the recent financial crises in Mexico, East Asia, and Russia. U.S. Treasury Secretary Lawrence Summers has cautioned that "countries are courting trouble when they reach for short-term capital. . . . Longer-term debt is the simplest and best kind of insurance,"[1] and Jason Furman and Joseph Stiglitz have warned that "virtually any country that has excessive levels of short-term debt relative to reserves can suffer a self-fulfilling balance of payments crisis if its creditors refuse to roll-over these loans."[2] Some observers believe that the level of short-term debt (relative to international reserves) is a reliable leading indicator of vulnerability to crises, since this component of capital flows can quickly reverse direction at the first sign of trouble in an economy. If true, such reversibility of short-term capital flows during

Correspondence should be addressed to dratha@worldbank.org. We would like to thank Eliana Cardoso, Stijn Claessens, Uri Dadush, Ashoka Mody, Carmen Reinhart, and Joseph Stiglitz for their helpful comments, and to Himmat Kalsi for Loanware data. The views expressed in the paper are the authors' own and not necessarily those of the World Bank.

1. Summers (1999).
2. Furman and Stiglitz (1998).

times of adverse shocks is contrary to the notion of consumption smoothing, which has always been an important argument in favor of global financial integration.

This paper addresses three important issues relating to short-term debt. First, it examines the factors that may be associated with the growth of short-term debt, with a view to understanding the benefits and risks of such debt. Second, it analyzes the behavior of short-term debt flows during times of favorable and unfavorable shocks. Finally, it examines the association between short-term debt and a country's vulnerability to liquidity crises.

In the section that follows, we describe some key features of short-term bank lending to the developing countries in the 1990s. In the third section, we undertake an empirical examination of various factors that are believed to influence the maturity structure of debt. The fourth section discusses the behavior of short-term debt during economic shocks, followed by an investigation of the association of short-term debt with financial crises in emerging economies. The paper concludes with a summary of findings. The appendix provides a brief discussion of the coverage (and shortcomings) of data on short-term debt.

Growth of Short-Term Debt in the 1990s

Broadly speaking, short-term debt comprises all cross-border debt with maturity of one year or less. Currently two conventions further define short-term debt. The Bank for International Settlements (BIS) uses the remaining maturity concept, according to which all cross-border debt becoming due within a year is counted as short-term debt. This includes liabilities with an original maturity of one year or less, as well as repayments falling due within the next twelve months on liabilities with an original maturity of more than a year. This concept is therefore useful for evaluating a country's total short-term external payments obligations (in other words, the liquidity position). Under the definition adopted by the Global Development Finance (GDF) report of the World Bank, by contrast, short-term debt comprises all cross-border liabilities that have an original maturity of one year or less. This definition highlights the amount of short-term debt contracted at the margin. The GDF definition also includes trade credits reported by the Organization for Economic Cooperation and Development (OECD).

The 1990s marked a boom in short-term lending by international banks to developing countries that lasted until the series of financial crises that began in 1997. The total debt of developing countries rose by approximately 60 percent—from about $1.5 trillion in 1990 to $2.3 trillion in 1997. During the same period, outstanding short-term debt by remaining maturity (the BIS definition of short-term debt) grew nearly 160 percent—from $176 billion to $454 billion. As a result, the share of short-term claims in total debt by BIS-reporting banks increased from 12 percent in 1990 to 20 percent in 1997 before declining to 15 percent in 1998, as short-term debt flows reversed dramatically in the aftermath of the financial crises (see table 11-1). Short-term debt also rose relative to other critical variables that indicate liquidity and debt-servicing capacity: exports and reserves. The ratio of short-term debt to exports in developing countries increased from 21 percent to 27 percent during the 1990–97 period. Whereas the average ratio of short-term debt to reserves declined markedly during the late 1980s for all developing countries and remained relatively stable during the 1990s—largely because of the decline in short-term debt to Latin America after the Brady bond conversions and larger additions to reserves—it remained precariously close to 1, the critical safe threshold identified in many studies.[3] In East Asia short-term debt not only exceeded the safe threshold but increased dramatically during the 1990s until the financial crisis of 1997–98.

The fastest growth in short-term debt occurred in East Asia and the Pacific, where between 1990 and 1996 the share of short-term debt in total debt outstanding rose from 20 percent to a peak of about 32 percent. The rapid buildup of short-term debt in this region is evident in the ratio of short-term debt to exports and even more dramatically in the ratio of short-term debt to reserves, which increased from 124 percent in 1990 to 214 percent in 1997. Although short-term debt also grew rapidly in Latin America between 1990 and 1997, albeit at a slower pace than in East Asia, the Latin American countries' larger additions to reserves helped to hold down the ratio of short-term debt to reserves. Between 1994 and the first half of 1997, 45 percent of all short-term debt flows went to East Asia and the Pacific; 31 percent went to Latin America and the Caribbean countries. The top ten recipients of short-term loans during this period were South Korea (with 15 percent of the total), Thailand (11 percent), Brazil (10 percent),

---

3. See, for example, Furman and Stiglitz (1998) and Rodrik and Velasco (1999).

Table 11-1. *Growth of Short-Term Debt in the 1990s*

Type of short-term debt	1986	1990	1994	1995	1996	1997	1998
Short-term debt (GDF) (U.S. $billions)[a]	154.2	244.6	360.5	424.4	460.8	469.3	411.9
Short-term debt (BIS) (U.S. $billions)[b]	159.9	175.6	293.9	351.9	410.6	454.1	369.1
Short-term debt (GDF)/total debt (percent)	14	17	18	20	21	20	16
Short-term debt (BIS)/total debt (percent)	14	12	15	16	18	20	15
East Asia and Pacific	16	20	25	29	32	30	18
Latin America and Caribbean	19	14	17	17	19	22	20
Short-term debt (BIS)/exports (percent)	33	21	25	25	26	27	23
East Asia and Pacific	26	24	28	30	33	29	n.a.
Latin America and Caribbean	76	39	44	39	42	45	44
Short-term debt (BIS)/reserves (percent)	198	119	91	91	88	91	68
East Asia and Pacific	181	124	123	143	153	214	92
Latin America and Caribbean	257	143	101	86	84	91	93
Memo items (U.S. $billions)							
Total debt outstanding of low- and middle-income countries	1,132.40	1,460.30	1,969.10	2,139.50	2,229.40	2,326.40	2,536.10
Exports of goods and services to developing countries	483.7	818.2	1,154.60	1,414.10	1,566.00	1,693.40	1,633.00

Sources: World Bank, GDF reports, various years; Bank for International Settlements.

n.a. Not available.

a. The GDF definition of short-term debt uses the original maturity concept and includes suppliers' credits.

b. The BIS definition of short-term debt uses the remaining maturity concept.

Indonesia (8 percent), Mexico (8 percent), China, Argentina, Russia, South Africa, and Malaysia (5 percent or less).

Short-term lending by international banks to developing countries during the 1990s increased rapidly despite a falling share of their lending in total private-debt flows and despite flat or declining ratios of indebtedness to exports and GNP in the developing countries.[4] The situation was very different from that of the 1970s, when international banks were the main source of private capital flows to all developing countries. Bank lending rose sharply during the years of the oil price increases as international banks recycled petrodollars from oil-exporting to oil-importing countries (see pp. 347–48). Following the collapse of such lending in the wake of the debt crisis of the early 1980s, international bank lending to developing countries fell precipitously. The 1990s witnessed a renewed upsurge in private capital flows but this time in the form of foreign direct investment (FDI), international bond placements, and portfolio equity flows.[5] As a result, the share of bank lending in total debt outstanding to developing countries fell continuously until about 1995 (figure 11-1). Developing country indebtedness surged during the 1970s and the first part of the 1980s, but the debt-to-GNP ratio has remained virtually flat since 1988, whereas the debt-to-exports ratio has declined sharply since the mid-1980s. The growth in the short-term debt of developing countries in the 1990s thus reflected the fact that international banks were lending more short-term funds while reducing their overall loan portfolios to developing countries as well as their capital-risk exposure.

Figure 11-2 shows the shortening of maturity of international bank lending to all developing countries during the 1990s, until the spate of global financial crises that began in 1997.[6] By 1997 close to 60 percent of all outstanding international bank claims on developing countries had a remaining maturity of less than one year, and some 50 percent of all new loans from international banks were being contracted on original maturity terms of a year or less. Regulatory distortions and cyclical influences were important reasons (among others) for this shift (see pp. 336–37). The result was that developing countries, especially in East Asia, became increasingly reliant on rollovers in short-term external debt and therefore

---

4. Although external indebtedness remained flat or declined in developing countries in the 1990s, it increased significantly in most transition economies during the same period.

5. See World Bank (1993, chap. 1); and Mussa and others (1999).

6. The data on remaining maturity of bonds also show a rising trend in the proportion of short-term bonds for all regions between 1985 and 1998: see Mussa and others (1999).

Figure 11-1. *Debt Stock Trends of Developing Countries, 1971–98*

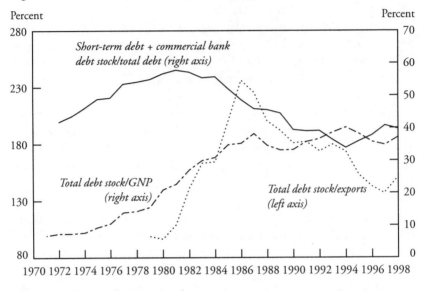

Source: World Bank Debtor Reporting System.

found themselves particularly susceptible to liquidity crises provoked by any sort of shock to international investors' confidence.

The other noteworthy trend in flows of bank debt in the 1990s was a substantial increase in the share of private sector borrowings, especially interbank transactions. Unfortunately, although BIS publishes the allocation of total bank claims to public agencies, commercial banks, and the private nonbanking sector in developing countries, very little information is available on the sectoral allocation of short-term debt. However, an examination of the subset of syndicated loan transactions reveals that in recent years more than 42 percent of short-term syndicated loans to emerging markets went to financial institutions (see table 11-2). Nearly a third of short-term syndicated debt was contracted by commercial banks. The shares of short-term debt contracted by oil and gas enterprises and by government agencies fell significantly relative to the situation a decade earlier, while the short-term debt of financial institutions increased.

Interestingly, external short-term debt (as a share of international bank lending to developing countries) going directly into the property sector has always been small, even though domestic credit to this sector has increased rapidly in recent years. This is consistent with the view that cross-

Figure 11-2. *Short-Term Debt as a Percentage of Bank Lending to Developing Countries, 1987–98*

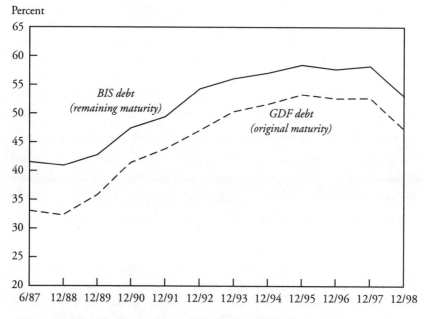

Percent

BIS debt
(remaining maturity)

GDF debt
(original maturity)

6/87 12/88 12/89 12/90 12/91 12/92 12/93 12/94 12/95 12/96 12/97 12/98

Source: Bank for International Settlements; World Bank Debtor Reporting System.

Table 11-2. *Sectoral Breakdown of Short-Term Syndicated Lending to Emerging Markets, 1980–99*

Percent

Sector	1980–84	1985–89	1990–94	1995–99
Financial institutions	8.1	24.7	32.7	42.2
Commercial banks	7.8	23.8	19.2	29.5
Commercial and industrial	55.7	53.4	46.2	36.3
Oil and gas	15.8	31.4	17.2	12.7
Property	0.3	0.0	0.9	0.7
Agribusiness	5.5	10.5	10.8	3.0
Utilities	14.1	0.0	3.2	7.2
Transportation	2.7	3.8	7.1	2.3
Government/agencies	11.1	18.0	10.2	11.8
Other	8.4	0.0	0.6	0.2

Source: Capital Data Loanware.

border intermediation by international banks to high-risk property sectors is exceedingly rare because of information and enforcement problems. Instead, domestic banks in emerging markets—especially in East Asia—borrowed short-term foreign debt at relatively low interest rates and on-lent to property companies (and others) at significantly higher rates. Such borrowing and lending activities involved risks of currency devaluation and maturity mismatch between assets and liabilities, but these were indirectly encouraged by pegged exchange rates and the belief that economic growth and asset booms would continue for a long time.

Determinants of Short-Term Debt

Several factors may have influenced the shortening maturity structure of international bank lending to developing countries during the 1990s. Examining these factors allows us to evaluate the risks and benefits of the growth in external short-term debt. The clearest benefits flow from the ability to match the maturity of an asset with the currency in which it is denominated (for example, inventories of imported raw materials or export accounts receivable in foreign currency). But if short-term debt is used for investments of longer maturity denominated in domestic currency, the liquidity and currency risks associated with such borrowing rise correspondingly. Moreover, it is the final use to which the money is put at the margin that determines the ability to repay the debt and that is therefore relevant for risk assessment.

Risks and Benefits of Shorter-Term Maturities

One reason that banks in industrial countries engage in short-term lending to emerging markets is that longer maturities carry greater risks. This is reflected in the pricing of debt: typically, the shorter the term of a loan, the lower the interest rate. Short-term lending by banks may also simply reflect the fact that a large share of the liability side of a bank's balance sheet consists of short-term deposits. From the perspective of borrowers in a developing country, short-term borrowing provides the advantage of lower interest rates, and to the extent that such short-term borrowing is used to finance short-term working capital needs (such as trade financing), the associated risks are low. Short-term lending, then, provides benefits to borrowers and reasonable returns to lenders, but in practice lending and borrowing decisions may also reflect the influence of policy-induced distortions and cyclical factors that may lead to excessive risk-taking and short-term borrowing.

On the basis of a survey of literature and interviews with several commercial bankers, we outline in table 11-3 a number of factors that in principle may affect the maturity structure of lending by international banks and borrowing by developing countries. These factors are summarized using a three-way classification: cyclical, structural, and policy factors and, within each of these categories, push versus pull factors, although the categories are by no means watertight. We have also tried to identify policy-induced distortions or cyclical influences that may have led to excessive and more risky forms of short-term borrowing, as distinguished from other factors that were more structural and market-driven. Many of these push-and-pull factors have been shown to have influenced the *level* of debt and nondebt capital flows to developing countries. The discussion that follows shows that these factors may have also affected the *maturity* of bank debt flows to developing countries by causing a larger change in short-term debt than in longer-term debt.[7]

STRUCTURAL FACTORS. Since the mid-1980s, the emerging market economies have undergone dramatic structural changes. The latter half of the decade saw a resolution of the debt crises in Latin America and the restoration of market access. During this period East Asia recovered from the sharp recession of the mid-eighties. Many countries in both regions began a process of comprehensive structural reforms, including lowering barriers to external trade, opening up domestic sectors to foreign investment, and liberalizing their capital accounts, which permitted greater mobility of capital; the reforms continued into the early 1990s. Many countries deregulated their banking sector, allowing banks to borrow from abroad and to lend to domestic customers; with the privatization of public enterprises, public debt gave way to private debt, and governments in emerging markets—particularly those in East Asia—began to pay off debt using fiscal surpluses. Soon, several countries received favorable ratings; rising per capita income and falling indebtedness, along with investor-friendly policies, improved these countries' access to global capital markets.

---

7. For example, the effect of cyclical drivers (international interest rates) on the share of short-term debt in total debt is much stronger than its effect on the level of longer-term debt in the 1990s (the respective coefficients are –0.5 and –0.01). The remaining maturity definition of short-term debt used here complicates this conclusion but does not alter it.

Table 11-3. *Determinants of the Maturity of Bank Lending to Developing Countries*

Determinants	Structural factors	Cyclical factors[a]	Institutional and policy factors[a]
Pull factors	Greater openness to trade leads to higher trade credits	High interest rates and rapid growth in emerging markets, often accompanied by high returns from asset booms, attract short-term capital inflows	Tax and other incentives for short-term borrowing (for example, BIBF)
	Deregulation of domestic sectors permitting foreign investment leads to higher requirement for shorter-term working capital finance	Lower interest rates abroad encourage substitution of domestic loans by external borrowing	Deregulation of domestic banks without adequate prudential regulations
	Rising per capita incomes and declining indebtedness improves access to international financial markets		Rapid capital account liberalization enables domestic borrowers to access the international capital markets
	Financial development leads to a deeper domestic debt market		Sterilization of capital inflows maintains high interest rate differential while preventing nominal currency depreciation
			Bailouts of banks by central banks (for example, in Thailand) create moral hazard
Push factors	New technology and telecommunications improve information sharing, reduce transaction costs, and encourage short-term trading	Low interest rates and low growth in industrial countries encourage investment in developing countries	Existing BIS regulation on capital adequacy encourages short-term exposures
	Technical innovation and new financial instruments improve risk monitoring and management of complex portfolios		International rescue packages (as in Sweden 1992, Mexico 1995) target short-term loans first, leading to a moral hazard problem

a. Policy-induced distortions or cyclical influences that may have contributed to short-term overborrowing.

Opening the capital account facilitates investment flows of all kinds, but it particularly tends to favor short-term debt flows over longer-term flows. On the one hand, it facilitates frequent trading activities in financial markets and allows investors to take advantage of interest rate differentials; on the other hand, by allowing foreigners to own domestic equity, it leads to the substitution of non-debt flows for longer-term bank loans. The share of short-term debt in total debt therefore tends to rise when restrictions on capital account transactions are lifted.

The 1990s were a period of important change among the industrial countries as well. The technological revolution improved communication and information-sharing between emerging markets and investors in developed countries. This, together with technical innovation and the emergence of new financial instruments, facilitated more productive and more rapid portfolio risk assessment across a wider range of asset classes. Against the backdrop of declining returns as the industrial economies entered a cyclical recession, international banks intensified their search for profits in the developing countries.

These structural changes in both industrial and the emerging economies set the stage for a surge in private capital flows to the developing world. These changes were particularly favorable for short-term flows. An increasing level of international trade meant a larger volume of short-term trade credits. Higher FDI flows were invariably accompanied by a larger demand for short-term working capital financing. The search for rapid returns encouraged frequent trading and liquid (short-term) investments, facilitated on the one hand, by faster and cheaper communication and, on the other, by more efficient computing power and financial tools that gave rise to more reliable systems for settling trades, enabled richer modeling of risk, and greatly reduced transaction costs.

Industrial country lenders extend credit to short-term suppliers in order to finance imports (typically essential commodities such as oil, food, and medicine) by developing countries. By definition, a positive relationship is expected between trade openness and short-term debt.[8] However, Dani Rodrik and Andrés Velasco find no such relationship; in fact, their estimated coefficient on the imports/gross domestic product (GDP) ratio is negative, suggesting that more open economies tend to engage to a lesser degree in short-term borrowing.[9] They argue that a higher degree of trade

8. Gooptu and Martinez Peria (1992).
9. Rodrik and Velasco (1999).

openness improves a country's creditworthiness, as well as its access to medium- and long-term financing. While this would also improve access to short-term financing, the net effect on maturity composition of debt could go either way.[10]

By reducing taxes on profits, eliminating barriers to entry by new companies, and allowing more foreign ownership of domestic equity, the deregulation of domestic industries promoted FDI flows to emerging markets during the 1990s. This was helped to a great extent by the liberalization of capital accounts, which allowed freer mobility of capital than before. This process tilted the maturity of debt toward the short-term in two ways: first, short-term debt tended to rise (in association with FDI, for example); second, longer-term bank debt declined or did not rise to the same extent when it was converted to equity and FDI at the margin.

The level of indebtedness (indicated by the debt-to-GDP ratio) also has a positive influence on short-term debt, albeit with a time lag. At one level, under the remaining maturity concept, higher debt levels mean more that debt is coming due over the short-term; this also implies a greater need to roll over or contract short-term debt (that is, the demand for short-term debt under the original maturity concept is also higher). At another level, indebtedness exceeding certain thresholds increases country risk and reduces access to longer-term financing, thus raising the share of short-term debt in total debt.[11] By definition, a higher level of medium- and long-term debt would imply a relatively smaller share of short-term debt.[12]

CYCLICAL FACTORS. Low interest rates in industrial countries during the 1980s and 1990s are widely credited as the most important push factor behind the global liquidity expansion and capital flows to the developing countries (see figure 11-3).[13] The absence of opportunities at home as their economies became mired in cyclical recessions prompted investors in developed countries to look outward and discover emerging markets that were experiencing rapid growth and offering very high rates of return (often accompanied by asset booms). Many of these economies needed

---

10. The main weakness in this argument is that higher imports may not necessarily be associated with an improvement in creditworthiness if the result is a higher current account deficit.

11. Rodrik and Velasco (1999).

12. Gooptu and Martinez Peria (1992).

13. World Bank (1997); Chuhan, Claesseans, and Mamingi (1993); Dasgupta and Ratha (1999); Eichengreen and Mody (1999); Sarno and Taylor (1999); Montiel (1993); and Mussa and others (1999).

Figure 11-3. U.S. Interest Rates, 1982–98

Percent

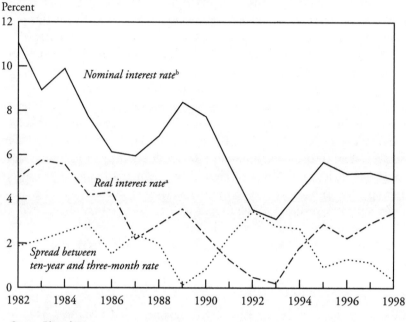

Source: Bloomberg.
a. Three-month rate minus CPI inflation.
b. Three-month rate.

credit from abroad to finance high investment rates (which were in excess of already high savings rates, particularly in Asia) and decided to borrow short-term in order to take advantage of the relatively low interest rates.

Why does a lowering of interest rates and expansion of liquidity promote lending at the short end? The answer seems to lie in the nature of the yield curve: a reduction in the short-term rate does not always lead to a proportionate decline in long-term rates because expectations about long-term inflation and growth (and risks in general) are revised at a much slower pace than short-term expectations. Therefore, a reduction in short-term rates would encourage shorter-term borrowing.

INSTITUTIONAL AND POLICY FACTORS. One would expect that domestic monetary policies pursued in the developing countries as well as developments in prudential regulation in G-10 countries would have affected the maturity structure of debt. Sustained growth in East Asia during the 1986–96 period led to overconfidence on the part of lenders and borrowers alike. Credit risk mechanisms became relaxed because of excess liquidity and euphoria in emerging markets. A large number of banks borrowed short-term to on-lend to domestic customers with medium- or long-term maturities. Such asset-liability mismatches were encouraged by the tendency of many central banks in developing countries to peg exchange rates and engage in massive sterilization efforts (to maintain a high interest rate differential and attract capital inflows). Some countries even actively promoted short-term borrowing to take advantage of low interest rates in industrial countries (the Bank of Thailand, for example, initiated the Bangkok Interbank Facility [BIBF] in 1993). Other countries (notably South Korea) discouraged long-term foreign investments for political reasons, which had the effect of shortening debt maturity. Sterilization attempts led to higher short-term interest rates at home, attracting more short-term flows, while adding to reserves through sterilization created an illusion of lower liquidity risks in foreign currency terms.[14]

Recent experiences with rescue packages also encouraged banks to take excessive risks. For example, during the Swedish banking crisis of 1987–89 the government guaranteed loans to local banks; during the Mexican crisis of 1994–95 the rescue package gave priority to honoring short-term paper in order to prevent default. Such instances have led investors to believe that short-term debt would be honored in future rescue efforts in the event of crisis. Thus lending to local banks—which on-lent to domestic corporates—rose on the belief that these banks had the backing of their governments.

The maturity structure of debt may have been influenced by a differential treatment of short-term debt in the BIS prudential regulations designed to reflect greater risks associated with longer-term debts. According to existing BIS regulations on minimum capital adequacy for banks, short-term lending to non-OECD countries carries a risk weight of 20 percent; loans with maturity of more than one year, by contrast, carry a risk weight of 100 percent; the risk weights do not apply to OECD countries. Thus, reducing the term of an interbank loan to a non-OECD counterparty from thirteen months to twelve months or less would reduce the risk weight from 100 percent to 20 percent. Similarly, short-term, self-liquidating trade-related contingent liabilities arising from the movement of goods carry a smaller risk weighting than comparable commitments

---

14. World Bank (1999); Calvo and Mendoza (1999); and Montiel and Reinhart (1999).

with original maturity of more than one year.[15] Such differential treatment of short-term debt may have encouraged short-term debt contracts.[16]

Empirical Evidence

In this subsection we examine the significance of some of the factors identified above on the maturity structure of borrowing by developing countries from international banks. A number of well-known problems are associated with such an exercise: the cause-and-effect relationships between maturity structure and some of the explanatory variables (such as growth, income levels, and trade) are often difficult to discern; demand and supply factors are both involved; and measures of some of the policy variables (for example, capital account openness or the effects of prudential regulations) are problematic. Therefore, these results need to be treated with caution (see also table 11-4 note, below).

Our analysis (following Rodrik and Velasco [1999]) is based on panel data for thirty-three developing countries that accounted for more than 80 percent of short-term borrowing by developing countries between 1986 and 1998. We regress the share of short-term debt (based on the BIS remaining-maturity concept) in total claims by BIS-reporting banks on these countries against a set of "explanatory" variables: (a) *structural*—the (log of) per capita GNP as a proxy for the level of development and trade openness; (b) *cyclical*—the growth differential between developing countries and the industrial countries, at the U.S. dollar London interbank offered rate (LIBOR); and (c) *institutional and policy factors*—borrowing by domestic banks (reflecting, imperfectly, effects of financial deregulation), capital account restrictions—a variable that takes the value 1 in the presence of restrictions and 0 otherwise (based on IMF [1997]), and a variable for BIS capital adequacy regulations that takes the value 1 during the period 1992–98 (when it became effective), and 0 earlier.

---

15. See Bank for International Settlements (1997, pp. 67–69). Off-balance sheet engagements are converted to credit risk equivalents by multiplying the nominal principal amounts by a credit conversion factor. For short-term trade-related contingent liabilities, the credit conversion factor is 20 percent. Commitments with original maturity of up to one year or commitments that can be unconditionally cancelled at any time do not have any capital requirement, whereas for those with maturity over one year, the conversion factor is 50 percent. Even the new capital adequacy framework being debated currently does not propose any changes in the existing standards: see Bank for International Settlements (1999).

16. Bank for International Settlements (1999); and Demirgüç-Kunt (1992).

Table 11-4. *Determinants of the Maturity Structure of Debt, 1986–98*[a]

Determinant	A[b]	B[b]
Per capita income (log GNP)	10.439***	10.952***
Trade openness (Trade/GDP, lagged)	0.0905*	0.119**
Borrowing by domestic banks from BIS banks as a share of GDP (reflecting financial deregulation)	0.792***	0.740***
Borrowing by public sector from BIS banks as a share of GDP	–0.270**	–0.281**
Difference between growth rate of each developing country and that of industrial countries as a group	0.281***	n.a.
International interest rates (U.S. dollar LIBOR)		–0.543*
BIS/capital adequacy regulation dummy (1992 – 98 = 1)	1.936*	n.a.
Capital account restrictions dummy	–3.473*	–4.619**
Adjusted R^2	0.31	0.3
Number of observations	413	414

Source: Authors' calculations.
n.a. Not available.
*** Significant at the 1 percent level.
** Significant at the 5 percent level.
* Significant at the 10 percent level.
a. The panel survey includes thirty-three countries—Algeria, Argentina, Bangladesh, Brazil, Bulgaria, Cameroon, Chile, China, Colombia, Ecuador, Egypt, Ghana, Hungary, India, Indonesia, Jordan, South Korea, Malaysia, Mexico, Morocco, Nigeria, Pakistan, Panama, Peru, the Philippines, Poland, Romania, South Africa, Thailand, Tunisia, Turkey, Venezuela, and Zambia.
b. Columns A and B report alternative specifications to account for some collinearity between cyclical variables.

Results are presented in table 11-4. The evidence tends to support the discussions above. Per capita income and trade structural variables appear to account for about half of the increase in short-term borrowing, suggesting the beneficial association of short-term debt with these factors; the other half appears to be accounted for by policy and cyclical factors (approximately 30 percent and 20 percent respectively). Among cyclical variables, faster GDP growth in borrowing countries seems to attract more short-term flows, while a decline in interest rates in industrial countries appears to provide an incentive for short-term lending and borrowing.

Among policy factors, an increase in short-term loans tends to be associated with the growth in interbank lending (reflecting financial deregulation), the opening of capital accounts, and with the effect of BIS regulations. When borrowing by domestic banks is replaced by a more direct financial liberalization indicator (a dummy variable), the results are again positive for seven major countries for which information is available; this is consistent with other findings that financial liberalization shortened the maturity of corporate debt in these countries.[17]

The coefficient of the dummy for the BIS regulation on capital adequacy (which is 1 for 1992–98 and 0 otherwise) is positive and significant, indicating that the BIS regulations may have led to a shortening of debt maturity. A BIS study mentions that pairwise comparisons of lending to equally rated OECD and non-OECD countries indicate a greater concentration of short-term lending to the latter.[18] This is evident at an aggregate level from figure 11-4, which shows a sharp rise in the share of short-term debt in total debt of developing countries since 1990. (The BIS targets were to be achieved by 1992, even though the initiative began in 1988.)

There are three main conclusions to be drawn from these empirical findings: first, the growth of short-term debt indeed accompanied a number of very desirable fundamental factors, such as GDP growth, trade, and FDI. However, it was also associated with some not-so-desirable outcomes, such as excessive lending from domestic banks that fueled unsustainable asset inflation, or circumvention of prudential capital regulations. Second, external push factors were also responsible for high levels of short-term lending to developing countries and raised the risk of capital flow reversal and self-fulfilling liquidity runs in the event of a crisis.

Finally, some of these results point to pro-cyclical behavior of short-term debt in response to adverse shocks. For example, the positive relationship between growth and shortening of debt maturity implies that an adverse shock to growth would lead to a reversal of short-term flows. Thus, instead of smoothing consumption, short-term debt flows would actually accentuate the impact of the shock. This is in line with the findings that short-term debt may not be the trigger for crisis, but that once a crisis happens, it can deepen the impact. The issue of the pro-cyclical response of short-term debt to shocks is explored in greater detail in the next section.

---

17. Schmukler and Vesperoni (2000).
18. Bank for International Settlements (1999, p. 25).

Figure 11-4. *Short-Term Debt as a Percentage of Total Debt, 1986–98*

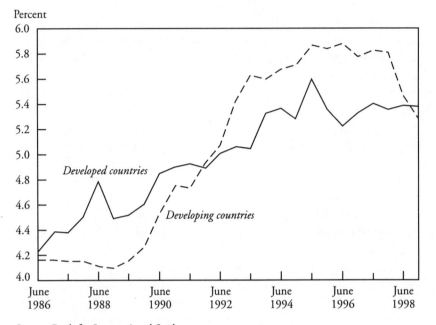

Source: Bank for International Settlements.

The Response of Short-Term Capital Flows to Economic Shocks

One important additional reason for why short-term capital flows could play a beneficial role is that in principle such flows could offer relief to countries requiring additional financing in the face of a temporary adverse shock. Such financing could offer residents of the affected country the opportunity to smooth their consumption.

Existing estimates of consumption-smoothing in industrial countries vary widely, from nearly zero percent of lifetime consumption,[19] to a very significant fraction of lifetime consumption[20]—indicative of the methodological problems in measuring such gains. Nonetheless, when the global capital market allows countries to smooth consumption, one would expect

19. Cole and Obstfeld (1991); Backus, Kehoe, and Kydland (1992); Mendoza (1995); and Tesar (1995).
   20. Van Wincoop (1994); and Obstfeld (1995).

the growth path of aggregate consumption to be less volatile than that of aggregate income. Second, one would expect the growth of consumption across countries that are financially integrated to show a much higher correlation than growth of income. These two implications of models of international risk-sharing are, however, rejected in practice, which sheds some doubt on whether financial markets are sufficiently integrated to allow consumption-smoothing through a counter-cyclical response of international capital flows.[21]

From the standpoint of a borrowing country, the benefits of integration arise mainly when short-term debt is counter-cyclical and determined by demand side (pull) factors. However, if lender decisions and other factors make access to short-term capital flows pro-cyclical, a favorable shock may attract huge capital inflows and encourage a level of consumption and investment that is unsustainable over the longer term; or, on the downside, countries may be forced to overadjust to adverse shocks (by reducing imports) when capital flees.[22] This is also consistent with findings in the literature that public debt (and fiscal policy) in developing countries, especially in Latin America, tends to be highly pro-cyclical (in sharp contrast to industrial countries) because access to international borrowing is tighter under adverse conditions and less tight under favorable conditions.[23]

There are two principal reasons why short-term capital flows respond pro-cyclically to economic shocks: the prevalence of large and frequent economic shocks in developing countries, on the one hand; and information asymmetry problems between lenders and borrowers on the other. Economic shocks tend to be larger and more frequent in developing countries, reflecting their narrower economic bases and greater dependence on primary commodity exports and often resulting in these countries' marginally creditworthy status. Thus changes in risk perception and rating downgrades under adverse shocks can lead to credit-rationing to such marginally creditworthy borrowers; such changes worsen, rather than smooth, their adjustment. These negative effects are exacerbated in the presence of information asymmetry problems between borrowers and lenders, which may cause herding and panic withdrawal of capital in response to an adverse shock.

---

21. Tamim Bayoumi (1997) studied consumption and growth paths in twenty-one OECD countries and concluded that there was little evidence in support of consumption-smoothing in these countries.

22. See World Bank (1993, p. 21).

23. Easterly, Islam, and Stiglitz (1999).

Jeffrey Sachs argues in the context of the Asian crises that the depletion of reserves, followed by the inevitable devaluation of the currency, revealed to investors holding short-term claims on the domestic financial sector that their investments were more risky than previously expected.[24] This in turn created a creditor panic as investors—unwilling to roll over short-term debt—suspended routine interbank lines and refused to continue with standard trade-financing operations.

Sometimes, small events may cause all information that was already in the hands of investors to become included in market prices.[25] This may explain why after a shock, investors seemingly all of a sudden withdraw capital from a country, while outsiders may judge this reaction as irrational given the size of the shock and the fact that no new information has arrived in the market. Such potential for agents to learn from the actions of other market participants may be reinforced if fund managers' performance is evaluated relative to that of others: this creates incentives for these managers to mimic the behavior of others if "beating the market" is less valued than being beaten by the market.[26]

Do short-term capital flows to developing countries, in particular, behave more pro-cyclically than counter-cyclically? Is this behavior exacerbated in the face of different types of shocks? And how do risk-ratings (which influence the quantity and price of capital flows) change in the face of favorable or adverse economic shocks? The evidence in answer to these questions is examined below.

We use a variant of the model described in table 11-4 for this empirical investigation. By expressing the dependent variable as well as the explanatory variables (except dummy variables) as growth rates, the elasticity with respect to a particular variable can be read directly from the estimated coefficients. We estimate this model using the panel data described in the previous section for thirty-three developing countries for the period 1987–98. The results are as follows:

(1) Short-term debt flows are pro-cyclical to growth in developing countries. As already anticipated in the results of the previous section, the relationship between growth in short-term debt and growth rates in developing countries is positive and significant in all developing countries. Under-

24. Sachs (1998).
25. See Romer (1994); and Caplin and Leahy (1994).
26. See also Calvo and Mendoza (1999).

Table 11-5. *Elasticity of Short-Term Debt (Original Maturity) with Respect to GDP Growth Rate, 1987-98*[a]

Thirty-three countries[b]	3.42
Twenty countries[c]	2.11
Latin America	2.39
East Asia	2.28

Source: Authors' calculations.

a. All reported elasticities are significant at the 1 percent level.

b. See p. 340, table 11-4, note a, for the list of countries.

c. Argentina, Brazil, Chile, China, Colombia, Ecuador, Egypt, Hungary, India, Indonesia, Korea, Malaysia, Mexico, Pakistan, Peru, the Philippines, Poland, South Africa, Thailand, and Venezuela.

standably this relationship is stronger in some countries than in others (see table 11-5 and figure 11-5).

(2) Short-term flows are usually more pro-cyclical than medium- and longer-term debt flows. The finding here is consistent: elasticity of short-term debt with respect to GDP growth rate is 2.1 compared to 0.9 for long-term debt. Thus, short-term debt is more reversible than long-term debt, and the volatility of short-term debt is greater. There is also some evidence that the pro-cyclicality of short-term debt to GDP growth has increased over time, especially in East Asia, where the elasticity of short-term debt with respect to GDP growth is 0.06 during the period 1988–93 and equal to 2.536 during the period 1994–98.

(3) Short-term flows are pro-cyclical to economic shocks, and pro-cyclicality is greater during adverse shocks. For the purposes of measuring the behavior of short-term flows during good or bad times, economic shocks are defined as periods of either favorable or adverse outcomes relative to the mean values of the economic variable under consideration. This involves partitioning the sample into good and bad times and then looking at the behavior of short-term debt flows within each partition.[27] Two types of economic shocks, in turn, are considered: (a) shocks to GDP

27. Results reported below for all twenty countries relate to the partitions obtained using mean plus or minus one-half standard deviation of the variable concerned. However, the results for specific regions—East Asia and Latin America—relate to a broader partitioning rule using above- or below-mean (to obtain sufficient degrees of freedom). Note that an adverse growth shock defined as mean minus one-half standard deviation may not necessarily imply that growth rate is negative, but it does imply that growth is relatively very low.

Figure 11-5. *Cyclicality of Short-Term Debt*

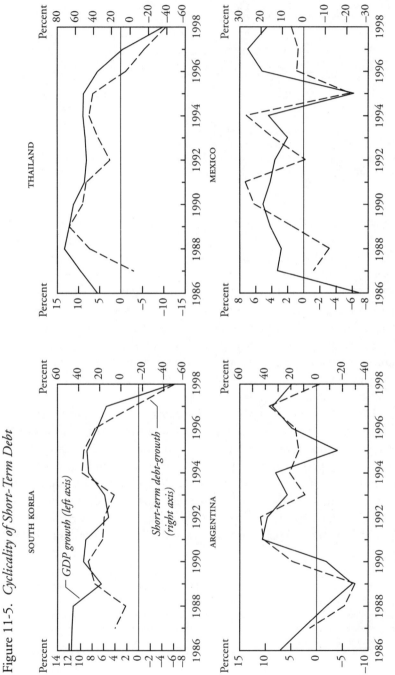

Source: Bank for International Settlements; World Bank, *Global Economic Prospects* (various issues).

growth; and (b) shocks to the terms of trade that a country faces. The key indicator used is the estimated elasticity of short-term debt with respect to GDP growth rate. We then infer the cyclical response of short-term debt to the different types of shocks from the size and sign of this estimated elasticity during favorable or adverse times, and we investigate the behavior of risk perception by foreign investors (that is, credit ratings) in response to economic shocks.

(a) Growth shocks. Short-term debt is highly pro-cyclical, and especially so during adverse growth shocks. When GDP growth experiences a positive shock (one-half standard deviation higher than mean growth rate), the elasticity of short-term debt growth with respect to GDP growth is about 0.9, but in adverse shock (when GDP growth is lower than the mean by one-half standard deviation), short-term debt growth falls twice as fast, with an elasticity of 1.8 in the latter case. By way of contrast, the elasticity of medium- and long-term debt with respect to GDP growth rate is negative (although statistically not significant) for both positive and negative shocks to GDP (at –0.41 and –0.3 respectively), suggesting weak countercyclical behavior to shocks to GDP. However, it is difficult to distinguish between demand and supply effects in the pro-cyclical response of short-term debt to growth shocks. Therefore an examination of terms of trade shocks is important, since they tend to be more exogenous.

(b) Terms of trade shocks. An analysis of terms of trade shocks reveals a similar pattern of pro-cyclicality as in the case of growth shocks, and greater pro-cyclicality during adverse shocks. The panel data are once again partitioned according to positive and negative terms of trade shocks, which are defined respectively as greater than the mean growth rate plus half the standard deviation of terms of trade growth, and less than the mean minus half the standard deviation. The estimated elasticity of short-term debt with respect to GDP for the partition with positive terms of trade shock is 0.8, compared to 1.8 for the partition with negative terms of trade shock.[28] Separating the oil-exporting countries from the others in the panel of twenty countries does not alter this conclusion—the elasticity of short-term debt to growth in either case is higher during below-average growth in terms of trade than during above-average growth—although pro-cyclicality in short-term flows is greater in the non-oil-exporting countries (see table 11-6). This asymmetry in pro-cyclicality between oil-exporting and non-oil-exporting

---

28. The direct relationship between short-term debt flows and terms of trade indexes is not significant. The relationship seems to operate through the GDP growth variable.

Table 11-6. *Elasticity of Short-Term Debt with Respect to*
GDP Growth Rate during Periods of Trade Shocks, 1987–98[a]

Country survey	Above-average trade growth	Below-average trade growth
Oil-exporting countries	0.52	3.29*
Non-oil-exporting countries	1.58**	3.62***

Source: Authors' calculations.
*** Significant at the 1 percent level.
** Significant at the 5 percent level.
* Significant at the 10 percent level.
a. Results based on a panel of twenty countries. See p. 345, table 11-5, note c.

developing countries may be explained in terms of the generally better access of the former to international capital markets.

(c) Responses of risk-ratings to economic shocks. Finally, there is evidence of a nonlinear relationship between risk perception by creditors and economic shocks in developing countries that lies at the heart of the greater pro-cyclical response of short-term debt to adverse shocks. Perceived risk may increase more during a large adverse shock than it may decline during a small adverse or even positive shock. Table 11-7 presents estimates of the responsiveness of one measure of risk perception, the Institutional Investor Risk Rating, to shocks in GDP growth.

The responsiveness of risk ratings is significantly adverse during times when GDP growth is below the average than it is positive when growth is above average. This is also consistent with other findings (see pp. 353–55) that credit-rating downgrades are associated with high volatility in loan spreads, and that the behavior of credit-rating agencies aggravated the East Asian crisis—by downgrading countries more than would have been justified by fundamentals alone, and thereby raising spreads and reducing access to capital sharply.[29] Risk rating goes up (that is, creditworthiness improves) if GDP growth is above the mean, but it falls even more (that is, creditworthiness worsens) when the growth rate dips below the average. This nonlinear response to change in growth rates is more pronounced in East Asia than in Latin America. Although not shown in the table, this relationship has become more important during the period 1993–98 compared to 1986–92.

29. Ferri, Liu, and Stiglitz (1999).

Table 11-7. *Elasticity of Risk Rating with Respect to Shocks in GDP Growth Rate, 1987–98*

Country survey	Above-average GDP growth	Below-average GDP growth
Twenty countries[a]	1.14	1.98***
Latin American countries	0.38	0.99**
East Asian and Pacific countries	1.09**	1.83***

Source: Risk ratings from *Institutional Investor*, various issues; authors' calculations.
*** Significant at the 1 percent level.
** Significant at the 5 percent level.
a. For the list of countries, see table 11-5, note c.

Short-Term Debt and Vulnerability to Crises

Short-term flows are potentially the most easily reversible component of private capital flows. Their shorter maturity enables the investor to withdraw quickly, whereas withdrawal of other types of capital can be costly during difficult times. For example, liquidating FDI may involve selling plants and machinery, and selling stocks or bonds during a crisis usually involves a loss for the seller. In contrast, short-term bank loans can be reversed at relatively minimal costs.[30] Many countries suffered large reversals in short-term capital flows during the recent financial crises, precipitating severe external liquidity crises. Short-term debt flows to all developing countries from BIS-reporting banks shifted from an inflow of $43.5 billion in 1997 to an outflow of $85 billion in 1998 (see table 11-8). Quarterly data suggest an even more dramatic swing.

The reversibility of short-term debt predisposes borrowers to the phenomenon of liquidity runs. The risks of such runs are greater the higher the level of short-term debt relative to the borrowing country's international reserves. Such runs can be self-fulfilling, because the chances of a borrower being repaid declines rapidly once a run has started.[31] High levels of short-term liabilities involving the financial system also involve risks of bank runs and systemic crisis. Therefore the risk of financial crisis is greater where the

30. Withdrawal of short-term bank lending may involve a setback in the relationship between the bank and its clients, which would impact the bank's business in the future, but the immediate pecuniary cost is relatively small.

31. Furman and Stiglitz (1998); Diamond and Dybvig (1983); Rodrik and Velasco (1998); and Eichengreen and Mody (1999).

Table 11-8. *Short-Term Debt Flows from Developing Countries,*
1997 and 1998
Billion of U.S. dollars

Region or country	1997	1998
All developing countries	43.5	–85.0
East Asia and the Pacific	0.8	–68.0
Indonesia	1.1	–11.8
Malaysia	3.4	–5.3
South Korea	–8.0	–29.9
Thailand	–6.9	–15.1
Latin America and the Caribbean	24.1	–5.7

Source: Bank for International Settlements.

level of short-term debt to reserves is excessive and the banking system is heavily involved in intermediating such flows.[32] Since residents may opt to liquidate their short-term assets in the banking system and move them abroad in the event that risks rise, the level of broad money relative to reserves is an additional indicator of vulnerability.

Early studies on crisis prediction did not find any strong evidence that maturity profile of external debt mattered for a crisis.[33] More recently, however, evidence is accumulating to the contrary—both because the influence of liquidity crises has become stronger in recent years and because of greater methodological attention to the subject.[34] Steven Radelet and Jeffrey Sachs, for example, find that the ratio of short-term debt to reserves is significantly associated with nine cases of crisis between 1994 and 1997

32. Short-term borrowing by corporations also involves significant risks, but the implications of such risks for systemic crisis are typically less than in the case of banks. The reason is that, unlike a commercial bank, a typical private corporation tends to be small, and its foreign currency liabilities tend to be hedged by export receivables or by real assets. However, unhedged foreign currency borrowings by *large* corporations may pose more serious risks, as was the case in the recent crises in Asia.

33. For example, Frankel and Rose (1996); Sachs, Tornell, and Velasco (1996a, 1996b, and 1996c); and Kaminsky, Lizondo, and Reinhart (1998).

34. Jason Furman and Joseph Stiglitz (1998) note that, at the end of 1996, eleven of the forty-two developing countries for which data were then available had short-term debt to BIS-reporting banks that exceeded their level of reserves. Several countries from this group subsequently faced severe financial difficulties, including Indonesia (with a ratio of short-term debt to reserves of 1.9), Korea (2.0), Thailand (1.2), South Africa (11.6), Pakistan (5.1), Russia (2.1), Bulgaria (2.1), and Zimbabwe (1.3).

for a sample of nineteen emerging markets.[35] Using a larger sample, Rodrik and Velasco find that when the ratio of short-term debt to reserves exceeds 1, there is a 10 percentage point higher probability of crisis than when the ratio is below that level.[36] They also find that the probability of crisis increases with total debt, the current account deficit, and real appreciation of the currency, suggesting that both liquidity and fundamentals factors play a role in inducing crises. This conclusion is also supported by Matthieu Bussière and Christian Mulder.[37] Their study finds that the ratio of short-term debt to reserves is not only a strong indicator of crises (see table 11-9) but that it is also significantly superior to alternative liquidity-risk specifications such as the ratio of imports to reserves and three different specifications of the ratio of money (M0, M1, and M2) to reserves.[38]

There are potential trade-offs between liquidity and fundamentals factors (see figure 11-6).[39] A safe threshold of short-term debt to reserves appears to be about 1: the crisis index would be zero with that level of short-term debt to reserves, no overvaluation of the currency, and the current account in modest surplus. But countries that have significant current account deficits, some overvaluation of the currency, or both need much larger reserves. Any country whose ratio of short-term debt to reserves significantly exceeds unity appears to be much more vulnerable to the onset of financial crises. These vulnerability windows are particularly important for private-to-private capital flows intermediated by the banking systems of the 1990s.[40]

These findings are robust to an extension of the analysis using a broader definition of the crisis index as a weighted average of the nominal depreciation and loss in reserves (similar to that proposed by Bussière and Mulder[41]), as well as an increase in domestic interest rates, weighted by the inverse of the standard deviation of these series. Interest rates are introduced as an added factor, since a rise in domestic interest rates is also closely associated with financial crises. This crisis index is found to be

35. Radelet and Sachs (1998b).
36. Rodrik and Velasco (1999).
37. Bussière and Mulder (1999a, 1999b).
38. It is also the case that a rise in short-term lending before an imminent crisis is partly endogenous to the rising risks of a crisis, so that more fundamental causes of a crisis remain important.
39. Since the probability of crisis is measured for a given year rather than over several years, these regressions may overstate the importance of proximate triggers as opposed to fundamental factors.
40. Bussière and Mulder (1999b).
41. Bussière and Mulder (1999a).

Table 11-9. *Ratios of Short-Term Debt to Reserves*[a]

Dependent variable: crisis index	Specification 1 (t statistic)	Specification 2 (t statistic)
Constant	−15.38** (−2.06)	−17.22*** (−2.80)
Real exchange rate index	−0.32* (−1.9)	−0.33* (−1.98)
Current account/GDP	1.65** (2.03)	1.55** (2.05)
Short-term debt/reserves	0.27*** (4.23)	0.28*** (4.75)
Export growth	−0.10 (−0.70)	. . .
Reserve change	0.00 (0.05)	. . .
R^2	0.43	0.43
Adjusted R^2	0.36	0.38

Source: Bussière and Mulder (1999a).
*** Significant at the 1 percent level.
** Significant at the 5 percent level.
* Significant at the 10 percent level.
a. The sample includes twenty developing countries for the period 1994–97 (see p. 345, table 11-5, note c). The crisis index is defined as the weighted average of a loss in reserves and exchange rate depreciation; t statistics are in parentheses.

strongly associated with the ratio of short-term bank debt (under the BIS definition) to reserves (note the case of Thailand in the third quarter of 1997 and of Mexico at the beginning of 1995 in figure 11-7). The qualitative results remain unchanged for a larger number of countries, including both developing and developed countries.

Conclusion

To summarize the findings of the above discussion relating to the growth and determinants of short-term borrowing by developing countries from international banks and the behavior of such debt during economic shocks:

—Short-term borrowing by developing countries from international banks nearly tripled between 1990 and 1997, with especially rapid growth in East Asia and Latin America.

Figure 11-6. *Trade-Off between Liquidity and Fundamentals*[a]

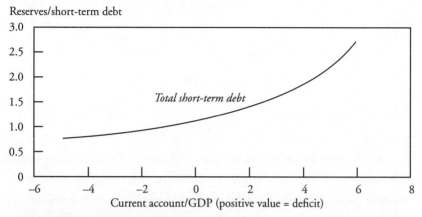

Reserves/short-term debt

Total short-term debt

Current account/GDP (positive value = deficit)

Source: Bussière and Mulder, 1999b.

a. The figure shows the equilibrium relationship between the ratio of reserves to short-term debt and current account deficit as a share of GDP when the crisis index is 0 and the real exchange rate is not overvalued.

—Some of this rapid rise was associated with significant benefits: it helped finance growing trade and supported faster economic growth. However, policy-induced distortions also contributed to the boom in short-term borrowing. These distortions stemmed from the rapid liberalization of domestic banking systems and the opening of capital accounts in borrowing countries without adequate supervision and risk-management practices in place, from the sterilization of capital inflows seeking to defend pegged exchange rates, and from international capital adequacy regulations that favored short-term lending. Cyclical influences, such as lower interest rates in industrial countries and asset market booms in borrowing countries, also stimulated growth in short-term borrowing.

—Short-term lending to developing countries tends to be pro-cyclical, rising during favorable times and falling even more sharply following adverse shocks. As a result, such lending often amplifies booms and busts rather than helping to smooth consumption. Such cyclical behavior of short-term flows may be due to asymmetric changes in risk perception in response to favorable and unfavorable economic shocks.

—Short-term debt in excess of short-term liquidity (as measured by holdings of foreign reserves) increases developing countries' vulnerability to financial crises. The risk of crises also appears to rise with the share of

Figure 11-7. *Liquidity Ratios and the Crisis Index, Thailand and Mexico*

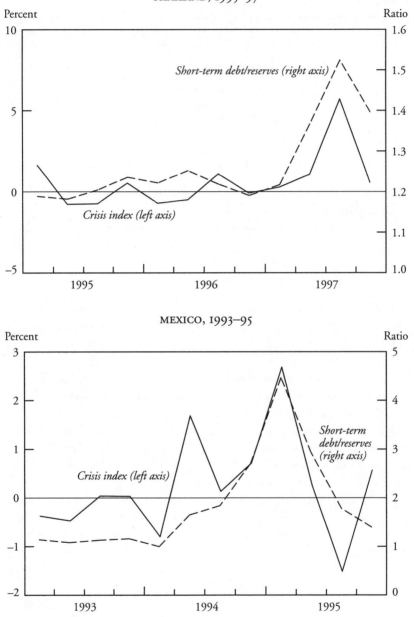

Source: Authors' calculations.

short-term borrowing by domestic banks. The interaction of deteriorating fundamentals (such as overvalued currencies and excessive public borrowing) and high levels of short-term debt appears to have played a significant role in recent crises. For countries with open capital accounts and high levels of financial intermediation, the level of broad money relative to international reserves is also important, because of the potential for domestic capital flight.

Given these risks, close monitoring and effective management of short-term debt (in particular, of short-term debt intermediated by domestic banks) are essential in developing countries in order to avoid currency and liquidity crises. This is not an easy task, however, considering that existing reporting systems fail to capture a significant part of potentially reversible short-term components of capital flows.[42] We provide a brief discussion of the data reporting systems in the appendix.

Although our discussion has focused exclusively on short-term debt, this is not the only reversible form of capital flows. Arguably almost all types of foreign investment can be withdrawn at a cost, and such costs have fallen rapidly as financial instruments and investment contracts have become increasingly complex in recent times. For example, our preliminary calculations on bond issuance show that the value of bonds with put options— which allows a long-term bond to be sold before the maturity date—has been significantly higher than that of short-term bonds in the 1990s.

Also to be borne in mind is that fact that most of the developing countries are only marginally creditworthy, and the only form of capital available to these countries is short-term debt from banks. Therefore, the only course of action for these countries may be to avoid policies that risk distorting the maturity pattern of debt flows toward the short end. This applies for industrial countries and international prudential regulations as well.

Appendix 11A
Shortcomings in the Reporting of Short-Term Debt

Given the large risks that developing countries run when borrowing short-term, improvements are needed in the reporting systems for short-term

---

42. The Inter-Agency Task Force on Finance Statistics (with participation by the BIS, the IMF, the OECD, and the World Bank) has recently been established to improve the quality, frequency, and coverage of debt information.

debt flows. Incomplete and partial information can provide a false sense of security. The three main debt reporting systems—operated by the BIS, the OECD, and the World Bank—report the short-term debt positions of developing countries. The BIS collects information on the international positions of banks in the reporting areas from the national banking authorities in eighteen major industrial countries plus six offshore centers[43] that report their claims on a worldwide consolidated basis. The creditor reporting system of the OECD provides semi-annual data on official and officially guaranteed non-bank export credits from twenty-one OECD member countries aggregated at the borrowing-country level. The World Bank uses this information on export to obtain its own estimates of short-term debt outstanding for some countries. The World Bank debtor reporting system obtains debt information from 129 debtor countries; this information is published annually in *Global Development Finance* and relies heavily on BIS and OECD information.

However, existing reporting systems may significantly understate the true extent of reversible short-term liabilities. Existing information systems rely primarily on BIS banking statistics and do not adequately capture short-term flows outside the banking sector. Significant omissions include investments in developing-country assets by international mutual funds, and non-BIS banks, cross-border deposits held by nonresidents, and inter-firm cross-border flows. Off-balance-sheet exposures are also omitted from the BIS definition, which may be especially significant with the rapid growth of derivatives transactions in developing countries in foreign exchange and interest rates.

During the Mexican peso crisis of 1994, swap and forward contracts on tesobonos (short-term local-currency bonds) increased by 40 percent before the end of 1994, at which point Mexican institutions held some $16 billion in swaps.[44] Similarly, before the Russian debt moratorium, both foreign and domestic creditors traded in over-the-counter derivatives amounting to perhaps as much as $90 billion. And U.S. data for nine East Asian countries suggest that, as of June 1997, before the onset of the crisis, in that region off-balance-sheet claims represented some 9 percent of total

43. Industrialized reporting countries are: Austria, Belgium, Canada, Denmark, Finland, France, Germany, Ireland, Italy, Japan, Luxembourg, the Netherlands, Norway, Spain, Sweden, Switzerland, the United Kingdom, and the United States. Other banking centers are the Bahamas, Bahrain, the Cayman Islands, Hong Kong, the Netherlands Antilles, and Singapore. These offshore banking centers are not covered in the semiannual or consolidated series.

44. Nussbaum (1997).

U.S. bank claims. They had risen to 28 percent of total claims by December 1997, clearly illustrating the importance that such transactions can have in crisis countries.[45] In addition to these factors, a serious challenge to estimating the potentially reversible component of capital arises from the use of put options in debt contracts, which allows investors to reduce or recall loans prior to maturity.

A second shortcoming is that the current system does not provide information on the nonresident holders of short-term liabilities owed by the private sector and in particular, by the domestic banks. Without such information, national authorities have no way of forestalling potentially excessive growth of such cross-border liabilities. Consequently, improvements in national debt-reporting systems, especially with regard to short-term liabilities of the national banking system, are equally important. But the role of hedge funds, offshore financial centers, and cross-border derivatives transactions will limit the extent to which national authorities can fully measure short-term liabilities.

References

Backus, David, Patrick Kehoe, and Finn Kydland. 1992. "International Real Business Cycles." *Journal of Political Economy* 100 (4): 745–75.

Bank for International Settlements. 1997. "International Convergence of Capital Measurement and Capital Standards." Publication 4 (July 1988 [1st ed.], updated to April 1997).

———. 1999. "Capital Requirements and Bank Behaviour: The Impact of the Basel Accord." Basel Committee on Banking Supervision Working Papers 1 (April).

Bayoumi, Tamim. 1997. *Financial Integration and Real Activity.* University of Michigan Press.

Bussière, Matthieu, and Christian Mulder. 1999a. "External Vulnerability in Emerging Markets Economies: How High Liquidity Can Offset Weak Fundamentals and the Effects of Contagion." Working Paper 99/88. Washington: International Monetary Fund.

———. 1999b. "Which Short-Term Debt over Reserve Ratio Works Best? Operationalizing the Greenspan-Guidotti Rule." Draft International Monetary Fund Working Paper (typescript).

Calvo, Guillermo. 1991. " The Perils of Sterilization." *IMF Staff Papers* 38 (4): 921–26.

———. 1998. "Capital Flows and Capital-Market Crises: The Simple Economics of Sudden Stops." *Journal of Applied Economics* 1 (1): 35–54.

---

45. Bank for International Settlements (1999).

Calvo, Guillermo, and Enrique Mendoza. 1999. "Rational Contagion and the Globalization of Securities Markets." Working Paper 7153. Cambridge, Mass.: National Bureau of Economic Research (June).

Caplin, Andrew, and John Heahy. 1994. "Economics of Adjustment." Working Paper 4687. Cambridge, Mass.: National Bureau of Economic Research (March).

Chuhan, Punam., Stijn Claessens, and Nlandu Mamingi. 1993. "Equity and Bond Flows to Latin America and Asia: The Role of Global and Country Factors." Policy Research Working Paper 1160. Washington: World Bank.

Cole, Harold, and Maurice Obstfeld. 1991. "Commodity Trade and International Risk-Sharing: How Much Do Financial Markets Matter?" *Journal of Monetary Economics* 28 (1): 3–24.

Dasgupta, Dipak, and Dilip Ratha. 1999. "What Factors Drive Private Capital Flows? And How Does IBRD Lending Respond?" Washington: World Bank (typescript).

Demirgüç-Kunt, Asli. 1992. "Creditor Country Regulations and Commercial Bank Lending to Developing Countries." Policy Research Working Paper 917. Washington: World Bank.

Diamond, Douglas, and Philip Dybvig. 1983. "Bank Runs, Deposit Insurance and Liquidity." *Journal of Political Economy* 91 (3): 401–19.

Easterly, William, Roomeen Islam, and Joseph Stiglitz. 1999. "Shaken and Stirred: Volatility and Macroeconomic Paradigms for Rich and Poor Countries." Michael Bruno Memorial Lecture presented at the Twelfth World Congress of the International Economic Association, Buenos Aires, August 27.

Eichengreen, Barry, and Ashoka Mody. 1999. "Lending Booms, Reserves and the Sustainability of Short-Term Debt: Inferences from the Pricing of Syndicated Bank Loans." Working Paper 7113. Cambridge, Mass.: National Bureau of Economic Research (May).

Ferri, Giovanni, Li-Gang Liu, and Joseph Stiglitz, 1999. "The Procyclical Role of Rating Agencies: Evidence from the East Asian Crisis." *Economic Notes* 28 (3): 335–55.

Furman, Jason, and Joseph E. Stiglitz. 1998. "Economic Crises: Evidence and Insights from East Asia." *Brookings Papers on Economic Activity, 1998:2,* 1–114.

Gooptu, Sudarshan, and Maria Soledad Martinez Peria. 1992. "Factors That Affect Short-Term Commercial Bank Lending to Developing Countries." Policy Research Working Paper 886. Washington: World Bank.

Kaminsky, Graciela, José Saul Lizondo, and Carmen M. Reinhart. 1997. "Leading Indicators of Currency Crises." Policy Research Working Paper 1852. Washington: World Bank.

Mendoza, Enrique G. 1995. "The Terms of Trade, the Real Exchange Rate, and Economic Fluctuations." *International Economic Review* 36 (1): 101–37.

Montiel, Peter J. 1993. "Capital Mobility in Developing Countries: Some Measurement Issues and Empirical Estimates." Policy Research Working Paper 1103. Washington: World Bank.

Montiel, Peter J., and Carmen M. Reinhart. 1999. "Do Capital Controls Influence the Volume and Composition of Capital Flows? Evidence from the 1990s." *Journal of International Money and Finance* 18 (4): 619–35.

Mussa, Michael, Alexander Swoboda, Jeromin Zettelmeyer, and Oliver Jeanne. 1999. "Moderating Fluctuations in Capital Flows to Emerging Market Economies." Paper presented at a Conference on Key Issues in Reform of the International Monetary and Financial System, May 28–29, Washington: International Monetary Fund.

Nussbaum, David. 1997. "Seeing is Believing: Why the IMF Sees Derivatives as Agents of Economic Change and Control." *Risk* 10 (9): 26–28

Obstfeld, Maurice 1994. "Risk-Taking, Global Diversification, and Growth." *American Economic Review* 84 (5): 1310–29.

———. 1995. "International Capital Mobility in the 1990s." In *Understanding Interdependence,* edited by Peter B. Kenen, 201–61. Princeton University Press.

Radelet, Steven and Jeffrey Sachs. 1998a. "The Onset of the East Asian Financial Crisis." Working Paper 6680. Cambridge, Mass.: National Bureau of Economic Research (August).

———. 1998b. "The East-Asian Financial Crisis: Diagnosis, Remedies, Prospects." *Brookings Papers on Economic Activity 1998:1,* 1–91.

Rodrik, Dani, and Andrés Velasco. 1999. "Short-Term Capital Flows." Working Paper 7364. Cambridge, Mass.: National Bureau of Economic Research (September).

Romer, Paul. 1994. "Origins of Endogenous Growth." *Journal of Economic Perspectives* 8 (Winter): 3–22.

Sachs, Jeffrey D., Aaron Tornell, and Andrés Velasco. 1996a. "The Collapse of the Mexican Peso: What Have We Learned?" *Economic Policy* no. 22 (April): 13–56.

———. 1996b. "The Mexican Peso Crisis: Sudden Death or Death Foretold?" *Journal of International Economics* 41 (3-4): 265–83.

———. 1996c. "Financial Crises in Emerging Markets: The Lessons from 1995." *Brookings Papers on Economic Activity 1996:1,* 147–215.

Sarno, Lucio, and Mark P. Taylor. 1999. "Hot Money, Accounting Labels, and the Permanence of Capital Flows to Developing Countries: An Empirical Investigation." *Journal of Development Economics* 59 (2): 337–64.

Schmukler, Sergio, and Esteban Vesperoni. 2000. "Globalization and Firms' Financing Choices: Evidence from Emerging Economies." World Bank.

Summers, Lawrence H. 1999. "Overcoming Volatility: Latin America and the IDB." Remarks at the Annual Meetings of the Inter-American Development Bank, Paris, March 15 (www.ustreas.gov/press/releases/pr3018.htm).

Tesar, Linda L. 1995. "Evaluating the Gains from International Risk-Sharing." *Carnegie-Rochester Conference Series on Public Policy* 42 (June): 95–149.

Van Wincoop, Eric. 1994. "Welfare Gains from International Risk-Sharing." *Journal of Monetary Economics* 34 (2): 175–200.

World Bank. 1993. *Global Economic Prospects and the Developing Countries.* Washington.

———. 1997. *Private Capital Flows to Developing Countries: The Road to Financial Integration.* Oxford University Press.

———. 1999. *Global Economic Prospects and the Developing Countries: Beyond Financial Crisis.* Washington.

PETER M. GARBER 12

What You See versus What You Get: Derivatives in International Capital Flows

T HE EXPLOSIVE GROWTH of derivative products during the last fifteen
years has paralleled the growth of cross-border capital flows. Indeed,
the use of derivatives has been a major factor in these movements for several reasons. First, by allowing the separation of various risks associated
with cross-border investment, the availability of derivatives makes such
investment more attractive; portfolio diversification is more easily accomplished, with a consequent increase in gross international flows. Second,
the use of derivatives weakens impediments to the movement of capital in
search of higher real yields, with a consequent increase in net capital flows.
Various dimensions of risk can be moved across borders to markets that
find them less unattractive, and such potential gains in the efficiency of the
international allocation of capital have redefined a major, profitable segment of the international wholesale banking market.

The problems associated with the rise of derivatives stem in part from
the same source as the benefits: the increased ability to separate and market risks means that some counterparties can assume riskier positions more
readily than in the past. Coupled with the existence of weak financial systems and the inherent opaqueness of derivative positions resulting from
obsolete accounting systems, slow reporting, and unprepared regulators,

This paper expresses the personal views of the author and not those of Deutsche Bank.

derivatives can be used to leverage financial safety nets in efforts to double-up lost financial bets. Often such activity must move offshore to evade detection and naturally generates a gross international capital flow. Derivatives can be used readily to evade onshore prudential regulation and capital or exchange controls, thereby generating yet more measured capital flows.

Interpretations of the causes and dynamics of the sudden capital flow reversals associated with balance-of-payments crises generally are based on on-balance sheet accounting data. In the presence of derivatives, however, such data can generate false inferences about the sources of a crisis and lead to misinformed policy prescriptions. They obscure the sources of the crisis—whether it stems from foreign speculators, panicked green-screen traders, or domestic insiders armed with knowledge about weak fundamentals. In addition, in the presence of large volumes of derivatives, claims that crises are generated by such inappropriate polices as an excessively short maturity of the public debt can be mirages of on-balance sheet accounting.

Even on-balance sheet data for measuring the quality of international capital flows—the capital accounts of the balance-of-payments data—are obscured by derivatives used to enhance risk or evade controls or even for benign purposes. Sub-account data, such as portfolio investment, equity investment, foreign direct investment, or long- or short-maturity fixed interest rate lending, can be illusory in the presence of substantial volumes of derivative products.

This paper focuses on the reliability of on-balance sheet versus off-balance sheet indicators of position-taking in the overall national balance sheet. Specifically, the paper examines how derivative transactions affect a country's foreign currency exposure, traditional measures of capital account flows, the distribution of both market and credit risk, and the ability to control risks through regulatory devices. A focus on off-balance sheet products is crucial in making sense of capital account data: trying to understand financial flows through on-balance sheet thinking is like trying to understand cosmology with reference only to visible light.

General descriptions of some of the basic derivative products follow.[1] After a discussion of the positive effects of derivatives—the ability to refine the management of risk—the paper examines the negative aspects of these products: their role in enhancing risk-taking, in evading prudential regulations, taxes, and controls, in channeling the dynamics of currency and

---

1. The paper is an adaptation and expansion of ideas developed in Garber (1996, 1999), Garber and Lall (1996), and Folkerts-Landau and Garber (1997).

financial crises, and in obscuring the meaning of capital account data from the standard balance-of-payments accounts.

Why Derivatives Can Increase Cross-Border Movement of Capital

It is worthwhile at this point to consider a brief set of examples of derivative products. These examples will be used through the remainder of the paper to show how derivatives might aid in the diversification of portfolios, to reduce or enhance risk, evade prudential regulations, and avoid capital controls and taxes. Derivatives can create gross international capital flows that otherwise might not have materialized, but they also can confound the nature of the cross-border flows that do occur. The derivative types described in the following examples were important in the Mexican exchange rate crisis of 1994–95, so they will be developed in the Mexican context, which is used as a backdrop for many of the succeeding conclusions. They are generic products, however, and are used worldwide for the same reasons they were used in Mexico.

Swaps and Repos

Interest rate swaps involve exchanging fixed-rate yields for floating-rate yields in a single currency, or fixed-rate yields for fixed-rate yields in two different currencies for relatively long maturities. Similar deals are made in large volumes for shorter maturities. The tesobono swap is a useful example of such deals.

Tesobono swaps were offshore derivative operations used by Mexican banks as a means of leveraging tesobono holdings—treasury bills issued by the Mexican government that were indexed to the peso-dollar exchange rate. In a tesobono swap, a Mexican bank received the yield earned on tesobonos and delivered dollars at the London Interbank Offered Rate (LIBOR) plus some additional basis points, multiplied by a notional amount of dollars.

The leverage involved in tesobono swaps can be most readily examined by analyzing the nearly equivalent tesobono repurchase agreement. As an example, consider a New York investment firm that is willing to lend dollars for one year against tesobono collateral through a repurchase agreement. The firm engages in a repurchase agreement with a Mexican bank to buy tesobonos at some agreed price and to resell them in a year at the original price plus a dollar interest rate.[2] A Mexican bank sells $1 billion of tesobonos to a New York firm for $800 million with an agreement to repurchase the tesobonos in one year for the original price plus the LIBOR plus 1 percent interest. The yield on tesobonos is 8 percent while dollar LIBOR is 5 percent. In effect, the Mexican bank has financed a $1 billion tesobono position by borrowing $800 million, although official data on tesobono holdings will indicate that a foreign address holds the tesobonos. The gain to the Mexican bank is that it pays LIBOR plus 100 basis points to finance tesobonos that may pay the equivalent of LIBOR plus 300 basis points. The gain to the U.S. lender is that it gets to place dollar funds at LIBOR plus 100 basis points against good collateral while it borrows at LIBOR.

A tesobono swap places both parties in the same risk position as a repurchase agreement. Another example indicates the positions taken if the financing of the Mexican bank's tesobono position takes the form of a tesobono swap. Suppose the New York firm swaps tesobono yield in return for LIBOR plus 100 basis points against a U.S. $1 billion notional principal. It requires U.S. $200 million as collateral from its Mexican counterparty—that is, a margin deposit of 20 percent to guarantee compliance with the contract. The payoffs to the two counterparties are identical to those of the repurchase agreement. To hedge, the New York firm will purchase U.S. $1 billion in tesobonos directly from the market, financed by the $200 million margin and $800 million borrowed at LIBOR. As before, the tesobonos will be held by a foreign address, although Mexican domestic residents will bear the tesobono risk.

In either form, these operations serve to channel a net flow of capital of $800 million into Mexico, which ultimately finances the government. Gross flow data picked up in the normal balance-of-payments operation will measure an inflow of $1 billion worth of tesobono purchases and an outflow (in the form of bank deposits) for the collateral of $200 million. The swap, however, disguises the nature of the flow. Superficially, it appears that foreign lenders are buying Mexican government debt in the form of tesobonos—that they are content to hold the indexed treasury bills at the maturities offered by the managers of the Mexican public debt. In fact, they are making short-term dollar loans, while Mexican residents are holding the tesobono risk. On the national balance sheet—consolidating the

---

2. In the swap form of the deal, of course, only net amounts are due in each settlement period.

government and domestic banking sector—Mexico is a short-term borrower of dollars.

Equity Swaps

An equity swap establishes a leveraged position in shares, with funding coming from an offshore source. Again, a Mexico-based example will be used with an eye on later exposition, but such cross-border transactions are commonplace.

Suppose that a Mexican bank agrees to swap the total return over one year on equity in a Mexican corporation—"Telmex," for purposes of this example—for dollar LIBOR plus 300 basis points on a notional amount of U.S. $1 billion. Its offshore counterparty, a New York investment firm, requires U.S. $200 million in collateral. To hedge its short equity position, the New York firm then directly buys U.S. $1 billion worth of Telmex shares, thereby appearing as a foreign investor in Mexican shares. The New York firm is taking a long position in short-term dollar loans, while the Mexican bank has a long position in Telmex shares and a short position in short-term dollar loans. The Mexican bank has acquired $1 billion of Telmex risk by putting up $200 million of collateral in the United States.

Again, balance-of-payments accounts will report a gross inflow of $1 billion worth of equity purchases for portfolio investment or perhaps foreign direct investment and an outflow of $200 million in bank deposits. The Mexican bank—and therefore the national balance sheet—holds the equity risk, while the foreign address is only a short-term dollar lender.

Structured Notes

Structured notes exist in many forms, but the example studied here will determine the payoff on what might be described as a bullish obligation on the peso.[3] A Mexican bank or its foreign subsidiary might buy a note with a twenty-nine-day maturity from a New York investment firm for $10 million. The coupon on the note and the principal on the note are payable in dollars. Suppose that the coupon offered in the note is 195 percent annually multiplied by the ratio of the current spot value of the peso to the peso-dollar exchange rate at maturity. Interest rates on peso paper such as cetes—

---

3. The description of this note is taken from an indicative term sheet issued by Donaldson, Lufkin and Jenrette on March 22, 1995.

peso-denominated treasury bills—are 85 percent per annum and 5 percent on dollar paper. The principal repayment also depends negatively on the peso value of the dollar at maturity: suppose it will be $[1 + 3(7.0 - P_m)/P_m] \times \$10$ million, where 7.0 is the initial peso value of the dollar and P_m is the value at maturity. In an extreme case, if the peso has depreciated by 50 percent at maturity, from say, 7.0 to 14.0 pesos per dollar, the principal repayment will be −$5 million. The overall payoff is then −$3.25 million.[4] Conversely, if the peso appreciates significantly, the payoff can be a multiple of the initial investment. Appendix 12A shows the payoff structure of a position that is currently short about $19.92 million at a market dollar interest rate of 5 percent per year and long 209.95 million pesos at a market peso interest rate of 85 percent per year. In effect, the initial $10 million investment has been leveraged threefold and invested in peso paper.

Through the payoff formula, the New York investment firm would have a position equivalent to being short 209.95 million worth of peso paper and long $19.92 million worth of dollar loans. In addition, it has the initial $10 million from the sale of the note. To hedge, it may wish to buy pesos by investing in one-month cetes while simultaneously selling dollars in the position. It would then appear in the on-balance sheet accounts as a foreign buyer of a peso-denominated asset rather than as a dollar-denominated lender, which is its true position.[5]

If the seller of the note hedges the position, the balance-of-payments accounts will report a net inflow of about $20 million. This will result from a gross inflow of about $30 million in the form of portfolio purchases of short-term, peso-denominated government paper and outflow of $10 million in the form of a Mexican bank's purchase of a short-maturity, dollar-denominated note.

Credit Derivatives

The structured credit market encompasses a broad range of capital markets products designed to transfer credit risk among investors through over-

4. As a safety feature for the buyer, such structured notes cap the potential losses. For example, in an actual bullish obligation, in no case would the principal redemption plus coupon payment be less than zero. This adds a put option feature to the note.

5. As an additional feature, such notes contain clauses that state that the notes will pay zero if there is a "default event" on cetes or an "exchange control event." This is a type of poison pill that automatically wipes out part of domestic bank capital in a country that imposes such policies.

the-counter transactions. The most common is the credit default swap. In addition, on-balance sheet products such as credit-linked notes provide a similar product for entities constrained from holding off-balance sheet positions.

Default Swaps

In a default swap, a *protection seller* makes a contingent payment to a *protection buyer* if there is a credit event associated with a *reference obligation* in exchange for a periodic fee tied to the credit spread of an instrument. For example, a bank might sell protection to the holder of a sovereign bond against a default or capital control event. Under some contracts, the protection buyer may deliver the reference asset to the protection seller for par if the event occurs. Under other contracts, the difference between par and the market value of the reference asset may be paid in cash.

Credit-Linked Notes

Not trusting the promise of the protection seller to pay off in case of a credit event, the protection buyer might require collateral. He can obtain this by selling a note at par to the would-be protection seller. The note has embedded in it the equivalent of a default swap that eliminates the obligation to repay principal on the note if a credit event occurs in the reference debt. The reference debt need not have any relation to the protection buyer or seller. The note will pay a credit spread tied to the reference debt if the event does not occur.

Circumventing Prudential Regulations and Capital Controls

In addition to their normal uses in portfolio diversification or risk reduction, derivatives can be used to increase risk: one party of the derivative deal may be speculating. In weakly regulated, undercapitalized financial systems, derivatives provide a perfect opportunity for financial intermediaries to take risky positions in attempts to recover capital. This section examines how derivatives such as those in the examples developed earlier can be used to evade prudential regulation and capital controls.

Evading Prudential Regulation

Prudential regulations of varying stringency are well accepted across different financial systems, but they are especially important in the presence of large capital inflows. With the rapid expansion of bank balance sheets into unfamiliar business, such inflows in particular increase the risk of systemic failures in the financial sector. A sudden flow into a country of a large amount of capital will give rise to general expansion of the financial system and investment projects, and there is no assurance that the capital will be placed in "good" projects. Many regulators and academics believe that the inflows are often the result of various investment fads and that disappointment about the payoffs from these investments will lead to investor attempts to withdraw their funds. Therefore, regulations are imposed—such as reserve requirements; limits on lending to individuals, firms, or sectors; liquidity requirements against domestic or foreign exchange liabilities; net foreign currency exposure limits; capital requirements—that aim at channeling inflows away from banks and risky projects. Similarly, a ban on holding securities on margin or on short sales will mean that holders of equities will not be forced to join the general scramble for cash in a liquidity crisis and thereby reduces the potential magnitude of the demand for cash. Banning margin buying outright, however, tends to push such activity offshore, through over-the-counter derivative markets.

Banks can readily avoid prudential regulations—either in a straightforward manner by going offshore or by engaging in off-balance sheet activities, which violate the intent, if not the letter, of regulations. I examine below how structured notes, equity swaps, credit derivatives, and similar instruments can be used to avoid such regulation.

STRUCTURED NOTES. As mentioned earlier, structured notes are investment vehicles with coupon payments and principal repayments driven by formulas that can leverage the initial capital invested. Nevertheless, in value accounting systems they can be booked as normal investments and in the currency denominated in the prospectus. More than simply magnifying the usual market risks associated with investment positions, structured notes provide an easy method for circumventing prudential regulations on currency positions or interest rate mismatches.

In the context of the last section's example, these notes, booked as claims of Mexican institutions with dollar principal and dollar payoffs, in fact were currency bets that created a short dollar and long peso currency position to take advantage of positive interest rate spreads between peso and dollar money markets. The notes were reported by Mexican banks as dollar assets, allowing them to offset short dollar positions in meeting regulatory limits on net foreign currency positions. In addition, some banks could count the note to satisfy their liquidity coefficient required for foreign currency–denominated liabilities because its short maturity allowed it to be classified as a liquid deposit. In the event of a depreciation of the currency, banks might have a much larger net short dollar position and greater losses than regulators had realized.

Held in this way, the structured note of the "bullish peso" example is a financial engineering device to circumvent prudential regulation. Only the principal was booked, in accordance with value accounting principles. The structured note's payoff formula component was not booked: it is an off-balance sheet item. That is the accounting trick—altering the nature of the booking through a complicated payoff formula. The use of the trick, however, requires an outflow of capital in the form of principal. Thus a net inflow of $20 million takes the form of a gross outflow of $10 million and a gross inflow of $30 million.

EQUITY SWAPS. As a means of taking a position in stocks, the market in equity swaps can be used to avoid financial market regulations against such positions. Such regulations may ban buying securities on margin or short selling, or they may limit the share positions of foreign addresses.[6] The benefits to market participants of the existence of this market are obvious. Speculators can leverage and gain larger positions, and hedgers of long positions held either directly or implicitly in the form of options can short stock to cover their positions. Again, net short-term dollar foreign borrowing for domestic stock purchases takes the form of a gross outflow in the form of dollar-denominated margin and a larger gross inflow in the form of a stock purchase by a foreign address.

The Role of Derivatives in the Korean Crisis

A common investment strategy for South Korean banks in 1996–97 was the acquisition of structured notes that involved taking leveraged positions on currencies. For example, a bank might buy a note tied to the Indonesian rupiah with a face value of $20 million. The note would pay a high coupon, but principal repayment would depend on the dollar-rupiah

6. Offshore equity swap markets also existed for Malaysia, South Korea, and Thailand, among others, in order to avoid curbs on short-selling and leveraging.

exchange rate: if the rupiah depreciated, principal and interest would be reduced, as in the Mexico example above. Such notes had implicit leverage of between five and ten times. Often the positions were leveraged even higher through the methods used to finance them: the foreign seller of the note would enter into a repurchase agreement with the buyer with a 20 percent haircut, thus providing five times more leverage.

Profit-hungry Korean banks were attracted to the seemingly sure high returns in a benign rupiah exchange rate environment. When the rupiah devalued, however, Korean banks took a double hit: they lost dollar capital in the structured note and had to deliver dollar margin or unwind their repurchase agreements. Such pressures came to a head in December 1997, when the rupiah collapsed, increasing the demand for dollars by Korean banks. This sudden drain on official reserves came as a surprise to the authorities, who were unaware of these derivative positions. Only in the third week of December did the Bank of Korea force the banks to disclose their full off-balance sheet positions.

Korean banks also took on Indonesian risk in the form of selling credit derivatives to counterparties. For example a counterparty might buy Indonesian bonds and pay 2 percent of the face value to a Korean bank for a credit swap—if the credit rating of the issuer fell, or if the market value of the bonds fell sufficiently, the counterparty had the right to sell the securities at the exercise price. Again, these were off-balance sheet items, so the dollar claims on Korean banks were unreported. (The Korean banks took on Brazilian credit risk as well through the use of credit derivatives.)

Avoiding Capital Import Taxes or Controls

Taxes or outright bans on the acquisition by foreign addresses of domestic securities have emerged in recent years as a means of stemming capital inflows. They sometimes have been imposed differentially by maturity of asset and by type of asset. Often, such taxes have been successful in that they have placed a wedge between domestic and foreign yields on similar assets. They can be breached by the usual invoicing subterfuges, but market participants have also used financial engineering to circumvent the taxes. Suppose, for example, that an enforceable tax is placed uniformly on all forms of gross inflows. Then, any positive net inflow will incur the tax, but gross transactions will move offshore. Instead of acquiring an equity position directly, a foreign investor will buy an offshore equity swap from a domestic resident who can hedge without a tax. If the domestic resident has a lower credit rating, an export of capital in the form of margin will be recorded. There will be no taxable inflow, but foreigners can take risk positions in domestic assets.

If the tax is differential across types of assets acquired from abroad, the net inflow will tend to take the form that incurs the lowest tax. Similarly, if differential controls are imposed, allowing equity investment but limiting short-term fixed-interest inflows, the flows will enter through the least restrictive door. The risk and maturity characteristics of the inflow can then be resculpted through offshore derivatives to a more desirable form. For instance, if equity investment is given a better treatment than short-term fixed-interest securities or bank deposits, the inflow will take the form of a stock acquisition together with an equity swap that converts it on net into a floating-interest loan of foreign currency. Even the maturity of the loan can be adjusted with an attachment by the lender of a stringent margining provision that permits the offshore creditor to realize cash on call.

The Role of Derivatives in Crisis-Driven Capital Outflows

Where such markets exist, forward contracts are the speculator's instrument of choice in implementing an attack on a currency, the beginning of a sudden outflow of capital. Positions in forward contracts can arise suddenly, or they can build up gradually in the expectation of an impending devaluation. Such derivatives serve merely to effect a crisis that is emerging from other causes. Other derivative products, already outstanding in large volumes, may reflect an environment in which such speculation may be successful and may even determine the dynamics of the currency and financial crisis that ensues.

Next, using the examples developed earlier from the Mexican case, I show how the existence of these products operated to determine the dynamics of exchange markets leading into the currency crisis of December 1994, to determine the magnitude of the final attack, and to drive the foreign exchange market turbulence in the months after the attack.

Derivatives and the Dynamics of Capital Flow Reversals

Even in countries in which currency forward contracts did not play a role in a sudden reversal in capital flows, other derivative products may be present in sufficient quantities to affect the dynamics of a crisis. The Mexican peso crisis of 1994 is such a case. Speculators did not use the forward market to suddenly short-sell the peso. Rather, outstanding products of the sort outlined earlier drove the near-in movements of capital going into and coming out of the devaluation of the peso. Similarly, derivatives played a key role in the Brazilian crisis of October 1997 (see box 12-1) and the trading dynamics of the 1998 Russian crisis (see box 12-2).

MEXICO: 1994. The derivative positions that drove the crisis were established by a weak banking system hungry for current income. Mexican groups financed their $12 billion purchase of Mexico's banks during the 1991–92 privatization though substantial borrowing. Interest due had to be paid through current bank income, and this led the banks into taking increased credit risk through on-balance sheet expansions and increased market risk through off-balance sheet growth.

Tesobono swaps. Industry sources in Mexico report that there was a stock of about U.S. $16 billion of tesobono swaps at the time of the peso's devaluation.[7] Of the U.S. $29 billion of tesobonos outstanding on December 19, 1994, about U.S. $16.1 billion were held by foreign addresses. Thus the value of tesobono swaps was sufficient to repackage the entire foreign holding of tesobono risk: foreigners held tesobonos primarily to hedge tesobono swaps and Mexican banks held the tesobono risk.

When the crisis arrived, tesobono market values in dollars suddenly fell. From December 1994 to January 1995, tesobono yields jumped from 8 percent to 24 percent, and several of the interim offerings failed. The fall in market value reduced the value of the collateral and triggered margin calls to deliver dollars or close out the positions.

If the typical tesobono fell by 15 percent in dollar value, the value of the collateral in the tesobono swap would have fallen significantly, and a margin call would immediately have been sent to the Mexican bank. Alternatively, anticipating margin calls, the Mexican bank would immediately have sought dollar liquidity in preparation. To restore margin, the $16 billion in swaps would instantly generate $16 × 0.15 = $2.4 billion of demand for dollars by the Mexican banks.

Equity swaps. Market participants have characterized the market in offshore Mexican equity swaps as very large; they have not been as explicit

7. Such numbers are guesswork because no one aggregates such data. Nevertheless, similar estimates were given to me by market managers at the top two banks in Mexico, which did a large fraction of the business.

Box 12-1. *Leveraged Brady Positions in the October 1997 Brazilian Crisis*

By October 1997 many domestic financial institutions and funds had established highly leveraged positions (ten or twenty times their capital) in Brazilian Brady bonds and Telebras shares through offshore repurchase agreements or swaps. The decline of Brady bond prices triggered large margin calls. Domestic institutions were forced to sell off domestic assets for dollars to meet the calls, putting strong pressure on the exchange rate market in Brazil. These positions were established primarily by investment banks and mutual funds, so they involved capital losses uninsured by the financial safety net. Initially, international economists ascribed this large reserve out-flow to panicked, twenty-five-year-old green-screen traders in New York irrationally spreading the Asian currency crisis to an unrelated Brazil. Another argument is that Brazilian investors, having acquired a taste for high real yields during the inflation-ary period, pressured their intermediaries into delivering high returns even as real yields started to decline after 1995.* To meet this demand in a regime of narrowing spreads, mutual funds took on more leveraged positions.

*Local inside information and a rumor concerning the possibility of an impending buy-back or conversion of Brazil's Brady bonds provide an alternative explanation for the number of highly leveraged positions. In an effort to get their piece of the pie, local institutions rapidly built up their Brady positions at precisely the wrong moment.

about orders of magnitude as in the case of tesobonos, though several par-ticipants have claimed a notional value of up to $3 billion in such contracts at the time of the crisis.

With the collapse of the peso, the stock market fell immediately by about 50 percent in dollars and by 66 percent within two months. With the margin in the equity swaps more than wiped out, margin calls or antic-ipations of margin calls again forced the Mexican banks to rush for dollar liquidity. Taking $3 billion as the notional value of outstanding equity swaps, this would have required the banks to find an additional $1.5 bil-lion at the time of the December 19, 1994, devaluation. Mexican institu-tions and individuals engaged in these swaps had to sell pesos to get mar-gin or close out their position, adding to the turmoil of the exchange and stock markets.

The total of margin calls from tesobono and equity swaps alone was about $4 billion. Coincidentally, this was approximately the amount that

Box 12-2. *The Trading-Dynamic and Derivatives Evolution of the 1998 Russian Crisis*

At the start of the crisis in May 1998, protracted difficulties in the Duma's approval of the appointment of Sergei Kiriyenko as prime minister caused yields in Russian Treasury bills (GKOs) to rise to 55 percent. The postponement until June 25 of the release of the International Monetary Fund's (IMF) extended finance facility tranche due in March added impetus to the rising yields.

By late May long positions in ruble-denominated securities were sustained solely by speculation that a new IMF loan program would be announced. This started a two-month, cat-and-mouse game among the markets, the Russian government, and the IMF—and a roller-coaster ride for ruble yields. At the end of May IMF officials announced that Russia did not need new loans. Those speculating with long positions on the ruble were driven by the view that there would be no devaluation before an IMF loan program was announced, which turned out to be accurate. Hedge fund buying based on this speculation rallied yields down to 42 percent.

As this game became protracted, successive GKO auctions were undersubscribed or failed altogether, with a consequent rise in yield level and volatility. Funds were provided to make up for the shortfall through several private placements with hedge funds and banks at unannounced terms. In one such makeshift deal, the Russian government, on June 10, privately issued a dual-currency bond similar to the bond that Mexico had successfully issued to reenter the markets. The characteristics of the security were that it could be treated as a dollar bond with a call option on the ruble. The Mexican issue worked because it had been placed with buyers who were willing to take peso positions—that is, to not hedge the long peso position implied by the call. The manager of the Russian bond, however, placed the issue (valued at approximately $250 million) with buyers who did not want ruble positions. This required the buyers to short GKOs in order to hedge their positions.

When positions were marked to market, margin calls were repeatedly made on outstanding repos with Russian banks. This created both a demand for dollars by the Russian counterparties and a further dumping of the securities on the markets. Regardless of the maturity of the debt structure, the existence of the repos put immediate pressure on the exchange market as yields on Russian securities rose.

The IMF loan program was finally announced on July 13 and made $5.6 billion immediately available. The result was an immediate effort to convert the GKOs into dollar bonds. The GKOs (depending on their maturity) were to be exchanged at a fixed price for a package of dollar bonds—half in twenty-year maturities, half in seven-year maturities. In all, some $4.4 billion worth of bills was swapped.

The attempt to lengthen the debt maturity structure was in line with the prevailing dogma that excessive short-term debt is a cause of crisis rather than simply a signal of distrust of the issuer. The exchange was an ill-conceived scheme in which issues were not carefully placed. Exposures in longer-maturity dollar bonds were already so large that it was not possible to increase exposure easily. Even if a holder of Russian dollar-denominated bonds was not a party to the deal, it perceived an increased risk in its holdings of these maturities and so immediately sold. The swap put a large amount of long-duration paper into the market and as a result drove down the price.

Alternatively viewed (and phrased in the debt crisis language of the 1980s), the swap converted junior claims on Russia into senior claims, with serious negative effect on existing dollar bond prices.

On July 20, the IMF pulled back $800 million from the program when its board approved disbursement of only $4.8 billion and skepticism was voiced about whether targets would be met. An attempt to hold another auction of GKOs failed immediately. Thus the negative market reaction was directly exposed. In the weeks following, the Russian government held another series of unsuccessful GKO auctions, funding maturing debt with its remaining foreign exchange. No new private money flowed in through conventional channels in the wake of the program

On July 24, two proprietary funds decided to close out their Russia business and liquidate, flooding the market with paper. Other traders, leery of the market's volatility, cut their own positions. Those who were still positive on Russia had filled the maximum positions allowed by their risk control systems, so there were no buyers for this added supply and the market crashed.

Markets in ruble debt became almost completely illiquid during the first week of August as the optimism of holders of ruble-denominated debt broke. On August 17 the intervention band for the ruble was moved to between 6.0 and 9.5, implying a potential depreciation of the currency by as much as 50 percent during 1998. Ruble-denominated securities—(GKOs) and coupon-bearing government paper (OFZs)—maturing before year-end 1999 were to be exchanged for new securities. Until the debt restructuring was complete, trade in GKOs and OFZs was suspended. A ninety-day moratorium was declared on servicing of foreign exchange contracts and repayment (especially by banks) of debt to nonresidents.

On August 26, the terms of the forced conversion were announced. The package was valued at no more than twenty cents on the dollar of the preconversion value of the domestic debt. Selling against Russia commenced immediately.

the Mexican central bank's reserves fell in the final attack just before the peso was allowed to float on December 21, 1994.[8]

Structured notes. During 1994 Mexican financial institutions took large positions in structured notes with New York investment firms. Because the notes were reported by the banks as dollar assets, however, the Mexican accounting rules allowed them to be booked as a dollar position, so that they were not counted against the regulatory net currency position limit of 15 percent of capital.

The first of these structures were known as ajustabono structures and were noticed when consolidated regulation was implemented in September 1994. The second group were similar to the structured note discussed earlier and came to the attention of authorities just after the December 1994 devaluation.

Ajustabonos—inflation-indexed Mexican government securities—had long been held by Mexican banks. In addition, to paying a relatively fixed real interest return, ajustabonos could be counted as foreign exchange assets in determining regulatory foreign exchange positions, so Mexican banks funded their ajustabono positions with dollar borrowings. When real interest rates rose in 1992, Mexican banks—unwilling to realize the capital losses on their investment portfolios—found that their ajustabono positions were effectively frozen. The solution was to contract structures with U.S. banks and investment firms through which the ajustabonos could be used as collateral.

For example, a U.S. investment firm and a Mexican securities firm associated with a bank might jointly organize a company in the Cayman Islands or in Bermuda that would agree to purchase ajustabonos at face value, with the funding provided from the sale of two series of securities, one senior and one junior, both denominated in dollars. Suppose that the deal involved a Mexican bank's selling $120 million par value worth of ajustabonos to the company. The Mexican partner might put up $20 million and receive $20 million par value of the junior securities, which it would sell to the Mexican bank. Denominated in dollars, the junior notes could be counted as a foreign exchange asset in determining regulatory positions. The U.S. firm would invest $100 million and receive $100 million par value of the senior securities. The senior securities would be

---

8. Other Mexico-oriented derivative products, such as cetes swaps and Brady bond swaps, also would have drawn margin calls at the same moment.

designed to pay a relatively secure dollar yield, which could be paid if the exchange rate did not depreciate excessively and would be sold for LIBOR plus. The payoff on the junior securities was like that of a structured note—if the exchange rate did not depreciate, it would pay a high yield and make good the losses on the ajustabonos. If the exchange rate depreciated, the yield or principal of the junior note would decline according to a pre-determined formula.

When the banking authorities became aware that the return on the junior notes was correlated with the peso, they required that 100 percent of the notes be covered with foreign exchange. Market sources estimate that $2 billion of the junior notes were outstanding in 1994. The banks began to cover their positions in September 1994 and throughout the autumn, which contributed significantly to the drain on official reserves during the several months preceding the devaluation.

After the devaluation, the Mexican central bank learned of the existence of large positions in structured notes resembling the "bullish obligation" example. Charged with enforcing regulations on domestic banks' net foreign exchange positions, the Banco de Mexico immediately ordered Mexican banks to cover their short dollar positions. This forced a scramble for several billion dollars of foreign exchange during the post-collapse floating period, leading to the highly volatile and illiquid foreign exchange market that dominated the first quarter of 1995.

Taken in sequence, the ajustabono structures, swaps, and structured notes account for most of the currency market dynamics in the months surrounding the collapse of the peso. The Mexican peso crisis is an example of a systemic crisis whose dynamics were driven by a structure of outstanding derivatives. The timing and magnitude of the near-in reserve drain, the final attack on foreign exchange reserves, and the post-collapse market turbulence are explainable by the automatic credit and market risk-covering programs attached to the contracts by counterparties and regulators themselves.

What Does "Proper Public Debt Management" Mean in the Presence of Derivatives?

Because Mexico had issued large amounts of short-term tesobonos that could not be rolled over in the aftermath of the devaluation, subsequent analyses have pinpointed improper management of public debt as a major

cause of this and succeeding financial crises.[9] The consequent policy prescription has been to restructure the public debt to longer maturities in a
modern version of the nineteenth-century British prescription for virtuous
public debt management: "all consols—no bills."

The example of the tesobono swaps, however, indicates that such a prescription can easily be circumvented. Even in the case of the relatively
short-term tesobonos, the yield apparently was not sufficient to encourage
foreign lenders to hold Mexican risk. Only the income-hungry Mexican
banks were willing to accept the low yields on tesobonos. Thus, vis-à-vis
the rest of the world, the Mexican national balance sheet was a borrower of
callable dollars through the tesobono-tesobono swap operation. The
tesobono debt of the government was balanced by the tesobono return
claims of the Mexican banks, leaving on net only the dollar debt. The sudden calls on the Mexican banking system to deliver dollars to restore margin in effect converted the average maturity of the tesobonos from six-
months to callable, and the only way to satisfy the call was to deliver official
reserves.

Suppose that instead of tesobono issues, the Mexican government had
structured its debt by issuing ten-year peso or even dollar-denominated
bonds. Foreign buyers, even more reluctant to absorb these issues than to
absorb tesobonos, would have required very high yields. Mexican banks,
however, proved that they would have been willing to take the risk at lower
yields than foreigners. The Mexican government, as a result, might have
found a market for the longer-term debt under a scenario like the following: Mexican banks would have entered into total return swaps with foreign banks to receive the yield on the long-term debt and pay dollar
LIBOR, delivering collateral to the foreign banks. Foreign banks would
then have been willing to buy the long-term debt. Any decline in value of
the debt would have instantly triggered margin calls to deliver dollars. In
effect, these operations would have converted these long-term claims
against the Mexican government into short-term, perhaps callable dollar
claims against the national balance sheet.

If the foreign lenders believe that the risks warrant only short-term lending, then a prescription to lengthen the debt is irrelevant. Even if it is
undertaken on-balance sheet, it will be undone off-balance sheet.

Of course, if the government is strongly committed to not bail out the
banking system, the construction of a national balance sheet itself is irrel-

9. See, for example, Calvo (1996); Calvo and Mendoza (1996); and Cole and Kehoe (1996).

evant; tesobono risk or the risk of government securities with any particular features would be priced properly by the domestic banks, and their dollar margin requirements would not be met by the central bank. The public debt could then be truly lengthened, if that is desirable.

What Do "Restructuring" and "Controls" Mean in the Presence of Credit Derivatives and Structured Products?

An undesired lengthening of maturity of public debt can be effectively undone in the national balance sheet through swaps with yield-hungry domestic banks. Similarly, the effectiveness of defaults and forced restructuring of sovereign debt and the imposition of controls can be curtailed through credit derivative positions of the domestic banking system. For example, an owner of a domestic bank can generally calculate that a sovereign default will be done in circumstances where, in any case, his bank is likely to fail and to be bailed out. Thus, it is natural for him to sell protection against a credit event to holders of the sovereign debt in the form of a credit-linked note so that he will win the risk premium in the good outcome. A minister of finance who thinks that he can force the foreign creditor to extend further credit through a forced restructuring will succeed merely in increasing the size of the hole in his own banking system. Similarly, the imposition of controls can be covered in a structured note held by a domestic bank.

Effects of Derivatives on Interpretation of Balance-of-Payments Accounting

Among the rationales of balance-of-payments accounting is to ascertain the stability of capital flows of on-balance sheet movements of assets. Typically, balance-of-payments accounting data are used to measure how long capital will remain in a country—to distinguish "good" money from "hot" money.[10] Various categories of the capital accounts have been interpreted as indicative of the nature of capital inflows or outflows. Foreign direct investment, for example, has been considered a more stable form of

---

10. Although the balance-of-payments capital accounts are set up to measure cross-border changes in legal ownership of claims to assets and liabilities, the classification system for financial items is designed to bring out the motivation of creditors and debtors. See International Monetary Fund (1994, p. xxii).

investment than portfolio investment or the foreign acquisition of bank claims. Foreign acquisition of short-term fixed-interest products is generally regarded as a speculative flow. Balance-of-payments accounts are also used to measure the foreign exchange position of a country's consolidated balance sheet and, in times of crisis, to determine the potential outflow of foreign exchange through speculation or covering operations by holders of domestic liquid assets.

The revolution in global finance and particularly the explosion in the use of derivative products have rendered the use of balance-of-payments capital account data even more problematic than it has been in the past.[11] Balance-of-payments accounting data use on-balance sheet categorizations, and they are based on value accounting principles to book and categorize asset values. They ignore almost completely the existence of derivatives and their role in reallocating who bears market risk.

For example, the acquisition of a large block of equity is classified as foreign direct investment, but a foreign buyer may be acquiring the block simply to hedge a short position in equity established through a derivative position. In the case of the equity swap described above, the foreign investment firm that sells the swap must acquire the shares to form a hedge. If the swap is large enough, the hedging operation may be booked as foreign direct investment because the offshore swap position is not included in the capital accounts, although the investment firm in fact is making a short-term floating rate loan in foreign currency.

Declines in equity values or exchange rate will then generate instantaneous exchange market pressure as margin calls are made or positions are closed. This is contrary to the general view among central banks that stock market investment will not likely generate exchange market pressure in a crisis because the losses will already have been absorbed in a resultant crash. Stock market money is therefore regarded as less "hot." If the buyer of the swap is a domestic resident, the capital import effectively takes the form of short-term, foreign currency-denominated borrowing, but the leveraged equity risk, and even the long-term control, remains in the hands of the domestic resident. Thus the "direct investment" turns

---

11. The usual problems concern omissions or miscategorizations of transactions. That these have been magnified in the presence of widespread use of derivatives has been duly recognized by authorities responsible for technical standards, as exemplified by the April 1996 meeting at the IMF of the Informal Group on Financial Derivatives.

into the hottest of money. In a similar manner, direct investment in the form of reinvestment of profits can be converted into short-term funding through an equity swap.

Alternatively, a foreign program trader may acquire the domestic stock index in the cash market while selling forward in the offshore over-the-counter index market. On net, he has a zero position in equities but in the balance-of-payments accounts appears as a portfolio investor in domestic equities. If the opposite positions are taken by a domestic residents—a sale of equities in the cash market and a forward purchase in the derivatives market—the net equity risk position for domestic residents is unchanged, though domestic residents are now in effect short-term foreign currency borrowers.

To the extent that they start with zero replacement values (as in the case of swaps and forwards), derivative products do not affect measured net capital inflows or outflows, but they blur the information in subcategories of the capital accounts.[12] In particular, they make a mockery of the use of capital account categories to attempt to measure the aggregate short foreign-currency position of an economy.

Conclusion

A blind spot in both national and international surveillance of capital markets has emerged from the explosion in the use of derivative products. Through derivatives, both individual institutions and financial systems can be put at risk in magnitudes and from directions completely unknown to regulators. This problem arises because derivatives are ideal means of avoiding prudential regulations, given the universally slow adjustment of accounting principles to the advent of these products. On a more parochial level, the accounting principles on which the balance-of-payments data gathering exercise is based are being made increasingly obsolete.

The illusion created by viewing the flow of capital solely through the on-balance sheet prism creates a dangerous potential for misinterpreting the implications of major events in capital markets. The information conveyed by the balance-of-payments accounts regarding the riskiness of the

---

12. An exception arises if a deposit of margin is required by a foreign counterparty; the margin will be counted as a capital export.

national balance sheet is confounded, so the susceptibility of an economy to capital-flow reversals cannot be known. When capital flows suddenly reverse, it is difficult to know which players are driving the flows and therefore to determine the appropriate short- and long-term policy responses.

Appendix 12A
Bullish Obligation on the Peso

1. i_{cetes} = .85 annual

2. $i_\$$ = .05 annual

3. Maturity of contract: 29 days

4. Overall payoff of the note = Coupon + Principal
$$= 1.95 * 7.0/P_m * 29/360 + 1 + 3\,[(7.0 - P_m)/P_m]$$

5. Some arithmetic to determine implied dollar and new peso (Npeso) positions:

Payoff = $(-2 + 3.157 * 7.0/P_m) \times$ \$10 million

= -\$20 million + \$31.57 million $* 7.0/P_m$

= -\$20 million + Npesos 221 million/P_m

Present values:

Current dollar position = -\$19.92 million

Current Npeso = 209.95 million = \$29.99 million

References

Calvo, Guillermo. 1996. "Capital Flows and Macroeconomic Management: Tequila Lessons." Working Paper 23. University of Maryland, Center for International Economics (March).

Calvo, Guillermo, and Enrique Mendoza. 1996. "Mexico's Balance-of-Payments Crisis: A Chronicle of a Death Foretold." Working Paper 20. University of Maryland, Center for International Economics (March).

Cole, Harold, and Timothy Kehoe. 1996. "Self-Fulfilling Debt Crises." Federal Reserve Bank of Minneapolis Staff Report 211 (December).

Folkerts-Landau, David, and Peter M. Garber. 1997. "Derivative Markets and Financial System Soundness." In *Banking Soundness and Monetary Policy*, edited by Charles Enoch and John N. Green, 290–304. Washington: International Monetary Fund.

Garber, Peter M. 1996. "Managing Risks to Financial Markets from Volatile Capital Flows: The Role of Prudential Regulation." *International Journal of Finance and Economics* 1 (3): 183–95.

———. 1999. "Derivatives in International Capital Flows." In *International Capital Flows,* edited by Martin Feldstein, 386–407. University of Chicago Press.

Garber, Peter M., and Subir Lall. 1996. "Derivative Products in Exchange Rate Crises." Paper prepared for Federal Reserve Bank of San Francisco's conference, "Managing Capital Flows and Exchange Rates: Lessons from the Pacific Basin," September 26–27.

International Monetary Fund. 1994. *Balance of Payments Statistics Yearbook.* Washington.

TIMOTHY S. WILSON 13

Financial Risk Management and Liquidity Crises

B OTH PRIVATE COMPANIES and developing country governments are exposed to "funding liquidity" crises. Three structural characteristics are primarily responsible for their shared vulnerability. First, future economic fundamentals—net income and net asset value for corporations, and external account flows and gross domestic product (GDP) for countries—are uncertain. Second, assets are financed in part with liabilities that require repayment in cash or, for a government, foreign currency. Third, assets cannot always be used to raise cash or foreign exchange on short notice. The interaction of these factors creates exposure to liquidity shocks, which, if not well managed, can lead to a funding liquidity crisis.

The liquidity crisis of 1997–98 had an enormous impact on market valuations for the equity of major global financial intermediaries and for debt of developing country governments. The line graph in figure 13-1 presents equity prices for three leading investment firms, as well as the value of the J. P. Morgan emerging markets bond index. These series look so similar that in the absence of the key, one is hard pressed to distinguish the financial firm equity values from the bond index. Figure 13-2, which provides

This paper expresses the personal views of the author and not those of Morgan Stanley Dean Witter. I am grateful to my colleagues at Morgan Stanley Dean Witter for stimulating discussions about various risk management issues addressed in this paper.

Figure 13-1. *Prices of Bank Equity and Emerging Markets Debt, 1997–99*

Share price or index value

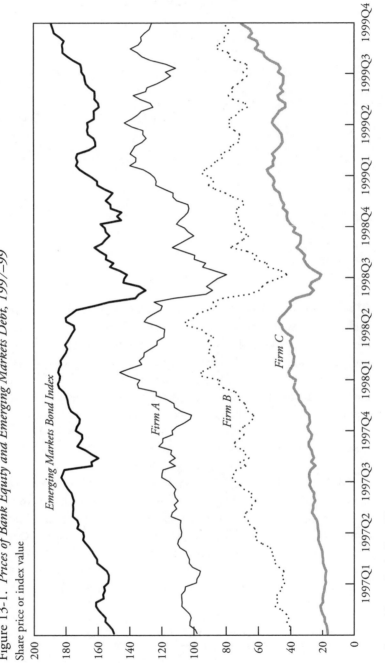

Source: Morgan Stanley Dean Witter.

Figure 13-2. *Quarterly Net Income for Selected Financial Firms, 1997–99*
Millions of dollars

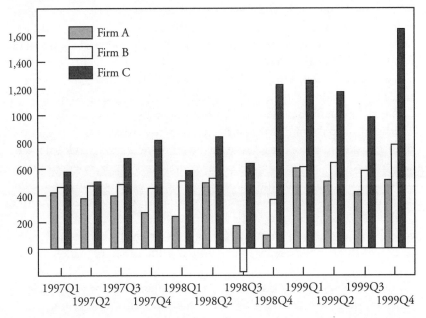

Source: Morgan Stanley Dean Witter.

quarterly net earnings for the firms with stock prices displayed in the figure 13-1, shows that a crisis can lead to severe stress even when an entity has sound economic fundamentals. Conservative market and credit risk management are necessary but not sufficient to deliver shareholder value and avoid crises over the long haul. Since markets can and will on occasion lose confidence in even a solvent firm, it is essential to maintain robust liquidity to allow time, as in this instance, for the quality of risk management and economic fundamentals to become evident to shareholders, analysts, and customers.

The central role of liquidity management has been brought home to securities firms by a series of incidents over the past dozen years. The liquidity of these firms had always been strong relative to that of most commercial banks because on average securities firm assets have a more ready market than bank assets. Nevertheless, in the equity crash of 1987, securities firms faced a large increase in immediate demand for cash to make margin and other payments. Short-term receivables from customers increased at the same time, but much of this cash was not due in for several days. Although securities firms succeeded in quickly securing sufficient funding in the market to cover the gap, they realized the need to strengthen their liquidity position to avoid being dependent on uncommitted bank lines in a future crisis. Their determination in this regard was reinforced by two further episodes involving liquidity stress: the collapse of the brokerage house of Drexel, Burnham, Lambert in 1990 and difficulties experienced by Salomon Brothers in the Treasury bond auction episode of 1991.

Assessment and management of exposure to a drying up of liquidity is clearly a principal strategic task for financial intermediaries and developing countries alike. This paper seeks to shed light on how modern global financial firms address these issues. The paper highlights the experience of nonbanks, which, like companies and governments in developing countries, cannot easily tap a central bank discount window for credit. The example of the 1987 equity market crisis illustrates that liquidity risk cannot be considered in isolation from market and credit risk. Therefore, the first section of this paper presents an overview of contemporary market, credit, and liquidity risk management with regard to financial firms. The second section of the paper considers the "macro" side of liquidity risk, with a focus on the global crises of 1997–98. This paper closes with some observations on the relative roles of financial intermediaries, asset management funds, and central banks in reducing the likelihood and scope of potential future systemic liquidity crises.

Key Principles of Financial Firm Risk Management

Risk management practices at financial institutions have changed dramatically over the past decade—driven by competition, a volatile global economy, and the availability of improved risk management tools. With the fall of regulatory barriers to competition in many countries, financial firms that were used to a relatively benign competitive environment faced intensified pressure to deliver shareholder value. Firms that fail to meet this challenge are apt to find themselves absorbed by more successful institutions as part of the wave of financial sector consolidation that is sweeping the globe. Delivering shareholder value requires achieving a high return on equity by making efficient use of capital. That, in turn, has fueled demand for securitizations and other innovative products to get less profitable risks off bank balance sheets and achieve better risk measurement and control as a means of optimizing capital held against retained risks.

Starting with the October 1987 equity market crash, global financial markets have experienced repeated episodes of high volatility. Dutch tulip-lovers would perhaps tell us that market volatility is hardly a new phenomenon. However, with the growth of capital markets relative to the size of the economy and the increased share of assets that are priced in transparent markets, market volatility has loomed larger on the radar screens of financial firm managers.[1] Likewise, as developing economies have gained greater access to global capital markets, volatility in these markets has become a greater concern for the governments and residents of such countries.

During the 1990s, in response to the heightened focus on the volatility of financial asset prices, financial intermediaries developed a wide range of new tools to address the problem of measuring market and credit risk in financial asset portfolios. These tools are grounded in portfolio theory as developed by William Sharpe, Harold Markowitz, and other financial economists. While this theory is not new, only in the past decade have firms overcome the practical challenges to estimating potential fluctuations in the value of a large and heterogeneous portfolio of financial assets and to using this information to make more effective risk management decisions.

The key elements of contemporary financial risk management practice can be usefully summarized as seven principles grouped into two categories: risk assessment and risk management. The discussion here focuses on the strategic, rather than technical, aspects of these principles. Some aspects of these principles are primarily relevant to major global banks and securities firms. However, other institutions—including smaller financial firms, asset management companies, nonfinancial firms, and governments—are increasingly finding it valuable to monitor and manage risk in a similar framework. The discussion below at times explicitly addresses how a principle may relate, or be developed to relate, to a management challenge facing an emerging market financial institution or government. Often, however, it is left to the reader to apply his or her own institutional and country expertise to develop relevant links and extensions.

---

1. This development should be seen as beneficial, since the volatility that has always been present in the economy and in real assets can now be better monitored and managed.

Risk Assessment Principle 1:
Know Your Current Economic Condition

Major financial institutions are finding it necessary to assess the estimated economic value of their assets and liabilities on a more frequent
basis. Financial statements produced quarterly or semi-annually according to existing accounting conventions are no longer, on their own, a
robust basis on which to manage a major financial institution in the
twenty-first century. Over time, accounting standards for financial assets
are moving toward broader and more timely recognition of fair market
value. It seems likely that in the not-too-distant future, most major
financial firms will operate on what would now be understood as a mark-
to-market basis. The unfolding of this trend will involve difficulties and
dislocations, but the result will be a more efficient, transparent, and
resilient financial system.

Mutual funds have for many years routinely made public on a daily
basis their mark-to-market value. Securities firms base internal financial
reporting and risk management, as well as external financial disclosure, on
mark-to-market valuations for the bulk of their portfolio. Banks and insurance companies have been slower to provide this level of transparency, in
part because it is more difficult to assess current market prices for substantial parts of their portfolios. Nevertheless, there is a clear trend at leading
commercial banks toward more frequent economic valuation of a steadily
expanding range of assets, if only for internal management purposes.
Although these valuations are necessarily approximate for parts of the portfolio for which market prices cannot be observed, it is often possible to
develop more accurate estimates of potential sales prices than traditional
accounting values.

The volatility of mark-to-market revenue or earnings provides substantial information about the risk exposure of a business unit. Tracking earnings volatility across business lines or products therefore can help a financial firm make better decisions regarding compensation, capital allocation,
and business development. In addition, the monitoring of this volatility by
firm management reinforces the incentive of mid-level managers to balance
risk relative to expected return in their business decisions. Finally, by mitigating the problem of asymmetric information between financial firm
insiders and outside creditors and investors, balance sheets and income
statements that are more soundly grounded in economic valuation can
help decrease a firm's borrowing costs and increase shareholder value.

Mark-to-market accounting is also valuable for financial regulators and the public at large. Regulators benefit from the strengthened incentives for effective risk management and efficient capital allocation. In addition, the enhanced transparency provided by economic valuation makes it more difficult for major losses to accumulate unacknowledged over time and facilitates timely regulatory intervention to force restructuring when necessary. Large systemic banking system failures have most often resulted not from sudden credit or market losses but from a long history of bad private or public sector lending decisions abetted by regulatory failure and inaccurate accounting. The history of national financial systems in developed and developing countries alike provides many instances in which such failures led to massive losses of shareholder and public funds and generated significant systemic risk.

Since financial firms in the world's more developed market economies are far from having universally implemented marking to market, one might argue that it is advisable for their counterparts in developing countries to wait before moving in this direction. On the other hand, traditional accounting balance sheets and income statements may be particularly misleading in the context of volatile developing economies.

Recommendation. Financial intermediaries in emerging markets should consider generating, initially on a quarterly or monthly basis, an approximate economic (or mark-to-market) balance sheet and income report as a risk management tool for the bank's senior executives.

Risk Assessment Principle 2: Measure Quantifiable Risks

If measures of mark-to-market valuation show where a financial firm currently is, measures of market, credit, and liquidity risk could be said to indicate its direction and how fast it is moving. Managing a firm knowing only its current condition is like driving a car guided only by the rear-view mirror. (Of course, even that is better than using only traditional accounting data, which amounts to a rear-view mirror that displays a distorted image with a time delay!)

MARKET RISK. Market risk can be defined as the risk that the future economic value of an asset (or liability) may differ from its current economic value. There is substantial consensus on the types of market risk metrics that are most valuable for financial firm managers. One useful measure, already mentioned above, is the volatility of revenue or net income. A second important measure is the sensitivity of portfolio value to movements in market prices or yields. Interest rate risk positions should be reported and tracked in "PV01" amounts, which represent the amount that the value of the position would gain or lose in the case of a single basis-point change in interest rates from current levels. By contrast, the notional value or market value of a set of assets does not generally provide a robust representation of market risk, especially for fixed income instruments. Risk position data should be reported appropriately aggregated, since it can be difficult for a manager to extract salient aspects of risk exposure from a sheet listing every position in a portfolio.

During the 1990s, many financial institutions developed value-at-risk (VAR) measures that estimate the maximum economic loss expected for a portfolio with a given probability over a given time horizon. Among the benefits of VAR are that it permits estimation of aggregate market risk exposure, incorporating a range of varied market risks; reflects risk reduction due to hedging and diversification; can cover a wide range of portfolio assets; yet is relatively easy to interpret. However, one must be careful to apply VAR models appropriately in light of the method's limitations. In particular, one must bear in mind that financial markets are always changing, so the past is not always a reliable guide to the future. It is also important to interpret the output of a VAR model with judgment and not treat the model as a "black box." The market risk measurement tools of stress testing and scenario analysis complement a VAR analysis. They can highlight market risk exposures, which may not show up in VAR, to potential extreme market shocks.

Initially, most financial firms applied VAR and stress testing only to their trading portfolios. In the United States, however, the Securities and Exchange Commission now requires that annual and quarterly public financial reports for most publicly traded companies include some form of market risk disclosure covering all financial assets, and VAR and stress testing are gradually being extended in this direction.

CREDIT RISK. Credit risk can be defined as uncertainty with regard to the future economic value of an asset arising from changing expectations about credit quality. While credit risk can be thought of as a component of market risk as defined above, in practice it is often managed somewhat separately from other aspects of market risk. In practice, it is difficult to measure pure credit risk in isolation from other influences on economic value, since available metrics, such as credit spreads, reflect considerations other than the obligor's credit quality. In particular, assetholders' expectations regarding liquidity, diversification, and correlations between credit events and other market events all influence economic value.

Measurement of credit exposure is a key building block in the measurement of credit risk. Exposure measures indicate the amount of credit that has been or could be extended to a borrower. Current credit exposure represents the amount of credit outstanding to the borrower at present. Potential future credit exposure is an estimate of the maximum amount of credit that is anticipated to be outstanding to a borrower at a specified future date with a given probability. Finally, current liquidation exposure represents the amount of credit exposure anticipated to arise if the borrower's position were liquidated. It may differ from current exposure because, for example, a timely sale of the collateral supporting a loan may require accepting a liquidation discount; if the collateral proceeds do not fully cover the credit extended, this discount increases the residual amount owed by the borrower.

Credit risk measures indicate the potential economic loss that could arise as a result of borrower default or changes in the likelihood of borrower default. Credit risk depends on expectations with regard to the magnitude of credit exposure in the event of default, probabilities of default, and recovery from a defaulting borrower.

A lender can quantify its credit exposure or credit risk at the level of one or more transactions with a single borrower. Credit risk can be measured, in addition, for all transactions with any chosen group of borrowers, including all borrowers together. (It is generally not useful to aggregate credit exposure across borrowers without factoring in borrower default probabilities and correlations, as is done in a credit risk calculation.)

A lender may take into account a range of legal considerations in calculating the magnitude of credit exposure and credit risk. The legal certainty associated with netting and collateral are particularly important. Netting agreements are legal contracts that in effect reduce a set of credit obligations between two firms down to a single net obligation. Gross credit exposures between firms, especially between major global wholesale financial companies, tend to be larger than net exposures. Without netting, a firm's credit exposure to a counterparty equals the sum of the gross exposures owed to the firm, ignoring the amounts the firm owes. But in the presence of a legally effective netting agreement, the exposure is only the (smaller) net amount owed to the firm. The legal efficacy of netting agreements between private parties depends on national and international legal and regulatory environments. It is relatively certain in some countries but uncertain in others. The taking of collateral is another important method of reducing credit exposure. As with netting, the legal certainty of the efficacy of collateral provisions varies depending on circumstances, and sophisticated credit risk management takes this variation into account.

Over the past decade public authorities in many jurisdictions have made progress on legal changes to enhance the certainty of netting agreements, but this issue still requires attention in some countries. More limited progress has been made in addressing legal concerns related to collateral, but the importance of this issue is now becoming better understood. Use of netting and collateral arrangements is already decreasing credit risk substantially for a number of international financial institutions. Additional improvements in national legal systems in some countries can further decrease credit risk and reinforce the resilience of the financial system. Finally, uncertainty and delay in determining the outcome of a bankruptcy proceeding can lead to costly dissipation of the assets of a financial institution and potential contagion that weakens other financial firms. To mitigate such problems, bankruptcy regimes in many countries need to be updated to ensure that bankruptcy proceedings, particularly with regard to financial institutions and transactions, are transparent, swift, and sure.[2]

The market turbulence of 1997–98 included defaults by developing country financial institutions and by Long Term Capital Management (LTCM). In many cases, creditors to these institutions experienced losses that resulted from the interaction of market and default risk operating through derivatives contracts. These events reminded lenders that having separate functions to assess market and credit risk may in some cases lead to insufficient attention being paid to the relationship between these risks. Major global financial firms have responded to this reminder by augmenting the market risk expertise of their credit departments, and in some cases by combining the two functions into a broader firm risk department.[3]

LIQUIDITY RISK. The extent to which a portfolio is liquid or illiquid can have a major impact on qualitative and quantitative measurement and management of both market and credit risk. Liquidity risk has in the past not been addressed, in the context of quantitative risk measurement, as extensively as pure price risk and credit risk. However, major financial firms

2. For a good survey of bankruptcy policy issues, see International Monetary Fund (1994).

3. For a valuable discussion of risk management issues related to the financial market events of 1997–98, see Counterparty Risk Management Policy Group (1999).

are now devoting substantial intellectual and financial resources to improved tracking and management of liquidity risk.

LIQUIDITY RISK INTERACTIONS. A particularly important challenge is to integrate liquidity considerations into calculations of market risk and potential credit exposure. Illiquidity can be factored into market risk VAR by estimating potential losses over a period sufficiently long to permit liquidation of an asset position without a large price impact. Thus the standard regulatory measure of market risk—3 times 99 percent per two-week VAR—implicitly provides capital to cover market risk over a position-unwind period much longer than the one-day horizon commonly used as a benchmark when VAR is used in applications other than capital adequacy calculations. A more differentiated approach now being implemented at a number of institutions assigns differing VAR time horizons, representing varied unwind periods, to asset classes depending on their liquidity. Finally, one can also capture liquidity in VAR by modeling the bid-offer spread by asset class as a function of position size. Similar approaches can be used to include liquidity effects in calculations of potential credit exposure. In addition, stress testing can be used to examine the potential impact of liquidity shocks that have never (or only rarely) been observed and that may therefore be difficult to integrate into a VAR framework. (Aspects of liquidity risk are explored in more detail below.)

FUNDING LIQUIDITY. One of the most important inputs to risk management for a financial firm is an assessment of the sources and uses of funding liquidity for a period of at least one year going forward.[4] A conservative analysis can be based on the assumption that in a crisis a firm would be unable to engage in any new unsecured borrowing, and that to avoid bankruptcy, cash outflows (for example, interest and principal payments) would be satisfied on contracted terms. "Cash capital usage" denotes the difference between the balance sheet value of a portfolio of assets and the maximum amount of cash that could be raised by selling the portfolio or using it as collateral for a secured loan. The amount of cash that can be raised will generally be less than accounting or current mark-to-market value, reflecting forced sale discounts and haircuts applied to

---

4. It is useful here to distinguish funding liquidity from asset liquidity. The latter corresponds to the discount to market value that must be accepted to turn an asset into cash. This is one element, but only one element, that must be taken into account in tracking funding liquidity, which refers to the ability to raise cash from any source to meet a contractual obligation as it comes due. Thus a committed unsecured line of credit contributes to funding liquidity even though for some purposes it would not be considered an asset.

assets used as collateral for a loan. Cash capital usage is normally compared with "cash capital availability," which consists of book equity, debt, and available contingent funding.[5]

With detailed information on the maturity structure of assets and liabilities and a set of assumptions about how the portfolio could be managed to economize on cash while satisfying all contractual obligations, a firm can develop an analysis of the balance of cash capital usage and availability over a crisis. Cash capital analyses are typically performed dynamically, aging the current portfolio over a one-year period. Cash capital usage and availability will typically decline, though not necessarily monotonically, over the period. Usage falls as assets are sold, while availability decreases as commercial paper and other short-term debt matures and is repaid.

BORROWERS' LIQUIDITY. Experience with LTCM has reinforced the understanding that a creditor should monitor the liquidity position of borrowers that are potentially exposed to liquidity problems. This involves assessing the borrower's liquidity management policies and its exposure to a firm-specific or market-wide liquidity shock. The weaker the policies and the greater the liquidity risk (relative to capital structure), the less current and potential credit exposure it is prudent to take with the borrower. Implementing such an analysis involves collecting information with respect to the borrower regarding maturity structure of borrowings (with a particular emphasis on maturities due within a year), exposure of the portfolio to liquidity shocks (for example, the size, and degree of hedging, of relatively illiquid positions such as real estate, loans, and certain securities), the magnitude of secured and unsecured loan commitments outstanding, and the net income risk facing the creditor (including market and credit risk).

Substantial insight into the liquidity risk exposures of major financial institutions can be gained from public documents and from discussions with the firm and with credit rating agencies. Analysis of liquidity positions for some borrowers, however, requires cooperation from the counterparty. This is particularly the case for certain leveraged investment vehicles, such as hedge funds, that are not regulated, are not rated by credit rating agencies, and may at times take on substantial market risk relative to capital. Since the events of the autumn of 1998, such funds are devoting more internal resources to assessing liquidity risk and are more forth-

---

5. As of the end of fiscal year 1999, for example, MSDW had available $17 billion in shareholders' equity, $28.6 billion in long maturity borrowings, $6 billion in committed secured lines of credit, and $6 billion in committed unsecured lines of credit.

coming in sharing this information with creditors. Moreover, most financial firms have reinforced their discipline with regard to granting lines for current and potential credit exposure when counterparty disclosure is less than ideal.

Recommendation. Developing country governments and financial firms should accord a higher priority to monitoring financial risk exposures. Financial firms should ensure that robust processes are in place for counterparty credit risk assessment and for review and approval of credit transactions. In addition, portfolio measures of market and credit risk should be developed (though these measures can reasonably be approximate at first, especially for smaller firms). For sovereign governments, risk assessment could involve estimation of the volatility of goods and services trade flows, capital flows, budget receipts and outlays, and GDP, among other economic variables. Both firms and governments should perform regular scenario analyses of how key economic and financial variables could move in a financial crisis—with particular attention paid to detailed tracking of available sources and uses of cash capital.

Risk Assessment Principle 3: Qualitatively Monitor Less-Quantifiable Risks

Operational risk can be taken to refer to potential losses that could result from the failure of a system or process. Business (or strategic) risk relates to the volatility of net income that is not allocated to market, credit, or operational risk. Often, important aspects of such risks cannot be captured adequately by simple quantitative measures. Although market and credit risk were the areas of risk management that saw the most rapid development during the 1990s, it is important to bear in mind that every financial firm has a large group of staff in accounting, operations, information technology, and related functions that contributes to the reduction of operational risk. Business risk is assessed firmwide as part of the overall financial planning and budgeting process, as well as on an ongoing basis by particular business units. As financial firms increasingly hedge and diversify market and credit risk, the relative risk management attention devoted to operational and business risk management will rise.

Recommendation. Financial firms in developing countries should implement a comprehensive, cross-divisional, senior-level review to identify and to develop recommendations for improving operational and business risk policies and processes.

Risk Management Principle 1: Hedge Risk

Table 13-1 shows the historical annual returns and standard deviation of returns for various systematic risk benchmarks. Shareholders of a financial firm can straightforwardly gain exposure to essentially all these varieties of market risk through mutual funds, and investors will generally prefer to take systematic market risk exposure through a fully transparent vehicle than by purchasing shares in a financial corporation. Financial firms do not deliver shareholder value by simply holding positions in liquid markets where the firm has no informational edge, but rather by cost-effectively providing financial services to clients and by leveraging the firm's expertise in financial transactions and markets. Therefore, optimal risk management should generally seek to transfer risk exposures to the market when possible and not excessively costly.

VAR, daily trading revenue volatility, and quarterly net income volatility figures published by leading global banks and securities firms tend to be moderate in size relative to equity capital. Taking account of diversification and hedging, most such firms appear to run significantly smaller systematic market risks relative to capital than does the average equity mutual fund.[6] Residual credit and liquidity-spread risks may also have systematic components. Increasingly, however, credit risk exposures in both trading and traditional banking portfolios are being sold or hedged through securitizations, asset swaps, credit derivatives, and related transactions. These trends toward improved market and credit risk management are farthest along at large global banks but are being rapidly taken up by smaller institutions.

Recommendation. Developing country banks and governments should strive to hedge large risk exposures where feasible and cost effective. Global investors can diversify away much of the risk from shocks unique to a particular developing country. Consequently, foreign investors can be expected to be willing to bear these shocks for compensation that is less than the value to undiversified domestic residents of avoiding these risks. Therefore, developing economies should seek to shift domestic economic and financial shocks to foreign assetholders. Among other avenues, this can be achieved

6. One example of the trend toward reduction of market risk through better hedging is that in many financial firms trading areas with credit-spread risks, such as corporate and mortgage desks, now hedge interest rate exposures with interest rate swaps rather than government bonds. Swaps cost more in interest paid, but were much more effective hedges during the market turmoil experienced in 1998, which involved a sharp widening of swap and credit-sensitive bond yields relative to the yields on government bonds.

by encouraging foreign direct investment, facilitating foreign ownership of domestic equities, and hedging major export and import price risks (such as oil price risk) using global commodity markets. Many countries have come to the view in recent years that foreign direct investment is particularly helpful in the financial sector. By diversifying local risk exposures through its parent, a foreign-owned local bank can economize on usage of risk capital, allowing it to provide services at lower cost while operating with enhanced safety and soundness. Finally, developing country governments, with the assistance of the international financial institutions, should review to what extent new risk-transfer mechanisms, such as securitization and derivative transactions, offer avenues for improved risk hedging.

Risk Management Principle 2: Diversify or Insure Unhedged Risk

Residual risk that remains after principal risks have been sold or hedged will consist of idiosyncratic risks that are not correlated with major systematic risks and systematic risks that are impossible or too expensive to sell or hedge. Financial economics suggests that bearing an idiosyncratic risk does not, in itself, yield a risk premium. Therefore, it is highly desirable to manage down an entity's aggregate exposure to such risk. Idiosyncratic risks that are not actively traded in financial markets (and that therefore cannot be hedged) can in many cases be effectively managed through diversification and insurance (which amounts to paying an insurance company to take the risk into its own diversified portfolio).

Recommendation. Companies and governments in developing countries should explore, with the assistance of international financial institutions, wider use of diversification, and, especially, insurance to protect against idiosyncratic risks (including certain weather, financial, and macroeconomic risks).

Risk Management Principle 3: Manage Capital Structure in Light of Risk

Risk exposures are a critical determinant of a financial firm's optimal capital structure. Most major financial firms seek to maintain a level of book equity that provides sufficient protection against default to achieve a targeted credit rating. Evaluating how much equity is sufficient takes into account estimates of potential losses from market risk and credit risk, extreme but possible future losses if operating revenues fall short of or

Table 13-1. *Estimated Annual Rates of Return for Various Asset Classes*
Nominal percentage returns (U.S. dollars unless otherwise noted)

Asset class	Post–World War II (varied dates)		Last twenty years (1979–98)	Last ten years (1989–98)	Last five years (1994–98)	1998 Total return
	Annualized return	Standard deviation	Annualized return	Annualized return	Annualized return	
Inflation	4.2	3.7	4.5	3.1	2.4	1.6
Equities						
Standard & Poor's 500 Index	13.2	16.6	17.8	19.2	24.1	28.6
Emerging growth	13.2	25.6	16.5	18.7	17.6	7.5
Small capitalization[a]	14.5	25.9	16.0	13.2	13.2	-7.3
Europe, Australia, and Far East[b]	11.5	25.8	13.2	5.5	9.2	20.0
European equities[c]	n.a.	n.a.	16.4	15.5	17.4	22.3
Japanese stocks[d]	14.3	34.1	9.4	-5.3	-3.7	5.1
Asian equities[b]	n.a.	n.a.	11.8	7.7	-5.2	-6.2
Emerging market equities	14.8	31.0	9.5	9.1	-10.1	-22.0
Venture capital	16.6	32.8	18.3	20.2	28.8	17.2

Fixed income						
Treasury bills	4.7	3.1	7.1	5.3	5.0	4.9
U.S. long Treasury bonds	5.7	10.3	11.1	11.7	9.5	13.1
Intermediate-term government bonds	5.9	6.4	9.9	8.7	6.2	10.2
Corporate bonds	5.9	9.9	10.9	10.9	8.7	10.8
High-yield bonds[e]	7.3	11.0	12.3	10.7	8.2	0.6
Foreign bonds[f]	n.a	n.a.	n.a.	8.8	8.3	5.8
Real estate						
Commercial real estate	8.2	5.7	9.0	5.4	10.8	16.1
Real estate investment trusts[g]	n.a.	n.a.	14.4	10.6	9.8	-17.5
Residential housing	7.0	4.0	5.1	3.9	3.9	5.2
Farmland	9.9	7.1	6.4	8.3	9.5	7.2
Real assets						
Collateralized commodities[h]	6.8	13.2	5.4	1.9	2.1	-20.2
Gold	n.a.	n.a.	1.2	-3.5	-5.9	0.6
Silver	4.6	53.3	-0.9	-1.7	-0.1	-15.1

Sources: Morgan Stanley Dean Witter Research, from sources noted.

n.a. Not available.

a. Dimensional Fund Advisors.

b. Morgan Stanley Capital International (MSCI).

c. MSCI—local currency.

d. Nikkei/MSCI.

e. First Boston.

f. Salomon Brothers.

g. National Association of Real Estate Investment Trusts.

h. Commodity Research Bureau (CRB) + Treasury bills.

operating costs exceed expectations, and potential extraordinary losses from unlikely but possible event risk. For assets that are not marked to market, equity also implicitly includes a buffer for the difference between economic and accounting value. For example, a slice of equity covers the difference between loan-loss reserves and the discounted present value of expected future credit losses. Equity capital is dynamically managed, through regular adjustments to issuance and to earnings retained versus earnings paid as dividends or share buybacks.

Once the level of equity is determined, issuance of long-term debt can be adjusted to maintain a robust supply of available cash or other liquid assets relative to the (evolving) demand of the firm for liquidity. As described earlier, liquidity is measured in terms of cash capital. For example, a shift of assets from liquid government bonds to illiquid loans would increase usage of cash capital. This would tend to spur a firm to issue long-term debt or equity in order to increase its supply of cash capital. Many major financial firms find it valuable to track the balance between sources and uses of liquidity on an ongoing basis. In addition, firms can perform regular stress test exercises to assess whether the available sources of funding would continue to be sufficient to support the portfolio of assets in the event of a hypothetical crisis that prevents the firm from issuing new short- or long-term debt over a specified period.

Recommendation. Developing country governments and financial institutions should establish liquidity management policies that take into account the market, credit, and liquidity risk assessments discussed in Risk Assessment Principle 2. On the basis of these analyses, sources of liquidity (such as foreign exchange reserves, lines of credit, and contingency funding arrangements) should ideally be managed on an ongoing basis to provide sufficient cash capital to permit a firm or country to meet obligations coming due over the next year.

Risk Management Principle 4: Communicate Information on Financial Condition and Risk

Poor communication of information generates unnecessary uncertainty. Therefore, global financial firms engage in regular communication with creditors, rating agencies, equity analysts, investors, journalists, and public officials about the firm's strategic orientation, financial condition, and risk exposures. Major financial firms provide a regular flow of information to external parties through annual and quarterly reports, intraquarter updates on material developments, and small and large group meetings. In these communications, firms disclose qualitative information about major strategies and business developments and provide data on current financial condition, mark-to-market trading revenue volatility, VAR, credit risk exposures, and liquidity risk management. A strong role for external audit in verifying data quality significantly enhances the credibility of information provided.

Recommendation. Developing country governments and firms should continue to improve the quantity and quality of information on economic condition, financial condition, and risk exposures made available to creditors, investors, and other interested parties. The International Monetary Fund and the International Bank for Reconstruction and Development should continue to facilitate better and more comparable disclosure of such data. Likewise, emerging markets companies should seek to conform their financial statements to global norms.

Having identified key principles of risk management, let us now analyze in more detail a particular aspect of risk that has been a focus of risk management attention in the wake of the market crises of 1997–98.

Liquidity Risk

Douglas Diamond and Raghuram Rajan, leading theorists in the field of liquidity and banking, define asset illiquidity as an inability to realize the full value of an asset through a sale or collateralized loan.[7] In this framework, full value for a purely liquid asset can be realized immediately, while full value for a purely illiquid asset can be realized only by collecting the cash flows that accrue over the life of the asset.

The Nature of Liquidity and Liquidity Risk

There are several reasons why the liquidation value of a portfolio could be less than the expected present value of its cash flows (discounted using an appropriate risk premium). One issue is the classic "lemons" problem that arises because a seller will tend to know more about the true value of the

7. Diamond and Rajan (1999).

portfolio than do potential buyers. A second factor is that when a sale is small relative to the market,[8] it is easy to find many competing buyers; if the sale is large, however, buyers may have relatively more power. Both of these problems are exacerbated if a sale must be conducted quickly, since this reduces the time that existing potential buyers have to become better informed about the portfolio and the time the seller has to find and educate new potential purchasers.

The actual discount to the present value of cash flows that will be realized should a portfolio be liquidated or used as collateral for a loan generally cannot be observed. At best, a distribution can be estimated for the discount. This distribution has an expected value and a residual variance. We can term the expected value the "liquidity valuation adjustment." This amount is a component of the current market value of a traded financial instrument. For example, it is a major determinant of the higher yields of off-the-run relative to more liquid on-the-run U.S. Treasury securities. The residual variance, which we can call "liquidity risk," reflects the potential difference between the discount that would actually be realized and the current liquidity valuation adjustment. In practice, concentrations of such risk are assessed by financial institutions today primarily through judgment and stress testing. Formal statistical modeling of this risk remains in its infancy, but over time it is likely to become better integrated as a risk factor in market and credit VAR calculations.

For trading portfolios, the liquidity valuation adjustment tends to be constant for asset position sizes up to a certain proportion of daily or weekly trading flows. For large positions, however, the liquidation discount tends to rise non-linearly with position size. Therefore, a financial firm should monitor the potential magnitude of such costs, and when they are material apply a liquidity valuation adjustment to mid-market value that is greater than half the bid-asked spread. It is common practice for financial firms to apply such adjustments to concentrated positions. Similarly, an equity trading business may employ a statistical liquidity model to estimate the discount that will arise in executing a large block trade for a client. In the context of a firmwide VAR calculation, the extra liquidity valuation adjustment associated with positions that cannot easily be liquidated or hedged in a day can be modeled by calibrating the simulation period applied to a position or set of positions to the length of time needed to eliminate the market risk associated with the position(s).

---

8. Here turnover is often more critical than amounts outstanding.

Trading Strategies and Liquidity Crises

In a market liquidity crisis, the risk premiums paid for holding less-readily traded assets increase sharply. Desired portfolio reallocations become much more correlated across investors than in normal markets. Investors become less certain about what market prices should be, especially for less liquid assets. Finally, trading is perceived to be costly given increased information asymmetries and bid-offer spreads. All these factors contribute to a sharp reduction in trading volumes. Low trading volume, in turn, has a feedback effect that magnifies market volatility by increasing the price impact of trades.

The role played by LTCM in the market turbulence of 1998 presents an interesting case study in liquidity trading and liquidity crisis. LTCM employed a variety of trading strategies in a range of markets and securities. However, most of these strategies shared a common characteristic: they offered very good risk-adjusted returns under normal market conditions in exchange for poor performance (potentially large negative returns and high volatility) in a market liquidity crisis. From a risk management perspective, LTCM's portfolio had a risk-return profile like that of selling a portfolio of out-of-the-money options. Shorting options generates immediate income in the form of the premium paid to the option writer in return for taking on risk of potential loss. If the options sold are well out of the money, losses by the option writer net of the option premium will tend to be infrequent but potentially large. Under normal market conditions, such positions may seem to have relatively modest risk using traditional risk metrics, such as the volatility of daily profit-and-loss or risk sensitivity exposure measures. But in an episode of extreme volatility that brings market prices or yields toward or past the option strike prices, such positions can rapidly generate significant losses.

Traders have long been acutely aware of the difficulty of managing short option positions. To avoid unpleasant surprises, good traders have learned to think through carefully the exposure of a portfolio under conditions of stressed and illiquid markets. In addition, stress testing—in which the portfolio is revalued assuming hypothetical large changes in market prices and yields—can shed light on the magnitude of potential losses in extreme market moves.

It is quite possible that if implemented in the context of a robust risk management and capital framework LTCM's strategies could have offered (and could still offer) investors superior risk-adjusted returns on average over time, even including the rare periods of market instability. However, such strategies would have the greatest economic value if executed by relatively liquid investment funds, in which case there would be a higher degree of confidence that neither market reversals nor investor need for cash would force illiquid assets to be sold quickly.

LTCM, by contrast, had relatively limited access to liquid resources. It was therefore not well positioned to withstand initial trading losses that eroded its equity base, brought about by margin calls, and increased absolute levels of portfolio risk as markets became more volatile. LTCM was forced to sell illiquid assets to raise cash for margin calls and to maintain a desired ratio of risk to capital. At that point a downward spiral set in. Selling in size led to liquidity-related losses and further moved market prices against the fund. In addition, as problems grew, creditors restricted credit availability, which made further sales necessary. (There was, however, one somewhat positive aspect to the fund's liquidity management policy: investors were not allowed to withdraw their capital on short notice, so the fund was able to avoid the symptoms of a classic bank run.) Had the managers of LTCM better assessed the risk they faced of entering a self-reinforcing spiral involving forced liquidation of positions, they might have maintained a more robust funding liquidity position. That is, of course, a statement more easily made after the fact than before, but it is more than 20/20 hindsight; after all, the managers of other funds and financial firms that made trades similar to LTCM's did a much better job of controlling their risk relative to their capital, precisely because they were aware of the risk of asset illiquidity turning into a funding crisis.

The failure of LTCM brought about a shift down in the aggregate demand curve for illiquidity. At first to raise cash, and then to close out the fund, LTCM had to sell relatively illiquid assets, such as certain mortgages, and purchase liquid assets that it had sold short as a hedge, such as government bonds. These actions led to higher risk premiums on assets perceived to have exposure to a liquidity crisis.

Figure 13-3, for example, shows yield spreads relative to Treasuries for AAA, AA, A, and BBB bank debt for 1997–99. Yield spreads trended up gradually during 1997 and the first half of 1998 and took off in the latter part of 1998 when Russia defaulted on its debt obligations and LTCM experienced financial difficulty. Yields spreads fell back as the crisis subsided in the winter and early spring of 1999. However, spreads then rose again and in the autumn of 1999 reached or surpassed their autumn 1998 peaks. Finally, in the winter of 1999, bank yield spreads fell back a good bit of the way toward pre-1998 levels. Yield spreads were particularly high at the peak of the crisis for BBB banks most exposed to asset and funding liquidity risk.[9]

With the LTCM failure having eliminated a large source of demand for certain illiquid assets, with banks and securities houses becoming more rigorous in pricing liquidity and credit risk, and with Treasuries becoming more valuable as their supply declines, it is not surprising that yield spreads on less liquid assets and for less creditworthy borrowers have remained higher than in the pre-crisis period. It is not evident, however, whether spreads are likely to remain in the range of current levels. One might see the LTCM period as the aberration and believe that the market is now more correctly pricing liquidity and credit risk. In that case, one would expect current spreads to persist. Alternatively, one might suspect that as memories of 1997–98 fade, the high premiums for holding less liquid and lower credit-quality assets will lead to increased demand for such assets, bringing about a decline over time in these spreads.

Mitigating and Managing Future Liquidity Crises

The mechanisms of liquidity crises are well understood with respect to financial firms and sovereign countries. In particular, it is now generally agreed that it is dangerous for a financial institution or a country to have a weak liquidity position, defined as having actual or potential short-term cash (or hard currency) liabilities exceeding cash (or hard currency) assets available in the short term. Academics and practitioners have stressed that with weak liquidity and no lender of last resort, a "bank run"-type crisis can readily occur.[10] On the other hand, with an active lender of last resort

9. Note that yield spreads would have declined to a greater extent post-crisis had Treasuries not benefited from increased scarcity value as the U.S. fiscal deficit declined faster than anticipated.

10. Nonbank financial firms typically maintain much stronger liquidity positions than do institutions subject to a bank safety net. This suggests that universal bank-style financial systems, which bring under the bank safety net many financial assets and activities that do not require safety net protection, tend to exacerbate private sector illiquidity. By contrast, a system based on securitization of financial assets and strong nonbank financial institutions can reinforce market discipline with regard to liquidity.

On balance, this latter approach may well lead to more sound and liquid national and global financial systems. Concerns about the safety of customer funds under such a system can be addressed by requiring nonbank financial firms to maintain private insurance for customer accounts and to maintain strict segregation of customer assets. For example, securities firms in the United States provide insurance, purchased from third parties, for funds in customer accounts and maintain a strong liquidity position. It is ironic that by encouraging many commercial banking institutions to maintain relatively illiquid funding policies, which are no longer necessary for banks to serve as effective financial intermediaries, the bank safety net is in some respects increasing the fragility of the global financial system.

Figure 13-3. *Yield Spreads: Ten-Year U.S. Dollar Bank Debt Indexes, 1997–99*

Basis points

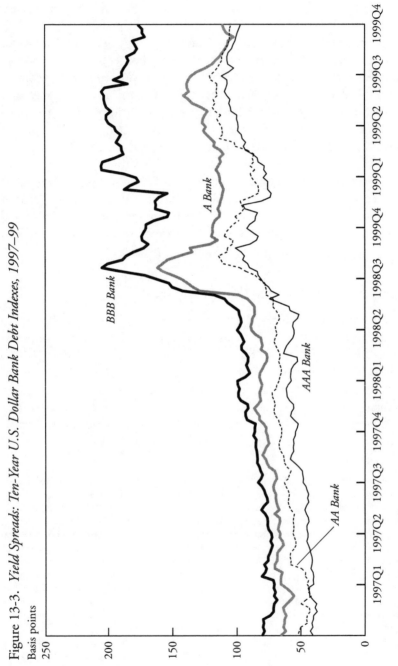

Source: Morgan Stanley Dean Witter.

generally comes moral hazard. Moral hazard can lead to inefficient and excessive risk-taking. It can also, experience with banking system failures indicates, lead to accumulating problems being swept under the rug, so that crises decrease in frequency but increase in severity. It therefore is unfortunately neither feasible nor desirable to eliminate the possibility of financial crisis, which makes it critical that the financial system be resilient in the face of episodes of market instability. Let us now review how some economic agents with various structural positions in the financial system can contribute to this goal.

ROLE OF FINANCIAL INTERMEDIARIES. A principal function of financial intermediaries is to provide liquidity risk management services to clients. These services encompass liquidity risk intermediation, hedging, and diversification, all of which on balance help make the financial system more robust in the face of liquidity risk. Liquidity risk is most dangerous when allowed to grow too large relative to available sources of liquidity. Modern financial firms help address this problem in three ways. First, they intermediate the transformation of illiquid assets into liquid assets. For example, credit card securitizations permit fund managers to purchase assets that otherwise would probably remain in relatively illiquid form on financial institutions' balance sheets.

Second, trading in financial assets permits a smooth and efficient reallocation of assets and liquidity risk in response to external shocks. In addition to trading various cash products, which has the effect of transferring liquidity within the financial system, financial intermediaries have increasingly developed their over-the-counter derivatives businesses as hedged portfolios whereby options sold to some clients are hedged with options purchased from others. Banks and securities houses actively seek out clients who are well positioned to write options—for example, equity pension funds that write covered calls. Since option writers as a group in effect provide liquidity in a market sell-off, trading options represent liquidity intermediation that can serve to better allocate liquidity risk in accordance with the ability of agents to bear this risk.

Third, under stressed market conditions a financial firm sells to customers liquidity from its own balance sheet. This liquidity is provided though traditional banking products such as contingent lines of credit and, increasingly, by dealers making markets in derivatives and cash inventory (where the dealer may accumulate less-liquid inventory as a result of customer sales during a crisis). A well-managed financial firm is likely to strive to secure available contingent liquidity during a crisis and, in normal markets, to hold a level of exposure to liquidity risk that is below its "carrying capacity." With these liquidity reserves, during a crisis the firm can provide the service of taking on liquidity exposure from customers. Concretely this would mean that the financial firm continues to make loans or to make markets in securities (or both), even if the net impact is an outflow of liquidity from the financial firm during the crisis. The net outflow of liquidity from the financial firm would be less than the gross flow to the extent that the firm is able to draw upon available supplies of contingent liquidity.

Role of Asset Managers

Asset managers tend to be a natural supplier of liquidity. Pension funds, for example, commonly hold a large part of their portfolio in less-liquid bonds. Since pension funds are unlikely to need to sell their portfolios rapidly, they tend to prefer to sacrifice some liquidity in return for the higher yields offered by less-liquid securities. Among asset managers, hedge funds have in the past been the most aggressive in opportunistically selling illiquidity when it is perceived to be expensive. However, it is quite possible that going forward unleveraged funds will increasingly invest in this type of trade. Having a wider group of investors actively seeking to purchase illiquidity when it is cheap and sell when it is dear can be expected to make the pricing of less-liquid assets more efficient. It should also promote more intermediation of liquidity—thereby helping to mitigate the chances and severity of liquidity crises.

Role of Central Banks

Central banks today have little comparative advantage in supplying liquidity in a typical firm-specific crisis. Financial markets are generally capable of reallocating liquidity reasonably quickly and efficiently in response to shocks to supply and demand for liquidity at the microeconomic level of a particular financial institution. They can handle a liquidity crisis at a medium-size bank without much difficulty—by, as the case may be, providing appropriate lending to a solvent but illiquid institution, finding a buyer for an institution as a whole, or facilitating the disposition of an institution's assets.

Modern financial markets are efficient enough that the costs of moral hazard probably outweigh efficiency gains that might arise from central bank liquidity lending to individual financial firms based on information that may be available to a supervisor but not to the market as a whole. Most major global central banks recognize these facts and therefore have in recent years kept a much tighter rein on credit to individual institutions facing liquidity problems. A stronger case can be made, however, for active central bank liquidity intervention, including discount window lending, in the context of a liquidity problem at a major global bank.

In contrast with the resolution of narrow "micro" crises, where a limited role for central banks is best, central banks' responsibility with respect to a broad "macro" liquidity crisis may be increasing as the scope of financial markets grows. In such a crisis, investors flee from illiquid instruments of many or all types, driving up the risk premiums for such assets. Central banks may have a comparative advantage relative to the private sector in bearing illiquidity and providing liquidity under such circumstances.

Central banks have traditionally provided liquidity in crises by increasing the money supply and discount window lending. Less obviously, liquidity also flows to banks that are under severe stress through the changing value of the put option that the central bank has written to the banking system. During a crisis, this formerly deep out-of-the-money and almost zero-value option moves closer to in-the-money and may become a much more valuable intangible bank asset, mitigating the tendency for deposits to flee in a bank run. In a major crisis, the change in the value of this put option may be a more important source of additional banking liquidity than either changes in money or discount window borrowing.

Today central banks have available new and potentially more efficient mechanisms for providing liquidity in a macro crisis. One of the most promising novel mechanisms is the explicit writing of options. As mentioned above, central banks have long been in the business of writing options on the value of individual banks and the banking system as a whole. Rarely has the option premium charged for this service represented a market price. As a result, banks have not held an optimal amount of liquidity on their own books and have underpriced liquidity services such as contingent guarantees.

It should generally be economically more efficient, and cheaper for the taxpayer, for a central bank to explicitly write options and collect option premiums, rather than implicitly and without adequate compensation, agreeing to provide liquidity in a crisis. This appears to have been, at least in part, the reasoning behind the path-breaking decision by the U.S. Federal Reserve System to sell liquidity options over the Year 2000 period.

Separate from this role as a mechanism for correctly pricing central bank liquidity services, the writing of options could also be an effective policy tool for dampening market volatility in cases where that is a central bank goal.

A risk management perspective on liquidity strongly suggests that central banks should assess the experience of the Federal Reserve with respect to Year 2000 liquidity options and consider whether explicit option writing by the official sector has a role to play in stabilizing financial institutions and financial markets.

References

Counterparty Risk Management Policy Group. 1999. *Improving Counterparty Risk Management Practices* (June). (www.jpmorgan.com/CorpInfo/Perspectives/linked_files/CRMPG.pdf [July 2000]).

Diamond, Douglas W., and Raghuram G. Rajan. 1999. "Liquidity Risk, Liquidity Creation and Financial Fragility: A Theory of Banking," Working Paper 7430. Cambridge, Mass.: National Bureau of Economic Research (December).

International Monetary Fund. 1994. *Orderly and Effective Insolvency Procedures: Key Issues.* Washington.

KENNETH M. KLETZER
ASHOKA MODY

14

Will Self-Protection Policies Safeguard Emerging Markets from Crises?

ALTERNATIVE MECHANISMS TO contain financial crises include international rescue packages, the "bail-in" of private creditors, and domestic safeguards. International rescue packages create moral hazard, and efforts to bail in private lenders have so far proved unsuccessful. To complement these international measures—and, perhaps, render them more effective—enhanced self-protection by governments against readily reversible capital flows has been proposed. Unlike international rescue packages and bail-in initiatives, which come into play mainly after a crisis is imminent, domestic safeguards are directed primarily toward crisis prevention.

The domestic proposals that we examine in this paper arise from three premises. First, financial crises are not always the consequence of fundamental inconsistencies in macroeconomic management and may be the by-product of ongoing, but incomplete, domestic financial reform and integration with international capital markets. Although liberalization is expected in the long run to foster the efficient working of financial markets, the short-run effect has often been a greater susceptibility to crises for

Parts of this paper were prepared as background for chapter 5 of the World Bank's *Global Development Finance 2000*. In turn, the paper draws on the findings of that report. For his valuable inputs, the authors are grateful to Robert Keyfitz. The authors are also grateful to Jonathan Eaton and Vincent Reinhart for their comments.

developing country financial sectors. Deregulation of the domestic financial sector is sometimes accompanied by imprudent lending practices, creating booms and busts, which may be amplified by highly responsive short-term international capital flows: international and domestic factors in combination create a "combustible mix," as noted by Barry Eichengreen.[1] Second, freely floating exchange rates—and the consequent insulation of domestic policy actions—are difficult to achieve in practice. Finally, although long-term fiscal prudence, sustainable public debt management, and a sound banking system are the most effective safeguards against crises, near-term measures are required to augment the capacity of governments to deal with capital flow volatility and thus reduce a country's exposure to crises.

As such, these new proposals go beyond traditional macroeconomic policies and include raising foreign currency reserves, establishing contingent lines of international credit, taxing short-term foreign capital flows, and instituting prudential capital controls. Martin Feldstein proposed the general concept of self-protection.[2] Pablo Guidotti and Alan Greenspan have suggested that it may be prudent for countries to hold foreign currency reserves in the amount of total external debt maturing within one year.[3] This proposal revises the traditional rule of thumb that foreign reserves should cover three to four months of imports to a rule based on short-term debt amortization. An alternative to holding reserves is for countries to arrange contingent lines of credit, effectively purchasing an option to borrow reserves if and when needed to avoid illiquidity during a crisis. These lines of credit could be arranged with private creditors or provided by the international financial institutions. Others have suggested restricting short-term capital inflows, drawing on the apparent success of Chilean controls in changing the composition of inflows toward those with longer maturities.[4] Prudential capital controls have been advocated by, among others, the World Bank and the International Monetary Fund.[5]

We deal in this paper principally with liquidity-enhancing measures, followed by a brief discussion of capital controls, and reach three main conclusions:

1. Eichengreen (1999).
2. Feldstein (1999).
3. Guidotti (1999); Greenspan (1999).
4. See Eichengreen (1999) for a review and an endorsement.
5. World Bank (1998); Ariyoshi and others (2000).

—Safeguards impose costs on the domestic economy either by raising the cost of capital or by reducing the flow of international capital and hence limiting the potential benefits from international integration. However, the rising frequency of crises—and the new coincidence of currency collapse and domestic financial distress—has been associated with high social costs: severe output losses in which the poor have borne a disproportionate burden. Safeguards are, therefore, appropriate. The adoption of policy safeguards is desirable particularly if they complement the transition from closed or repressed financial systems to efficiently functioning financial markets.

—A higher level of liquidity is most appropriate when a crisis is one possibility among "multiple equilibria," that is, when unfavorable outcomes are not a necessary consequence of government policies and actions. Access to liquidity can prevent an unwarranted crisis or contain the amplification of one where weak "fundamentals" create vulnerability. Contingent credit lines are superior to the holding of international reserves, since reserves create higher fiscal costs, which, in turn, can further weaken fundamentals and contribute to crises rather than alleviating them. Governments can, however, lower their costs of reserves by requiring banks to hold high-quality foreign assets. In contrast to higher liquidity, capital controls more directly address concerns arising from weak banking or corporate governance systems.

—The design of the safeguards is likely to be highly country-specific, taking into account both cyclical and structural country characteristics.

In the next section we discuss the motivation for the proposals considered. We note the growing importance of "twin" currency and banking crises, which typically reflect fundamental weaknesses in the domestic financial sector but which may be amplified by short-term capital flows. Following a discussion of the role of reserves both in the context of weak fundamentals and liquidity crises, we review the uses and limits of contingent credit lines and the recent experience with such facilities. Capital controls are briefly considered in the next section, followed by some concluding remarks.

Sources of Crises

The frequency of emerging market crises has risen progressively over the last 120 years. During the Bretton Woods era, crises resulted mainly from

speculative attacks on exchange rates that had become increasingly inconsistent with macroeconomic policies. The frequency of pure currency crises
has declined as countries have chosen more flexible exchange rate regimes.
However, banking crises, which were relatively rare between 1945 and 1971
because of capital controls and tight banking regulations, have reemerged as
companions to currency crises in the large majority of cases since 1973.[6]
Problems in the domestic financial sector appear to be largely responsible for
the sudden capital flow reversals that precipitated the Asian financial crisis.

Any argument for safeguards should be based on the substantive social
costs of crises. Though the share of annual foreign capital inflows to gross
domestic product (GDP) in emerging market economies falls in the range
of 3 to 5 percent of GDP, the turnaround in flows following a crisis is
much larger. Moreover, since this capital is leveraged by the domestic system, the withdrawal of funds contributes to systemic disruption, with large
and persistent impact on the crisis economies. World Bank estimates place
the average cost of an emerging market currency crisis at 8 percent of GDP,
rising to 18 percent when a banking crisis occurs simultaneously.[7] For the
five crisis countries of East Asia—Indonesia, Malaysia, the Philippines,
South Korea, and Thailand—the costs of crises range from 7.8 percent of
pre-crisis-year GDP for the Philippines to 30.2 percent for Indonesia.
These costs are comparable to the benefits of capital account openness estimated by Maurice Obstfeld.[8] The costs of crises may be even worse when
their impact on the poor is recognized.[9]

The analysis of policy safeguards depends on the causes of financial
crises. If a mismatch of macroeconomic policies with an exchange rate peg
is the proximate cause of a crisis, then a reasonable approach might be to
reform fiscal or monetary management or allow greater exchange rate flexibility. However, if crises are endemic to the process of financial liberalization and development, then safeguards may play a critical role. Two competing views of how domestic financial markets and foreign capital inflows
interact to create currency and financial crises have emerged in the theoretical literature in recent years.[10] One view is based on the conventional

---

6. Kaminsky and Reinhart (1999).
7. World Bank (1998, box 3-1, p. 127).
8. Obstfeld (1986).
9. Lustig (1999).
10. See, for example, Calvo (1998a, 1998b); Caballero and Krishnamurthy (1998); Chang and
Velasco (1999); Corsetti, Pesenti, and Roubini (1998a, 1998b, 1998c); Furman and Stiglitz (1998);
Mishkin (1996); among many others.

speculative-attack currency crisis model of Paul Krugman.[11] In this view, economic fundamentals are the source of a currency crisis and its consequent financial crisis, but the inconsistency between fiscal policies and a pegged exchange rate regime arise endogenously with external capital inflows to the domestic financial sector. Capital account and financial liberalization without adequate domestic prudential regulation can lead to a banking crisis as intermediaries take on excessive levels of debt and risk in the presence of moral hazard. The government accumulates implicit liabilities that must be financed through domestic credit expansion after a crisis. An ultimate government bailout is expected and, along with a surge in capital inflows, creates the environment that makes the country vulnerable to a financial crisis.

The second view regards recent financial and currency crises as financial panics that result from the simultaneous actions of creditors and need not have occurred. The lack of liquid resources available to the government to meet the sudden reversal of international credit has highlighted the role played by short-term capital flows in the Mexican crisis of 1994 and the Asian crises of 1997–98. These experiences have also stimulated theoretical work on explanations of currency and financial crises that do not rely on a mismatch of an exchange rate peg and other macroeconomic policies. The extension of currency crisis models by Obstfeld demonstrates the possibility of multiple equilibria so that a crisis may occur but is not inevitable.[12] A financial crisis is one possible outcome in an international economy with multiple equilibria. Illiquidity of the financial sector, rather than policy unsustainability, plays the central role in recent theoretical models that take this perspective. In these models there is a maturity mismatch between the foreign liabilities and domestic assets of the private or public sector. In the pure liquidity view, short-term borrowing to finance long-term investments is the system's Achilles heel, exposing nations to potential financial panics.

The diversity of macroeconomic conditions preceding currency crises suggests that both views, separately or in combination, deserve attention in policy analysis. It is also evident that the impact of policy prescriptions may be quite different, depending on the source of financial crises. Both approaches can be used to analyze the vulnerability of national economies to rapid financial capital inflows and outflows. The traditional model (also

11. Krugman (1979).
12. Obstfeld (1986).

known as the first-generation model) can yield either an inevitable, fundamentals-driven crisis or a crisis that occurs as one possible but not inevitable equilibrium. The role of short-term lending for generating a liquidity crisis is discussed second.

Financial Liberalization: Long-Term Benefits and Short-Term Costs

Financial sector liberalization has proceeded in parallel with capital account liberalization. Though such liberalization is necessary—and inevitable—in the long run, recent events in Mexico, the East Asian countries, and Russia show that in the early stages of liberalization banking systems remain fragile, and such fragility can be powerfully amplified by volatile international capital flows. In each of these countries, but especially in East Asia, the depth of the crisis reflected the withdrawal of foreign funds from the distressed domestic banking system. Implicit government guarantees of the liabilities of the banking system can generate "twin" currency and banking crises.

The deregulation of domestic financial sectors is an important and key element for achieving long-term economic growth. However, liberalization of domestic financial systems in emerging markets has been accompanied by an increased incidence of financial crises. A substantial number of countries deregulated their interest rates from 1985 to 1995. This coincided with an impressive expansion in bank lending to the private sector (as a share of GDP). However, Asli Demirgüç-Kunt and Enrica Detragiache show that the probability of a banking crisis increases and remains high for three or four years following interest rate deregulation.[13]

Regulatory failure enables banks to invest in excessively risky projects, knowing that if they fail the public will absorb the cost. Ronald McKinnon and Huw Pill, Paul Krugman, and others argue that elements of moral hazard and weak supervision combine to produce speculative asset price bubbles and crashes.[14] Demirgüç-Kunt and Detragiache find that when the domestic institutional environment is weak, financial liberalization is especially prone to banking crises.

The potential benefits of capital account openness are also well known. These include the efficient allocation of world savings to the most produc-

---

13. Demirgüç-Kunt and Detragiache (1998).
14. McKinnon and Pill (1997); Krugman (1999).

tive investment opportunities (often in capital-poor regions), the ability to smooth consumption against fluctuations of national income, and the diversification of risk for savers.[15] Among the many benefits that international investors acting in their self-interest bring to recipient countries is a market-imposed discipline on governments and domestic businesses. Ultimately, Michael Klein and Giovanni Olivei argue, one of the main benefits of capital account openness is the development of the financial sector itself, as international capital brings skills and discipline that help long-term financial sector discipline.[16]

However, foreign capital can amplify the weaknesses of an unsophisticated or inadequately regulated financial sector. Private capital inflows are subject to surges and sudden reversals, both of which cause severe stress. During periods of inflows, weak domestic regulatory frameworks and distorted incentives allow lenders to build up poor-quality loan portfolios and channel investment to low-yielding, speculative projects. When inflows are reversed, the resulting credit contraction causes widespread defaults in the banking, corporate, and real estate sectors. Both Klein and Olivei and Dani Rodrik find that contrary to theoretical analysis, capital account openness has not been beneficial for developing countries.[17] One problem with both the Klein and Olivei and the Rodrik studies is that they measure capital account openness as a binary variable (open or not) when, in practice, the measure is much more nuanced. As a result of the measurement error, the estimated benefit from openness is biased downward. Nonetheless, these results suggest that developing countries are unable to fully exploit the benefits of financial openness available to the rest of the world.

Government Contingent Liabilities and Crises

The most recent version of the fundamentals view emphasizes government subsidization of private sector foreign borrowing. The importance of implicit or explicit public sector guarantees of foreign debt repayment for developing country financial crises was raised by Carlos Diaz-Alejandro.[18] His observations and arguments form the basis for recent models that emphasize the role of governments as underwriters of foreign

---

15. See Obstfeld (1998) for a summary.
16. Klein and Olivei (1999).
17. Klein and Olivei (1999); Rodrik (1995).
18. Diaz-Alejandro (1985).

debts accumulated by private banks and firms.[19] In particular, Diaz-Alejandro argues that it is at best difficult for a debtor-country government to refuse to assume private foreign debt in the event of a financial crisis. Ex post debt guarantees may be implicit even if explicitly denied ex ante.

While the subsidization of foreign borrowing may be subject to cronyism or other forms of corruption, distortions in the flow of capital to developing countries due to sovereign risk can also provide a rationale for public sector intervention. The value of loans made to domestic intermediaries is sensitive to domestic monetary, fiscal, and regulatory policies that are chosen by the government to advance domestic interests. When sovereign immunity is a binding constraint on financial integration, we should expect the domestic rate of return to capital to exceed the foreign opportunity cost of financial capital. Foreign creditors are naturally reluctant to lend in domestic currency because the sovereign determines its own monetary policy. Even if all loans are denominated in foreign currency, the ability of domestic intermediaries or firms to service foreign debts is impaired by sudden devaluations or depreciations of the domestic currency. Exchange rate pegs are often adopted as part of a policy package to provide a stable monetary environment for foreign creditors. Experience has shown that when an exchange peg is abandoned, governments guarantee foreign currency liabilities in part or whole. A government may seek to promote efficiency-enhancing capital inflows by insuring foreign creditors against losses caused by its own policy changes but not against individual project risk or bank failure.

A government debt guarantee must be calculated into the public sector budget as a contingent increase in public debt. When a government guarantee is invoked, there is an increase in outstanding public debt and subsequent interest obligations. In the event that the guarantee is invoked and the subsequent increase in the public sector budget deficit is monetized, a conventional speculative attack on a pegged exchange rate can occur. The details of how the government accumulates contingent liabilities determine whether such guarantees might actually be invoked.

A standard monetary model of the exchange rate that takes account of the public sector solvency constraint is useful for illustrating the role of government guarantees in financial crises. A simple discrete-time model is given by equations 1 through 4:

19. See, for example, Calvo (1998b); Burnside, Eichenbaum, and Rebelo (1999); Dooley (2000).

(1) $m_t - p_t = \varphi y_t - \delta i_t,$

(2) $p_t = s_t + p_t^*,$

and

(3) $i_t = i_t^* + E_t s_{t+1} - s_t,$

where m, p, p^*, y, and s are the logarithms of the monetary base, price level, foreign price level, real income, and spot nominal exchange rate, respectively. The shadow exchange rate is given by

(4) $\bar{s}_t = (1 + \delta)^{-1}[\bar{m}_t - p_t^* - \varphi y_t + \delta i_t^* + \delta E_t \bar{s}_{t+1}].$

The monetary base, if an attack just occurs at time t, is given by $\bar{m}_t = \log(M_t - S_t R_t)$, where M_t is the level of the money supply, R_t is the stock of central bank reserves, and S_t is the pegged exchange rate.

The public sector budget identity is given by

(5) $S_t(B_{t+1} - B_t) = i_t^* S_t B_t + D_t + S_t(R_{t+1} - R_t) - r_t^* S_t R_t$
                        $- (M_{t+1} - M_t),$

where B_t is outstanding stock of public debt denominated in foreign currency at the beginning of period t, and D_t is the primary public sector budget deficit. i^* is the nominal (in foreign currency) rate of interest for domestic government debt, while r^* is the foreign nominal rate of interest paid to reserves. It is assumed that $i^* \geq r^*$. If $i^* = r^*$, the government pays no interest premium on its debt relative to foreign reserves. For developing countries, we expect i^* to exceed r^*.

Under the contingent government liabilities story, domestic credit expansion,

(6) $(M_{t+1} - S_t R_{t+1}) - (M_t - S_t R_t) = i_t^* S_t B_t + D_t - r_t^* S_t R_t$
                        $- S_t(B_{t+1} - B_t),$

is consistent with the pegged rate before a crisis occurs. The deficit and required domestic credit creation rise conditionally on the crisis and lead to depreciation afterwards.

First, consider a case in which the contingent increase in the deficit, ΔD, is a one-time event. Suppose that the exchange rate peg is consistent with pre-crisis fiscal policy. That is, the peg would be sustainable in the absence of the contingent insurance. In this case, when initial reserves are sufficiently large, the shadow exchange is less than the pegged rate and will never rise above the peg. A currency crisis will never occur. However, if the shadow rate equals the pegged rate, then multiple equilibria are possible. In one equilibrium, there is no crisis and the shadow rate does not rise above the pegged rate. In another equilibrium, the crisis occurs and the deficit increases by ΔD. This is an example of a second-generation model of a collapsing exchange rate regime, as in Obstfeld.[20] Given the fiscal policies and the structure of the economy, an exogenous increase in the reserves that the central bank commits to defending the exchange rate regime lowers the shadow exchange rate. If the increase in committed reserves is sufficiently large, then the crisis equilibria are eliminated.

Things are different if the contingent liability can rise over time. In many countries, the cost of government guarantees appears to have risen with outstanding private foreign currency debt. Menzie Chinn and Kletzer, and Craig Burnside, Martin Eichenbaum, and Sergio Rebelo consider currency crisis models in which private banks accumulate foreign debt that is guaranteed implicitly by the government in the event of a collapse of the exchange regime.[21] The ratio of nonperforming assets to liabilities for the banking system rises endogenously over time. The government's contingent liabilities rise over time until the reserves that the central bank will use in defending the peg and the implied post-crisis increase in domestic credit expansion just make the shadow exchange rate, $\tilde{S}_t$, equal to the pegged rate, S_t. In these models, crises are inevitable, and banking crises and currency crises are simultaneous. Output growth collapses with the financial crisis in the endogenous growth version of Chinn and Kletzer.

Short-Term Lending and Crises

Short-term lending by commercial banks to the domestic financial sectors of emerging markets appears to have accentuated crises in recent years. A strong trend toward shorter maturity lending by commercial banks to developing countries occurred between 1989 and 1997. This pattern is especially pronounced for the Asian crisis countries, where the share of bank lending composed of short-term debt rose from around 40 percent in the late 1980s to more than 65 percent by the mid-1990s. The share of short-term debt was approximately level between 1992 and the end of 1996. Thus while the East Asian economies enjoyed rapid growth, the accumulation of short-term debt was treated as relatively benign by the

---

20. Obstfeld (1986).
21. Chinn and Kletzer (1999); Burnside, Eichenbaum, and Rebelo (1999).

markets.[22] However, the positive interaction of short-term debt with growth also generated the basis of instability. Short-term borrowing, in other words, created a vulnerability that made the crises more severe than would otherwise have been the case.

The standard model of the liquidity view of recent financial crises is based on Douglas Diamond and Phillip Dybvig's model of bank runs.[23] Short-term debt finances long-term productive investments. Risky capital is productive after two periods, yielding an expected return in excess of the riskless rate of return. If a project is liquidated early, the return is significantly less than the riskless rate. Such time-to-build models demonstrate that the withdrawal of funding can strand incomplete projects and hence cause a sharp downturn in output.

An investment of size k made at date t yields $r < i^*$ in period $t + 1$ and R in period $t + 2$, where $E_t(1 + R) > (1 + i^*)^2$. r may be negative (but larger than -1). A domestic bank makes this loan using credit extended by foreign savers. It is assumed that a lender receives net interest i^* for each period as long as the bank has liquid resources to meet withdrawal demand. An early withdrawal of size xk requires the liquidation of part of the capital to pay the amount $(1 + i^*)xk$. This reduces the remaining capital by the amount

$$(7) \qquad \frac{(1 + i^*)xk}{(1 + r)}.$$

The present value net return to a domestic investor equals

$$(8) \qquad E_t\left[\left(\frac{1 + R}{(1 + i^*)^2}\right)\left(1 - \frac{(1 + i^*)x}{(1 + r)}\right) - (1 - x)\right]$$

per unit invested in period t, where x is the ratio of short-term debt that is liquidated in period $t + 1$. This is decreasing in x if

$$(9) \qquad E_t\left(\frac{1 + R}{(1 + r)(1 + i^*)}\right) > 1,$$

which is assumed so that long-term investments are desirable. Whenever x satisfies the condition

22. Eichengreen and Mody (1999).

23. Diamond and Dybvig (1983). See, for example, Chang and Velasco (1999); Goldfajn and Valdes (1997); Sachs, Tornell, and Velasco (1996).

(10) $(1 + r)(1 + i^*)(1 - x) > E_t(1 + R)\left(1 - \dfrac{(1 + i^*)x}{(1 + r)}\right),$

every lender that can should withdraw her funds, receiving $(1 + r)$ per unit lent in period t and earning the opportunity gross interest $(1 + i^*)$ between periods $t + 1$ and $t + 2$. Long-term lenders receive a net rate of return less than i^* if

(11) $E_t\left(\dfrac{(1 + R) - (1 + i^*)^2}{(\frac{1 + i^*}{1 + r})(1 + R) - (1 + i^*)^2}\right) = \bar{x} < x,$

where $\bar{x} < 1$.

Therefore, if all debt is short-term, self-fulfilling runs are possible in this economy. In one equilibrium, no lender withdraws her funds in period t and the project yields maximum surplus. In another, all lenders withdraw in period t, receiving a total return of $(1 + r)k$, and there is no period $t + 2$ production. In this approach, a currency crisis takes place in the same fashion as in Obstfeld: if all participants demand reserves, reserves are exhausted, forcing the central bank to abandon an exchange rate peg that would have been otherwise sustainable.[24] Financial crises arise because domestic liquid assets are insufficient to cover the short-term liabilities of the domestic financial sector, leading to a run on central bank reserves. Gestation lags in investment generate a collapse in output consequent to a financial crisis.

In the absence of government intervention, the Diamond-Dybvig model of bank runs provides a rationale for self-fulfilling currency and financial crises. However, liquidity crises can only occur if market imperfections restrict the use of long-term debt contracts. Under optimal loan contracts, the possibility of Pareto-inferior multiple equilibria is eliminated. Short-term lending can dominate in an equilibrium with imperfect financial markets. Dani Rodrik and Andrés Velasco demonstrate that short-term borrowing can arise in the equilibrium of the model outlined above as a consequence of the possibility of bank panics.[25] Sovereign risk can also lead to short maturity loans by creating a short leash on govern-

24. Obstfeld (1986).
25. Rodrik and Velasco (1999).

ment or private behavior. Appendix 14A explains why short-maturity foreign debt may dominate capital inflows from the private sector.

Why Exchange Rate Flexibility May Not Be Enough

The adoption of more flexible exchange rate regimes can work to reduce crisis vulnerability because it reduces the likelihood of speculative attacks against domestic currencies. The cost of capital to the borrowing country is higher because greater uncertainty is associated with foreign lending in domestic currency. Ceteris paribus, this reduces the flow of capital into the country. Flexibility also reduces the incentives for speculation and the taking of unhedged positions. Both factors lower the likelihood of a pure currency crisis, and a true float should eliminate externally triggered crises.

Since 1973 there has been a trend toward greater exchange rate flexibility, and the incidence of pure currency crises has simultaneously declined. However, susceptibility to externally generated crises has not disappeared, because, in part, under flexible exchange rates, international borrowing is often contracted directly in foreign currency. The currency risk is thereby transferred to domestic borrowers, such as banks and others in nontradable sectors, and takes the form of credit risk.

Moreover, most currencies are flexible only to a limited extent. As Guillermo Calvo and Carmen Reinhart note, countries appear to fear floating, and central banks tend to maintain nominal exchange rates within bands while still seeking to achieve domestic policy independence.[26] Jacob Frenkel and Michael Mussa point out that freely floating exchange rates do not necessarily increase policy autonomy and that the true limitation to achieving domestic policy goals arises inherently from the openness of the economy.[27] They distinguish between the ability to achieve monetary targets and the ability to achieve real economic effects. Under a fixed exchange rate, the domestic money supply is endogenous—that is, domestic interest rates equal foreign rates. In contrast, money supply and interest rate targets may be achieved in a floating exchange rate regime. However, real effects may still be illusory if optimal nominal contracts respond to exchange rate variability. If exchange rate variability is associated with more nominal flexibility, then real balances adjust more quickly, so monetary policy is less

26. Calvo and Reinhart (1999).
27. Frenkel and Mussa (1981); Frenkel (1983).

effective. Thus, to achieve production and income goals—as distinct from merely money supply and interest rate targets—policymakers may wish to contain nominal exchange rate movements, requiring safeguards such as sufficient international reserves. Frenkel finds that the demand for international reserves remained unchanged after the shift from the Bretton Woods period of fixed exchange rates to more flexible exchange rates.[28]

Reserves Accumulation

Both government guarantees and short-term lending can be explained as responses to financial market imperfections arising from sovereign risk. Appropriate prudential regulation of the domestic financial industry may be the best way to mitigate the potential problems of volatile short-term international capital flows. Another may be overcoming the "fear of floating" by developing country governments during financial liberalization and reform. However, as discussed above, managed flexibility and exchange rate pegs have their own justification at times, and sophisticated financial regulation requires significant administrative capacity to achieve. Several alternative policy remedies have been proposed to help debtor nations to manage volatile short-term capital flows and reduce the incidence of financial crises in either magnitude or frequency. The recent approaches to understanding how financial crises arise sketched above are useful for analyzing two important proposed safeguards: reserve accumulations and contingent credit facilities.

One approach to policy intervention that has been widely advocated is the accumulation of larger levels of reserves by developing countries and the creation of contingent credit lines.[29] The Guidotti and Greenspan proposals call for the accumulation of reserves equal to the amount of debt maturing within one year. Lines of credit could be provided by official sources, private financial institutions, or a combination of the two.

A sufficiently high level of foreign currency reserves held by the central bank would allow a country to avoid a currency crisis generated as an inferior equilibrium in a multiple equilibrium world. In the government guarantees model or the liquidity crisis model, a sufficiently high level of reserves ensures that the shadow exchange rate always remains below the

---

28. Frenkel (1983).
29. See, for example, Feldstein (1999).

pegged rate when macroeconomic policies are consistent with the chosen exchange rate regime. In such cases, the central bank has the resources to successfully fend off an attempted attack on the exchange parity or to act as a domestic lender of last resort meeting the demands of all foreign creditors to the private sector. If fundamentals disfavor the exchange rate, then the regime is ultimately unsustainable. The simple model from the literature shows that higher reserves postpone the day of reckoning for the peg.

These proposals for higher liquidity should be viewed in the context of a more general government borrowing strategy that takes into account not only the short-term costs but also refunding risk.[30] Since governments need to be sensitive to potential contingent liabilities on account of private sector actions, a consolidated asset and liability management strategy is necessary. Policymakers can use traditional tools to limit risk, including the amount, maturity, and currency composition of the country's liabilities and reserves. Modern tools to hedge risk can provide useful complements through the purchase of insurance by buying or selling options, arranging contingent lines of credit, including call provisions in its debt, and using regulatory and tax policies to encourage equity, as opposed to debt, financing. Modern financial engineering also suggests that authorities should perform stress tests to gauge residual exposure to risk. Continued work is required to determine if simple rules provide useful benchmarks for good debt and reserve management.

Reserve Adequacy in Practice

Though the simple short-term debt rule proposed by Guidotti and Greenspan may serve as a benchmark, countries will be best served by maintaining the level of reserves that meets their particular requirements. In addition to short-term debt, the factors to be considered in determining reserve adequacy include the current account deficit, the variability of the balance of payments, and the uncertainty associated with the measurement of the country's short-term debt and its reserves. It is important, moreover, that the traditional concern with reserve adequacy in relation to imports also be a consideration, though the analysis below shows that when reserves are adequate from a short-term debt point of view they also provide sufficient cover for imports. For some countries, the costs of holding adequate

---

30. Personal communication from Vincent Reinhart.

reserves may be high and will require innovative approaches to reserves management as well as a shift in the burden of holding reserves to banks.

RESERVES AND CURRENT ACCOUNT DEFICITS. Reserves may be required not just to repay debt but also to meet the obligations due to the current account deficit. In an empirical analysis, Matthieu Bussière and Christian Mulder show that the Greenspan-Guidotti rule of reserves equal to short-term debt will work best to limit crisis when the country also runs a current account surplus of about 2 percent of GDP.[31] However, where the current account is just balanced, the required reserves for containing crises rise to about twice the level of short-term debt. With higher current account deficits, the required reserves may rise nonlinearly to large levels.

RESERVES AND VARIABILITY IN THE BALANCE OF PAYMENTS. A traditional reason for holding reserves is to deal with the variability in the balance of payments. Empirical studies find that the higher the variability, the greater the observed level of reserves.[32] In these empirical studies, the past variability in reserves is used as a proxy for the variability in the balance of payments. Figure 14-1 shows the level (right-hand side) and standard deviation (left-hand side) of reserves/short-term debt. The levels are those from June 1999. The standard deviations are calculated over the period June 1994–June 1999. Note, as earlier studies suggested, that the two measures are highly correlated across this sample of countries, with a correlation coefficient of 0.85.

THE AMBIGUITY IN THE MEASUREMENT OF RESERVES AND SHORT-TERM DEBT. There are some other reasons why reserves may need to be higher than proposed under the Greenspan-Guidotti rule. First, adequate measures of debt that has to be repaid in the coming year are not always readily available. Short-term debt reported by the Bank for International Settlements (BIS) refers to debt owed to specified banks and hence does not cover other short-term repayment obligations, such as supplier credits, bonded debt, and equity outflows, that create demands on the country's foreign exchange earnings and reserves. Second, short-term debt can fluctuate sharply. For example, Ukrainian debt repayments fluctuate significantly because the country has borrowed using bullet bonds. The rule would require either large maintained reserves, which are costly, or a rapid increase in reserves just prior to the time of repayment, which may not be feasible. Third, the level of reserves can be depleted rapidly. For example,

---

31. Bussière and Mulder (1999).
32. See, for example, Frenkel (1983); Frenkel and Jovanovic (1981).

the level of Korean reserves were relatively low in the early part of 1997 and began to fall sharply just before the crisis in November when the Korean central bank began using its foreign exchange reserves to provide liquidity to the foreign branches of Korean banks. Similarly, the level of Thai reserves was lower than appeared since the Thai authorities had undertaken to buy the baht at a fixed exchange rate.

OTHER INDICATORS OF RESERVE ADEQUACY. Traditional rules for reserve adequacy look to import coverage. Figure 14-2 compares the reserves to import ratio to the reserves to short-term debt ratio and reveals a strong association. The axes in the figure intersect at reserve/imports = 4 months and reserves = short-term debt. Thus, any point to the right of the vertical axis represents reserves in excess of a year's repayment of outstanding short-term debt. Any point above the horizontal axis represents import coverage greater than four months. Using these two widely accepted benchmarks as a reference, any point in the upper right quadrant represents adequate reserves and any point in the lower left quadrant represents inadequate reserves. Of the thirty-six countries represented in the figure, twenty-seven are in either the upper right or lower left quadrants. This is not surprising: a country's short-term debt and imports tend to be highly correlated. In other words, while the new focus on short-term debt is appropriate, for many countries conventional reserve management to cover three or four months of imports appears to be a relevant rule. Moreover, since estimates of imports are likely to be more accurate than short-term debt and to be available sooner than short-term debt measures, the reserves-to-import ratio could be a leading proxy for the ratio of reserves to short-term debt.

Also relevant is the ratio of reserves to money supply (M2). Country rankings along this measure often vary significantly from rankings on reserves/short-term debt and reserves/imports. For example, before the crisis Malaysia had relatively high reserves in relation to short-term debt, but the level of reserves were more modest in comparison with M2. The controls on capital outflows instituted in September 1998 were motivated by the concern that international reserves would be inadequate if domestic residents chose to convert large sums of domestic currency assets into foreign currency assets.

The Costs of Holding Reserves

There is a cost to holding central bank reserves. This is the difference between the interest paid on the country's public debt and the interest earned

Figure 14-1. *Level and Variability of Reserves to Short-Term Debt*

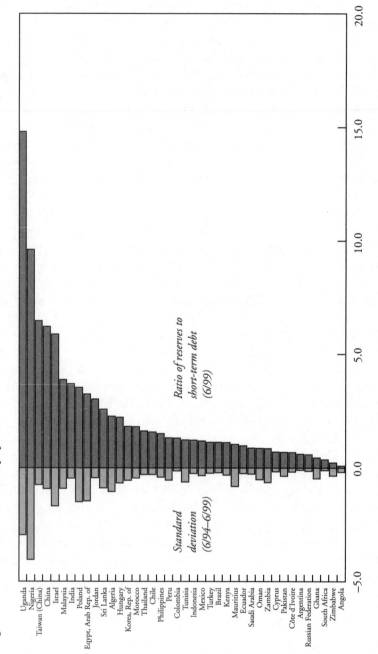

Sources: IMF, *International Financial Statistics*; BIS, *International Banking Consolidated Statistics.*

Figure 14-2. *Reserves to Short-Term Debt versus Reserves to Imports, 1999*
Ratio of reserves to imports (months of import cover)

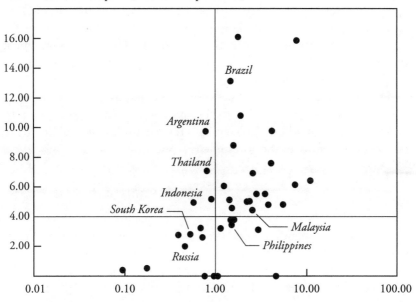

Source: BIS, IMF statistics.

on foreign reserves, typically the rate of interest for U.S. Treasury or similar debt. This is the interest rate differential, $i^* - r^*$, included in equations 5 and 6. An increase in reserves implies an equal increase in public debt; equivalently, if the additional reserves were not added to the central bank's assets, then the same amount of government debt could have been purchased by the central bank. For all purposes, a debtor government borrows to increase central bank reserves for self-protection under this proposal.

The act of accumulating reserves when $i^* > r^*$ is identical to the problem of sterilizing capital inflows in the presence of quasi-fiscal costs, as defined by Calvo.[33] The costs of sterilizing capital inflows have been estimated by Mohsin Khan and Reinhart for Latin American countries and by Kletzer and Mark Spiegel for Pacific Basin countries.[34] Both studies find

33. Calvo (1991).
34. Khan and Reinhart (1995); Kletzer and Spiegel (1998).

that the net costs of sterilization were between 0.25 percent and 0.5 percent of GDP during periods of large capital inflows post-1985. Kletzer and Spiegel find further that these costs can be as high as one percent of GDP for brief episodes of capital inflows. Because these estimates represent the quasi-fiscal costs of reserve accumulated during attempts to sterilize capital inflows, the costs of raising reserves to match one year of debt amortization are likely to be much higher.

The interest rate differential between developing country debt and foreign reserves has consequences for using reserves for self-protection. To show this, begin by adding an increase in reserves in the amount ΔR_t to the flow budget identity of the government:

$$(12) \quad (M_{t+1} - S_t R_{t+1}) - (M_t - S_t R_t) = i_t^* S_t (B_t + \Delta R) + D_t - r_t^* S_t (R_t + \Delta R) - S_t (B_{t+1} - B_t).$$

The costs of borrowed reserves, $(i_t^* - r_t^*) S_t \Delta R$, can be financed by current or future public spending cuts, tax revenue increases, or monetization. Given fiscal policies, solving this forward and imposing the conventional solvency criterion on the government implies a net present value increase in domestic credit creation due to borrowing foreign reserves given by

$$(13) \quad E_t \sum_{s=t}^{\infty} \left(\prod_{j=t}^{s} \frac{1}{1 + i_j^*} \right) \Delta(M_{s+1} - M_s) = E_t \sum_{s=t}^{\infty} \left(\prod_{j=t}^{s} \frac{1}{1 + i_j^*} \right) (i_s^* - r_s^*) S_s \Delta R.$$

When $i^* > r^*$, current or future monetization of the increase in the public sector budget deficit must rise.

This increase in the growth rate of the monetary base is a change in fundamentals. Suppose that a pegged exchange rate was consistent with macroeconomic fundamentals before the accumulation of reserves. The borrowing of reserves now makes that peg unsustainable in the absence of fiscal adjustment. Eventually, following the models of Krugman or of Robert Flood and Peter Garber, the exchange rate regime will collapse.[35] If the accumulation of reserves was undertaken to avoid a possible liquidity crisis, it is self-defeating. The additional reserves cause a financial crisis instead of preventing one.

In the case of a self-fulfilling crisis unjustified by fundamentals, increasing central bank reserves can be helpful if the interest rates are equal. Whether this can work depends on the maturity of government debt. If the

35. Krugman (1979); Flood and Garber (1984).

government borrows long-term, then foreign creditors only demand immediate repayment of private debts. In this event, the government spends its reserves and assumes private debts (either through government guarantees or by providing liquidity to the domestic financial sector). However, if government debt is short-maturity, then foreign creditors demand repayment by the government, leaving no extra resources from the borrowed reserves for bailing out the private sector. Short-term public borrowing to accumulate foreign reserves is at best costly and useless.

If the exchange rate peg is inconsistent with macroeconomic fundamentals, then borrowing reserves can either postpone or advance the date of a currency crisis. This has been shown by Willem Buiter for the Flood and Garber model when domestic and foreign government debt pay the same rate of interest ($i^* = r^*$).[36] Borrowing reserves, ΔR, raises the post-crisis rate of domestic credit creation by the amount $i^*\Delta R$, although it does not raise the pre-crisis rate of domestic credit creation. This is because the interest-bearing reserves are gone after the defense of the exchange regime is over, but the public debt incurred raising them remains. Before a crisis, there are two opposing effects of reserve accumulation: the rate of growth of the shadow exchange rate rises and current reserves are higher. If the reserves are borrowed close to the onset of a speculative attack, it is postponed because the reserve increase dominates. Accumulating reserves well in advance of the date of the attack brings the crisis forward because the rate of growth of the shadow exchange rate is the dominant effect.

Martin Feldstein proposes that these costs could be reduced by investing reserves in higher return and higher risk securities than government debt issued by the United States or similar countries.[37] While this generates some risk, he argues that the risk is much less than that of being caught with inadequate reserves.

Another way to reduce the government's costs of holding reserves is by requiring the private sector (including the banking sector) to hold more reserves. Increasing reserve requirements for banks during periods of rapid capital inflows could achieve this. The burden of holding reserves is then shifted to depositors and borrowers from the banking system. Carmen Reinhart and Vincent Reinhart find that deposit rates fall and lending rates rise when reserve requirements are increased, thereby creating incentives to

36. Buiter (1987).
37. Feldstein (1999).

bypass the banking system in favor of other means of financial intermediation.[38] However, where banks hold high-quality foreign assets as part of their liquidity portfolio, they may be perceived as safer and hence may be able to increase their level of intermediation.

Contingent Credit Lines

Drawing on official contingent credit lines during a crisis can be effective for stopping a self-fulfilling liquidity crisis. If the government borrows reserves from a contingent credit facility at the same interest cost that foreign reserves earn, then the shadow exchange rate,

$$(14) \qquad \bar{s}_t = (1 + \delta)^{-1}[\bar{m}_t - p_t^* - \varphi y_t + \delta i_t^* + \delta E_t \bar{s}_{t+1}],$$

falls because $\bar{m}_t = \log(M_t - S_t R_t)$ falls with a rise in reserves, R_t. A fundamentals-driven crisis will be postponed, as demonstrated by Buiter. This may be a superior policy reform for preventing or stopping liquidity crises, but it is costly if crises are caused by inconsistencies in macroeconomic policies.

Some proposals have called for the private provision of contingent credit facilities for the purpose of bailing private creditors into the resolution of financial crises. These have been contracted by Argentina, Indonesia, and Mexico and can be less costly than borrowed foreign reserves, although there are offsetting factors. When contracted, a contingent credit line incurs a commitment fee, which is the fee for the right to borrow under specified circumstances. This commitment fee is typically less than one percent of the contracted amount and, as such, is much smaller than the cost of holding reserves, which is approximated by the sovereign risk spread on the borrowed reserves. This large difference reflects an efficiency gain. By holding the money on behalf of the potential borrower, the international lender does not incur sovereign risk during the holding period; also, the money can be invested in a diversified portfolio that can be optimized continuously. When a borrower draws against the contingent credit, the precontracted interest rate is used, which, in practice, has had a lower spread (over the relevant risk-free rate) than sovereign bond borrowings. However, contingent credit lines have been arranged by commercial banks, who may charge a lower rate than bondholders.

---

38. Reinhart and Reinhart (1999).

Argentina established a $6.1 billion contingent credit line with thirteen banks in December 1996. This was a substantial amount, since Argentina held $18.1 billion in foreign exchange reserves and had $23.0 short-term debt to BIS-reporting banks. Thus the contingent line took Argentina over the Greenspan-Guidotti threshold, at least in terms of commercial bank debt. The line of credit has not been utilized, and has subsequently been rolled over once with an increase in the commitment fee from around 30 to 60 basis points during a period of heightened risk perception following the Asian crisis. The line of credit backstops liquidity to the domestic banking sector in the event of a liquidity crisis. In effect, the Argentine government can act as an intermediary, channeling reserves into the banking system, with the timing, extent of usage, and cost determined by need.

The other significant benefit of a contingent credit is that it only specifies a maximum amount that would be borrowed in the event of an emergency. An emergency may be averted by borrowing only a fraction of the contracted amount. This suggests that if the maximum amount is set to be large enough (against which only a commitment fee is paid), the additivity problem may be reduced. To allow dynamic hedging in the contingency that the credit line is used, the same creditors to the country should choose a level of lending that can be reversed to offset the increase in exposure in the emergency. This level should be based on the expected use of the contingent facility and not necessarily chosen to cover its maximum. This could reduce the risk of a liquidity crisis, although it implies that the contingency fund would exceed short-term debt exposure.

Contingent credit lines have been criticized on the basis that private creditors can hedge against the contingent loans they write. This hedging, called dynamic hedging, consists of reducing other loans to the country in an amount equal to the contingent credit when the contingency arises. Dynamic hedging has already appeared as a threat to the usefulness of contingent credit lines. In the case of Mexico, participating banks warned against exercising the credit because bank lending to Mexican corporations would contract as a result.[39] As such, it is possible that contingent lines of credit will not increase the resources available to the government in the event of a crisis. This problem of nonadditivity is identical to the neutrality of issuing short-term debt to borrow reserves at equal rates of interest noted above. The contingent borrowing facilities would be of no consequence if the offset is complete. If, however, the offsetting positions less

---

39. International Monetary Fund (1999 p. 33).

than match the full maximum amount of the credit or if they are taken as a crisis approaches (in which case, lenders incur significant costs), then the lines could add net resources to provide liquidity to avert a crisis.

While contingent credit lines may not provide additional resources during a crisis in the presence of dynamic hedging, they may still help to protect countries against a liquidity crisis. Under dynamic hedging, a lender avoids increasing the total credit it extends to the country when the contingent credit is drawn against. However, if the lender seeks to reduce its short-term lending to the country in the event of a crisis, the contingent credit is invoked, thereby replacing that short-term debt. The contingent credit line is effectively a contingent maturity extension. It can be used to replace short-term debt when the lender is unwilling to roll over existing short-term debts during a liquidity crisis. For example, if a country has short-term external debt of $10 million, it can face an outflow of capital up to this amount in a crisis. By arranging $5 million of contingent credits, one-half of its short-term debt exposure can be automatically rolled over by invoking the credits in the event of a liquidity run, halving the short-term capital outflow. If dynamic hedging is to unravel this effect, then lenders need to increase their short-term exposure by $5 million to raise the maximal liquidity shortfall to $10 million. Thus, in equilibrium, contingent credits do not have a beneficial effect if they induce lenders as a whole to increase their total exposure to the countries by the amount of the contingent credits. The purpose of contingent credit lines is to create a portion of the debt that cannot be subtracted in a crisis by allowing for a pre-arranged conditional maturity extension.

A second, related, issue is that collateral has been required to back credit lines. This has the effect of precommitting resources for the repayment of the debt. The Argentine agreement commits the participating banks to purchase Argentine government securities from the central bank as collateral; the value of the collateral, which is marked to market, has to be maintained above the level of the contingent credit line. Since the collateral held by the beneficiary banks is in the form of Argentine government debt, Argentina is under an obligation to repay following the triggering of the credit. The risk of this obligation led the Argentine government to arrange backstop funding from the World Bank.

The IMF also created a contingent credit facility in April 1999.[40] These contingent credit lines are intended to provide protection against adverse

40. International Monetary Fund (1999).

developments in international capital that pose a risk to member countries not of their own making. As of this writing, these have not been used. The commitments would normally be in the range of 300 to 500 percent of the member's quota. Countries would be expected to repay each tranche within twelve to eighteen months.

Capital Controls

The analogue of bank runs to developing country financial and currency crises suggests that a remedy lies in attaining a better match between the maturities of domestic assets and foreign liabilities. Restrictions on short-term borrowing address this issue and have drawn renewed interest from economists and policymakers since the onset of the Asian financial crisis.

Four types of capital account restrictions have received the most attention. The first of these is a Tobin tax, a proportionate tax on capital inflows or outflows.[41] The second is a one-time tax on capital inflows as adopted by Chile and recently relaxed. The third are contingent controls on capital outflows as imposed by Malaysia during the Asian crisis. Lastly, other direct controls on short-term bank borrowing have been proposed. Each of these is subject to concerns that it can be circumvented and will not effectively control capital flows as intended. That issue has been discussed widely.[42] The Chilean approach has received the most attention since it seeks directly to restrict short-term capital flows.

Consider, first, the implications of restricting short-term capital on aggregate capital flows. As noted, short-term debt may be an equilibrium solution for capital mobility under market imperfections associated with sovereign risk. Short-term lending may provide a short leash, allowing lenders to withdraw funds quickly in anticipation of a policy or regime change that would reduce their returns. Longer-term lending is associated with countries whose policy regimes are perceived to be more stable and pose a lower risk of sovereign default. The consensus on Chile appears to be that capital controls changed the maturity composition of capital inflows with limited long-run impact on the volume of net inflows.[43] In

41. Eichengreen, Tobin, and Wyplosz (1995).
42. See, for example, Garber and Taylor (1995); Ariyoshi and others (2000).
43. See, for example, Budnevich and Lefort (1997); Montiel and Reinhart (1999); Gallego, Hernandez, and Schmidt-Hebbel (1999).

countries with greater political risk, capital flows may decline—and such a decline may also be perceived as desirable.

As observed by Rodrik and Velasco, individual investors do not take into account the social costs of borrowing short. In this case, eliminating short-term debt for all but short-maturity investments is also beneficial. Thus the models of financial crises do imply that there are benefits of achieving superior maturity matches. In the time-to-build economy, discouraging short-term in favor of long-term lending reduces the possibility of bank runs, ceteris paribus.

Sebastian Edwards argues that the controls did not insulate Chile from the disturbances to international capital markets of the Asian financial crises.[44] He notes that the interest rate response was greater in Chile than in Hong Kong and interprets this as evidence that the controls were ineffective. However, it seems more appropriate to argue that the change in the maturity structure of capital inflows and interest rate volatility are evidence that the controls worked as intended. The controls appear to have reduced short-term debt exposure without eliminating integration with international capital markets. The interest rate responses are consistent with maintaining integration of the domestic economy with international capital markets. This may be a desirable, rather than undesirable, aspect of short-term restrictions relative to other forms of capital controls. Appendix 14B discusses the impact and potential costs of this type of capital control when it is effective.

Conclusion

This paper provides a preliminary and partial assessment of the costs and benefits of policy interventions aimed at reducing the impact of crises generated by (implicit or explicit) government commitments to honor the liabilities of their domestic banking systems and by short-term capital mobility. Reserve accumulations and contingency funds can guard against unexpected and limited shocks that lead to the realization of government contingent liabilities and can also protect against the sharp downturns that result from the inability to roll over short-term debt. However, they cannot protect from endemic and unsustainable vulnerabilities. Reserve accumu-

44. Sebastian Edwards, "Abolish the IMF," *Financial Times*, November 13, 1998, p. 12.

lations suffer from the further limitation that by creating a significant fiscal cost, they may bring about the very currency collapse they are intended to protect against. In this respect contingent credits are superior. They serve as a mechanism to enforce a rollover of funds when private capital seeks to leave in the midst of a crisis. Taxation of short-term capital inflows raise the costs of investment, especially to small and medium firms, but it may allow countries to limit short-term debt accumulation without significantly interfering with capital market integration. The limits on short-term debt thus achieved reduce government contingent liabilities and hence lower the costs of a crisis.

Appendix 14A
Rationale for Short-Term Lending

There are several reasons why we might observe short-term lending in an economy with gestation lags in capital formation. One is uncoordinated borrower behavior when there are a large number of borrowers. It is easy to calculate equilibrium interest rates for short- and long-term debt given a probability of a bank run. This has been done by Rodrik and Velasco.[45] In the notation used in this paper, if $\bar{x} \le x \le (1 + r)/(1 + i^*)$, the short-term interest rate is i^* and the long-term interest rate (expressed as a single-period rate) is given by

$$(15) \quad p(1 + R)\left(1 - \frac{(1 + i^*)x}{(1 + r)}\right)\frac{1}{1 - x} + (1 - p)(1 + i^L)^2 = (1 + i^*)^2.$$

If $x > (1 + r)/(1 + i^*)$, the short-term interest rate is given by

$$(16) \quad 1 + i^S = \frac{1}{1 - p}\left[(1 + i^*) - p\frac{(1 + r)}{x}\right],$$

where it has been assumed that short-term lenders are paid proportionately in a run. The long-term interest rate is simply

$$(17) \quad (1 + i^L)^2 = \frac{1}{1 - p}(1 + i^*)^2.$$

45. Rodrik and Velasco (1999).

A simple calculation shows that the investor maximizes expected surplus by taking only long-term debt in this model when she takes account of the endogeneity of the long-term and short-term interest rates to x given p. If she does not internalize the effect of her financing decision on i^S and i^L, then the expected return to borrowing short-term is positive.

Sovereign immunity provides a reason why lenders will prefer to lend on short maturities. In reputational models of sovereign borrowing, threats of lending moratoria provide repayment incentives. Kletzer and Brian Wright demonstrate that punishments that are proof to renegotiation provide the same incentives as permanent exclusion from credit market access in a very general model.[46] The borrowing moratorium needs to last only one period. The important quantity for determining how much consumption-smoothing is achievable through international borrowing and lending is the surplus gained through borrowing itself. The greater the cost of a cut-off from access to international credit, the more that can be lent under the threat of potential repudiation or default.

Using this logic, with long-term loans the short-run cost to a default in period t is the forgone output from new investments undertaken in period t. This loss equals

$$(18) \qquad k_t E_t\left[\left(\frac{1 + R}{(1 + i^*)^2}\right) - 1\right],$$

where k_t is equilibrium foreign lending in period t in the equilibrium constrained by sovereign risk. There is no default on loans due in period $t + 1$.

Suppose that an input of capital is needed in the second period of a project to bring the project to completion. In this case, the project yields the uncertain net output R in period $t + 2$ if investments equal to $1/2$ are made in each of periods t and $t + 1$. If no investment is made in period $t + 1$, then net output is r. In this situation, assume that a long-term loan commits foreign capital for both periods even if the country defaults on other debts coming due. The additional output loss that can be imposed on the country using short-term loans equals

$$(19) \qquad k_{t-1}^S E_t\left[\left(\frac{1 + R}{(1 + i^*)}\right) - (1 + r/2)\right],$$

where k_{t-1}^S is short-term debt contracted in period $t - 1$.

46. Kletzer and Wright (2000).

Using only short-term debt increases capital flows in a simple extension of Jonathan Eaton and Mark Gersovitz's model by the proportion[47]

$$(20) \qquad \frac{\Delta k}{k} = \frac{1}{(1 + i^*)^2} \, E_t \left[\left(\frac{1 + R}{(1 + i^*)} \right) - (1 + r/2) \right].$$

As in all models of sovereign debt in which punishment does not actually occur in equilibrium, there is an incentive to increase the penalties for default. This is because a larger penalty sustains higher levels of lending, which are more efficient whenever the constraints imposed by sovereign immunity are binding. Short-term lending increases the costs of default in the time-to-build model.

Another issue involving sovereignty is the desire to influence policy choices that might adversely affect foreign creditors. The ability to keep a short leash is essentially the same as increasing the penalties that can be imposed in the short run. Typical changes in fiscal and regulatory policies do not constitute default, but they can impair the value of long-term loans. Short-term lending allows a run on banks that may be optimal conditional on an expected policy change. The cost of the run given in equation 17 can increase the cost of such a policy change, discouraging its adoption. The prospects of a bailout also can generate a bias toward short-term debt. Other reasons for short-term lending despite a potentially troublesome maturity mismatch include regulatory and tax treatment that favors short-term borrowing.

Appendix 14B
Controls on Short-Term Capital Inflows

Chilean-style capital controls can be represented by a tax that is diminishing with maturity. This differential tax is easy to represent in time-to-build models. The contractual interest for a loan made in period t and held for T periods satisfies

$$(21) \qquad \prod_{j=t+1}^{t+T} (1 + i_j^*) = (1 - \tau) \prod_{j=t+1}^{t+T} (1 + i_j)$$

if repayment in full is certain.

47. Eaton and Gersovitz (1981).

The potential benefits of this policy can be seen by considering a given probability p of a panic. The short-term interest rate is given by

$$(22) \qquad 1 + i^S = \left(\frac{1 + i^*}{1 - \tau}\right),$$

if $x \le (1 + r)(1 - \tau)/(1 + i^*)$, and by

$$(23) \qquad 1 + i^S = \left(\frac{1}{1 - \tau}\right)\frac{1}{1 - p}\left[(1 + i^*) - p\frac{(1 + r)}{x}\right],$$

if $x > (1 + r)(1 - \tau)/(1 + i^*)$. The long-term interest rates are given by

$$(24) \qquad (1 + i^L)^2 = (1 + i^*)\left(\frac{1 + i^*}{1 - \tau}\right),$$

for $x \le x'$, where x' satisfies

$$(25) \qquad \frac{(1 + i^*)^2}{1 - \tau} = \left(\frac{1 + R}{1 - x'}\right)\left(\frac{(1 + i^*)x'}{(1 - \tau)(1 + r)} - 1\right).$$

For $x' \le x \le (1 + r)(1 - \tau)/(1 + i^*)$, the long-term interest rate is given by

$$(26) \quad p(1 + R)\left(1 - \frac{(1 + i^S)x}{(1 + r)}\right)\frac{1}{1 - x} + (1 - p)(1 - \tau)(1 + i^L)^2 = (1 + i^*)^2,$$

and for $x > (1 + r)(1 - \tau)/(1 + i^*)$ by

$$(27) \qquad (1 + i^L)^2 = \frac{1}{1 - p}(1 + i^*)\left(\frac{1 + i^*}{1 - \tau}\right).$$

These expressions imply that the gap between the long-term equilibrium interest rate and the short-term equilibrium interest rate decreases with the capital inflows entry tax. The term structure of interest rates favors longer-term borrowing. This has the correct incentive effects if short-term borrowing is socially inefficiently high.

References

Ariyoshi, Akira, Karl Habermeier, Bernard Laurens, Inci Otker-Robe, Jorge Ivan Canales-Kriljenko, and Andrei Kirilenko. 2000. "Country Experiences with the Use and Liberalization of Capital Controls." Occasional Paper 190. Washington: International Monetary Fund (May).

Budnevich, Carlos, and Guillermo Lefort. 1996. "Capital Account Regulations and Macroeconomic Policy: Two Latin American Experiences." Working Paper 6. Santiago: Banco de Chile.

Buiter, Willem H. 1987. "Borrowing to Defend the Exchange Rate and the Timing and Magnitude of Speculative Attacks." *Journal of International Economics* 23 (August): 221–39.

Burnside, Craig, Martin Eichenbaum, and Sergio Rebelo. 1999. "Hedging and Financial Fragility in Fixed Exchange Rate Regimes." Working Paper 7143. Cambridge, Mass.: National Bureau of Economic Research (May).

Bussière, Matthieu, and Christian Mulder. 1999. "Which Short-Term Debt over Reserve Ratio Works Best? Operationalizing the Greenspan-Guidotti Rule." Draft Working Paper. Washington: International Monetary Fund.

Caballero, Ricardo, and Arvind Krishnamurthy. 1998. "Emerging Markets Crises: An Assets Markets Perspective." Working Paper. Massachusetts Institute of Technology, Department of Economics.

Calvo, Guillermo A. 1991. "The Perils of Sterilization." *International Monetary Fund Staff Papers* 38 (4): 921–26.

———. 1998a. "Balance of Payments Crises in Emerging Markets: Large Capital Inflows and Sovereign Governments." Paper prepared for the National Bureau for Economic Research Conference on Currency Crises, Cambridge, Mass., February 6 and 7 (www.bsos.umd.edu/econ/ciecrp5.pdf [June 2000]).

———. 1998b. "Varieties of Capital-Market Crises." In *The Debt Burden and Its Consequences for Monetary Policy,* edited by Guillermo Calvo and Mervyn King, 181–202. Basingstoke: Macmillan.

Calvo, Guillermo, and Carmen M. Reinhart. 1999. "When Capital Inflows Come to a Sudden Stop: Consequences and Policy Options" (www.bsos.umd.edu/econ/ciecpp6.pdf [June 2000]).

Chang, Roberto, and Andrés Velasco. 1999. "Illiquidity and Crises in Emerging Markets: Theory and Policy." Economic Research Report 99-14. New York University, Department of Economics (June).

Chinn, Menzie D., and Kenneth M. Kletzer. 1999. "International Capital Inflows, Domestic Financial Intermediation and Financial Crises under Imperfect Information." Paper prepared for the Federal Reserve Bank of San Francisco Pacific Basin Conference, September 23–24 (www.frbsf.org/econrsrch/pbc/conferences/1999/papers/chinn_ kletzer.pdf [June 2000]).

Corsetti, Giancarlo, Paolo Pesenti, and Nouriel Roubini. 1998a. "Paper Tigers? A Preliminary Assessment of the Asian Crisis." Working Paper 6783. Cambridge, Mass.: National Bureau of Economic Research.

———. 1998b. "What Caused the Asian Currency and Financial Crisis? Part I: A Macroeconomic Overview." Working Paper 6833. Cambridge, Mass.: National Bureau of Economic Research.

————. 1998c. "What Caused the Asian Currency and Financial Crisis? Part II: Theory and Policy Responses." Working Paper 6834. Cambridge, Mass.: National Bureau of Economic Research.

Demirgüç-Kunt, Asli, and Enrica Detragiache. 1998. "Financial Liberalization and Financial Fragility." Working Paper 98/83. Washington: International Monetary Fund (June).

Diamond, Douglas, and Phillip Dybvig. 1983. "Bank Runs, Deposit Insurance, and Liquidity." *Journal of Political Economy* 91 (June): 401–19.

Diaz-Alejandro, Carlos. 1985. "Goodbye Financial Repression, Hello Financial Crash." *Journal of Development Economics* 19 (112): 1–24.

Dooley, Michael P. 2000. "A Model of Crises in Emerging Markets." *Economic Journal* 110 (460): 256–72.

Eaton, Jonathan, and Mark Gersovitz. 1981. "Debt with Potential Repudiation: Theory and Evidence." *Review of Economic Studies* 48 (2): 289–309.

Eichengreen, Barry. 1999. *Toward a New International Financial Architecture: A Practical Post-Asia Agenda.* Washington: Institute for International Economics.

Eichengreen, Barry, and Ashoka Mody. 1999. "Lending Booms, Reserves, and the Sustainability of Short-Term Debt. Inferences from the Price of Syndicated Bank Loans." Working Paper 7113. Cambridge, Mass.: National Bureau of Economic Research (May).

Eichengreen, Barry, James Tobin, and Charles Wyplosz. 1995. "Two Cases for Sand in the Wheels of International Finance." *Economic Journal* 105 (428): 162–72.

Feldstein, Martin. 1999. "Self-Protection for Emerging Market Economies." Working Paper 6907. Cambridge, Mass.: National Bureau of Economic Research (January).

Flood, Robert, and Peter Garber. 1984. "Collapsing Exchange Rate Regimes: Some Linear Examples." *Journal of International Economics* 17 (August): 1–138.

Frenkel, Jacob. 1983. "International Liquidity and Monetary Control." In *Money and Credit: The Policy Rules,* edited by George M. von Furstenberg, 65–109. Washington, International Monetary Fund.

Frenkel, Jacob, and Boyan Jovanovic. 1981. "Optimal International Reserves: A Stochastic Framework." *Economic Journal* 91 (362): 507–14.

Frenkel, Jacob, and Michael Mussa. 1981. "Monetary and Fiscal Policies in an Open Economy." *American Economic Review* 71 (May, *Papers and Proceedings*): 253–58.

Furman, Jason, and Joseph Stiglitz. 1998. "Economic Crises: Evidence and Insights from East Asia." *Brookings Papers on Economic Activity, 2:1998,* 1–115.

Gallego, Francisco, Leonardo Hernandez, and Klaus Schmidt-Hebbel. 1999. "Capital Controls in Chile: Effective? Efficient?" Working Paper 59. Santiago: Banco de Chile.

Garber, Peter, and Mark P. Taylor. 1995. "Sand in the Wheels of Foreign Exchange Markets: A Sceptical Note." *Economic Journal* 105 (428): 173–80.

Goldfajn, Ilan, and Rodrigo Valdes. 1997. "Capital Flows and the Twin Crises: The Role of Liquidity." Working Paper 97/87. Washington: International Monetary Fund (July).

Greenspan, Alan. 1999. "Currency Reserves and Debt." Speech to the World Bank Conference on Recent Trends in Reserves Management, April 29, Washington, D.C.

Guidotti, Pablo. 1999. "Currency Reserves and Debt." Speech to the World Bank Conference on Recent Trends in Reserves Management, April 29, Washington, D.C.

International Monetary Fund. 1999. *World Economic Outlook 1999.* Washington.

Kaminsky, Graciela L., and Carmen M. Reinhart. 1999. "The Twin Crises: The Causes of Banking and Balance-of-Payments Problems." *American Economic Review* 89 (3): 473–500.

Khan, Mohsin S., and Carmen M. Reinhart. 1995. "Capital Flows in the APEC Region." Occasional Paper 122. Washington: International Monetary Fund (October).

Klein, Michael, and Giovanni Olivei. 1999. "Capital Account Liberalization and Economic Growth." Working Paper 7384. Cambridge, Mass.: National Bureau of Economic Research (October).

Kletzer, Kenneth M., and Mark M. Spiegel. 1998. "Speculative Capital Inflows and Exchange Rate Targeting." In *Managing Capital Flows and Exchange Rates,* edited by R. Glick, 409–35. Cambridge University Press.

Kletzer, Kenneth M., and Brian D. Wright. 2000. "Sovereign Debt as Intertemporal Barter." *American Economic Review* (forthcoming).

Krugman, Paul. 1979. "A Model of Balance-of-Payments Crises." *Journal of Money, Credit and Banking* 11 (August): 311–25.

———. 1999. "Balance Sheets, the Transfer Problem and Financial Crises." Massachusetts Institute of Technology, Department of Economics (January) (web.mit.edu/krugman/www/flood.pdf [June 2000]).

Kupiec, Paul H. 1995. "Noise Traders, Excess Volatility, and a Securities Transactions Tax." Finance and Economics Discussion Paper 95-26. Washington: Board of Governors of the Federal Reserve System.

Lustig, Nora. 1999. "Crisis and the Poor: Socially Responsible Economics." Presidential Address to the Fourth Annual Meeting of the Latin American and Caribbean Economics Association, Santiago, Chile, October 29, 1999 (www.lacea.org/presidential.pdf [June 2000]).

McKinnon, Ronald I., and Huw Pill. 1997. "Credible Economic Liberalizations and Overborrowing." *American Economic Review* 87 (2): 189–93.

Mishkin, Frederic. 1996. "Understanding Financial Crises: A Developing Country Perspective." In *Annual World Bank Conference on Development Economics 1996,* edited by Michael Bruno and Boris Pleskovic, 29–62. Washington: World Bank.

Montiel, Peter, and Carmen M. Reinhart. 1999. "Do Capital Controls Influence the Volume and Composition of Capital Flows? Evidence from the 1990s." *Journal of Money and Finance* 18 (4): 619–35.

Obstfeld, Maurice. 1986. "Rational and Self-Fulfilling Balance-of-Payments Crises." *American Economic Review* 76 (1): 72-81.

———. 1998. "The Global Capital Market: Benefactor or Menace?" *Journal of Economic Perspectives* 12 (4): 9-30.

Reinhart, Carmen M., and Vincent Reinhart. 1999. "On the Use of Reserve Requirements in Dealing with Capital Flow Problems." *International Journal of Finance and Economics* 4 (1): 27–54.

Rodrik, Dani. 1995. "Getting Interventions Right: How South Korea and Taiwan Grew Rich." *Economic Policy* 20 (April): 55–107.

Rodrik, Dani, and Andrés Velasco. 1999. "Short-Term Capital Flows." Working Paper 7364. Cambridge, Mass.: National Bureau of Economic Research (September).

Sachs, Jeffrey, Aaron Tornell, and Andrés Velasco. 1996. "Financial Crises in Emerging Markets: The Lessons from 1995." *Brookings Papers on Economic Activity, 1:1996,* 147–215.

World Bank. 1998. *Global Economic Prospects.* Washington.

MANSOOR DAILAMI

15

Managing Risks of Global Financial Market Integration

The revolutionary idea that defines the boundary between modern
times and the past is the mastery of risk.

PETER L. BERNSTEIN,
Against the Gods—The Remarkable Story of Risk

INTERNATIONAL FINANCIAL POLICY is currently in a state of introspec-
tion and revisionism. It is in search of a new paradigm to enlighten,
explain, and draw lessons from the novel financial developments of the
1990s—perforce, the increased volume and mobility of capital flows across
national boundaries, financial innovation and advances in information
technology, and heightened exposure to global financial risk. Given the
policy consensus and conventional wisdom of the 1980s, emphasizing
sequencing of financial liberalization and macroeconomic stabilization, the
financial crises of the 1990s came as a total surprise, if not in kind, certainly
in frequency and severity. The crises affecting emerging market economies
in 1997–98, for instance, were unprecedented in several important

The views expressed in this paper are the author's alone and in no way reflect those of the World
Bank, its executive directors, or the countries they represent. The author would like to thank Andres
Becker and Ilya Lipkovich for expert research assistance.

447

respects, including the extent of initial depreciation of local currencies, the plunges in asset values on local equity and bond markets, the severe distress in the corporate and banking sectors, and the contraction of economic activity.

Many developing countries embraced globalization in the 1980s through trade in goods and services and began to liberalize their domestic financial markets. They achieved considerable macroeconomic stabilization and enjoyed steady high economic growth. In the 1990s, they moved to relax or remove restrictions on capital transactions, without having achieved the macroeconomic, regulatory, and institutional prerequisites for capital account openness. Such weaknesses on the domestic front, coupled with the changing nature and composition of capital flows, rendered these economies vulnerable in the 1990s to cycles of investor euphoria and panic, as exemplified in the high degree of volatility in both the volume and the price of foreign capital. The subsequent crises imposed extremely high social and economic costs on affected countries in terms of lost output and jobs, and above all, an increase in poverty.

The crises have also catalyzed interest in the broader debate on the functioning, architecture, and regulation of international financial markets. Fifty-five years after the postwar institutional reconstruction that launched the Bretton Woods consensus, the international community must again contemplate how to design a new international financial architecture that would promote financial stability and long-term economic growth. Just as the postwar reconstruction was driven and shaped principally by the United States' adherence to an open international system, managed by multilateral institutions, and was sustained by its "hegemony of vision and initiative as well as power and wealth,"[1] American hegemony in global finance today places the nation in a unique position. The underlying conditions, trends, and forces at play, however, have changed substantially since 1944. Global financial markets have grown significantly in the size, complexity, and range of services and products that they offer. Private capital has emerged as the dominant source of development finance, surpassing official finance by a factor of five to one in recent years. The eleven member countries of the European Union culminated their move toward monetary and economic integration with the launching of the Euro, which

1. See Calleo (1984, p. 392).

could potentially rival the U.S. dollar in both the international payment system and international finance.

Equally important, the triumphant spread of democracy worldwide and the corresponding increase in political and civil liberty means that for the first time in human history, electoral democracy is the world's predominant form of government.[2] This consolidation of democratic governance, in turn, leads to an increased demand by citizens for political voice, for national economic security, and for social insurance against the hazard of exposure to international financial volatility. Seen collectively, these developments underline the need for a greater understanding and appreciation of the interrelationships between domestic politics and an openness to international finance. If the potential gains from an openness to cross-border capital flows are to be realized in developing countries, as they have been in member countries of the Organization for Economic Cooperation and Development (OECD), there will need to be strong efforts to enhance the stability of capital flows and improve risk management through better crisis prevention and containment and the orderly resolution of crises when they do occur. An effective risk management framework needs to recognize the benefits of financial openness, while at the same time safeguarding against the hazard of exposure to international financial volatility. The basic elements of this risk management framework are articulated below.

Identify the risks. Two broad categories of risk are important for understanding the dynamics of capital flows to developing countries. The first source derives from various weaknesses in the host government's own domestic policies and regulatory and macroeconomic environment, which induce banks and corporations to take on excessive risk on their balance sheets through an excessive buildup of short-term external liabilities relative to short-term assets. The second relates to certain features of international financial markets that generate an amplified price and quantity dynamic in flows of foreign capital to developing countries that are not necessarily conditioned or warranted by a particular country's long-term creditworthiness or its underlying fundamentals. These two categories of

2. According to a recent survey by the Freedom House, 88 of the world's 191 countries (46 percent)—the largest number ever recorded—were rated as free, meaning that "they maintain a high degree of political and economic freedom and respect for civil liberties." A majority of the world's population is governed by democratically elected governments—thus, today, 2.354 billion people (40 percent of the world's population) now live in free societies, 1.57 billion (26.5 percent) live in countries that are partially free, and 1.984 billion (33.5 percent) live in nonfree countries. See Karatnycky (1999).

risk correspond, respectively, with the first- and second-generation models of financial crisis,[3] emphasizing the role of fundamentals in triggering a liquidity crisis and debtor-creditor incentive and coordination problems.

Elucidate strategic objectives. Having identified these risks to developing countries' integration into global financial markets, the second step in evolving an effective risk management strategy is to elucidate the overall objectives that the strategy is supposed to serve. These objectives can be defined broadly—openness to international capital movements, democratic forms of governance, and policy autonomy. They command a wide degree of respect among scholars and policymakers dealing with international finance. And their appearance at the center of the policy debate clearly reflects the remarkable success in the global advance of democracy, political freedom, and financial integration.

Develop mechanisms to mitigate and share risks. The third step in this risk management strategy involves the development of appropriate institutional and regulatory frameworks to minimize the likelihood of future crises—and mechanisms to contain their associated socioeconomic costs. The framework developed in this paper favors a moderate view: an orderly opening of financial markets accompanied by an appropriate regulatory framework and instruments for controlling short-term capital flows; and a building of public support for openness by providing cushions against risks, through social safety nets and redistribution policies.

On the international front, since capital account liberalization implies welfare gains globally, there exists a justification and rationale for international action—of policy coordination, prudential financial regulation and supervision, and lender-of-last-resort activity to provide liquidity and emergency financial assistance.

Historical Antecedents and the Changing Nature of Risk

Global financial risk and the strategies for managing it have changed substantially over the past fifty years. Three distinct periods, each unique in the way the global financial system changed, and the way in which countries dealt with the changes, can be discerned. The first period, from 1945

---

3. A large body of literature has developed over the past two years discussing the causes and consequences of recent financial crises in emerging market economies. For a sample of such studies, see Sachs, Tornell, and Velasco (1996); Calvo and Mendoza (1996); Radelet and Sachs (1998); and Haldane (1999).

to 1973, entailed the post–World War II era Bretton Woods system of fixed exchange rates. The second period, which lasted throughout the 1970s and well into the 1980s, consisted of high, volatile inflation along with macroeconomic instability. The third distinct period is the post–cold war era of the 1990s.

1945–73: Risk Management through Capital Controls and Fixed Exchange Rates

From the standpoint of risk management, the Bretton Woods period exhibited a remarkable degree of stability, by effectively combining fixed exchange rates with capital controls on the external side and Keynesian welfare-state macroeconomics on the domestic side.[4] The solution devised at Bretton Woods gave priority to fixed exchange rates and national policy autonomy. As put forth by several scholars, capital controls were an accepted norm of the international monetary system in the 1950s and 1960s, as the Bretton Woods Agreement did not grant the International Monetary Fund (IMF) jurisdiction over capital movements.[5] It was not until September 1997 that the Interim Committee of the IMF "agreed that the Fund's Articles [of Agreement] should be amended to make the promotion of capital account liberalization a specific purpose of the Fund and to give the Fund appropriate jurisdiction over capital movements."[6] Thus the relative closure of national economies to the free flow of capital in that era—with a few exceptions—afforded governments the scope for deploying the instruments of fiscal and monetary policy, including progressive taxation and public expenditures, in pursuit of national objectives of full employment and social equity, without fear of the exit of capital. The analytical underpinnings of Bretton Woods were the classical open economy

---

4. This policy mix was referred to by John Ruggie (1983) as "a compromise of embedded liberalism." It connotes a commitment to a liberal order different from both the economic nationalism of the 1930s and the liberalism of the gold standard. For further elaboration, see Garrett (1998). Razeen Sally (1998) also referred to embedded liberalism as "mixed system thinking." See also Dailami (2000).

5. Reflecting the understanding of the time, John Maynard Keynes expressed the issue succinctly in his often-quoted 1944 speech to Parliament, stating that "Not merely as a feature of the transition, but as a permanent arrangement, the plan accords to every member government the explicit right to control all capital movements. What used to be heresy is now endorsed as orthodox. . . . It follows that our right to control the domestic capital market is secured on firmer foundations than ever before, and is formally accepted as a part of agreed international agreements" (Gold 1977, p. 11).

6. Quoted in Polak (1998, p. 47).

models of Robert Mundell and J. Marcus Fleming, according to which countries can attain only two of the following three conditions: capital mobility, fixed exchange rates, and monetary policy autonomy. The relatively high degree of policy autonomy served the cause of democracy well, particularly in Western Europe, where it advanced to a high degree of maturity. It was not until the 1970s, after Western European countries had achieved currency convertibility on their current balance-of-payment accounts that free movement of capital across national boundaries emerged as an important policy priority.

The 1970s and 1980s: Financial Risk Management through Market Solutions

The 1973 collapse of the Bretton Woods system, floating exchange rates, rising oil prices, chronic inflation, and slumping global economic conditions intensified currency and interest rate risks in global financial markets during the 1970s and 1980s. The responses were principally "market solution" types of action, exemplified by the drive toward international diversification of capital and the impressive expansion of derivative markets (interest and currency forwards, options, and swaps). These steps occurred along with an important shift in the direction of macroeconomic policy away from its traditional focus on full employment and toward price stability. The success of these actions has been considerable on both fronts. Derivative markets today provide a broad range of hedging instruments for managing currency- and interest rate risks in major currencies. On the macroeconomic front, industrial countries and many developing countries have had considerable success in attaining stability, with smaller fiscal deficits and lower inflation and interest rates. Indeed cross-country empirical research shows that during the 1990s volatility in main macroeconomic variables—economic growth, export growth, and inflation—was down more than 60 percent from the 1980s.

The 1990s: Massive Growth and a Technological Revolution Change the Landscape

The acceleration in the globalization of capital markets and the resulting increase in the volume of cross-country capital flows and financial transactions in the 1990s have profoundly altered the structure of international financial markets. This globalization of finance is partly the result of advances in communication and information technologies, which reduced cross-border transaction costs and information asymmetry.[7] It has also come from financial innovations. The creation of the euro-currency money market centers linking national money and capital markets of major industrial countries, the spread of modern risk management techniques, and the rapid extension of hedge funds have facilitated cross-border capital flows. The liberalization of insurance and pension sectors in developed countries increased liquidity and the supply of capital to developing countries. Domestic reforms in the developing world also contributed to the globalization of finance, with the privatization of public enterprises, macroeconomic stabilization, and the relaxation of barriers to cross-border trade in financial instruments for both sovereign and private entities. All this, in turn, improved country creditworthiness and expanded investment opportunities. Reflecting the influence of these developments, international financial markets have grown significantly in recent years. The volume in international lending in new medium and long-term bonds and bank loans reached $1.2 trillion in 1997, up from $0.5 trillion in 1988.[8] International financial transactions, at more than five times the value of world gross domestic product (GDP), now dwarf world trade. The average daily turnover in foreign exchange markets reached $1.6 trillion in 1995 (up from $0.2 trillion in 1986), compared with the $4.7 trillion a year in trade in goods and services. The ratio of total global market capitalization of stock markets relative to world GDP rose from 23:1 in 1986 to 68:1 in 1996, while derivative markets expanded from $7.9 trillion in 1991 to $40.9 trillion in 1997 (see table 15-1).

Barriers to the free flow of capital across national boundaries, such as capital controls and foreign exchange restrictions have also been significantly dismantled.[9] In the OECD countries, progress toward liberalization of capital controls accelerated, particularly during the 1980s, as members' liberalization obligations under the Code of Liberalization of Capital Movements were broadened to include virtually all capital movements, including short-term transactions by enterprises and individuals.[10] Thus

---

7. From a historical perspective, the globalization of finance in the 1990s is equivalent to the level reached during the gold standard period from 1870 to 1914. However, the latter applied only to a few industrial countries. See Verdier (1998).

8. Bank for International Settlements, *Annual Report* (1998).

9. In 1974 the United States removed the temporary capital restrictions that had been imposed in the mid-1960s. See Helleiner (1994).

10. See Organization for Economic Cooperation and Development (1990).

Table 15-1. *Growth of Derivatives Markets, 1991–97*
Notional values in billions of U.S. dollars

	Instruments traded on exchanges					Over-the-counter (OTC) instruments			
Year	Interest rate futures	Interest rate options	Currency futures and options	Stock market index futures and options	Total	Interest rate options	Interest rate swaps	Currency swaps	Total
1991	2,157	1,073	81	109	3,519	577	3,065	807	4,449
1992	2,913	1,385	98	238	4,635	635	3,851	860	5,346
1993	4,959	2,362	110	340	7,771	1,398	6,177	900	8,475
1994	5,778	2,624	96	366	8,863	1,573	8,816	915	11,303
1994	5,863	2,742	82	502	9,189	3,705	12,811	1,197	17,713
1996	5,931	3,278	97	574	9,880	4,723	19,171	1,560	25,453
1997	7,489	3,640	85	993	12,207	5,033	22,116	1,585	28,733

Source: Bank for International Settlements, *Annual Report* (various issues).

the United Kingdom abolished all exchange controls and achieved capital account convertibility in 1979, Japan in 1980; the timeline for the rest of the OECD stretched until 1992, when the last group—comprising Greece, Ireland, Portugal, and Spain—completed the abolition of their capital controls. Thus, by the early 1990s, the capital accounts of OECD countries were open to a wide range of cross-border financial transactions including capital market securities, money market operations, forward operations, swaps, and other derivatives. This process of liberalization, coupled with internationalization of financial markets, means that today in OECD countries borrowers can raise financing in their desired currency at competitive terms, and investors have the opportunity to achieve their desired degree of portfolio diversification in terms of currencies, maturities, and risk profile.

Regarding emerging market economies, the overall trends have also been toward reform of local financial markets and liberalization of cross-border capital movements, but the progress, the pace, and the scale of liberation measures have not been even. The underlying liberalization trends have been most clear with regard to the rapid increase in the number of countries that have assumed the IMF's Article VIII, thereby declaring their currencies convertible on current accounts, an action that often precedes capital account convertibility. In 1970 only 34 countries, or 30 percent of the IMF membership, had declared their currency convertible on current account transactions. By 1997, 143 countries had done so (see table 15-2). In the 1990s alone, 38 countries, including India, Israel, Greece, the Philippines, Russia, and Turkey, assumed IMF Article VIII (see appendix, table 15A-1). With regard to liberalization of capital controls in emerging market economies, two sets of indicators are of interest. First, actual flows of capital witnessed a significant expansion in the 1990s, with sharp drops in 1997 and 1998, and recovering once again in 1999.[11] Second, the deliberate policies of national governments in the 1990s clearly reflect a considerable degree of opening up, relaxing, and easing of exchange restrictions, controls, and barriers to the entry of foreign financial players to engage in commercial banking, securities, asset management, and other financial services.

---

11. The net flow of foreign capital to developing countries rose from $98 billion in 1990 to $335 billion in 1997, a major part of it originating from foreign direct investment (FDI), portfolio investments in domestic stocks and bonds, commercial bank lending, and the issues of equity and bonds in offshore markets. FDI flows to developing countries increased more than sixfold from 1990 to 1998, and their share of global FDI flows has risen from 25 percent in 1991 to an estimated 42 percent in 1998, compared with 18 percent in the mid-1980s (World Bank [1998]).

Table 15-2. *Number of Countries Assuming Article VIII, 1970–97*

Countries	1970	1975	1980	1985	1990	1997
Article VIII members	34	44	51	61	70	143
All member countries	115	129	142	150	155	186
Article VIII members as percent of member countries	30	34	36	41	45	77

Source: IMF, *Annual Report on Exchange Arrangements and Exchange Restrictions* (various years).

How Open Are Emerging Market Economies to International Capital Movements?

Evidence regarding the degree or level of openness of emerging market economies to cross-border capital flows is scanty and fragmented. Informational and methodological problems have hindered the proper development of quantitative measures of the degree of financial openness. In contrast to measures of trade openness (or protection), for which a fair degree of consensus exists on both methodology and systematic data availability, research on measuring the degree of countries' openness to international finance remains in its infancy and requires attention. Most studies in the past have relied on measures of incidence of capital controls, that is, whether a particular transaction is subject to restrictions rather than the degrees of intensity of such restrictions and controls.[12] In practice, controls can take a variety of forms, ranging from direct quantitative limitations on certain transactions or associated transfers, to indirect measures (such as withholding taxes or reserves on external assets or liabilities) that are intended to influence the economic incentives of engaging in certain transactions. Such controls could apply to the transfer of funds associated with financial transactions or to the underlying transactions themselves. Of course, no single measure of a country's level of openness exists. Researchers have relied on a variety of proxies and indicators to assess the degree of openness to capital flows. There are, however, important benchmarks, such as a country's assumption of the IMF's Article VIII, or currency convertibility on capital accounts. A viable measure of a country's level of financial openness to international capital markets needs to incorporate, at the least, the distinc-

12. See, for instance, Razin and Rose (1994); Alesina, Grilli, and Milesi-Ferretti (1994).

tion between the severity of controls and the different types of transactions contributing to capital flows. Table 15-3 provides preliminary information on such a measure for a sample of ninety-six countries in 1997.

The measure referred to as the Financial Openness Index is constructed using disaggregated measures of capital controls based on the classification and information contained in the IMF's *Annual Report on Exchange Arrangements and Exchange Restrictions* (AREAER) and draws on the coding methodology developed by Dennis Quinn and A. Maria Toyoda.[13] The measure is a composite index of our coding of rules, regulations, and administrative procedures affecting capital flows (both inflows and outflows) for a total of twenty-seven individual transactions in the current and capital accounts of the balance of payments for each country in the sample. Thus out of ninety-six countries in the sample, it is interesting to note that forty-six can be classified, as of 1997, as open and ten as semi-open, with both of these categories including emerging market economies in Latin America and Eastern Europe. The Financial Openness Index has a correlation of 0.51 with the length of time that a country has accepted the conditions of IMF Article VIII.[14]

Toward a Broader Framework for Financial Risk Management

Among scholars and policymakers concerned with international finance, openness to international capital movements, democratic forms of governance, and national policy autonomy command respect. How attainable are these goals? And under what conditions? These two questions have been much debated in the literature on international economics and politics. That these goals occupy such official and scholarly attention clearly reflects the remarkable global success in the advance of democracy, political and civil liberty, and financial integration.

Fundamental Objectives and Trade-offs

A closer look at cross-sectional evidence uncovers a robust, positive association between indicators of financial openness and political and civil liberty

---

13. Quinn and Toyoda (1997).

14. Correlation is calculated between the Financial Openness Index and the logarithm of the number of years since a country has assumed the IMF's Article VIII.

Table 15-3. *Financial Openness in Selected Developed and Developing Countries, 1997*

Country	Index[a]	Country	Index[a]	Country	Index[a]	Country	Index[a]
Open[b]							
Argentina	1.78	France	1.73	Lithuania	1.85	Singapore	1.78
Australia	1.77	Germany	1.84	Luxembourg	1.93	Spain	1.82
Austria	1.92	Greece	1.91	Mauritius	1.82	Sweden	1.86
Bahrain	1.73	Guatemala	1.73	Mexico	1.69	Switzerland	1.88
Belgium	1.88	Guyana	1.72	Netherlands	1.87	Trinidad and	
Bolivia	1.79	Iceland	1.74	New Zealand	1.90	Tobago	1.67
Canada	1.92	Ireland	1.93	Nicaragua	1.82	United	
Denmark	1.92	Italy	1.84	Norway	1.83	Kingdom	1.86
Egypt	1.81	Jamaica	1.76	Panama	1.90	United States	1.85
El Salvador	1.91	Japan	1.73	Paraguay	1.81	Uruguay	1.77
Estonia	1.88	Kuwait	1.77	Peru	1.90	Venezuela	1.84
Finland	1.83	Latvia	1.88	Portugal	1.84	Zambia	1.79
Largely open[c]							
Croatia	1.54	Israel	1.59	Poland	1.54	Slovenia	1.50
Ecuador	1.54	Mongolia	1.56	Slovak		Turkey	1.52
Honduras	1.56	Philippines	1.59	Republic	1.58		
Partially closed[d]							
Bahamas	1.36	Colombia	1.38	Indonesia	1.46	Romania	1.48
Belize	1.44	Congo,		Korea,		Russian	
Benin	1.48	Democratic		Republic of	1.42	Federation	1.43
Botswana	1.48	Republic	1.42	Lesotho	1.41	South Africa	1.44
Bulgaria	1.46	Costa Rica	1.48	Mali	1.49	Sri Lanka	1.43
Burkina Faso	1.49	Czech		Malta	1.40	Thailand	1.46
Burundi	1.39	Republic	1.48	Moldova	1.46	Tunisia	1.39
Cameroon	1.41	Dominican		Mozambique	1.41	Ukraine	1.36
Cape Verde	1.39	Republic	1.49	Namibia	1.33		
Chile	1.43	Ghana	1.43	Papua New			
China	1.37	Hungary	1.49	Guinea	1.36		
Largely closed[e]							
Bangladesh	1.21	Brazil	1.19	Malawi	1.26	Pakistan	1.31
Barbados	1.28	Ethiopia	1.12	Malaysia	1.34	Syria	1.20
Bhutan	1.19	India	1.20	Morocco	1.27		

Source: Author's calculations based on data from IMF, *Annual Report on Exchange Arrangements and Exchange Restrictions* (various years).

a. The Financial Openness Index scoring draws on the methodology originally developed by Quinn and Inclan (1997), and is based on information contained in IMF, *Annual Report on Exchange Arrangements and Exchange Restrictions*, 1998. For a full explanation of the scoring, see appendix 15A.

b. Open: Little or no regulation for outward or inward transactions, with a generally nondiscriminatory environment.

c. Largely open: Some regulations are exercised on outward and inward transactions requiring documentary support but not governmental approval.

d. Partially closed: Regulation with governmental approval required for outward and inward transactions and usually granted.

e. Largely closed: Substantial restrictions, with governmental approval required but seldom granted for outward and inward transactions.

across a large sample of countries, as shown by figure 15-1. Such partial correlation coefficients are statistically significant (at a 99 percent confidence level), and lend credibility to the argument that countries that are more open to international capital flows are also open in offering a high degree of political and civil liberty to their citizens, and indeed, such countries scale high on the democracy index, where democracy is defined as a composite index of civil and political liberty.[15] Much current debate probes how best to achieve this "triangle," and balance the benefits with the risks inherent in its pursuit.

The economic benefits of open capital accounts are well articulated and widely known for both individual countries and the global economy as a whole. Major benefits for developing countries include access to a broader menu of investment sources, options, and instruments. They also include enhanced efficiency of domestic financial institutions, and the discipline of capital markets in conducting domestic macroeconomic policy. And by easing financing constraints, the greater availability of international finance can extend the period for countries to implement needed adjustments.[16]

---

15. For more detailed discussion on the link between financial openness and democracy see Dailami (2000). Our measure of democracy follows the recent literature exploring the role of democracy on economic growth (Helliwell [1992]), income levels (Londregan and Poole [1996]), and wages (Rodrik [1999]). This measure defines democracy as a composite index and draws on the Freedom House measures of political and civil liberty; that is:

$$\text{Democracy} = \frac{14 - civil\ rights - political\ rights}{12}.$$

This index will be defined from 0 to 1, with 0 indicating low democracy and 1 indicating high democracy. Political and civil liberty indexes are from the *Comparative Survey of Freedom* that Freedom House has published annually since 1973. The survey rates each country on a seven-point scale for both political rights and civil liberties (1 representing the most free and 7 the least free) and assesses a country's freedom by examining its record in these two areas. A country grants its citizens political rights when it permits them to form political parties that represent a significant range of voter choice and whose leaders can openly compete for and be elected to positions of power in government. A country upholds its citizens' civil liberties when it respects and protects their religious, ethnic, economic, linguistic, and other rights, including gender and family rights, personal freedoms, and freedoms of the press, belief, and association. The survey divides the world into three broad categories: "free" (countries whose ratings average between 1 and 3); "partly free" (countries whose ratings average between 3 and 5.5); and "not free" (countries whose ratings average between 5.5 and 7). For more detail, see Karatnycky (1999).

16. Markets will be willing to provide this leeway, however, only if they perceive that countries are truly undertaking adjustments that fundamentally address existing and prospective imbalances. Otherwise, markets will eventually exert their own discipline, in such a way that the time period for adjustment may be brutally shortened. See Dailami and Haque (1998).

Figure 15-1. *Correlations of Capital Openness with Political Rights and Civil Liberties*[a]

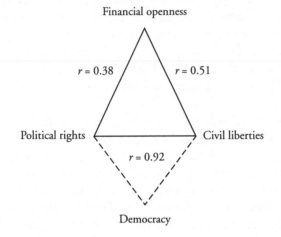

Source: Author's calculations.
a. The estimated correlation coefficients are statistically significant at 1 percent (based on the z test).

For the global economy, open capital accounts support the multilateral trading system, expanding the opportunities for portfolio diversification and efficient allocation of global savings and investment.[17] There is also an important property rights issue related to the free movement of capital across national boundaries. As Richard Cooper states, "individuals should be free to dispose of their income and wealth as they see fit, provided their doing so does not harm others."[18] This view, embodying the thinking behind a liberal order, constitutes the "ideal" for the reconstruction of the international financial system toward which to aspire.[19]

Another perspective questions whether the benefits of closer financial integration outweigh its socioeconomic costs. Volatility in capital flows creates uncertainty in economic growth, and this perception of vulnerability

17. Fischer (1998).
18. Cooper (1998, p. 12).
19. Lawrence Summers, U.S. Secretary of the Treasury, has emphasized the importance of a liberal paradigm in building a new international financial architecture, as well, stating, "We should all be able to agree on the danger of . . . denying a country's own citizens the capacity to convert their own currency and invest abroad. Such measures represent substantial intrusions on freedom." Summers (1999).

to the internationalization of capital flows sees developing countries on the periphery. In the design and functioning of the post–World War II international monetary and financial system, developing countries exerted little influence. The supply of foreign capital to them was mostly in the form of official aid, grants, and loans intended for governments or public entities through multilateral or bilateral agencies. Private capital was marginal, and it surged only in the 1970s with an expansion of commercial bank lending that ended with the debt crisis in the 1980s. That was followed by a resumption of capital flows to emerging markets that culminated in a currency crisis in Mexico during the winter of 1994–95 and a deeper financial crisis in East Asia in 1997–98. Thus it is increasingly being argued that under some circumstances—that is, weakness in local financial markets, euphoria and panic behavior of foreign investors, and structural balance-of-payments problems—there exists a case for deploying capital controls, particularly on short-term flows, to reduce volatility. In this respect, Chile's capital controls experience, as will be argued later, has attracted considerable interest, partly because of its market-based nature, transparency, and the fact that it is easier to phase out restrictions based on taxation than those on quantitative controls, as discussed below.

Mechanisms and Arrangements

In the present, risk management demands more judicious strategies, both at the institutional level (that is, corporate and financial institutions) and the national policy level. The global financial landscape has witnessed significant changes: the internationalization of the banking business; the breakdown of traditional boundaries between different sectors, such as banking, insurance, and underwriting; the rise of emerging markets as important investment opportunities; and the broader investor base in emerging market economies, which includes commercial banks, pension funds, hedge funds, and mutual and insurance industries. All pose new challenges and require a more effective risk management approach.

Particularly striking in the 1990s have been the numerous liquidity and currency crises, such as those experienced by the European Monetary System in 1992–93, Mexico in 1994–95, East Asia (Indonesia, Malaysia, the Philippines, South Korea, and Thailand) in 1997, and Brazil and Russia in 1998. All these emerging markets first had a surge in capital flows (from the early- to mid-1990s) and then fell victim to sudden reversals—

on the order of 10 percent of GDP in East Asia. The episodes in 1997–98 offer examples of how one of the largest markets in the world—the market for capital—could fail at several levels. Borrowing countries were not properly monitoring the high exposure of their domestic banks and corporations to foreign currency risk. Major international players, such as credit rating agencies, failed to properly assess the country risk in the globalizing financial environment of the 1990s. The financial risk management specialists failed to identify the causes of the contagion effect in emerging market economies by underestimating the positive correlations that existed between individual private sector credit quality and the broader sovereign or country credit quality. Regulators failed because of the weakness of their regulatory and supervisory frameworks.

Four other salient features of international finance in the 1990s have helped to shape its character and warrant further discussion. First, high risks of contagion across countries exist in international capital and loan markets. During the Asian crisis, the world witnessed financial meltdowns spreading from one country to another. Second, these crises and their corresponding shocks were largely unforeseen and unexpected by market participants. Credit spreads on emerging market debt declined, and international bank lending continued to expand until just before the beginning of the Asian crisis.

A third feature is the extent to which capital flows into many developing countries were channeled through short-term banking instruments, as banks were perceived to have implicit government guarantees. As a result, credit standards and prudent project appraisals were often compromised, leading to overinvestment in sectors with surplus capacity or declining demand. Indeed, it appears that many market participants, if not most, succumbed to the inherent moral hazard in these perceived government guarantees. This accounts for the simultaneous incidence of foreign exchange liquidity crises in countries with fixed exchange rates and collapses of their domestic banking systems.

Fourth, the primary sources of instability originated in the capital account, unlike the current account problems that, historically, Bretton Woods institutions were designed to prevent. This recognition has implications for the design of policy responses—and for the traditional approach to country risk assessment. In today's globalized financial environment, a better measure of a country's external payments position is the condition of its total balance sheet—that is, its assets and liabilities, with liabilities including both debt and equity.

In summary, looking deeper into why the decade proceeded in such a manner, it can safely be stated that many developing countries moved in the 1990s to liberalize financial markets and relax restrictions on capital transactions without putting into place adequate institutional frameworks on money, foreign exchange markets, and capital markets. As countries liberalized, access to a broader menu of foreign financing was opened to banks and corporate borrowers, with strong incentives for recourse to foreign finance. The desirability of longer-maturity foreign capital for funding infrastructure projects in particular provided a strong competitive advantage to foreign capital, particularly in countries with an exchange rate regime pegged to the U.S. dollar. As the private sector has increasingly become the main recipient of foreign capital, the vulnerability to financial risk has increased. However, neither the maturity nor the foreign exchange risk associated with foreign capital was taken into account or properly priced.

Such weaknesses on the domestic side, coupled with changes in the composition and nature of capital flows has generated amplified cycles of boom and bust, not only in the volume of capital flows, but also in the pattern of spreads in emerging market economies' foreign currency obligations. To provide a quantitative estimate of the extent of this shift in sentiment among international investors and creditors, table 15-4 shows estimates of the default probabilities associated with indicative values of spreads on emerging market economies' dollar-denominated bonds, as tracked, for instance, by the J. P. Morgan EMBI+ index.[20] As measured by this often-used benchmark index, spreads on emerging market economies' dollar-denominated bonds spiked in 1995 and 1998 as a result of the Mexican and Russian crises respectively to about 1600 basis points, which was clearly not warranted by the deterioration in credit quality or economic fundamentals of these emerging market economies. Thus when spreads are in the range of 100 to 300 basis points, as was the case before the crisis in Asia, the implicit default probabilities are estimated to be between 2 and 5 percent. As the spreads spiked in September 1998 to 1600

20. The J. P. Morgan EMBI+ index is an extension of the Emerging Markets Bond Index and includes emerging market non-Brady bond spreads. EMBI+ tracks total returns for external currency-denominated debt instruments from sixteen emerging market economies: Argentina, Brazil, Bulgaria, Colombia, Ecuador, Mexico, Morocco, Nigeria, Panama, Peru, the Philippines, Poland, Russia, South Korea, Turkey, and Venezuela.

Table 15-4. *Summary Results of Simulated Spreads and Default Probability*[a]

Percent

Spread	Default probability	Volatility
1.0	2.0	7.4
1.5	3.0	9.0
2.0	4.0	10.3
2.5	5.0	11.5
3.0	6.0	12.6
6.0	12.0	17.2
10.0	20.0	21.3
16.0	32.0	25.2
20.0	40.0	26.7

Source: Author's calculations.

a. Based on a stylized credit risk model, in which a default-no default process is assumed to follow a binomial event, and the rate of recovery—in the event of a default—is assumed to be a random variable of between 0 and 100 percent and is specified as a beta distribution. The spread over a benchmark rate is interpreted as the mean of the unconditional loss distribution function, incorporating both the probability of default and the rate of recovery. This model is available from the author on request.

basis points, the implied probability of default increased to the high level of 32 percent.[21]

Firm-Level Risk Management

Financial risk management at the institutional level advanced significantly in the late 1990s. Today, financial and nonfinancial institutions use quantitative risk measurement techniques such as value at risk (VAR), volatility and beta measures, option-pricing models, and Sharpe ratios. Using these tools, financial institutions have the ability to systematically measure and

21. Shifts in the supply of foreign capital have been triggered by exogenous factors, such as the increase in oil prices in the 1970s, the deregulation of pension funds and insurance companies in major industrial countries in the late 1980s, or by shifts in investors' sentiments and expectations. The latter problem could happen because of incomplete information between creditors that could render their decision to run or flee from a particular country dependent on the behavior of others. This dependence can generate a run, analogous to a bank run in domestic settings during the 1990s, adding a noncooperation premium on top of other country risk premiums. See Haldane (1999) for further elaboration of this point.

control market-related risk under normal volatility. At the same time, with innovation and the advances in technology and communications, financial risk management practice has improved significantly in recent years. The evolution of VAR in the mid-1990s has led to a significant improvement in financial institutions' ability to measure market-related risk under normal volatility conditions in a systematic manner. It has also stimulated a wealth of literature and computer-based modeling with applications particularly in the banking sector for regulatory capital calculation (allowed under the January 1996 amendment to the Basel Committee on Bank Supervision) and as a benchmark for market risk.[22] Also, with the increasing corporate focus on shareholder value and the expansion in the number and complexity of financial instruments, the emerging perspective on risk management at a corporate level is shifting toward a companywide integrated approach, encompassing credit, market, and operational risks in a holistic manner, integrating more closely market risk, credit risk, and measurement processes. The rapid expansion in the credit derivatives market is fundamentally changing the banking business by providing opportunities to trade credit risk.

Risk Management at the National Level

From the national perspective, a dilemma facing democratic societies is how to best manage financial market integration to benefit from the economic efficiency associated with integration while safeguarding against the risks of capital flow volatility and associated economic instability. To cope with such risks, countries can resort to capital controls or to the provision of social insurance through the marketplace or through redistribution.

The Role of Redistribution in Mitigating Risk

The motivation for redistribution as income insurance—as distinct from altruism and other poverty reduction–related motives—is induced

---

22. VAR summarizes the worst expected loss over a specific time horizon, within a pre-defined confidence level, such as 99 percent or 95 percent. The literature on VAR is vast; see Jorion (1996); recent application of VAR has also raised important questions. For example, how can extreme market situations, that is, low probabilities, and high loss events that occur beyond the 99 percent or 95 percent confidence level—that might affect portfolio value—be incorporated in the modeling process through stress testing, extreme value theory, scenario testing? How might a widespread use of VAR affect contagion?

by volatility and insecurity in underlying economic conditions and by citizens' aversion to risk.[23, 24] Uncertainty over future economic position and income level can be an important source of demand for insurance-like redistribution. An important source of volatility in economic conditions can be volatility in capital flows, as demonstrated most radically by the recent Asian financial crises. The basic argument can be elaborated more clearly in Albert Hirschman's terminology of exit and voice.[25] In a world with a high degree of capital mobility across national borders, open democratic societies face a dilemma in how to balance the threat of exit of capital (made more credible by the opening of capital markets) with the political demands for voice and increased political incentives for government intervention in cushioning market dislocation. Financial market integration has increased the exit potential of capital, as investors' ability to shift their financial resources to other countries has increased by virtue of the openness of capital markets. The threat of the exit of capital in this sense refers not only to investors' decisions regarding existing foreign assets that can be liquidated or un-wound but also to domestic liquid assets, such as money, and other liquid assets that can be converted and transferred.[26]

Arguments about the link between redistribution and financial openness can also be anchored in the median voter model with risk aversion.[27] Thus, in its simplest form, the median voter model predicts that in a democratic system, the median voter will use the ballot box to facilitate self-interested redistribution. Citizens face a trade-off between the costs and benefits of income redistribution. The main benefits consist of a reduction in the variance of future levels of income, and the costs are the deadweight costs associated with government intervention, as well as the fiscal costs associated with financing such redistributive schemes. Any

---

23. The idea of distribution as insurance has, of course, a long tradition in welfare economics going back to Lerner (1994); Harsanyi (1953); and Rawls (1971). More recently, this issue has been analyzed from the perspective of constitutional political economy: see Mueller (1998); Wessels (1993).

24. See Wessels (1993) for a justification of this type of redistributive scheme, within the realm of methodological individualism.

25. Hirschman (1970).

26. The exercise of exit of capital can be seen as a function of the degree of the "liquidity" of the underlying assets—the more liquid the assets, the less transaction costs involved—and the degree of financial openness of the country. For fixed assets, such as investments in plants and equipment with high sunk-in costs, the transaction cost for liquidating an investment is much higher.

27. Bishop, Formby, and Smith (1991). The median voter model has been used in the literature on the politics of income redistribution as a framework for analyzing political choice.

involuntary redistribution—that is, one not motivated by altruism—is bound to entail deadweight economic costs. One type of cost is the cost related to the government bureaucracy needed to administer transfers— the enforcement costs—or as Bruce Benson has categorized them, rent seeking and rent avoidance.[28] There is also an important dynamic cost: there is less incentive to invest when property rights are not secure and a possibility exists for involuntary income transfers. In addition, redistribution policy is often financed through discretionary taxation, which is associated with fiscal and macroeconomic costs that need to be taken into account. How this trade-off between the costs and benefits of redistribution is resolved remains an important question, on which the experience of OECD countries could shed some light.

The counterbalance to the threat of exit of capital is the political voice by citizens demanding protection against external risk through redistribution, social safety net programs, and other insurance-like measures.[29] Indeed, critical in easing the tension between politics and financial openness in OECD countries has been the role of their redistributive policies in mitigating and redistributing risk through massive transfer payments and other insurance-like government involvement. Government expenditures on health, education, social security, and welfare in high-income OECD countries during recent years (1991–97) have averaged about 25 percent of their GDP, with smaller open European countries such as Denmark, Norway, and Sweden spending as much as 30 percent of their GDP.[30]

Table 15-5 reports the statistical summary of the key variables classified by countries' degree of openness. Of interest here is the wide difference in countries' degree of redistribution as measured by the ratio of government social expenditure to GDP. Thus countries classified as financially open spend on the average 22.3 percent of their GDP on social expenditure, as compared to 6.7 percent among financially closed countries. The view that financial openness, democracy, and government social spending go hand in hand is confirmed by the econometric results shown in figure 15-1. The cross-country data, with sample size ranging from 70 to 140, show statistically significant

28. Benson (1999).

29. In this interpretation "voice" belongs to the political sphere; the form that it takes and how it is exercised are a function of the underlying political institution and particularly the degree of political and civil liberty.

30. Focusing on globalization through trade, Rodrik (1997) also emphasizes the relationship between redistribution and openness.

Table 15-5. *Taxonomy of Financial Openness*[a]

Variable	Open	Largely open	Largely closed	Closed
		Country grouping		
Democracy index[b]	0.81	0.71	0.63	0.48
Civil liberties index[c]	2.28	3.30	3.38	4.55
GDP per capita (U.S. dollars)[d]	13,147	3,051	2,317	1,557
Social expenditure (percent of GDP)[e]	22.3	23.5	12.5	6.7
Total government expenditures (percent of GDP)[f]	26.0	19.9	23.4	27.7
General government consumption (percent of GDP)[g]	16.1	17.9	15.5	14.7
Number of countries	46	10	34	11

a. The table displays group averages computed for the countries for which data were available.

b. Democracy index ranges from 0 (lowest) to 1 (highest) and is computed on the bases of political rights and civil liberties indexes. See note 15.

c. See note 15.

d. Average 1990–97.

e. Includes the sum of health, education, and social security and welfare, average 1991–97.

f. Average of central government and budgetary accounts plus state or provincial government, 1990–97.

g. Includes all current expenditures for purchases of goods and services by all levels of government, excluding most government enterprises. It also includes capital expenditure on national defense and security, 1990–97.

results for all three relationships based on a z test, with the highest correlation between political liberty and government social expenditures.

Moving from an analysis of correlations to a reflection on the significance of redistribution on the degree of financial openness and democracy in countries, we first group countries in a 2×2 classification along the democracy and financial openness axis. Figure 15-2 shows the number of countries in each category, as well as the mean value for the countries in each quadrant, of average government expenditures on health, education, and transfer payments as a percentage of GDP for the period 1991–97 (in parentheses). From the matrix, it could be argued that the difference in mean between the two groups (High Democracy and High Financial Openness versus Low Democracy and Low Financial Openness) was highly significant at the 0.1 percent level.

Figure 15-2. *Country Classification: Political Rights and Financial Openness*[a]

Financial openness

		Low	High
Democracy	Low	23 (8.86)	9 (9.09)
	High	32 (18.24)	37 (25.59)

a. A high level of democracy means a democracy index greater than 0.6. A high level of financial openness is defined by a score greater than 1.6 in the Financial Openness Index. An alternate measure of openness of an economic nature is the Fraser Institute's Economic Freedom of the World rankings. These rankings are strongly correlated with the Financial Openness Index (0.70) and show a correlation of 0.49 with the Democracy Index. The 95 percent confidence interval for the difference in means is 11.15–21.74.

The empirical evidence reported in table 15-5 also supports the proposition that the relationship between financial openness and democracy is partly a function of the level of income, and more precisely, per capita income: rich countries are, with few exceptions, democratic in government, either presidential or parliamentarian in type. Rich countries are also open to international capital movement, as they have a high degree of financial sector development, currency convertibility on capital accounts, and enjoy macroeconomic stability and highly developed and stable expectations of peaceful regime change, domestic rule of law, and stable institutions that guarantee civil and political liberty.[31]

Yet at a deeper level of analysis, the link between democracy and financial openness proves to be complex, revealing more than just the influence of the level of income. International policy coordination in macroeconomic policy and in financial regulation and supervision is part of the answer, but not all. Controlling for the level of income, one factor that figures prominently in

31. For a more detailed discussion of the link between democracy and financial openness, see Dailami (2000).

the linkage between democracy and financial openness is redistributive policy, in the form of social security, health, housing, welfare, education, and transfer payments. Empirical investigations, based on a multinominal logit model[32] of country classifications along the two axes of democracy and financial openness, as shown in figure 15-2, confirm the proposition. Both per capita income and the ratio of social expenditures to GDP have a statistically significant impact in explaining the likelihood that a country falls into the high-high category.[33] The model also performs well in predicting the percentage of countries that are correctly classified as belonging to the high democracy-high financial openness group,[34] that is, out of twenty-seven countries in the high-high group, nineteen were correctly predicted to be in that group (based on the threshold probability of 0.5), thus producing a 70.37 percent correct classification rate.

Capital Controls as an Instrument of Risk Management

An alternative approach for resolving the tension between capital market integration and national policy autonomy is the use of capital controls. Interest in this approach has been rekindled by recent financial crises in Asia and Latin America in both academic and policy circles. Thus it is increasingly being argued that under some circumstances (that is, weakness in local financial markets, euphoria and panic behavior of foreign investors, and structural balance-of-payments problems), there is a case for deploying capital controls, particularly on short-term flows, to reduce volatility. In this respect, a range of market-based capital flow interventions are available, ranging from contingent liquidity facilities (less severe) to tax and reserve requirements on selected inflows. Chile's capital controls experience has attracted considerable interest, partly because of its market-based nature, transparency, and the fact that it is easier to phase out restrictions based on taxation than those based on quantitative controls. Recent analy-

32. See Dailami (2000), for a more detailed analysis.

33. Using these estimates, we can also estimate the probabilities of each country belonging to the high-high group, as opposed to all other groups. Given this probability, one can classify a country to the group that has the predicted probability greater than or equal to 0.5. This classification can be compared with the actual grouping of the data, and the percentages of correctly predicted countries can be computed for both target and nontarget groups.

34. It is important to note that our estimated results are based on the logit model and the 2×2 country classification along the democracy and financial openness indexes. As with such categorical dependent variable models, the results may be sensitive to the particular standard of classification adopted.

sis indicates that the Chilean experience has been made partially effective by changing the debt composition—reducing short-term capital inflows while increasing long-term ones—and by allowing for a larger wedge between domestic and foreign interest rates. Many of these effects are likely to be temporary, as controls are bound to lose their effectiveness in today's highly mobile capital environment.

The Role of International Policy Coordination

International policy coordination in macroeconomic policy and in financial regulation and supervision merits special attention. As generally recognized, macroeconomic policy coordination among major industrial countries has been instrumental in reducing payment imbalances, in stabilizing expectations for currency and interest rate movements, and in lessening the volatility of capital flows across their borders.[35] In the same vein, the coordination of international banking regulation in industrial countries has been significant, as exemplified by the Basel Capital Accord of 1992 and the subsequent Core Principles for Effective Banking Supervision. With the memory of the 1980s debt crisis and its prolonged resolution still alive, the international policy and regulatory responses to the 1997–99 crises were prompt. These included an easing of monetary policy in the major industrial countries; extension of large standby and direct multilateral and bilateral rescue loans; development of internationally agreed codes and standards of good practice, transparency, and disclosure; and establishment of a plethora of high-level committees with the aim of strengthening the safety and soundness of banks and other financial firms involved in international capital flows. The international financial assistance committed from August 1997 to December 1998 to Brazil, Indonesia, Thailand, Russia, and South Korea amounted to $190 billion—1.4 times their foreign exchange reserves and 30 percent of the reserves of all developing countries at the end of 1997.[36] The Miyazawa Plan, unveiled by the government of Japan in October 1997, committed $30 billion in yen-denominated assistance loans to Asian countries affected by the crisis. Furthermore, in February 1999 the G-7 finance ministers and central bank governors endorsed the creation of a Financial Stability Forum to bring

35. See Webb (1994) and Bryant and Hodgkinson (1989) for a discussion of international policy coordination in macroeconomics; and Kapstein (1989) for international coordination of banking regulation.

36. See Dailami (1998); and Eichengreen (1996) for further elaboration.

together the monetary authorities from the G-7, principal regulatory agencies, and the multilaterals and to serve as a focal point for assessing vulnerabilities affecting the global financial system and identifying and overseeing the required actions.

Conclusion

The enormous expansion of international financial markets in the 1990s and the higher mobility of capital across national borders relative to both national economic activity and world GDP means that any sustained disruption in financial flows will have far-reaching implications for growth, investment, and employment. As demonstrated by recent financial crises in emerging market countries, the costs to affected countries can be staggering and provide a strong basis for evolving better mechanisms and strategies for managing global financial risks, with a view toward minimizing the likelihood of such crises in the future. The analysis in this paper has sought to provide a framework for managing financial risks with regard to developing countries.

The challenge facing the emerging economies in forging closer integration of their capital markets can be seen in two areas. The first encompasses the pace at which these countries should dismantle administrative controls over short-term capital flows and move toward full capital-account convertibility. The second area includes the overall incentive system and regulations that could govern international financial flows to minimize future risks and panics. Countries, both internally and under the rules of an international financial framework, need to develop suitable mechanisms for balancing the benefits of globalization with the risks. These mechanisms must work in a way that reduces the risks of panic and crisis, while remaining committed to free markets, free capital flows, and the principle of individual choice. Though technological advances and the sheer size of financial markets make the risk of panic and crisis an ever-present one, there are various options governments can follow to reduce that risk significantly.

Pursuing sound macroeconomic policies is an obvious first step— indeed, an essential prerequisite. But recent experience also shows that macroeconomic stability alone is not sufficient to guarantee sustainable growth unless reinforced by actions to strengthen domestic regulation and supervision of banks and other intermediaries, to rebuild the information infrastructure of financial markets (including accounting norms), and to improve corporate governance. With the increasing trend toward democracy worldwide, equally important is the availability of mechanisms through which insurance is provided to citizens, either through the marketplace or through redistributive policy, to avert political pressure for capital controls. In the long run, the globalization of capital requires an open institutional framework to ensure transparent accounts, secure property rights, enforceable contracts, as well as regulations to control risk, yet such institutions do not exist or are only in the early stages of development.

This paper presents information suggesting that there is a positive and statistically significant correlation between democracy, open capital flows, and redistributive domestic social policies. This correlation, notwithstanding some data limitation, is significant in unveiling the positive forces at work in generating the convergent trends toward greater democracy and financial openness, as well as the critical role of redistribution—confirmed also by the more rigorous multinomial logit model. One should keep in mind the experience of OECD countries. Capital mobility as a policy objective gained currency and support only after significant trade liberalization and only in democratic countries in which the states had established the ability to respond to citizens' demands for national economic security. By the time all OECD members had achieved full capital openness and convertibility, there was a sophisticated system of state responsibility for risk sharing in place. This must be taken into account when pondering the status and future of developing countries along the road to full capital account convertibility in today's international financial environment.

Table 15A-1. *Date on Which Selected IMF Member Countries Assumed IMF Article VIII*

El Salvador	11/06/46	Iceland	09/19/83
Mexico	11/12/46	Spain	07/15/86
Panama	11/26/46	Indonesia	05/07/88
United States	12/10/46	Portugal	09/12/88
		Republic of Korea	11/01/88
Honduras	07/01/50		
Canada	03/25/52	Turkey	03/22/90
Dominican Republic	08/01/53	Thailand	05/04/90
		Switzerland	05/29/92
Belgium	02/15/61	Greece	07/22/92
France	02/15/61	Tunisia	01/06/93
Germany	02/15/61	Morocco	01/21/93
Ireland	02/15/61	Israel	09/21/93
Luxembourg	02/15/61	Mauritius	09/29/93
Netherlands	02/15/61	Barbados	11/03/93
Sweden	02/15/61	Trinidad and Tobago	12/13/93
Italy	02/15/61	Ghana	02/02/94
United Kingdom	02/15/61	Sri Lanka	03/15/94
Austria	08/01/62	Bangladesh	04/11/94
Jamaica	02/22/63	Lithuania	05/03/94
Kuwait	04/05/63	Latvia	06/10/94
Japan	04/01/64	Pakistan	07/01/94
Nicaragua	07/30/64	Estonia	08/15/94
Costa Rica	02/01/65	India	08/20/94
Australia	07/01/65	Paraguay	08/23/94
Guyana	12/27/66	Malta	11/30/94
Denmark	05/01/67	Croatia	05/29/95
Norway	05/11/67	Poland	06/01/95
Bolivia	06/05/67	Moldova	06/30/95
Argentina	05/14/68	Slovenia	09/01/95
Singapore	11/09/68	Philippines	09/08/95
Malaysia	11/11/68	Czech Republic	10/01/95
		Slovak Republic	10/01/95
Ecuador	08/31/70	Botswana	11/17/95
Bahrain	03/20/73	Malawi	12/07/95
South Africa	09/15/73	Hungary	01/01/96
Bahamas	12/05/73	Mongolia	02/01/96
Papua New Guinea	12/04/75	Benin	06/01/96
Venezuela	07/01/76	Burkina Faso	06/01/96
Chile	07/27/77	Cameroon	06/01/96
		Mali	06/01/96
Uruguay	05/02/80	Russian Federation	06/01/96
New Zealand	08/05/82	Namibia	09/20/96
Belize	06/14/83	Romania	03/25/98

Source: IMF, *Annual Report on Exchange Arrangements and Exchange Restrictions* (1998).

Table 15A-2. Multinomial Logit Results[a]

Variable	Financial openness (high), democracy (high)			Financial openness (low), democracy (high)			Financial openness (high), democracy (low)		
	Co-efficients	Marginal effect	z statistic	Co-efficients	Marginal effect	z statistic	Co-efficients	Marginal effect	z statistic
Log of social expenditure per GDP	2.348*	0.148	2.664	1.739**	0.169	2.195	-0.523	-0.011	-0.538
Log of GDP per capita	1.2091*	0.076	2.725	0.318	0.031	0.826	1.085**	0.022	2.241
Constant	-15.209*	-0.960	-4.186	-6.430**	-0.627	-2.406	-7.860**	-0.158	-2.358

Source: Author's calculations.
* Significant at 1 percent for a two-tailed z test.
** Significant at 5 percent for a two-tailed z test.
a. The reference category is financial openness (low)–democracy (low).

Table 15A-3. Prediction Performance of the Multinomial Logit Model

Actual dependent variable	Predicted dependent variable				Total	Percent correct
	0	1	2	3		
0: Financial openness (low), democracy (low)	13	2	0	2	17	76.5
1: Financial openness (low), democracy (high)	5	3	1	6	15	20.0
2: Financial openness (high), democracy (low)	4	0	1	2	8	14.3
3: Financial openness (high), democracy (high)	1	2	0	25	28	89.3
Total	23	7	2	35	67	62.7

It can be seen that the multinomial logit provided a satisfactory prediction of the two extreme groups (low-low and high-high) but underpredicted the other two groups.

Box 15A-1

We used the multinomial logit model to estimate the likelihood that a given country would fit into each of the 2×2 classifications. This is an extension of the binomial logistic model and can be specified as

$$\Pr(y_{ij} = 1 \,|\, \mathbf{x}_i) = p_i^{(j)} = \frac{\exp(z_i^{(j)})}{1 + \exp(z_i^{(2)}) + \exp(z_i^{(3)}) + \exp(z_i^{(4)})}, \, j = 2,...4$$

$$z_i^{(j)} = \mathbf{a}^{(j)'} \mathbf{x}_i, \, j = 2,3,4 \quad i = 1,...,n,$$

where $p_i^{(j)}$ = the probability that the country i falls in the jth classification; y's are the set of binary response variables, $y_{ij} = 1$ if the country i belongs to the group j and $y_{ij} y_{ij}$ = 0, otherwise; and $\mathbf{x}_i$ is the vector of explanatory variables for the ith country; and n is the total number of countries.

Note that one of the k groups (here it is the first) has to be fixed as a *reference group* (or base category). This means that the coefficients of the corresponding equation must all be set to zero, so that we actually estimate the set of $k - 1$ equations, which in the case of the regular logit model with two groups reduces to a single equation with coefficients $\{a_0, a_1, a_2, ...a_m\}$. It can be easily shown, then, that $\exp(z_i^{(j)})$ expresses the probability that country i belongs to a group j relative to the probability that it belongs to the reference category (here the reference category is the *low-low* group), namely, $\exp(z_i^{(j)}) = \Pr(y_i = j)/\Pr(y_i = 1)$.

$\Delta\Pr(l,j)$ is the marginal change in the probability $\Pr(y_{ij} = 1) = p_i^{(j)}$ resulting from an infinitesimal change in the lth explanatory variable.

$$\Delta\Pr(l,j) \, a_i^{(j)} \frac{\exp(z_i^{(j)})}{\left(1 + \exp(z_i^{(2)}) + \exp(z_i^{(3)}) + \exp(z_i^{(4)})\right)^2}, j = 2,3,4.$$

The values of z are computed at the mean values of the explanatory variables.

The maximum likelihood associated with the above multinomial logit model is given as

$$\ln L = \sum_{i=1}^{n} \left(\sum_{j=1}^{4} y_{ij} \mathbf{a}^{(j)'} \mathbf{x}_i - \ln \sum_{j=1}^{4} e^{\mathbf{a}^{(j)'} \mathbf{x}_i} \right), \text{ under the constraint that } \mathbf{a}^{(1)'} \mathbf{x}_i = 0.$$

We estimate the equation with the explanatory variables defined as (1) per capita GDP, and (2) the log of the ratio of social expenditures to GDP, using cross-country data for a sample of 67 countries for which consistent data on all explanatory variables were available.

Box 15A-2. *Financial Openness Index*

This index is based on information contained in the IMF *Annual Report on Exchange Arrangements and Exchange Restrictions* (1998) and distinguishes between twenty-seven individual transactions, classified into five groups, as shown below.

1. *Imports and Import Payment*
   Foreign exchange budget
   Financing requirements for imports
   Documentation requirements for
     release of foreign exchange for
     imports

   Import licenses and other nontariff
     measures
   Import taxes and/or tariffs
   State import monopoly

2. *Exports and Export Proceeds*
   Repatriation requirements
   Financing requirements
   Documentation requirements

   Export licenses
   Export taxes

3. *Payments for Invisible Transactions and Current Transfers*
   Controls on these payments

4. *Proceeds from Invisible Transactions and Current Transfers*
   Repatriation requirements
   Restrictions on use of funds

5. *Capital Account Transactions*
   Capital market securities
   Money market instruments
   Collective investment securities
   Derivatives and other instruments
   Commercial credits
   Financial credits
   Guarantees, sureties, and financial
     backup facilities

   Direct investment
   Liquidation of direct investment
   Real estate transactions
   Personal capital movements
   Commercial banks and other
     credit institutions
   Institutional investors

The scoring draws on the methodology developed by Quinn and Inclan (1997). It is based on a five-tiered scale of openness that ranges from 0 (highly controlled) to 2 (highly liberal) for each item, indicating the degree of openness as follows:

0.0: Laws or regulations that impose quantitative or other regulatory restrictions on a particular transaction, such as licenses or reserve requirements, that completely forbid such economic transaction;

0.5: Laws or regulations that impose quantitative or other regulatory restrictions on a particular transaction, such as licenses or reserve requirements, that partly forbid such economic transaction;

1.0: Laws or regulations requiring the particular transaction to be approved by authorities or subjecting it to heavy taxes when applicable, whether in the form of multiple currency practices or other taxes;

1.5: Laws or regulations requiring the particular transaction to be registered but not necessarily approved by authorities and also taxed when applicable;

2.0: No regulations requiring the particular transaction to be approved nor registered with authorities and free of taxation when applicable.

The financial openness index for a given country is derived as the arithmetic average overall total score divided by 27, the number of items (see table 15A-2).

References

Alesina, Alberto, Vittorino Grilli, and Gian Maria Milesi-Ferretti. "The Political Economy of Capital Controls." In *Capital Mobility: The Impact on Consumption, Investment, and Growth*, edited by Leonardo Leiderman and Assaf Razin, 289–328. Cambridge University Press.

Benson, Bruce L. 1999. "To Arbitrate or to Litigate: That Is the Question." *European Journal of Law and Economics* 8 (2): 91–151 (September).

Bernstein, Peter L. 1996. *Against the Gods—The Remarkable Story of Risk*. Wiley.

Bishop, John A., John P. Formby, and W. James Smith. 1991. "Incomplete Information, Income Redistribution, and Risk Averse Median Voter Behavior." *Public Choice* 68 (1–3): 41–55.

Bryant, Ralph C., and Edith Hodgkinson. 1989. "Problems of International Cooperation." In *Can Nations Agree? Issues in International Economic Cooperation*, 1–11. Brookings Institution.

Calleo, David P. 1984. "Since 1961: American Power in a New World Economy." In *Economics and World Power: An Assessment of American Diplomacy since 1789*, edited by William H. Becker and Samuel F. Wells Jr., 391–457. Columbia University Press.

Calvo, Guillermo A., and Enrique G. Mendoza. 1998. "Petty Crime and Cruel Punishment: Lessons from the Mexican Debacle." *American Economic Review* 86 (May, Papers and Proceedings): 170–75.

Cooper, Richard. 1998. "Should Capital-Account Convertibility be a World Objective?" In *Essays in International Finance* 207, 11–19. Princeton University, Department of Economics, International Finance Section (May).

Dailami, Mansoor. 1998. "Euphoria and Panic: Developing Countries' Relationship to Private Finance." *EDI Forum* 3 (Fall): 1–3, 6.

———. 2000. "Financial Openness, Democracy, and Redistributive Policy." Policy Research Working Paper 2372. Washington: World Bank (June) (http://wbln0018.worldbank. org/research/workpapers.nsf/[July 2000]).

Dailami, Mansoor, and Nadeem ul Haque. 1998. "What Macroeconomic Policies Are 'Sound'?" World Bank and IMF Policy Research Working Paper 1995. Washington: World Bank.

Eichengreen, Barry. 1996. *Globalizing Capital: A History of the International Monetary System*. Princeton University Press.

Fischer, Stanley. 1998. "Capital Account Liberalization and the Role of the IMF." In *Should the IMF Pursue Capital-Account Converitibility?* Essays in International Finance 207, 1–10. Princeton University, Department of Economics, International Finance Section (May).

Garrett, Geoffrey. 1998. "Global Markets and National Politics: Collision Course or Virtuous Circle?" *International Organization* 52 (Autumn): 787–824.

Gold, Joseph. 1997. *International Capital Movements under the Law of the International Monetary Fund*. Washington: International Monetary Fund.

Haldane, Andy. 1999. "Private Sector Involvement in Financial Crisis: Analytics and Public Policy Approaches." *Financial Stability Review* 7 (November): 184–202.

Harsanyi, John C. 1953. "Cardinal Utility in Welfare Economics and in the Theory of Risk-Taking." *Journal of Political Economy* 61 (5): 434–35.

Helleiner, Eric. 1994. *States and the Reemergence of Global Finance: From Bretton Woods to the 1990s.* Cornell University Press.

Helliwell, John F. 1992. "Empirical Linkages between Democracy and Economic Growth." Working Paper 4066. Cambridge, Mass.: National Bureau of Economic Research (May).

Hirschman, Albert O. 1970. *Exit, Voice and Loyalty: Responses to Decline in Firms, Organizations and States.* Harvard University Press.

Jorion, Philippe. 1996. "Risk^2: Measuring the Risk in Value at Risk." *Financial Analysts Journal* (November–December): 47–56.

Kapstein, Ethan B. 1989. "Resolving the Regulator's Dilemma: International Coordination of Banking Regulations." *International Organization* 43 (Spring): 323–47.

Karatnycky, Adrian. 1999. "The 1998 Freedom House Survey: The Decline of Illiberal Democracy." *Journal of Democracy* 10 (January): 112–25.

Lerner, Abba P. 1944. *Economics of Control.* Macmillan.

Londregan, John, and Keith T. Poole 1996. "Does High Income Promote Democracy?" *World Politics* 49 (1): 1–30.

Mueller, Dennis C. 1998. "Constitutional Constraints on Governments in a Global Economy." *Constitutional Political Economy* 1998 (9): 171–86.

Organization for Economic Cooperation and Development. 1990. *Liberalization of Capital Movements and Financial Services in the OECD Area.* Washington.

Polak, Jacques J. 1998. "The Articles of Agreement of the IMF and the Liberalization of Capital Movements." In *Should the IMF Pursue Capital-Account Convertibility?* Essays in International Finance 207, 47–54. Princeton University, Department of Economics, International Finance Section (May)

Quinn, Dennis, and Carla Inclan. 1997. "The Origins of Financial Openness: A Study of Current and Capital Account Liberalization." *American Journal of Political Science* 41 (July): 771–813.

Quinn, Dennis, and A. Maria Toyoda. 1997. "Measuring International Financial Regulation." Washington: Georgetown University.

Radelet, Steven, and Jeffrey Sachs. 1998. "The East Asian Financial Crisis: Diagnosis, Remedies, Prospects." In *Brookings Papers on Economic Activity 1:1998*, 1–90.

Rawls, John. 1971. *A Theory of Justice.* Belknap Press of Harvard University Press.

Razin, Assaf, and Andrew K. Rose. 1994. "Business-Cycle Volatility and Openness: An Exploratory Cross-Sectional Analysis." In *Capital Mobility: The Impact on Consumption, Investment and Growth,* edited by Leonardo Leidermann and Assaf Razin, 48–75. Cambridge University Press.

Rodrik, Dani. *Has Globalization Gone Too Far?* 1997. Washington: Institute for International Economics.

Ruggie, John G. 1983. "International Regimes, Transactions, and Change: Embedded Liberalism in the Postwar Economic Order." In *International Regimes,* edited by Stephen D. Krasner, 195–231. Cornell University Press.

Sachs, Jeffrey, Aaron Tornell, and Andrés Velasco. 1996. "Financial Crises in Emerging Markets: The Lessons from 1995." Discussion Paper 1759. Harvard University, Harvard Institute of Economic Research.

Sally, Razeen. 1998. "Classical Liberalism and International Economic Order: An Advance Sketch." *Constitutional Political Economy* 9 (1): 19–44.

Summers, Lawrence. 1999. Speech delivered October 22, 1998, at the Cato Institute's Sixteenth Annual Monetary Conference, Washington (www.ustreas.gov/press/releases/pr2770.htm [July 2000]).

Verdier, Daniel. 1998. "Domestic Responses to Capital Market Internationalization under the Gold Standard, 1870–1914." *International Organization* 52 (Winter): 1–34.

Webb, Michael C. 1995. *The Political Economy of Policy Coordination: International Adjustment since 1945.* Cornell University Press.

Wessels, Joachim H. 1993. "Redistribution from a Constitutional Perspective." *Constitutional Political Economy* 4 (3): 425–48.

World Bank. 1998. *Global Development Finance 1998.* Washington: World Bank.

Contributors

Charles Adams
International Monetary Fund

Anand Adiga
Thomson Financial BankWatch

Joel A. Binamira
Barents Group

Dennis P. J. Botman
World Bank

Mansoor Dailami
World Bank

Dipak Dasgupta
World Bank

Bernhard Eschweiler
J. P. Morgan & Co.

Benjamin M. Friedman
Harvard University

Peter M. Garber
Deutsche Bank

Paul Grela
Thomson Financial BankWatch

William C. Haworth
Barents Group

Dong He
International Monetary Fund

Stefan Ingves
International Monetary Fund

Mark Jones
Thomson Financial BankWatch

Masahiro Kawai
World Bank

Kenneth M. Kletzer
*University of California,
Santa Cruz*

Ira Lieberman
  World Bank

Robert E. Litan
  Brookings Institution

William P. Mako
  World Bank

Gerald E. Meyerman
  World Bank

Ashoka Mody
  World Bank

Ashish Narain
  World Bank

Michael Pomerleano
  World Bank

Richard Portes
  London Business School;
  Haas School of Business, Berkeley;
  and Centre for Economic Policy
  Research

Dilip Ratha
  World Bank

Gregory Root
  Thomson Financial BankWatch

David Scott
  World Bank

Timothy S. Wilson
  Morgan Stanley Dean Witter

Index

Ajustabonos, 376–77
AMCs. *See* Asset management companies
Argentina: contingent credit lines, 434,
435, 436
Asian crisis *(1997–98):* bailout packages,
56, 471–72; corporate overexpansion
preceding, 77–78, 139, 141, 172–73,
462; costs, 416; development of,
77–78, 129, 416, 461–62; impact on
investment, 226, 230–31; lessons,
127–34; market reactions, 51–55,
385–87; reactions of credit-rating agencies, 348; recovery, 123–24, 146–47,
218, 223, 226; short-term capital flows
reversed, 327, 349, 417; structural
issues, 44; unemployment, 142;
unprecedented aspects, 447–48. *See also*
Indonesia; Korea; Malaysia; Thailand
Asian economies: additional reforms
needed, 223–24; close ties between
banks and corporations, 140, 187, 192,
196, 200, 305; conflict avoidance attitudes, 314–15; corporate/government
relationships (Asian Model), 137–38,

141, 187, 192, 312; cyclical drivers of
recovery, 235; economic development
models, 225; financial sector liberalization, 418–19, 448, 453, 455, 463; foreign direct investment, 237–39; future
prospects, 235–36, 239, 240–42;
growth in *1990*s, 137, 141, 337–38;
growth in past, 224, 239; importance
of personal relationships, 138; short-
term debt, 327–29, 422–23; state-
owned companies, 137–38; trade openness, 236–37. *See also* Indonesia;
Korea; Malaysia; Thailand
Asset management companies (AMCs):
approaches, 94–95, 97, 215–16; benefits, 283, 284; bonds issued, 285; challenges, 125; drawbacks, 283, 284, 285;
establishment, 144; private, 94, 125,
174, 308; purchases of nonperforming
loans, 93–94, 95, 105, 283–85, 292;
purposes, 283, 284, 285; resolution of
banking crises, 93, 284; roles, 93–96,
133, 261–62, 284; sales of assets,
17–18, 147–48, 206, 210, 216; in